Nurses' Handbook

of

FLUID BALANCE

Nurses' Handbook

of

FLUID BALANCE

NORMA MILLIGAN METHENY, R.N., M.S.

*Department of Nursing, St. Louis Junior College, St. Louis, Mo.
Formerly Medical-Surgical Coordinator, Missouri Baptist Hospital
School of Nursing, St. Louis, Mo.*

W. D. SNIVELY, JR., M.D., F.A.C.P.

*Clinical Professor of Pediatrics, University of Alabama Medical
Center, Birmingham, Alabama, and Vice President, Medical Affairs,
Bristol-Myers Company International Division, Evansville, Indiana*

J. B. LIPPINCOTT COMPANY
Philadelphia   Toronto

Distributed in Great Britain by
Blackwell Scientific Publications
Oxford ● London ● Edinburgh

ISBN-0-397-54063-9

Library of Congress Catalog Card No. 66-26769

Printed in the United States of America

9   11   10   8

Preface

The authors' goal for this textbook is to provide the nurse, student and graduate alike, with an *inviting, clear, comprehensive* and—above all—*practical* handbook on body fluid disturbances. With this goal ever in mind, we have first presented general information concerning body fluid disturbances —their nature, pathogenesis, clinical manifestations and diagnosis, and the principles of medical therapy. Our approach is *systematic*, for only such an approach can bring order from the apparent chaos that is so often synonymous with the subject. Sir William Osler might well have been speaking of body fluid disturbances (although he was not) when he said: "System, or as I shall term it, the virtue of method, is the harness without which only the horses of genius travel."

After laying the foundation, we have built on it the nurse's management in the eminently practical matters of observation, interpretation and intervention. We have dealt with the more important clinical areas in which body fluid disturbances play such a cogent role. Always, we have laid great emphasis on the *how*, as well as the *why*, and with generous use of illustrations. The surgical patient, the badly burned patient, the patient with digestive, urologic, cardiac, endocrine, respiratory disease—each has his day in court. Problems associated with drowning and with excessive exposure to heat are not forgotten, nor is the child, with his peculiar proneness to body fluid disturbances.

To avoid cluttering the text, we have used a minimum of footnotes; but following Chapter 24, the reader will find a comprehensive list of references for looking up moot points as well as for additional reading.

Our tack cannot but reveal our conviction that the nurse's role in the management of patients is becoming an increasingly complex and crucial one, especially so for the patient with a body fluid disturbance, whose status changes from hour to hour. The unique contribution of the nurse, who is with the patient around the clock, includes not only the physical care of the patient, but also her intelligent observations and judgments—knowing *what* to look for and *how* to look for it. The careful recording of fluid intake and output, and the understanding of the purely nursing problems posed by the patient's condition and treatment are also part of her comprehensive care plan. All this is essential not only to the patient, but also to the physician, who bears the primary responsibility for management. Clearly, the nurse's contributions will be infinitely greater if she has more than a casual familiarity with body fluid disturbances.

We hope our book might be epitomized by something Oliver Wendell Holmes said: "Science is a first-rate piece of furniture for a man's upper chamber, if he has common sense on the ground floor." We have tried to provide the nurse both with science for her upper chamber, and with the practical information that will enable her to exercise common sense on the ground floor, as she goes about her work with patients suffering from body fluid disturbances.

This book, like the proper care of the patient with a body fluid disturbance, represents the joint efforts of a nurse and a physician. It could not have been written without both contributors; nor can the hospitalized patient with a fluid imbalance receive optimal care without such a team effort.

N. M. M.
W. D. S., Jr.

Contents

"Water . . . is the image of the ungraspable phantom of life; and this is the key to it all."

—Herman Melville in *Moby Dick*

Much Ado About Something

Although Thomas Latta treated cholera "by the copious injection of aqueous and saline fluids into the veins" in 1832, it has been only during the past quarter century that disturbances of water and electrolytes have been accorded the attention their importance deserves. Especially in the decade beginning in 1950 did interest reach a high intensity. The realization had dawned at last that body fluid disturbances represent the common denominator of a host of illnesses; that every seriously ill patient is a candidate for one or more of these disturbances; that many patients with moderate or even mild illnesses can develop them; that whether many patients live or die depends upon how their medical attendants solve the problems posed by body fluid disturbances. It has become clear that a working knowledge of body fluids is required for the intelligent management of most of the diseases listed in the diagnostic nomenclature.

The list of clinical problems in which body fluid disturbances tend to be especially important is a long one. It includes the seriously burned patient, the patient with ulcerative colitis, the diabetic patient, the patient with congestive heart failure, the patient undergoing surgery, the patient with hypertension and the patient taking potent diuretics. Indeed, in many respects medical progress has *increased* the potential number of body fluid disturbances. For example, sulfonamide diuretics, such as the thiazides, cause a dangerously increased excretion of potassium in nearly half the patients taking these diuretics for a prolonged period. The resultant body fluid disturbance, potassium deficit, can cause permanent damage to the heart muscle and to the kidney tubules.

However, this is only one of some 50 important causes of potassium deficit. Therapy involving several hormones of the adrenal cortex represents a great triumph for medicine, yet it has brought in its train a significant increase in body fluid disturbances.

Because many hospitalized patients are seriously ill, the incidence of body fluid disturbances in hospitals is often high. Surveys of 2 hospitals revealed that more than 20 per cent of the patients were suffering from potassium deficit that was largely undiagnosed by the attending physician! In these studies, other imbalances were not sought out. It is interesting to speculate what the incidence of *other* fluid imbalances would have been, had they been investigated. Since the early diagnosis of body fluid disturbances depends upon close observation of the patient, the nurse carries a heavy responsibility. She must be alert to untoward events in the patient's progress and must understand the significance of those events.

Observations that might once have been regarded as of little or no importance now rank with TPR as vital signs. At one time, sweating called only for the application of nursing comfort measures; now its potentially serious clinical result has to be considered. The same statement applies to losses of body fluids from whatever source. The nurse is the on-the-spot observer not only of the patient's output of fluids, but also of his intake. All this clearly means that the nurse must know what the various body fluid disturbances are, how they develop and what characterizes them. This knowledge is required so that she can take the proper action, which includes the accurate reporting of significant facts to the physician.

1

The nursing profession has been prompt to respond to the challenge of the new knowledge of body fluid disturbances. Splendid courses in body fluids are being taught in schools all over the land. Numerous articles on the various aspects of body fluid disturbances are appearing in the nursing literature. Certainly the subject deserves the increased interest, which represents *much ado about something*—something of vital importance to every nurse, every physician, and every patient who entrusts himself to their professional care.

TERMINOLOGY

The old bugbear of terminology plagues everyone who writes a book on a technical subject. The problem is at least as formidable in the medical field as in any other. All too frequently, identical entities are described by entirely different terms. Sometimes a term that has one meaning for one group of workers has exactly the opposite meaning for another. Inconsistency of terminology appears at times to mount into a 20th century Tower of Babel.

Of all the fields of medicine, none has suffered more confusion in terminology than fluid balance. For years we desperately needed a classification that was at once *systematic, clear, logical, clinical, all-inclusive,* and perhaps most important of all, *not susceptible to misinterpretation.* The ideal classification had to be eminently practical, having to serve as a useful basis for understanding, diagnosis and treatment.

A classification meeting many of these criteria was introduced by Moyer in 1952 in his classic *Fluid Balance: A Clinical Manual.* It was modified and extended considerably by Snively and Sweeney in 1956, in their book *Fluid Balance Handbook For Practitioners.* This classification has since been further modified by Snively, and that modification is employed in this text, with its rationale being described in detail in Chapter 5. In Chapter 7 is presented a comparative table showing, in parallel columns, body fluid disturbances described by our terminology under the heading of *physico-clinical imbalance;* the less realistic and more confusing *conventional terminology;* and, in the third column, *closely related clinical states.*

There are lesser problems caused by the fact that several perfectly correct terms may be used interchangeably. For example, the ubiquitous term *glucose* is usually referred to as *dextrose* when it occurs as part of the name of a parenteral solution, because it is the U.S.P. designation for glucose of requisite purity. *Solution of sodium chloride* is usually designated by the shorter term *saline;* but when used as part of a solution description, it is described by the longer term. The old term *uremia* has been replaced—in part, at least—by the more modern term *azotemia.* Roughly equivalent to the term *plasma* are *intravascular extracellular fluid, serum,* and *intravascular space,* and the term *interstitial fluid* is approximated by the terms *extravascular extracellular fluid* and *interstitial space.* Yet, in the strictly technical sense, *plasma* has had an anticoagulant added, at least as it occurs when prepared for intravenous administration; *serum,* upon which laboratory determinations are performed, has not. And certainly, if one wants to be technical, a fluid is not a *space,* nor a space a fluid. Throughout the book we have endeavored to use these roughly synonymous terms in the natural way in which they would be employed by nurses and physicians in the hospital.

Now let us plunge boldly into our subject, with the consideration of body fluid, our heritage from the sea.

Chapter 1

Body Fluid, Our Heritage From the Sea

Every one of us contains within his body a constricted little pond that probably was once part of the great ocean. We call that pond the *body fluid*; it accounts for two-thirds of the weight of the average person. Its contents are essential to us in our daily lives. As long as the quantity and the chemical ingredients of the fluid remain within narrow limits, we remain healthy; but if the volume or chemical composition of the pond departs even slightly from normal limits, we become ill. This body fluid pond represents our little personal inlet, cut off from the sea. How did this come about?

Scientists tell us that life began in the sea over a billion years ago. It probably consisted of simple microscopic plants, yet it was life. The sea was a kind mother: its waters, with their rich concentration of chemical substances, cradled and nourished the primitive forerunners of the plant and animal kingdoms.

Millions of years passed while the simple, single-celled forms of life used their gigantic ocean bath for food, as a sewer into which they discharged their wastes, and as a great chemical reaction vat. Their requirements for life were simple, and the sea was their mother.

Later, spurred by an unknown life force, the single-celled creatures divided into those that were destined to become plants and those that were to become animals. Some of the early animal forms took a step of gigantic importance for all of us when they banded together to form many-celled creatures, the metazoa. Later the metazoa took another great stride; they enclosed sea water within their bodies as *body fluid*. This was a step essential for progress, but it had its penalties, since the possession of body fluid forced the creatures to develop a blood circulation system, a system for removing waste materials, a breathing or respiratory system, a system for digesting foods, and new methods of reproduction and locomotion. Yet, by enclosing sea water within the bodies, these ancient pioneers anticipated an event that was still millions of years away—the first dramatic landfall.

This story of evolution, if it be the correct one, makes it clear why human body fluid bears such a striking resemblance to the salty seas, in which it originated so many geologic periods ago. But there are striking differences between body fluid and present-day sea water. The latter, for example, is several times as salty as body fluid, which explains why we can't drink it with equanimity. There are differences in the proportions as well as in the actual quantities of the several electrolytes. In general, these changes are due to the fact that the electrolyte content of the sea has increased drastically as the continental land masses have been gradually dissolved and washed into it. If we could obtain a sample of the ocean water from that remote day when life first came ashore and could compare it chemically to human body fluid, we would probably find that the two would be strikingly similar. Our *sea within* is, indeed, an ancient fluid.

Chapter 2

Cellular and Extracellular Fluid; Secretions and Excretions

Cellular and Extracellular Fluid

Body fluid consists chiefly of water and certain dissolved substances, sometimes referred to as salts, sometimes as minerals, but more properly designated *electrolytes*. Electrolytes are so named because they develop tiny electrical charges when they are dissolved in water. Some of the electrolytes develop positive charges. These include sodium, potassium, calcium and magnesium. They are called *cations*. Other electrolytes develop negative charges. These include chloride, bicarbonate, sulfate, phosphate, proteinate, carbonic and other organic acids. They are called *anions*. The term *ion* covers both cation and anion.

One can determine which electrolytes carry positive charges and which carry negative charges by placing the electrolyte in question in a wet electric cell through which an electric current is conducted. (Fig. 1) Such a cell has a negative pole called a *cathode* and a positive pole called an *anode*. In the field of electricity, perhaps as in life, unlikes attract, hence positively charged particles travel to the negative pole, or cathode. Such particles are therefore designated as *cations*. Negatively charged particles, on the other hand, migrate to the positive pole, or anode. Such particles are therefore known as *anions*. Cations and anions balance each other electrically. (Fig. 2)

The body fluid is divided between two major *compartments*. The first so-called compartment, the *cellular fluid*, comprises the fluid contained within the billions of body cells. It might be envisioned as a vast multitude of tiny, encapsulated droplets, suspended in the extracellular fluid. The cellular fluid accounts for about three-fourths of the total body fluid. The *extracellular fluid*, comprising one-fourth of the total body fluid, has two subdivisions. The first is made up of the fluid contained within the blood vessels, the intravascular extracellular fluid, which we designate the *plasma*. The second subdivision consists of the fluid lying outside the blood vessels, the extravascular extracellular fluid, which we designate the *interstitial fluid*. The interstitial fluid has about three times the volume of plasma. (Figs. 3 and 4)

We may live on dry land and breathe air and regard ourselves as highly-complex, highly-civilized organisms, the goal of creation, yet our body cells still cling to their ancient oceanic habits of feeding themselves and of getting rid of wastes by exchanging materials with their environment. The environment of the cells is, of course, the extracellular fluid, be it plasma or interstitial fluid. These exchanges of water, electrolytes, and other dissolved chemical materials between the cells and their bath water are continuous and of tremendous magnitude. Scientists cannot entirely explain the basis for them. There must be a fantastically complex system of delicate "pumps" that provide the energy for the vital transfers. Perhaps the exchanges are based on differences in electrical potential between the cells and their environment. Perhaps they are

FIG. 1. In a wet electric cell cations go to the negative pole or cathode, anions to the positive pole or anode.

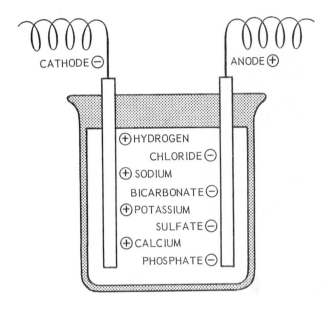

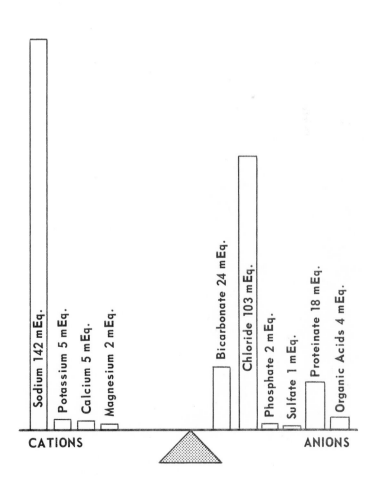

FIG. 2. The cations and anions of the extracellular fluid balance each other when expressed in milli-equivalents.

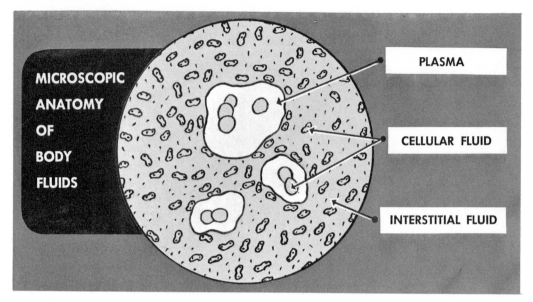

FIG. 3. Microscopic anatomy of body fluids.

based on biologic factors of which we do not yet have an inkling. Whatever the mechanisms, it is fascinating to speculate on the nature of the ghostly pumps that begin their work months before we are born and, like the old grandfather's clock, keep faithfully on the job, never stopping, never resting, until death.

The chemical reactions occurring within single cells in a body of water, be that body

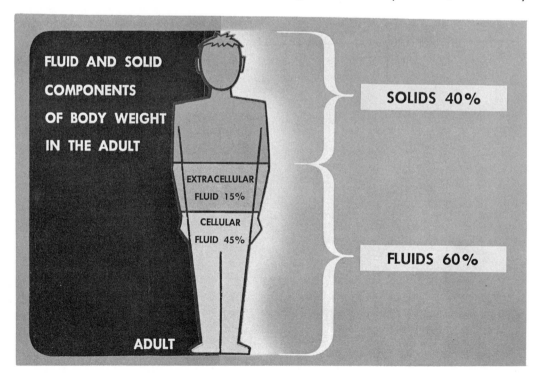

FIG. 4. Fluid and solid components of body weight in the adult.

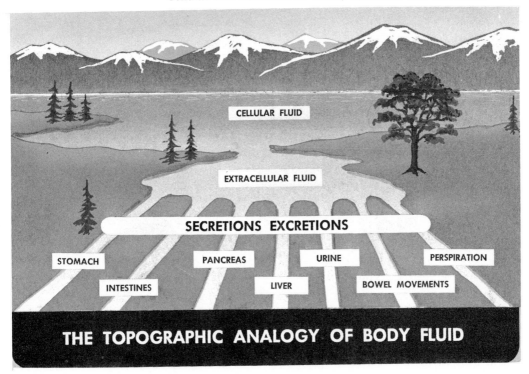

FIG. 5. The topographic analogy of body fluid.

of water an ocean or a farm pond, do not importantly change the composition of the water, which provides an unlimited source of food as well as a vast sink for the disposal of waste products. The activity of our body cells, on the other hand, does affect the composition of the extracellular fluid in which they float. Indeed, the products of the cells' chemical activities would exert a catastrophic effect on the composition of this extracellular fluid if it were not for chemical regulatory activities that are carried out by the body homeostatic mechanisms, to which we will refer later. These mechanisms enable the tiny, overcrowded pond within the skin to maintain its compositional integrity and, at the same time, to keep the body cells just as healthy as if they were still floating around in the wide blue sea, under the towering Cambrian clouds.

Secretions and Excretions

Since the extracellular fluid carries material to and from the cells, we might call it the middle-man fluid of the body. It is a middle-man fluid in another sense, since it communicates with various tiny rivers that derive their water and electrolytes from it. These rivers contain special fluids—the familiar secretions and excretions such as saliva, gastric juice, intestinal juice, bile, pancreatic juice, nasal secretions, perspiration, urine and feces. Just as the extracellular fluid and the cellular fluid each has its own characteristic chemical composition, so each one of these special secretions or excretions has a composition that is relatively constant during health, but which may deviate widely from normal during disease. Figure 5, a topographic analogy, shows graphically how the cellular fluid and extracellular fluid communicate one with the other, and how the extracellular fluid communicates with the secretions and excretions. The topographic analogy appears to indicate that when the little rivers—the secretions and excretions—are depleted, they deplete the extracellular fluid; that when the extracellular fluid is depleted, it draws from its reservoir, the cellular fluid. The analogy is correct: this is precisely what happens. (Fig. 6)

When one is discussing the composition of a secretion or excretion, the quantities of

ELECTROLYTE COMPOSITION OF VARIOUS BODY SECRETIONS OR EXCRETIONS

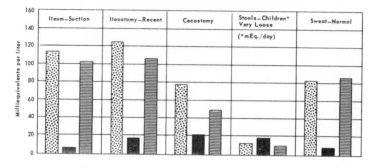

KEY:

Sodium   Potassium   Chloride   Bicarbonate

Fig. 6. Electrolyte composition of various body secretions or excretions.

electrolytes per unit volume mean nothing unless they can be related to a constant. We like to use as a constant the levels of sodium, potassium, chloride and bicarbonate in plasma. On this basis we find that gastric secretions have about half the sodium concentration of plasma. We find also that for all practical purposes they have about the same potassium, about half again as much chloride, and only a fraction of the bicarbonate. We find that pancreatic secretions have about the same sodium and potassium, about a third the chloride, and about three times the amount of bicarbonate. We find that perspiration, a dilute secretion, has a little over half the sodium and the chloride of plasma, and about the same potassium. We find that diarrheal stools in children have a tiny fraction of the sodium in plasma, have several times as much potassium as plasma, have a small fraction of the chloride of plasma. Furthermore, they most likely contain large amounts of bicarbonate, certainly much more than is in plasma.

The time that it takes depletion of a secretion or excretion to affect the extracellular fluid, and the time that it takes depletion of the extracellular fluid to affect the cellular fluid, vary widely and depend, in general, upon the magnitude and the rapidity of the depletion. In severe infantile diarrhea, or in Asiatic cholera, loss of intestinal secretions through vomiting and diarrhea can deplete the extracellular fluid so as to cause fatal shock within a few hours. On the other hand, gradual losses of intestinal secretions can require days to seriously affect the extracellular fluid. Reduction in the volume of the extracellular fluid or a serious loss of one of its electrolytes usually does not affect the cellular fluid for several days. But when the cellular fluid has been adversely affected, a replenished extracellular fluid takes several days to repair the defect.

Chapter 3

Units of Measure

A long time ago, a gentleman named John Selden said,

. . . if they should make the standard for the measure we call a "foot" a Chancellor's foot; what an uncertain measure would this be! One Chancellor has a long foot, another a short foot, a third an indifferent foot . . .

Master Selden was pointing out, quite correctly, that we must have standard, invariable units of measure or we shall get nowhere. Certainly we shall get nowhere in attempting to understand, diagnose and treat body fluid disturbances unless we have simple, accurate units of measure.

Now, what is it we want to measure? Chiefly, we are interested in the extracellular fluid. The cellular fluid is divided among the billions of cells of the body and is not readily available for examination. Not only is the extracellular fluid easily accessible; the disturbances in this fluid are accurately reflected in the symptoms and findings shown by a person when he becomes ill. For this reason, physicians focus their chief attention upon the extracellular portion of the body fluid when they study imbalances of water and electrolytes.

What units of measure do we need? First of all, we must have a unit of measure for volume. The European system of weights and measures is being used more and more in science; it uses the *liter* (L.) for volume measurement. The liter is broken down into 1,000 parts or milliliters (ml.), each milliliter representing 1/1,000 of a liter. A milliliter is virtually identical with a cubic centimeter (cc.), but the milliliter is preferable to the cubic centimeter, since the centimeter is a linear rather than a volumetric unit of measure. Expressed in terms of weight rather than volume, a liter of water weighs 1,000 grams (Gm.), or about 2.2 lbs.

Next, we must have a unit of measure for the electrolytes of the body fluid. These electrolytes are active, dynamic chemicals. Since we are interested in their activity, we must have a unit that expresses *chemical activity*, or *chemical combining ability*. This ability is really the power of cations to unite with anions to form molecules. Virtually any cation can unite with any anion. The cation sodium, for example, mixed with the anion proteinate, forms the molecule sodium proteinate; potassium unites with chloride, magnesium with sulfate, hydrogen with nitrate, and so on. Why could we not merely use as our unit of measure the weight of the ions in which we are interested? Unfortunately, this does not solve our problem, since the *weight* of a chemical bears no relation to its *chemical activity*. *One* mg. of sodium unites chemically with *180* mg. of proteinate to form the compound sodium proteinate, for example.

So, we must search for a different sort of unit of measure, a unit of chemical activity. We do not have to look far: the chemists have a unit they call the *milliequivalent* (mEq.). Now, the unit of physical power in our civilization is traditionally the power of an imaginary average horse. Our unit of chemical power, the milliequivalent, is *equivalent* to the activity of 1 *milligram* of hydrogen. Our *chemical horse is 1 mg. of hydrogen* (Fig. 7). Put another way, 1 milligram of hydrogen exerts 1 milliequivalent of chemical activity; so do 23 mg. of sodium, 39 mg. of potassium, 40 mg. of calcium, 35 mg. of chloride, or 4,140 mg. of

FIG. 7. One milligram of hydrogen represents the unit for chemical combining power: it is the electrolyte horsepower.

proteinate. Each of these weights represents 1 mEq. of the ion in question.

How large is a milliequivalent? Actually, 1 mg. is only 1/30,000 of an ounce. Although the sizes of the units of which we are speaking are tiny indeed, an excess of only a few milliequivalents of an electrolyte per liter of

body fluid can have a profound effect on the state of one's health. And here is something we ought to memorize:

> One Milliequivalent of Any
> Cation Is Equivalent
> Chemically to One Milliequivalent
> of Any Anion

It matters not a bit whether the cation is sodium, potassium, calcium, or magnesium, or whether the anion is chloride, bicarbonate, phosphate, sulfate, or proteinate.

Interestingly enough, the milliequivalent is not only useful as a measure for chemical activity, but it is also a rough unit of measure for osmosis, or the drawing power of water. A quick way of describing osmosis is to say, "Water goes where salt is." This means that if there are two solutions, separated by a special membrane, which we call a semipermeable membrane, the solution

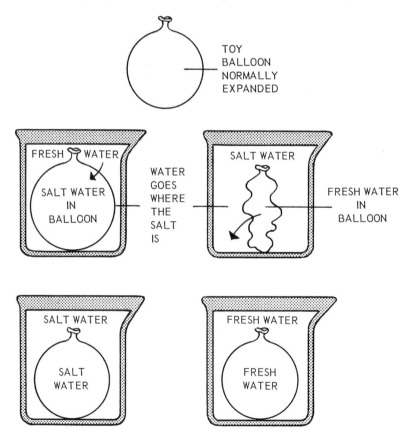

FIG. 8. The principle of osmosis: "Water goes where the salt is."

with the greatest concentration of electrolyte draws water from the solution with the lesser concentration of electrolyte. It is almost as if there were an effort on the part of each electrolyte particle to surround itself with its fair share of the available water.

Osmosis is highly important in the body. (Fig. 8) If pure water not containing electrolytes were injected directly into the bloodstream, the red blood cells would absorb water, swell and burst. If, on the other hand, an extremely salty solution were injected into a vein, the red blood cells would find themselves in a bath saltier than their contents. They would lose water to their salty environment and would shrink, just as your fingers do if they have been in water too long. Osmosis is particularly important when, because of disease or some accident such as drowning, the extracellular fluid develops an electrolyte content lower or higher than normal.

Chapter 4

Gains and Losses of Water and Electrolytes

Most of the mechanisms by which body fluid disturbances develop are basically simple. The consideration of a farm pond helps us to envision them. A farm pond gains water from rain falling directly into it or flowing into it from an adjoining hillside. It also gains water from underground springs. Like the body fluid pond, the farm pond contains electrolytes and gains additional electrolytes from its environment—in this case, the adjoining fields and hillsides. Some of the electrolytes come from the earth itself; others, from fertilizer that the farmer has put on his fields, which rain washes into the pond. Sometimes a pond owner will add fertilizer to the pond to keep weed growth down and to encourage the development of algae, on which the fish feed.

A farm pond loses water through evaporation; in a year, it loses a great amount this way. It also loses water from seepage into the earth. Every farm pond must have a spillway into which it can overflow when the water level rises sharply following a heavy rain. Both water and electrolytes can be lost from a farm pond when they are consumed by creatures living in the pond, or by plants growing in the waters.

Just as the body fluid pond can develop abnormalities, so can the farm pond. In times of drought, when there has been little or no rain and excessive evaporation, the volume may decrease. The electrolyte content of the pond will rise sharply in such a case, and may even kill the fish. When it rains heavily, the pond may fill to the brim, suffering an excess of volume. The pond be- comes abnormally dilute; the growth of underwater weeds is favored and an unpleasant scum appears, which may cover the lake unless electrolytes are added.

These same principles apply to the body fluid pond: it can suffer a deficit in volume or an excess. It can suffer deficits in the quantities of individual electrolytes, or it can suffer excesses of them. Bear in mind:

It Is Abnormal Differences Between Gains and Losses of Water and Electrolytes That Cause Body Fluid Imbalances

We gain water and electrolytes when we drink water. If the water is distilled, we gain water alone. If it is well water, softened water, mineral water, or most city water, we gain water plus electrolytes. We gain both water and electrolytes when we eat food, for food consists largely of water, yet is rich in electrolytes and nutrients such as protein, fat, carbohydrate and vitamins. Hospitalized patients are frequently given water and electrolytes, as well as other materials, by special routes such as nasogastric tube, intravenous needle, or rectal tube.

Water alone is gained within the body as a result of the chemical processes to which foodstuffs are subjected. In starvation, when the body is consuming its own tissues, the chemical reactions that occur release water. The chemical breakdown of a gram of fat, for example, creates more than a gram of water.

The list of routes through which water

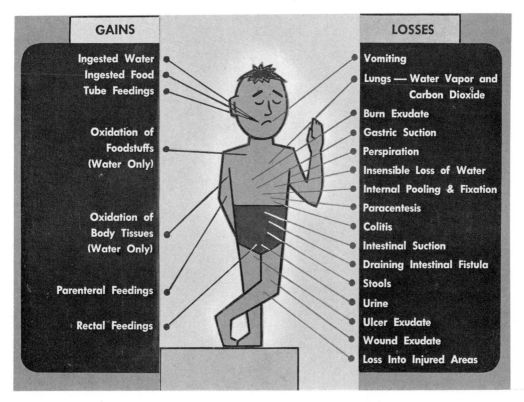

FIG. 9. Gains and losses of water.

and electrolytes are lost from the body is a long one. Both water and electrolytes are lost from the eyes in tears, from the skin in perspiration, from burns, from wounds and from ulcers. They are lost from the mammary glands as milk and from cuts as blood. They are lost in considerable quantities from the lungs—normally in breathing, abnormally in various diseases affecting the lungs. With the rapid breathing that accompanies high fever, large amounts of water and carbon dioxide are exhaled. (Fig. 9)

Especially important in the loss of water and electrolytes is the digestive tract. Vomiting causes their loss; so does the use of a gastric or intestinal suction tube. Water and electrolytes are lost from the intestinal tract with enterostomy, colostomy, or cecostomy. They are lost as a result of surgical operations, as in drainage from the biliary tract. They are lost in normal bowel movements, and in greater than normal quantities in diarrhea. They are lost from the kidneys in urine, and from the fluids surrounding the brain and spinal cord when there is an abnormal opening to the exterior.

Water and electrolytes are lost in draining abscesses or by way of paracentesis. They are sometimes lost within the body itself in abnormal closed collections of fluid which are just as unavailable to the body economy as if they were outside the body. They are lost in the swelling that occurs in injured or burned areas and in the skin with various skin diseases. Water alone is lost through the skin in *insensible perspiration*, which goes on continually night and day. It is also lost from the lungs as water vapor.

The general state of the fluid balance of the healthy adult (Fig. 10) can readily be assessed by comparing the *volume of fluid consumed by mouth* with the *volume of urine*. This simple rule holds because the other chief sources of fluid in health,

- water derived from solid food and water obtained from chemical reactions in the body approximately equal

- the normal losses of water lost as vapor through the lungs and the skin, and water lost in the bowel movements.

When one becomes ill, he almost always decreases his intake of water and food. At the same time, the illness itself—through vomiting, diarrhea, or similar mechanisms—may enhance his losses of water and electrolytes. With the intake decreased and the output increased, it is no wonder that ill patients frequently develop imbalances of the body fluids. Sometimes the imbalance may be so great as to kill the patient within a matter of days, or even hours.

Just as differences in weather significantly affect our little farm pond, so do the changes wrought by disease affect our body fluid pond. Robert Burton said it well:

. . . attenuate our bodies, dry them, wither them, shrivel them up like old apples, make them so many anatomies.

For one to remain healthy, the volume and electrolyte composition of the extracellular fluid must be maintained within a narrow corridor of normality, in spite of the many events that conspire to cause abnormalities of water or electrolytes. The difficulties involved in maintaining the volume and chemical composition of the extracellular fluid at a constant stagger the imagination. The billions of cells of the body constantly pour the results of chemical reactions into the extracellular fluid; they constantly withdraw from it substances needed for specific organ or cell activities. We eat and drink a wide variety of materials not matched against the needs of our body. Our digestive tract is, to a large measure, nonselective, absorbing most of the substances offered it.

The volume of the liquids we drink would drown us if there were no mechanism for maintaining a constant extracellular fluid volume. These problems in health are multiplied over and over in disease, which adds to the already gigantic task of maintaining a

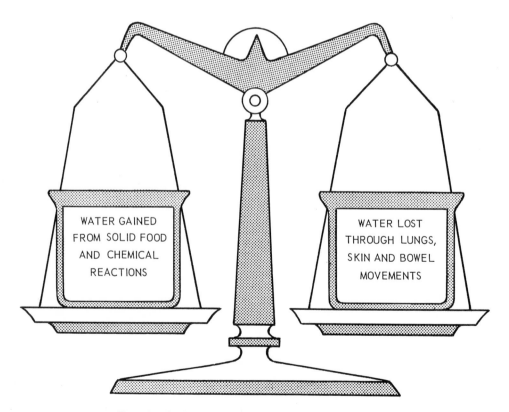

FIG. 10. The balance portrays water balance in health.

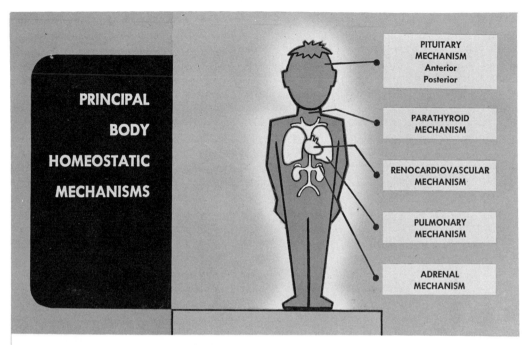

FIG. 11. Principal body homeostatic mechanisms.

constant volume and chemical composition of the extracellular fluid.

Fortunately, nature has provided each one of us with a set of complicated controls—a system of *body automation*, which demonstrates the wisdom of the body. This system, in its handling of an unbelievably complex task, puts man-made automation to shame.

What are the chief organs of the body that maintain a constant volume and chemical composition of the extracellular fluid? (Fig. 11) The lungs serve to maintain the composition of the blood with respect to oxygen and carbon dioxide. Since carbon dioxide stems from the carbonic acid of the blood, the lungs play an important role in maintaining the balance between acid and alkali in our extracellular fluid.

Other organs play a somewhat different role. The kidneys carry the lion's share of the responsibility of maintaining a constant volume and chemical composition of our extracellular fluid. They are the master chemists of the body pond. They excrete the ashes of the chemical fires of our body. They remove from the extracellular fluid a great variety of foreign substances indiscriminately absorbed by our digestive tracts. But still

more important, they preserve chemical balance in the extracellular fluid. We can exist for hours, days, or even longer, without the use of our bones, muscles, digestive organs, nerves, endocrine glands, and even the brain. However, if the kidneys cease their chemical regulation of the extracellular fluid for a single hour, physiologic oblivion promptly

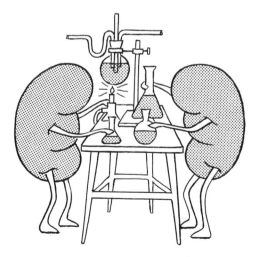

FIG. 12. The kidneys are the master chemists of our *sea within*.

overtakes us. The story of the way the kidneys go about their regulation of extracellular fluid and why they go about it in the way they do is too long to be told here, but it is a fascinating tale that reminds one of a chapter from *Alice In Wonderland*. (Fig. 12)

There are other organs of body automation: the adrenal glands, the parathyroid glands, and the pituitary gland. They perform their several functions efficiently and silently, and, fortunately, seldom suffer malfunction. Nevertheless, when any of the organs of body automation—lungs, kidneys, adrenals, parathyroids, or pituitary—do break down, the physician caring for the patient faces a formidable task. He faces this problem because these organs mediate the wisdom of the body, which is considerably greater than the wisdom of the most learned physician who ever lived.

Chapter 5

Volume Changes in Extracellular Fluid

THE CLINICAL PICTURE APPROACH

Despite the frequency and the importance of body fluid disturbances, there is probably no group of clinical problems that has been so poorly understood. Why is this?

Much of the early knowledge concerning imbalances of the body fluids came from teachers who were biochemists first and clinicians second—if, indeed, they were clinicians at all. Quite naturally, they presented body fluid disturbances in the light of their own research, which had usually been carried out in highly circumscribed fields. As a result, much of the early teaching about body fluid disturbances was concerned with detailed descriptions of all the possible imbalances that could occur in the one or two diseases on which the teacher had concentrated. Body fluid disturbances began to be regarded as *biochemical appendages* of disease states, rather than as a broad group of problems representing the common denominator of many ailments. No over-all view of these universal disturbances was presented. The subject as taught was so complex, so saturated with the interests of the teacher-investigator, and presented in such depth, that most members of the medical and nursing professions came to regard comprehension of body fluid disturbances by the non-investigator as something difficult, if not impossible. The instruction concerning the disturbances appeared to many persons as it did to one student in the class of a famous pediatrician-biochemist: "as clear as if written backwards by Gertrude Stein in Sanskrit."

A completely different approach to learning body fluid disturbances, one which is a highroad to their understanding, might be termed the *clinical picture approach*; first introduced by Carl Moyer, it was enlarged upon considerably by Snively and Sweeney. In understanding the clinical picture approach, one should first recognize that disturbances of water and electrolytes are produced by a fairly small number of mechanisms, most of which are simple and readily understandable. Some of these disturbances might be termed primary—for example, the sodium deficit that occurs when one sweats excessively and drinks only water. Other body fluid disturbances occur secondary to other ailments, such as the base bicarbonate deficit (metabolic acidosis) that we find in uncontrolled diabetes mellitus. Although produced by a wide variety of etiologic factors, body fluid disturbances can be divided into 16 *clinical entities*. To recognize these entities we employ the clinical picture approach.

There is nothing new to this pedagogic technique for studying disease. When ailments such as rheumatic fever, appendicitis, lobar pneumonia, or the contagious diseases are presented to nursing students, they are presented as clinical pictures, and the students learn them as clinical pictures. Each picture represents a composite that includes the history, the symptoms—both subjective and objective—and the laboratory data. When the student learns body fluid disturbances by this method, she analyzes the underlying mechanisms responsible for the disturbances—she learns the imbalances as clinical pictures.

Essential to the application of the clinical picture approach is a simple diagnostic classification. Our classification divides body fluid disturbances into some 16 basic imbalances, or clinical pictures. Each has its own set of causative mechanisms; its own symptoms, subjective and objective; its own laboratory findings. Sometimes one of these disturbances exists by itself; at other times, it occurs in combination with one or more additional imbalances. Frequently, body fluid disturbances are associated with other disease states and, indeed, interact intimately with them. Sometimes a succession of body fluid disturbances occurs, one after another. Clearly, one must understand single imbalances if he is to understand the combinations.

Because the extracellular fluid is primarily involved in body fluid disturbances and is available to us for laboratory examination, and because it is variations in the water and the electrolytes of the extracellular fluid that produce our clinical pictures, our diagnostic classification focuses attention on the extracellular fluid. The classification is as follows:

1. Changes in Volume of Extracellular Fluid
   A. Deficit
   B. Excess
2. Changes in Properties of Extracellular Fluid
   A. Changes in sodium concentration
      a. deficit
      b. excess
   B. Changes in potassium concentration
      a. deficit
      b. excess
   C. Changes in calcium concentration
      a. deficit
      b. excess
   D. Changes in base bicarbonate concentration
      a. deficit (metabolic acidosis)
      b. excess (metabolic alkalosis)
   E. Changes in carbonic acid concentration
      a. deficit (respiratory alkalosis)
      b. excess (respiratory acidosis)
   F. Change in protein concentration
      a. deficit
   G. Change in magnesium concentration
      a. deficit
3. Changes in Position of Extracellular Fluid
   A. Shift of water and electrolytes from plasma to interstitial space
   B. Shift of water and electrolytes from interstitial space to plasma

CHANGES IN VOLUME

Extracellular Fluid Volume Deficit

This imbalance (Fig. 13) represents a deficit—not of water alone—but of water and electrolytes in roughly the same proportion as they exist in extracellular fluid. It is erroneous to designate extracellular fluid volume deficit as dehydration, which means loss of water only.

In the history of the patient with extracellular fluid volume deficit, one usually finds that there has been one or more of the following: decreased water intake, vomiting, diarrhea, a systemic infection (with its attendant fever and increased utilization of water and electrolytes), fistulous drainage, or intestinal obstruction. (In intestinal obstruction, the deficit develops not because water and electrolytes are lost to the outside, but because they are pooled in a distended intestine, which makes them just as unavailable to the body economy as if they *were* outside the body.)

The symptoms of this imbalance include dry skin and mucous membranes, longitudinal wrinkles or furrows of the tongue, oliguria or anuria, acute weight loss (which may be in excess of 5 per cent in the child or adult, or in excess of 10 per cent in the infant), lassitude, and a drop in body temperature. The formed elements of the blood, including the red blood cell count, the packed cell volume and the hemoglobin, are increased, since they find themselves in a lesser volume of plasma because of the deficit in extracellular fluid volume.

Clinical Example. An 18-month-old baby was admitted to the hospital with a history of onset of severe diarrhea and vomiting 24

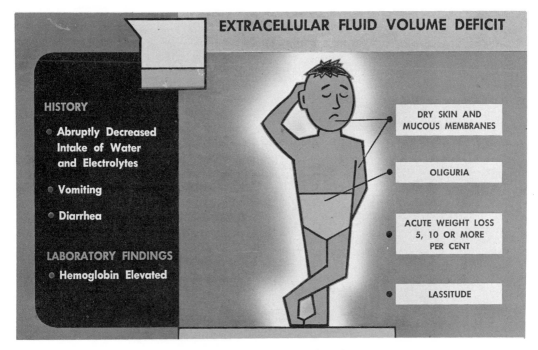

Fig. 13. Extracellular fluid volume deficit.

hours before admission. The infant had been well up to that time. During the preceding 24 hours, the mother stated, he had had an almost continuous running off of the bowels with frequent spells of vomiting. The baby took a few sips of water, but refused food. On examination, the infant was found to have lost approximately 6 per cent of his pre-illness body weight. His skin and mucous membranes appeared dry. The skin was inelastic. Body temperature was 98°F. The diaper was not wet, and the mother felt there had been a definite decrease in urination. A red blood cell count revealed 6,500,000 cells, and the hemoglobin was found to be 14 Gm.

Extracellular Fluid Volume Excess

This imbalance (Fig. 14) represents an excess in the volume of extracellular fluid, and is caused by an increase in both water and electrolytes in roughly the same proportions as they exist in extracellular fluid. It is not over-hydration, since this term would imply an increase in water only.

In the history of volume excess of extracellular fluid, one may find that the patient has been given excessive quantities of an isotonic solution of sodium chloride (so-called "normal saline" or "physiological solution of sodium chloride") intravenously. This solution is highly concentrated, possessing about the same tonicity as extracellular fluid. Moreover, its electrolyte pattern is strikingly different from extracellular fluid, chiefly in that it provides 154 mEq./L. of chloride, while extracellular fluid normally has only 103. It therefore imposes a chloride excess on the kidneys. *It is extremely easy to exceed the renal tolerances by administering isotonic solution of sodium chloride.* Other factors that may cause volume excess include congestive heart failure, excessive ingestion of sodium chloride or of electrolyte mixtures, administration of adrenal cortical hormones (especially for long periods), hyperaldosteronism, or renal disease.

The symptoms of this imbalance include puffy eyelids, shortness of breath, edema, edema of tissues at surgical operation, moist rales in lungs, and acute weight gain, which can be in excess of 5 per cent. The formed elements of the blood, as reflected by the red blood cell count and the packed cell volume,

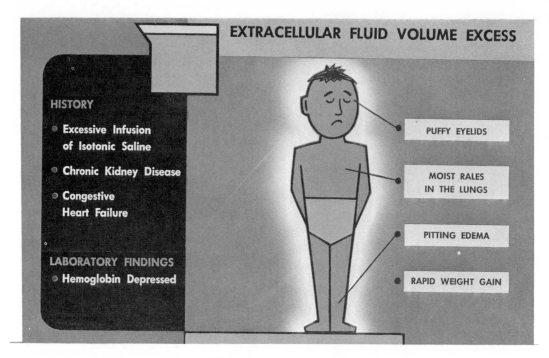

FIG. 14. Extracellular fluid volume excess.

and the hemoglobin, are decreased since they find themselves in an abnormally large volume of extracellular fluid.

Clinical Example. An 8-year-old boy was unable to retain liquids following appendectomy, and he was therefore maintained on parenteral fluids. For 2 days he was given an intravenous infusion of 5 per cent dextrose in isotonic solution of sodium chloride in the amount of 4 L. On the morning of the third day, he complained of shortness of breath. His eyelids were puffy, and his cheeks appeared full. Moist rales were heard in the lungs. He was weighed and was found to have gained approximately 6 per cent over his admission weight. His red blood cell count was found to be 4,000,000, and his hemoglobin was 10.5 Gm.

Chapter 6

Composition Changes of Major Extracellular Electrolytes

SODIUM, POTASSIUM AND CALCIUM IMBALANCES

Sodium Deficit of Extracellular Fluid

It must be borne in mind that the compositional changes to be discussed in this chapter represent changes in concentration of the electrolytes in question, as expressed in mEq./L. A change in the concentration of an electrolyte can be produced either by a change in the total quantity of the electrolyte or in the total quantity of the water in the extracellular fluid. For example, one could develop a sodium deficit (Fig. 15) because either of decreased intake or increased loss of sodium, or because of excessive intake or decreased loss of water. Similarly, one could develop an excess of sodium in the extracellular fluid because either of increased intake or decreased output of sodium, or because of decreased intake or increased loss of water. These mechanisms apply not only to changes in sodium concentration, but to all the other extracellular electrolytes.

In the history of sodium deficit of extracellular fluid, we find that there has been excessive sweating plus drinking of plain water, gastrointestinal suction plus drinking of plain water (an unfortunately common occurrence), administration of repeated water enemas, administration of a potent diuretic, infusion parenterally of an electrolyte-free solution, or inhalation of fresh water (as occurs in fresh water drowning).

Symptoms include apprehension (sometimes a bizarre indefinable feeling of im-pending doom), abdominal cramps, convulsions, oliguria or anuria. In a pronounced deficit, symptoms may occur of vasomotor collapse, such as hypotension, rapid thready pulse, cold clammy skin and cyanosis. An interesting finding that may be observed is fingerprinting over the sternum. This consists of a visible fingerprint apparent after pressure is applied with the finger or thumb on the skin overlying the sternum. Fingerprinting is due to increased plasticity of the tissues, which occurs as a result of the transfer of water from the abnormally dilute extracellular fluid into the cells. As a result of this osmotic transfer of water, an abnormally large portion of the body fluids lies within the confines of the cells. The fluid volume of the extracellular fluid—both plasma and interstitial fluid—is decreased. Consequently, tissues tend to retain any shape attained by pressure deformation, that is, they become more plastic than normal.

The laboratory findings reveal a plasma chloride usually below 98 mEq./L., a plasma sodium below 137 mEq./L. The specific gravity of the urine is characteristically below 1.010.

Clinical Example. Following the removal of her gallbladder, a 35-year-old woman complained of considerable gas and general abdominal discomfort. A gastric tube was inserted, and suction drainage instituted. The woman was given water to sip. Over a period of two days, approximately 2 L. of fluid were removed from the stomach by means of the gastric tube. During this period, the patient had nothing by mouth ex-

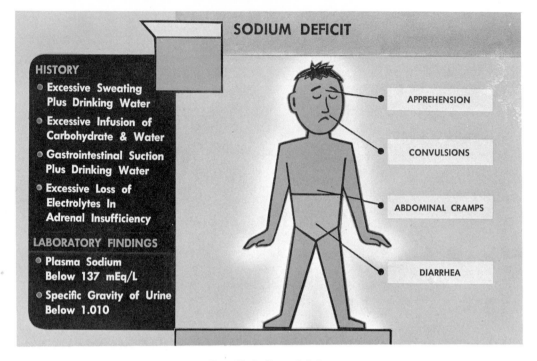

FIG. 15. Sodium deficit.

cept sips of plain water. On the morning of the third day, she complained of abdominal cramps. Nursing records showed that she had passed only 400 ml. of urine during the previous 24 hours. Physical examination revealed the finding of fingerprinting over the sternum. (After the physician pressed his thumb over the sternum, a thumbprint remained.) The plasma sodium was found to be 132 mEq./L. The plasma chloride was 90 mEq./L. Urine was not available for a specific gravity determination.

Sodium Excess of Extracellular Fluid

In this imbalance (Fig. 16) we find there has been a decreased water intake, an excessive ingestion of sodium chloride, or perhaps a tracheobronchitis in which the rapid breathing and high fever have caused the loss of great amounts of water by way of the lungs. The imbalance may follow profuse watery diarrhea, in which water is lost in excess of electrolytes. It may occur with unconsciousness when the patient simply does not drink liquids, or it may happen to the patient who has inhaled ocean water as a result of drowning.

The symptoms of this imbalance include dry, sticky mucous membranes, a flushed skin, intense thirst; the tongue is rough and dry, and oliguria or anuria is present. The temperature is elevated.

The laboratory findings include a plasma sodium above 147 mEq./L., plasma chloride above 106 mEq./L., and a specific gravity of the urine above 1.030.

Clinical Example. A 6-year-old girl was brought into the hospital because of extreme agitation and inability to sleep. The history revealed that for the past 4 days, she had had a mild diarrhea, which her mother was treating by the administration of a solution of salt and soda in water. Apparently, the mother had added a tablespoon full of salt and a tablespoon full of baking soda to each pint of water and had been forcing the child to drink about a pint of this mixture a day. On physical examination, the child was found to have dry, sticky mucous membranes. The tongue was rough and dry. Her skin was flushed. She complained of thirst.

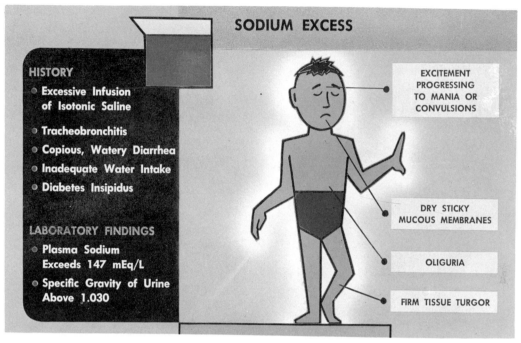

FIG. 16. Sodium excess.

The mother stated the child had not urinated for the past 24 hours. The plasma chloride was found to be 112 mEq./L., and the plasma sodium, 160 mEq./L.

Potassium Deficit of Extracellular Fluid

The potassium ion is one of the most interesting and important of all the body electrolytes. Although it is present in the cellular and extracellular fluid, it is within the cells that it is especially active. Potassium is the chief cation of the cells. Since the body conservation mechanism is, at best, inefficient, potassium deficit (Fig. 17) inevitably occurs when there has been no ingestion of potassium for several days. Naturally, the onset of the deficit is hastened if there have been abnormal losses of potassium from the body. As the extracellular fluid is depleted of potassium, a cellular deficit develops.

Although there are at least fifty important historical antecedents for potassium deficit, it is most frequently observed following the use of a potent diuretic—especially one of the thiazide group—or when there has been vomiting, ulcerative colitis, or diarrhea. The deficit is encouraged by the administration parenterally of a solution not containing potassium, by the loss of potassium through fistulas of the small intestine or colon, by the metabolic changes that occur in diabetic acidosis, or in a burn after the fifth day.

Early symptoms of potassium deficit are nonspecific, consisting chiefly of malaise, "just not feeling well." As the deficit develops, symptoms relating to the muscle systems appear:

1. Symptoms involving the skeletal muscles include:
   - Generalized weakness
   - Diminished to absent reflexes
   - Muscles flabby like half-filled water bottles
   - Patient lies flat like a cadaver, not rounded
2. Symptoms relating to the heart muscle:
   - Weak pulse
   - Faint heart sounds
   - Heart block
   - Falling blood pressure

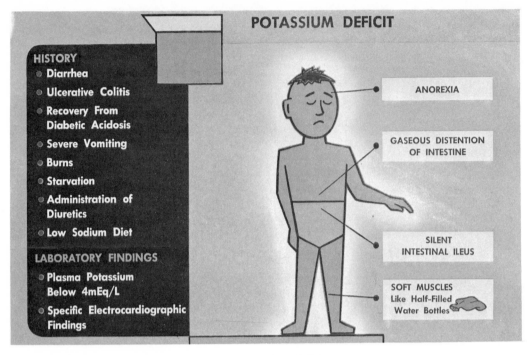

FIG. 17. Potassium deficit.

3. Symptoms involving the gastrointestinal tract:
   • Vomiting
   • Paralytic ileus
4. Symptoms involving the muscles of respiration are shallow respirations.

In addition to the above symptoms, thirst may be present.

The laboratory findings include a plasma potassium below 4 mEq./L. The chloride is often below 98 mEq./L. The electrocardiograph reveals evidence of potassium deficit.

Clinical Example. A 60-year-old man was admitted to the hospital because of extreme weakness and a complete loss of appetite. The history revealed that he had been receiving a thiazide-type diuretic for his hypertension for the past 6 months. Weakness and anorexia had been gradual in onset. The man had eaten an average diet with no particular emphasis on potassium-containing foods, nor did he receive a potassium supplement. Physical examination revealed a patient with soft, flabby muscles, which felt much like half-filled water bottles. Intestinal sounds impressed the physician as less than normal. There was minimal gaseous distention of the intestines. The plasma potassium was found to be 3 mEq./L. An electrocardiogram presented findings consonant with potassium deficit.

Potassium Excess of Extracellular Fluid

We often observe an excess in the potassium of the extracellular fluid (Fig. 18) in advanced kidney disease. It may occur early after a severe burn, or with a massive crushing injury. Potassium excess can be caused by an unduly large dose of potassium administered parenterally. It can occur with adrenal insufficiency, as a result of oliguria or anuria, or because of the kidney damage caused by mercuric bichloride poisoning.

Symptoms include irritability, nausea, intestinal colic, and diarrhea in mild excess. As excesses become severe, weakness and flaccid paralysis occur. There may be difficulty in phonation and respiration. Oliguria occurs and progresses to anuria. Finally, cardiac arrhythmia followed ·by standstill terminate the picture.

The laboratory findings reveal the plasma

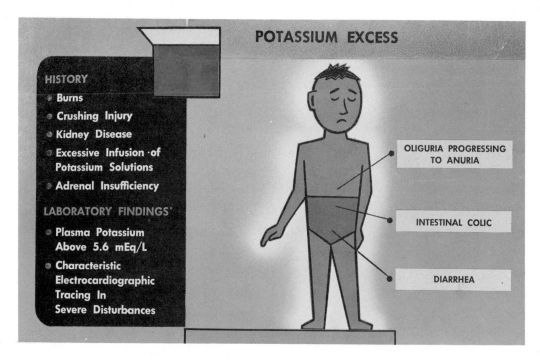

FIG. 18. Potassium excess.

potassium to be above 5.6 mEq./L. Renal function tests show severe renal impairment in most cases of potassium excess. The electrocardiograph reveals a high T wave and a depressed ST segment.

Clinical Example. A 40-year-old man was admitted to the hospital because of extreme irritability, abdominal cramps, and nausea. His urination had been scanty for the past month, and during the previous 24 hours had ceased altogether. He gave a history of having had chronic disease of the kidneys on and off since childhood. The plasma potassium was found to be 7 mEq./L. The electrocardiogram showed a high T wave and a depressed ST segment.

Calcium Deficit of Extracellular Fluid

This deficit (Fig. 19) can be caused by the loss of excessive quantities of calcium, as in the diarrhea of sprue, or by the extraction of calcium from the extracellular fluid, as occurs in acute pancreatitis or in massive infections of subcutaneous tissues. Correction of acidosis sometimes causes calcium

deficit; this occurs when the patient's extracellular supply of calcium has been abnormally low but functionally adequate because of the high ionization of calcium that accompanies acidosis. When the acidosis is corrected, the ionization is reduced and the patient develops manifest calcium deficit. We also see calcium deficit with the parenteral administration of calcium-free solutions, which wash out calcium. Calcium deficit occurs when citrated blood is administered in excessive quantities, because the citrate binds the extracellular fluid calcium. We also see it as a result of the metabolic changes accompanying primary hypoparathyroidism.

The symptoms of calcium deficit include tingling of the ends of the fingers, tetany, abdominal cramps, muscle cramps, carpopedal spasm and convulsions.

The Sulkowitch test on the urine reveals no precipitation, and the plasma calcium is usually below 4.5 mEq./L. The electrocardiograph is helpful in diagnosing calcium deficit; so is the x-ray.

Clinical Example. A patient was admitted to the hospital because of sprue of some 2

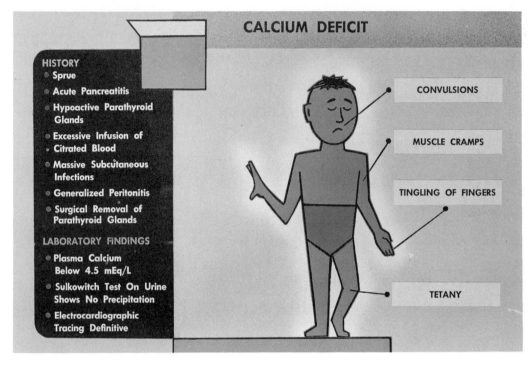

FIG. 19. Calcium deficit.

months' duration. During a period of 2 weeks in the hospital, the patient had numerous large, foul-smelling stools daily. Because of the frequent bowel movements, he was given a potassium supplement in addition to a regular diet. During his third week in the hospital, he complained of tingling of the ends of his fingers and of abdominal cramps. Physical examination revealed hyperactive deep reflexes and bilateral carpopedal spasms. A Sulkowitch test on the urine revealed no precipitation. The plasma calcium level was found to be 3.8 mEq./L.

Calcium Excess of Extracellular Fluid

This excess (Fig. 20) can be seen as a result of the metabolic changes following hyperparathyroidism, parathyroid tumor, or the excessive administration of Vitamin D. It may result from the retention of calcium because of kidney disease. Multiple myeloma may produce excessive calcium; prolonged immobilization may encourage its retention. A pathologic fracture may be the first indication of a parathyroid tumor and calcium excess.

The symptoms of calcium excess include hypotonicity of the muscles, kidney stones, flank pain, deep bony pain, and bone cavitation.

The Sulkowitch test on the urine reveals heavy precipitation; the plasma calcium is characteristically above 5.8 mEq./L. The electrocardiograph is helpful in diagnosing calcium excess; so is the x-ray.

Clinical Example. A 55-year-old female was admitted to the hospital with a fracture of the right femur. She stated that she had suffered a slight fall, but hardly enough, in her opinion, to bruise her. Yet, her right femur was shown to be fractured on x-ray examination. Physical examination revealed that her muscles were hypotonic. When the femur was x-rayed to determine if a fracture was present, numerous areas of decalcification were observed. The Sulkowitch test on the urine revealed heavy precipitation. The plasma calcium level was found to be 6.4 mEq./L. A parathyroid tumor was suspected and was found at operation.

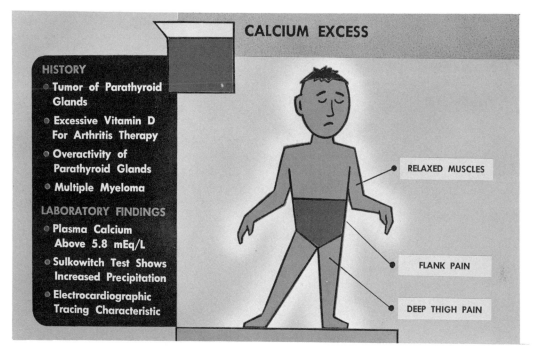

FIG. 20. Calcium excess.

NATURE OF THE ACID-BASE IMBALANCES

Deficits or excesses of base bicarbonate or of carbonic acid are usually designated the *acid-base imbalances*. They stem from abnormalities in the hydrogen ion concentration of the extracellular fluid. The cation hydrogen, although present in extracellular fluid in extremely tiny quantities, is immensely important from the standpoint of health. When its concentration lies within certain narrow limits, the patient's extracellular fluid is chemically and physiologically neutral. When the concentration of hydrogen increases (pH decreases), the extracellular fluid becomes acid, and the patient is in acidosis. When the concentration of hydrogen ion decreases (pH increases), the reaction of the extracellular fluid becomes alkaline or basic, and the patient is in alkalosis.

What is it that determines the concentration of hydrogen ions? Carbon dioxide unites with water in the extracellular fluid to form carbonic acid. The cations sodium, potassium, calcium and magnesium unite with the anion bicarbonate to form an extracellular fluid complex, which Snively and Sweeney have designated as *base bicarbonate*.

It Is the Ratio of Carbonic Acid to the Base Bicarbonate of the Extracellular Fluid That Determines the Concentration of Hydrogen Ions

Although other factors enter in, this is the prime determinant. As long as there is 1 mEq. of carbonic acid for each 20 mEq. of base bicarbonate in the extracellular fluid, the hydrogen ion concentration lies within normal limits. Picture an imaginary acid-base balance with 1.33 mEq. of carbonic acid resting on the left side and 27 mEq. of base bicarbonate on the right, the situation in health. Each carbonic acid block represents .333 mEq./L. of carbonic acid; each base bicarbonate block represents 6.75 mEq./L. of base bicarbonate. This is the 1 to 20 ratio required for normal acid-base reaction of extracellular fluid.

Any condition that tilts the balance to the

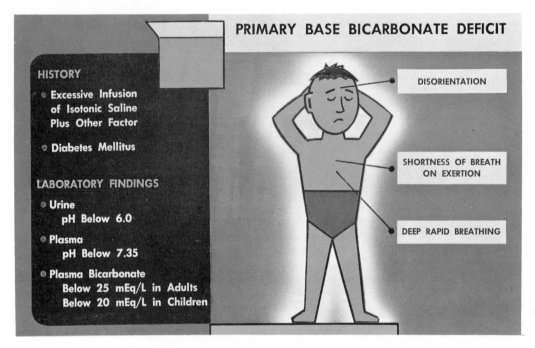

PRIMARY BASE BICARBONATE DEFICIT

HISTORY

● Excessive Infusion of Isotonic Saline Plus Other Factor

● Diabetes Mellitus

LABORATORY FINDINGS

● Urine pH Below 6.0

● Plasma pH Below 7.35

● Plasma Bicarbonate Below 25 mEq/L in Adults Below 20 mEq/L in Children

DISORIENTATION

SHORTNESS OF BREATH ON EXERTION

DEEP RAPID BREATHING

Fig. 21. Primary base bicarbonate deficit.

left causes acidosis; any condition that tilts it to the right causes alkalosis. The balance can be tipped by two types of disturbances: metabolic (systemic) and respiratory. The metabolic disturbances affect the base bicarbonate, or right side of the balance, by either adding to the base bicarbonate or subtracting from it. The respiratory disturbances affect the carbonic acid or left side of the balance, by adding to the carbonic acid or subtracting from it.

Primary Base Bicarbonate Deficit of Extracellular Fluid

A primary deficit in the base bicarbonate concentration of the extracellular fluid (Fig. 21) is usually called *metabolic acidosis.* It is caused by a clinical event that decreases the amount of base bicarbonate. Thus, it can result from decreased food intake, from diabetic acidosis, or from a systemic infection. It can be caused by the parenteral infusion of isotonic solution of sodium chloride, in combination with one or more other etiologic factors. A ketogenic diet can produce it; so can renal insufficiency

or salicylate intoxication after the initial stages.

The symptoms of metabolic acidosis include stupor; deep, rapid breathing of Kussmaul type; shortness of breath on exertion; weakness; and, if severe, unconsciousness.

The laboratory findings include a urine pH below 6.0, a plasma bicarbonate below 25 mEq./L. in adults and below 20 mEq./L. in children, and a plasma pH below 7.35.

Clinical Example. A 3½-year-old girl was admitted to the hospital approximately 2 hours after having ingested 10 5-grain tablets of sodium salicylate. At the time of admission, the child was stuporous. Her breathing was both deep and rapid, of the typical Kussmaul variety. A pH determination on the urine revealed a reading of 5. The plasma bicarbonate was found to be 10 mEq./L. The plasma pH was 7.25.

Primary Base Bicarbonate Excess of Extracellular Fluid

A primary excess of base bicarbonate concentration (Fig. 22), usually called *metabolic alkalosis,* can be caused by any clinical event

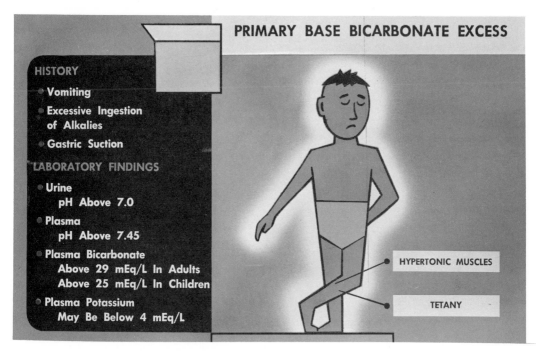

FIG. 22. Primary base bicarbonate excess.

that weights the base bicarbonate side of the balance. It can also be caused by the loss of a chloride-rich secretion, such as gastric juice. When chloride is lost, bicarbonate increases in compensation, since the total anions of the extracellular fluid must always equal the total cations to preserve chemical-electrical equality. We find metabolic alkalosis following excessive ingestion of sodium bicarbonate or other alkalies; after vomiting; following the infusion of a potassium-free solution; when the taking of a potent diuretic for a long period has caused potassium deficit; following gastrointestinal suction; and with the administration of adrenal cortical hormones.

There is a close association between metabolic alkalosis and potassium deficit. Potassium deficit does not of itself *cause* base bicarbonate excess, but it does make the body peculiarly vulnerable to base bicarbonate excess should chloride loss occur. This is because potassium deficit makes it difficult or impossible for the kidneys to excrete alkali for reasons still obscure. Suppose large amounts of chloride are lost from the body,

as in vomiting. Base bicarbonate increases in compensation since the total anions must always equal the total cations. Usually the body would tend to correct the situation by retaining dietary chlorides. However, if a potassium deficit is present, the kidneys will excrete dietary chlorides and other acid materials, but will retain bicarbonate and other alkaline materials. Only the correction of the potassium deficit will permit the kidneys to retain needed acids and excrete alkalies.

The symptoms of metabolic alkalosis include hypertonicity of the muscles, tetany and depressed respiration. Correction of metabolic acidosis may precipitate tetany or convulsions for the following reason: Calcium deficit of the extracellular fluid causes hyperirritability, manifesting itself in tetany and convulsions if the deficit is severe. The effective calcium of the extracellular fluid is the ionized calcium. The degree of ionization of calcium is directly proportional to the acidity of the fluid. In the acid body fluid of acidosis, calcium ionization is high. In the alkaline fluid of alkalosis, ionization is greatly decreased. A patient can, therefore,

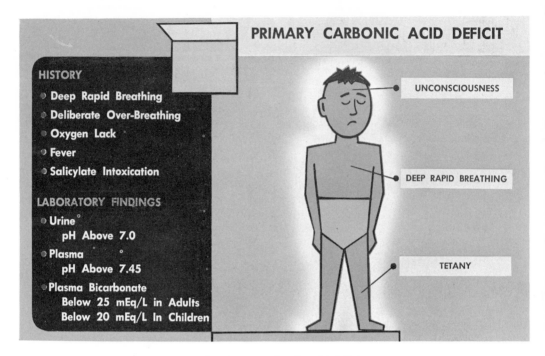

FIG. 23. Primary carbonic acid deficit.

have a calcium deficit of extracellular fluid not manifested by symptoms if the patient is acidotic. With the correction of the acidosis to neutral, or with its overcorrection to alkalosis, the calcium deficit becomes manifest and symptoms of hyperirritability occur.

The laboratory findings include a urine pH above 7.0, plasma bicarbonate above 29 mEq./L. in adults and above 25 mEq./L. in children, plasma pH above 7.45, and a plasma potassium below 4 mEq./L. The chloride will be under 98 mEq./L. if the alkalosis is hypochloremic.

Clinical Example. A 22-year-old woman was admitted to the hospital with the diagnosis of anorexia nervosa. During the first three days of her hospital stay, she ate very little and vomited what she did eat. She was given no supplements or parenteral fluid therapy. On the fourth day, she was seen to have tetanic movements of the fingers. Physical examination revealed that her muscles were hypertonic. The physician thought that breathing was depressed. The urine pH was found to be 7.5. The plasma bicarbonate level was determined as 35 mEq./L. The plasma potassium was 3.5 mEq./L.

Primary Carbonic Acid Deficit of Extracellular Fluid

This deficit (Fig. 23), usually called *respiratory alkalosis,* is caused by any condition that results in an increased rate and depth of breathing, with the resultant blowing off of carbon dioxide. This loss of carbon dioxide depletes the carbonic acid of the extracellular fluid. We see respiratory alkalosis with oxygen lack, with fever, in hysteria, early in salicylate intoxication, with anxiety, with intentional overbreathing and following extreme emotion.

The symptoms include tetany, convulsions and unconsciousness.

The laboratory findings include a urine pH above 7.0, plasma bicarbonate below 25 mEq./L. in adults and below 20 mEq./L. in children, and a plasma pH above 7.45. The plasma bicarbonate is depressed in an effort to compensate for the decreased extracellular fluid carbonic acid. Depression of the bicarbonate tends to restore the carbonic acid: base bicarbonate ratio to normal.

Clinical Example. An 18-year-old girl was admitted to the hospital for study because of

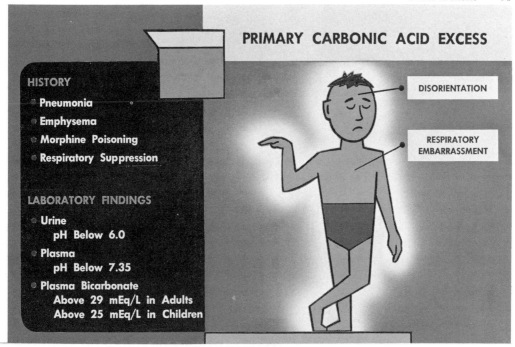

FIG. 24. Primary carbonic acid excess.

tetanic spasms of the fingers and occasional convulsions. The history revealed that she had been extremely apprehensive because of her fear of failing in school. Her mother noticed that she had been breathing deeply and rapidly for several weeks. Physical examination revealed hyperactive reflexes. The urine pH was 7.5, and the plasma bicarbonate, 20 mEq./L.

Primary Carbonic Acid Excess of Extracellular Fluid

This excess (Fig. 24), usually called *respiratory acidosis*, occurs when there is any impairment to the exhalation of carbon dioxide. It is caused, in general, by conditions which depress respiration, such as pneumonia, emphysema, occlusion of the breathing passages, morphine poisoning, barbiturate poisoning and asthma. It can also come from breathing excessive carbon dioxide.

The symptoms include disorientation, respiratory embarrassment, coma and weakness. Laboratory findings reveal a urine pH below 6.0; the plasma bicarbonate is above 29 mEq./L. in adults and above 25 mEq./L. in children, and the plasma pH is below

7.35. Elevation of the plasma bicarbonate represents an attempt on the part of the body to compensate for the elevated extracellular fluid carbonic acid. This elevation tends to restore the carbonic acid: base bicarbonate ratio to normal.

Clinical Example. A patient was admitted to the hospital because of coma. The history revealed that he had suffered from emphysema for the past six years, that during the past 2 weeks he had become increasingly weak and disoriented. His urine pH was 5.5. The plasma bicarbonate reading was 40 mEq./L. The plasma pH was 6.8.

OTHER DEFICITS

Protein Deficit of Extracellular Fluid

Protein deficit (Fig. 25) can result from the repeated or chronic loss of whole blood, from decreased food intake, or as the aftermath of a severe burn, severe trauma, or fracture. It can occur as a result of wound drainage or decubitus ulcers.

Its symptoms include ready fatigue, pallor, soft flabby muscles and emotional depression. The protein-deficient patient fre-

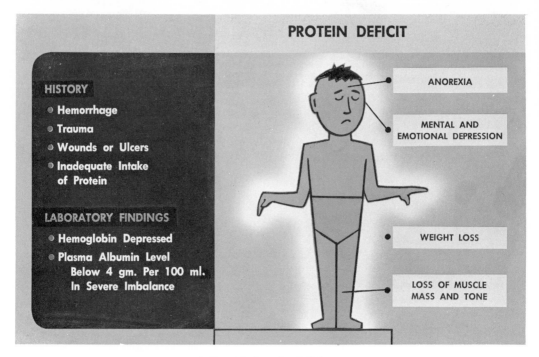

FIG. 25. Protein deficit.

quently appears to have decreased resistance to infection; he also shows chronic weight loss.

With respect to laboratory findings, the plasma albumin is sometimes, though not necessarily, below 4.0 Gm./100 ml.; the packed cell volume, hemoglobin, and red blood cell count are decreased. This decrease is significant only if the iron stores of the patient are adequate; if the iron stores are inadequate, the patient may well be suffering from iron deficiency anemia.

Clinical Example. A 28-year-old female was severely injured in an automobile accident, suffering considerable loss of blood and multiple fractures, one of which was compound. She was given multiple blood transfusions during the first few days in the hospital, but after this period her only source of nutrients was the usual hospital diet, at which she only nibbled. Her fractures were slow in knitting, and her flesh wounds healed slowly. She was emotionally depressed and pale. Her muscles were soft and flabby. She lost 20 lbs. during the period of her stay in the hospital. Her plasma albumin was determined and found to be 3.8 Gm./100 ml. Her hemoglobin was found to be 9 Gm., and her red blood cell count, 3,000,000. (Recall that a depression of the hemoglobin or red blood cell count is indicative of protein deficit only if the patient has been receiving adequate iron.)

Magnesium Deficit of the Extracellular Fluid

This deficit (Fig. 26) is not common, but should be considered if it is not to be missed —it can easily be mistaken for potassium deficit. The history frequently reveals the presence of chronic alcoholism, vomiting, or diarrhea. There may be impaired gastrointestinal absorption, either because of disease of the small intestine or because of surgical removal of portions of the intestine. It may occur with enterostomy drainage, or following prolonged parenteral administration of magnesium-free solutions.

Symptoms are due to hyperirritability of the muscles and central nervous system.

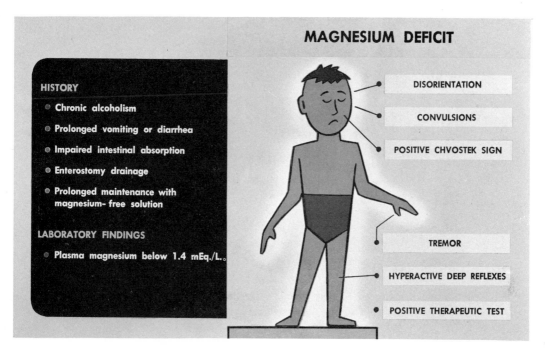

MAGNESIUM DEFICIT

HISTORY

- Chronic alcoholism
- Prolonged vomiting or diarrhea
- Impaired intestinal absorption
- Enterostomy drainage
- Prolonged maintenance with magnesium-free solution

LABORATORY FINDINGS

- Plasma magnesium below 1.4 mEq./L.

DISORIENTATION

CONVULSIONS

POSITIVE CHVOSTEK SIGN

TREMOR

HYPERACTIVE DEEP REFLEXES

POSITIVE THERAPEUTIC TEST

FIG. 26. Magnesium deficit.

They include tremor, hyperactive deep reflexes, positive Chvostek sign, and convulsions. Confusion—even hallucinations—may occur; so may elevated blood pressure and tachycardia. There is a positive therapeutic response to magnesium sulfate.

The laboratory findings reveal a plasma magnesium below 1.4 mEq./L.

Clinical Example. A patient was admitted to the hospital with regional enteritis accompanied by considerable diarrhea. He was given the usual hospital diet plus a potassium supplement. After a month in the hospital, the patient began to have periods of disorientation. Physical examination revealed a tremor of the fingers. His deep reflexes were found to be hyperactive, and his Chvostek sign was positive. On one occasion, the patient had a convulsion of brief duration. Plasma potassium was normal. A plasma magnesium was found to be 1 mEq./L. Magnesium sulfate was administered as a therapeutic test, and immediate improvement was noted.

Chapter 7

Position Changes of Water and Electrolytes of Extracellular Fluid

Normally, about one-fourth of the extracellular fluid exists as plasma and about three-fourths as interstitial fluid. Under certain circumstances, water and electrolytes of the plasma can shift into the interstitial space. In other circumstances, water and electrolytes shift from the interstitial fluid to the plasma. The mechanisms for these shifts are obscure. If they have a useful function, it is difficult to discern. These mysterious tides of disease represent a curious response to unseen, unfathomed forces set in motion by certain illnesses and injuries.

Plasma-to-Interstitial Fluid Shift

This shift (Fig. 27) is frequently seen on the first or second day of a severe burn, or following a massive crushing injury, perforated peptic ulcer, or severe trauma. It may be observed with intestinal obstruction, or following the acute occlusion of a major artery.

The symptoms of the shift are virtually synonymous with those of shock, with which it is identifiable. They include pallor, low blood pressure, tachycardia, weak to absent pulse, weakness, cold extremities and unconsciousness.

The red blood cell count is increased in this shift, as are the packed cell volume and hemoglobin. The reason why these formed elements of the blood are increased is this: With the shift of water and electrolytes from the plasma to the interstitial space, the formed elements find themselves in a lesser volume of extracellular fluid.

Clinical Example. An 11-year-old girl was admitted to the hospital with two-thirds of her body covered by second- and third-degree burns, suffered when an inflammable party dress caught fire. The burn team of the hospital immediately took charge of this patient and carried out the usual excellent burn program of that hospital. Nevertheless, during her second 24 hours in the hospital, her hemoglobin and red blood cell count were found to be rising rapidly. Her blood pressure dropped to 90/70. Her pulse rose to 125. She complained of cold hands and feet. The burned area appeared boggy, as if filled with fluid. (This is an example of the plasma-to-interstitial shift that almost invariably occurs early during a severe burn. On the third to fifth day, the opposite shift occurs—interstitial space-to-plasma shift, the so-called remobilization of edema fluid.)

Interstitial Fluid-to-Plasma Shift

This shift (Fig. 28) may occur in a severe burn after the third day, in which case it is often called remobilization of edema fluid. It is also seen after the loss of whole blood and following the excessive infusion of large molecular solutions, such as plasma or dextran. It is likewise seen as the aftermath of a fracture.

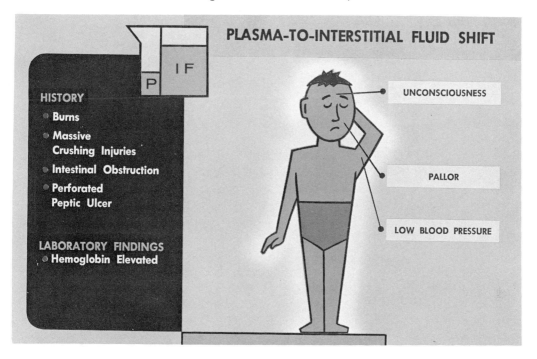

FIG. 27. Plasma-to-interstitial fluid shift.

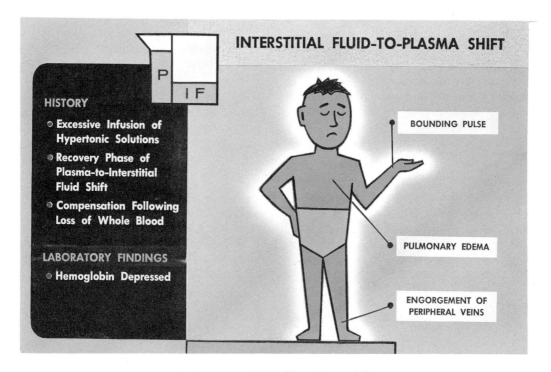

FIG. 28. Interstitial fluid-to-plasma shift.

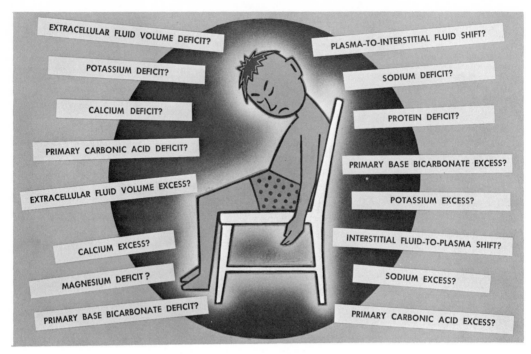

Fig. 29. The systematic approach to understanding body fluid disturbances brings order out of confusion.

The symptoms include pallor, weakness, air hunger, and bounding pulse. The peripheral veins are engorged, there are moist rales in the lungs. Cardiac dilatation and ventricular failure can occur.

Since there is a volume increase in the plasma portion of the extracellular fluid, the red blood cell count is decreased, as are the packed cell volume and the hemoglobin.

Clinical Example. A 14-year-old boy was admitted to the hospital with a 60 per cent second- and third-degree burn. His initial water and electrolyte therapy was, perhaps, over-zealous. On the third day, he complained of being unable to get his breath. Physical examination at that time revealed a bounding pulse, with engorgement of the peripheral veins. Moist rales were heard in both lungs. The red blood cell count was found to be 3,500,000, and the hemoglobin, 10 Gm. (This patient was suffering from the well-known remobilization of edema fluid that occurs during the third to fifth day following a severe burn. This shift will be more severe if the patient has received ex-

cessive quantities of water and electrolytes during the first one or two days of his treatment.)

Comment

The clinical examples of body fluid disturbances were chosen so as to represent relatively pure examples of single disturbances. Actually, these relatively pure examples are not uncommon. Sometimes, of course, one sees combined imbalances, and in some patients a considerable number of imbalances can be present simultaneously. Usually, however, one or two imbalances dominate the clinical picture. The infant with an acute onset of vomiting and diarrhea, for example, early has volume deficit of extracellular fluid. Shortly thereafter, however, if he is not properly treated, he will develop primary base bicarbonate deficit. If potassium is not given and the diarrhea continues, he will, after 3 or 4 days, develop potassium deficit. If he continues to have loose watery stools and, particularly, if he is

PHYSICO-CHEMICAL IMBALANCE	CONVENTIONAL TERMINOLOGY	CLOSELY-RELATED CLINICAL STATES
Extracellular Fluid Volume Deficit	• Fluid deficit • Dehydration (incorrect term, since ECF volume deficit means loss of water *and* electrolytes) • Hypovolemia	
Extracellular Fluid Volume Excess	• Fluid volume excess • Overhydration (incorrect term, since this imbalance means an excess of both water *and* electrolytes)	
Sodium Deficit	• Electrolyte concentration deficit • Hyponatremia • Low sodium syndrome • Hypotonic dehydration	• Heat exhaustion • Sodium-losing kidney
Sodium Excess	• Hypernatremia • Hypertonic dehydration • Salt excess • Oversalting	
Potassium Deficit	• Hypokalemia • Potassium deficiency	• Potassium-losing kidney
Potassium Excess	• Hyperkalemia	
Calcium Deficit	• Hypocalcemia	• Calcium deficiency leg cramps
Calcium Excess	• Hypercalcemia	• Pathologic fractures
Primary Base Bicarbonate Deficit	• Metabolic acidosis • Acidemia	• Diabetic ketosis • Renal acidosis
Primary Base Bicarbonate Excess	• Metabolic alkalosis • Alkalemia	
Primary Carbonic Acid Deficit	• Respiratory alkalosis • Alkalemia	• Hyperventilation
Primary Carbonic Acid Excess	• Respiratory acidosis • Acidemia	
Protein Deficit	• Hypoproteinemia • Protein malnutrition	• Kwashiorkor • Pluri-carencial syndrome • Hypoproteinosis
Magnesium Deficit	• Hypomagnesemia	
Shift of Water and Electrolytes from Plasma to Interstitial Space	• Hypovolemia	• Shock • Edema
Shift of Water and Electrolytes from Interstitial Space to Plasma	• Hypervolemia	• Remobilization of edema fluid

also given salt mixtures by mouth, he may well develop a sodium excess.

The addition of each one of these fluid balance disturbances has the effect of importantly increasing, perhaps doubling, the mortality. Various disease states are characterized by a wide variety of body fluid disturbances, depending upon the severity of the disease. Among these conditions might be mentioned burns, severe trauma, diabetes mellitus, gastrointestinal disease and intestinal obstruction. As an example, obstruction of the large intestine can manifest the following disturbances:

- Extracellular fluid volume deficit
- Extracellular fluid volume excess
- Sodium deficit
- Sodium excess
- Potassium deficit
- Potassium excess
- Calcium deficit

- Primary base bicarbonate excess
- And, perhaps, others.

It cannot, however, be overemphasized that if one is to understand combined, complex body fluid disturbances, he must understand the single imbalances, the mechanism of their development, plus their relationships to each other and to disease. (Fig. 29)

Terminology Problems

Understanding body fluid disturbances is made considerably more difficult since so many terms frequently apply to the same condition. The chart on page 39 attempts to resolve this problem by showing in parallel columns each chemical imbalance, then the conventional term applied to the imbalance, and finally, the related clinical term, if such exists. A careful study of this chart will help to resolve apparent conflicts in terms.

Chapter 8

The Role of Nursing Observations in the Diagnosis of Body Fluid Disturbances

FORMULATION OF NURSING DIAGNOSIS

Although her role is not diagnostic in a medical sense, the nurse must possess enough knowledge of body fluid disturbances to make an intelligent nursing diagnosis. Such a step is necessary to locate pertinent nursing problems. Once the problems (or potential problems) are identified, the nurse can plan for meaningful observations, measures to prevent imbalances, intelligent execution of medical directives, and other effective nursing care measures. The emphasis in this chapter is on meaningful observations.

The nurse must be a careful observer in all areas of nursing—fluid balance is no exception. Changes in the patient developing a fluid imbalance are often subtle and perceptible only to those familiar with him and his condition. Therefore, observations made by the nurse are particularly valuable, because she spends more time with the patient than does the physician. The observations must be planned and based on an understanding of basic physiologic processes; otherwise, they are of little or no value.

To assist in the formulation of the nursing diagnosis, the nurse should attempt to answer these questions:

1. What, if any, disease state is present that can disrupt body fluid balance? (For example: diabetes mellitus, emphysema, or fever) What type of imbalance does this condition usually result in? (See Table 1)

2. Is the patient receiving any medication

TABLE 1. IMBALANCES LIKELY TO OCCUR IN VARIOUS CLINICAL CONDITIONS

CONDITION	IMBALANCES LIKELY TO OCCUR
Acute Illnesses:	
Uncontrolled severe diabetes mellitus	Metabolic acidosis Potassium deficit
Adrenal insufficiency	Potassium excess
Acute pancreatitis	Calcium deficit
Perforated peptic ulcer	Plasma-to-interstitial fluid shift
Pneumonia (exudate blocks exchange of CO_2)	Respiratory acidosis
Occlusion of breathing passages (inability to exchange CO_2)	Respiratory acidosis
Tracheobronchitis	Sodium excess
Oxygen lack with hyperpnea	Respiratory alkalosis
High external temperature with physiologic hyperpnea	Respiratory alkalosis
Fever	Respiratory alkalosis Fluid volume deficit
Systemic infection	Metabolic acidosis Fluid volume deficit
Acute occlusion of major artery	Plasma-to-interstitial fluid shift
Massive infection of subcutaneous tissues	Calcium deficit

TABLE 1—(*Continued*)

CONDITION	IMBALANCES LIKELY TO OCCUR
Chronic Illnesses:	
Emphysema	Respiratory acidosis
Asthma	Respiratory acidosis
Congestive heart failure	Fluid volume excess
Pulmonary edema	Respiratory acidosis
Renal disease	Metabolic acidosis Potassium excess Fluid volume excess Calcium excess
Hyperaldosteronism	Fluid volume excess
Hyperparathyroidism	Calcium excess
Primary hypopara- thyroidism	Calcium deficit
Meningitis	Respiratory alkalosis
Encephalitis	Respiratory alkalosis
Multiple myeloma	Calcium excess
Gastric disease with re- peated vomiting	Metabolic alkalosis Potassium deficit
Chronic alcoholism	Magnesium deficit
Burns or Injuries:	
Burn, early	Potassium excess Plasma-to-interstitial fluid shift
Burn after third day	Potassium deficit Protein deficit Interstitial fluid-to- plasma shift
Massive crushing injury	Potassium excess Plasma-to-interstitial fluid shift
Severe trauma	Protein deficit Plasma-to-interstitial fluid shift
Fractures	Protein deficit Plasma-to-interstitial fluid shift
Inhalation of fresh water (drowning)	Sodium deficit
Inhalation of salt water (drowning)	Sodium excess

or treatment that can disrupt body fluid balance? (For example: steroids or thiazide diuretics) If so, how might this therapy upset fluid balance? (See Table 2)

3. Is there an abnormal loss of body fluids and, if so, from what source? What type of imbalance is usually associated with the loss of the particular body fluid or fluids? (See Table 3, p. 42.)

4. Have any dietary restrictions been imposed? (For example: low sodium diet) If so, how might this affect fluid balance?

5. Has the patient taken adequate amounts of water and other nutrients orally or by some other route? If not, for how long?

6. How does the total intake of fluids compare with the total fluid output?

ANTICIPATION OF FLUID IMBALANCES ASSOCIATED WITH SPECIFIC BODY FLUID LOSSES

Because the anticipation of an imbalance makes its appearance easier to detect, the nurse should learn to anticipate imbalances. It is extremely difficult to recognize significant changes in the patient when one does not know what to look for. Also, prevention is easier to practice when one knows which imbalance is likely to occur.

Water and electrolyte imbalances are often due to abnormal losses of body fluids. The type of imbalance (or imbalances) that accompanies the loss of a specific body fluid varies with the content of the lost fluid. The nurse can learn to anticipate specific imbalances when she knows the chief constituents of the lost fluids and how they function.

Table 3 lists the sodium, chloride, potassium and bicarbonate concentration of many of the body fluids.

A brief discussion of some of the body fluids and types of imbalances associated with their loss may help to clarify how the nurse can learn to anticipate fluid disturbances.

Gastric Juice

The usual daily volume of gastric juice is 2,500 ml. and the pH is usually 1 to 3. The amount of gastric fluid can vary from 100 to

TABLE 2. IMBALANCES CAUSED BY MEDICAL THERAPY

CONDITION	IMBALANCES LIKELY TO OCCUR
Administration of adrenal cortical hormones	Fluid volume excess Potassium deficit Metabolic alkalosis
Administration of potent diuretics	Potassium deficit Sodium deficit Metabolic alkalosis
Morphine or demerol in excessive doses	Respiratory acidosis
Barbiturate poisoning	Respiratory acidosis
Oral intake of potassium exceeding renal tolerance	Potassium excess
Early salicylate intoxication	Respiratory alkalosis
Salicylate intoxication (not early)	Metabolic acidosis
Mercuric bichloride poisoning	Potassium excess
Excessive administration of vitamin D	Calcium excess
Excessive parenteral infusion of isotonic solution of sodium chloride	Fluid volume excess Metabolic acidosis
Excessive parenteral administration of calcium-free solutions	Calcium deficit
Excessive parenteral administration of magnesium-free solutions	Magnesium deficit
Excessive parenteral administration of potassium	Potassium excess
Excessive infusion of large molecular solution	Interstitial fluid-to-plasma shift
Excessive administration of citrated blood	Calcium deficit
Excessive ingestion of sodium chloride	Sodium excess Fluid volume excess
Excessive ingestion of sodium bicarbonate	Metabolic alkalosis
Gastrointestinal suction plus drinking water	Sodium deficit Metabolic alkalosis Potassium deficit
Water enemas	Sodium deficit Potassium deficit
Recent correction of acidosis	Calcium deficit
Mechanical respirator inaccurately regulated (causing too deep or too fast breathing)	Respiratory alkalosis
Mechanical respirator inaccurately regulated (causing too shallow or too slow breathing)	Respiratory acidosis
Prolonged immobilization	Calcium excess

TABLE 3. ELECTROLYTE CONTENT OF BODY FLUIDS EXPRESSED
IN MILLIEQUIVALENTS PER LITER

BODY FLUID	NA+	K+	CL−	HCO$_3$−
Saliva	9	25.8	10	10–15
(fasting) Gastric juice	60.4	9.2	84	0–14
(suction) Small bowel	111.3	4.6	104.2	31
(recent) Ileostomy	129.4	11.2	116.2	..
(adapted) Ileostomy	46	3.0	21.4	..
(fistula) Bile	148.9	4.98	100.6	40
(fistula) Pancreatic juice	141.1	4.6	76.6	121
Cecostomy	79.6	20.6	48.2	..
Urine: normal	40–90	20–60	40–120	..
abnormal	0.5–312	5–166	5–210	..
(normal) Perspiration	45	4.5	57.5	..
Plasma*	137–147	4–5.6	98–106	..
Transudates**	130–145	2.5–5	90–110	..

* Also contains protein, 6–8 Gm./100 ml.
** Protein content is similar to plasma.

Weisberg, H.: Water, Electrolyte, and Acid-Base Balance. Ed. 2, p. 143, Baltimore, Williams & Wilkins, 1962.

6,000 ml. in abnormal states. Gastric juice contains hydrogen (H+), chloride (Cl−), sodium (Na+) and potassium (K+) ions. Imbalances that may result from severe vomiting or prolonged gastric suction include:

1. *Extracellular Fluid Volume Deficit:* This imbalance is due to the loss of both water and electrolytes.

2. *Metabolic Alkalosis (Primary Base Bicarbonate Excess):* Alkalosis develops because H+ and Cl− are lost from the body. Remember that pH is a measure of H+ concentration; the more H+ present, the more acid the solution. Conversely, with the loss of H+ from the body the pH becomes more alkaline. The Cl− loss is compensated for by an increase in the number of bicarbonate (HCO$_3$−) ions. Remember that both Cl−

and HCO$_3$− are anions (negatively charged ions) and that they equal the total number of cations (positively charged ions). The increase of HCO$_3$−, then, is an attempt to maintain chemical-electrical equilibrium. Because HCO$_3$− is basic, however, the pH becomes more alkaline.

3. *Sodium Deficit:* Note in Table 3 that sodium is rather plentiful in gastric juice.

4. *Potassium Deficit:* There is sufficient potassium in gastric juice to result in a potassium deficit if vomiting or gastric suction is prolonged.

Sodium is more plentiful in gastric juice than is potassium (see Table 3). Recall that sodium is the chief extracellular ion and that potassium is the chief cellular ion. The loss of sodium occurs more rapidly because extracellular ions move easily out of the body.

5. *Tetany (if metabolic alkalosis is present):* Although there is no loss of calcium in gastric juice, the patient may develop tetany from a deficit of *ionized* calcium. This fact may be difficult to comprehend unless it is remembered that calcium ionization is readily influenced by pH. Calcium ionization is decreased in alkalosis and increased in acidosis. Thus, a patient in acidosis may have a shortage of calcium with no symptoms of calcium deficit, since the acid pH has caused a high degree of ionization of the available calcium. Converting this acidosis to alkalosis, or even to a normal pH, reduces the ionization of calcium and brings about the manifestations of calcium deficit. The tetany accompanying alkalosis is corrected when the pH is restored to normal.

6. *Ketosis of Starvation:* Ketosis results from the excessive catabolism of body fat during starvation. The accumulation of ketone bodies in the blood stream may tend to counteract metabolic alkalosis caused by loss of gastric juice if vomiting has occurred. Indeed, since ketosis is a form of acidosis, the accumulation of sufficient ketones can convert the alkalosis into acidosis.

7. *Magnesium Deficit:* Although this imbalance is rare, it can occur with the loss of gastric juice. It is particularly apt to occur when prolonged nasogastric suction is used. There is 1 mEq./L. of magnesium in gastric juice.

Intestinal Juice

The daily volume of intestinal juice is usually about 3,000 ml. and its pH is usually alkaline. Diarrhea, intestinal suction and fistulas can result in the loss of Na^+ and HCO_3^- in excess of Cl^-. Losses from these sources can lead to:

1. *Extracellular Fluid Volume Deficit:* This imbalance is due to the loss of both water and electrolytes.

2. *Metabolic Acidosis (Primary Base Bicarbonate Deficit):* The loss of HCO_3^- is compensated for by an increase in the number of Cl^-. (As mentioned earlier, this change occurs to keep the total number of anions equal to the total number of cations in the body). The loss of HCO_3^-, which is basic, results in acidosis.

3. *Sodium Deficit:* The amount of sodium lost from the intestines in diarrhea or intestinal suction can be great.

4. *Potassium Deficit:* This imbalance develops because relatively large amounts of potassium are lost in the secretions.

Bile

The normal daily secretion of bile is 500 ml. and the pH is alkaline. Abnormal losses of bile can occur from fistulas or from T-tube drainage following gallbladder surgery. Imbalances that can result from excessive loss of bile include:

1. *Sodium Deficit:* Note in Table 3 that the sodium content of bile is quite high.

2. *Metabolic Acidosis:* This imbalance develops because of the loss of HCO_3^- and the relative increase of Cl^-.

Pancreatic Juice

The normal daily secretion of pancreatic juice is 700 ml. and the pH is 8 (alkaline). Losses of pancreatic juice result in depletion of Na^+, HCO_3^- and Cl^-. The loss of HCO_3^- exceeds the loss of Cl^- because it is more plentiful in pancreatic juice. (See Table 3) Pancreatic juice is an integral part of intestinal secretions; thus, loss of pancreatic juice is accompanied by losses of other intestinal secretions. Imbalances that can result from pancreatic fistulas include:

1. *Metabolic Acidosis:* This imbalance occurs because the basic ion, HCO_3^-, is lost in excess of Cl^-.

2. *Sodium Deficit*

3. *Calcium Deficit*

4. *Decrease in Extracellular Fluid Volume*

Sensible Perspiration

Excessive sweating due to fever or to high environmental temperature can result in large losses of water, sodium and chloride. Normally, sweat is a hypotonic fluid containing sodium, chloride, potassium, ammonia and urea. Severe perspiration can lead to:

1. *Extracellular Fluid Volume Deficit:* Both water and electrolytes are lost in sweat.

This imbalance may result if there is no provision for fluid (water and electrolyte) intake.

2. *Sodium Deficit:* Sodium deficit is especially apt to occur when plain water is ingested in large amounts after profuse sweating. Plain water replaces the lost water but not the electrolytes.

Insensible Water Loss

The invisible loss of water without solute through the lungs and skin is normally about 600 to 1,000 ml. daily. Insensible water loss is increased by anything that accelerates metabolism. For example, the increase in insensible water loss is roughly 50 to 75 ml., per degree of Fahrenheit temperature elevation for a 24-hour period.

Increased respiratory activity causes an increased loss of water vapor by way of the lungs. Damage to the skin's surface also results in an increased insensible water loss.

Increased insensible water loss can lead to:

1. *Water Deficit (Dehydration):* Because only water is lost by means of the insensible route, water deficit results.

2. *Sodium Excess:* Sodium is the chief extracellular ion; a loss of water alone results in an increased concentration of sodium in the extracellular fluid.

Large Open Wounds

Considerable quantities of water, electrolytes and protein are lost in the drainage from large open wounds. Such drainage has a composition similar to plasma. (Note the similarity between transudates and plasma in Table 3.) Severe losses from wound drainage can lead to:

1. *Protein Deficit*
2. *Sodium Deficit*
3. *Fluid Volume Deficit*

Ascites

Ascites is the accumulation of fluid within the abdominal cavity. The composition of ascitic fluid is similar to plasma; the amount varies, but occasionally as much as 20 L. can form in a week. The amount of protein lost in the formation of this much ascitic fluid can be enormous. The accumulation of large quantities of ascitic fluid requires periodic paracentesis, which can result in considerable losses of protein and electrolytes. Sodium deficit has been observed following paracentesis. Ascites can lead to:

1. *Protein Deficit*
2. *Sodium Deficit*
3. *Plasma to Interstitial Fluid Shift:* This imbalance may be serious if the formation of ascites is rapid.
4. *Fluid Volume Deficit*

PLANNED NURSING OBSERVATIONS RELATED TO BODY FLUID DISTURBANCES

Provided that the nurse is familiar with the material covered previously, she should now be able to consider a systematic method of nursing observations. A summary of familiar nursing routines and areas amenable to objective scrutiny shows how meaningful observations can reveal a wealth of information concerning the patient's fluid balance status. The summaries point out only a few of the significant nursing observations; many others, too extensive to list here, are more appropriately discussed in later chapters.

When the nurse detects significant symptoms, she can relay them to the physician, thus facilitating early diagnosis and treatment. The ability to sort out observations demanding urgent action comes with a working understanding of fluid balance and experience in applying this knowledge. The tables presented in this section refer to symptoms and the diagnoses that they may possibly indicate.

Body Temperature

The oral method for measuring body temperature is most often used for patients who are not acutely ill. The nurse should be aware of extraneous variables that may affect the accuracy of oral temperatures, such as drinking hot or cold liquids, smoking, or mouth breathing. Unless such variables are recognized, temperature readings are meaningless.

The rectal method is usually preferred for patients who are seriously ill; it is more ac-

TABLE 4. SIGNIFICANCE OF BODY
TEMPERATURE VARIATIONS

SYMPTOM	IMBALANCE INDICATED BY SYMPTOM
Depressed body temperature	Fluid volume deficit Sodium depletion
Elevated body temperature	Sodium excess (excessive water loss)
Extremities cold to touch	Plasma-to-interstitial fluid shift Profound sodium depletion Profound fluid volume deficit

TABLE 5. SIGNIFICANCE OF PULSE
VARIATIONS

SYMPTOM	IMBALANCE INDICATED BY SYMPTOM
Bounding, easily obliterated pulse	Impending circulatory collapse
Rapid, weak, thready pulse, easily obliterated	Circulatory collapse Sodium deficit Hemorrhage Plasma-to-interstitial fluid shift
Bounding pulse (not easily obliterated)	Fluid volume excess Interstitial fluid-to-plasma shift
Weak, irregular, rapid pulse	Severe potassium deficit
Increased pulse rate	Sodium excess Magnesium deficit

curate than the oral method. To assure accuracy, a rectal temperature should be taken for 3 minutes and an oral temperature for 3 to 5 minutes. It should be remembered that the rectal temperature is at least one degree higher than the oral temperature.

Usually the temperature is checked at least 4 times daily; when indicated, it is checked every 4 hours or oftener. Because fever increases loss of body fluids, it is important that temperature elevations be reported and appropriate orders be sought.

Changes in the temperature of the extremities may be noted by touch; external skin temperature gives some insight into the state of peripheral circulation.

Pulse

The pulse should be evaluated in terms of rate, volume, regularity and ease of obliteration. The average rate for the adult at rest is 70 to 80 beats per minute. When abnormalities are noted, the pulse should be checked for a full minute. It is wise to observe it for no less than 30 seconds even though the patient does not appear to be seriously ill; a shorter period might not reveal an irregularity. (Variables that may have influenced the pulse, such as activity and emotional upsets, should be considered.)

Careful observation of the pulse reveals much. Hence, the pulse should be checked whenever the temperature is taken, more often if indicated. Certainly the nurse should check the pulses of all seriously ill patients when she makes rounds.

Because the nurse often delegates TPRs to auxiliary personnel, it is important to teach them the importance of observing pulse volume and regularity as well as pulse rate. See Table 5 for possible implications of pulse variations.

Respiration

The nurse should become skilled in observing respiration for indications of body pH changes. It should be remembered that the lungs play a major role in regulating body pH by varying the amount of carbon dioxide retention.

In order to detect variations from normal, the nurse must evaluate respiration in terms of rate, depth, and regularity. It is important that the nurse be familiar with the respiratory changes accompanying both metabolic alkalosis and metabolic acidosis.

Severe metabolic alkalosis affects all aspects of breathing: (1) the rate is decreased, (2) the depth is shallow, and (3) the respiratory pattern is disrupted by periods of apnea lasting from 5 to 30 seconds. Note that the lungs attempt to compensate for the alkalosis by retaining carbon dioxide. (Slow, shallow respiration favors carbon dioxide retention.)

Severe metabolic acidosis affects primarily the rate and depth of breathing: (1) the breathing rate is increased and may be as fast as 50 per minute, and (2) the depth is greatly increased. The increased volume of

TABLE 6. SIGNIFICANCE OF VARIATIONS
IN BREATHING

SYMPTOM	IMBALANCE INDICATED BY SYMPTOM
Deep rapid breathing (close observation reveals an effort with expiration)	Metabolic acidosis
Shallow, slightly irregular, slow breathing	Metabolic alkalosis
Shortness of breath on exertion (in absence of cardiopulmonary disease)	Mild metabolic acidosis
Shortness of breath (in absence of cardiopulmonary disease)	Fluid volume excess
Moist rales	Fluid volume excess Interstitial fluid-to-plasma shift Pulmonary edema
Air hunger	Interstitial fluid-to-plasma shift
Severe dyspnea	Acute pulmonary edema
Shallow breathing (secondary to weakness or paralysis of respiratory muscles)	Potassium deficit (severe) Potassium excess (severe)
Respiratory stridor	Calcium deficit (severe)

lung ventilation is striking; all of the respiratory accessory muscles are used to increase the capacity of the thorax. Note that the lungs attempt to compensate for the acidosis by "blowing off" carbon dioxide. (Fast, deep respiration favors a loss of carbon dioxide from the lungs.)

Usually, respiration is observed for 30 seconds and multiplied by two for a full minute's count; when abnormalities are noted, respiration should be observed for two full minutes. More accurate results are obtained if the patient is unaware that his breathing is being observed. Variable factors that may influence respiration should be

noted, such as increased activity or emotional upsets.

Respiration is checked routinely when temperatures are taken and more often if indicated. Again, because auxiliary personnel frequently take TPRs, the importance of observing depth and rhythm as well as rate should be impressed upon them. The nurse should make it a practice to observe the respiration of seriously ill patients when she makes rounds.

Other factors related to fluid balance may also influence respiration. See Table 6.

Blood Pressure

Blood pressure measurement is usually taken over the brachial artery. Normal adults have an average systolic pressure of 90 to 145 mm. Hg. and an average diastolic pressure of 60 to 90 mm. Hg. The pulse pressure (difference between systolic and diastolic pressures) is usually between 30 to 50 mm. Hg. The systolic pressure indicates the pressure within the blood vessels when the heart is in systole. The diastolic indicates

TABLE 7. SIGNIFICANCE OF BLOOD
PRESSURE VARIATIONS

SYMPTOM	IMBALANCE INDICATED BY SYMPTOM
Hypotension	Sodium deficit Plasma-to-interstitial fluid shift Contracted plasma volume due to hemorrhage Severe potassium deficit or excess *Late* interstitial fluid-to-plasma shift
Hypertension	*Early* interstitial fluid-to-plasma shift Fluid volume excess Magnesium deficit
Normal blood pressure while patient is flat in bed—hypotension develops when head of bed elevated	Contracted plasma volume Impending circulatory collapse

the pressure when it is in diastole. Pulse pressure varies directly with cardiac output.

Blood pressure variations are immensely helpful in evaluating body fluid disturbances. The nurse should use this means of evaluation often when there is a real or potential water and electrolyte balance problem. When an abnormal reading is obtained, it is wise to check the pressure in both arms. Variables that may influence blood pressure, such as increased activity, position change and emotional upsets, should be considered.

The physician may order blood pressure checks at regular intervals, or he may request them when special situations arise, such as a surgical procedure or the development of new symptoms. Symptoms such as dizziness while standing, sudden apprehension, or a weak pulse are indications to check the blood pressure. See Table 7 for possible implications of blood pressure variations.

Peripheral Veins

Observation of peripheral veins can be helpful in evaluating the patient's plasma volume. Usually, elevation of the hands causes the hand veins to empty in 3 to 5 seconds; placing the hands in a dependent position causes the veins to fill in 3 to 5 seconds. (See Figs. 30, 31.)

A decreased plasma volume causes the hand veins to take longer than 3 to 5 seconds to fill when the hands are in a dependent position. The decreased plasma volume may be secondary to an extracellular fluid volume deficit or to a shift of fluid from the plasma to the interstitial space. The veins are not readily apparent when plasma volume is reduced. The slow filling of hand veins often precedes hypotension when the patient is in the early stage of shock.

An increased plasma volume causes the

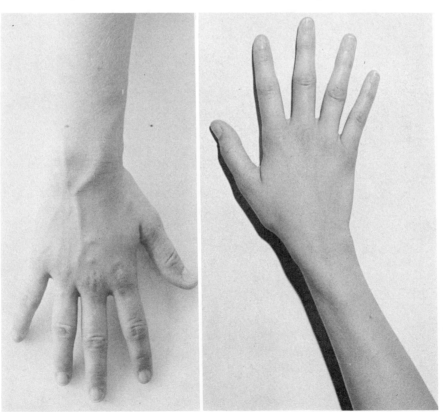

FIG. 30. (*Left*) Appearance of hand veins when the hand is held in a dependent position.
FIG. 31. (*Right*) Appearance of hand veins when the hand is held in an elevated position.

hand veins to take longer than 3 to 5 seconds to empty when the hands are elevated. The increased plasma volume may be secondary to an increased extracellular fluid volume or to a shift of fluid from the interstitial space into the vascular compartment. When this is the case, the peripheral veins are engorged and clearly visible.

Skin and Mucous Membranes

Changes in skin elasticity and in mucous membrane moisture are important for evalu-ation of changes in fluid volume and elec-trolyte concentration, as pointed out in previous chapters. It is important for the nurse to look for such changes and evaluate them.

In a normal person, pinched skin will fall back to its normal position when released. In an individual with fluid volume deficit, the skin may remain slightly raised for many seconds. (See Fig. 32, Parts A and B.) In part A, the skin of the forearm is picked up; in part B, 30 seconds later, the skin has not returned to its normal position. This patient

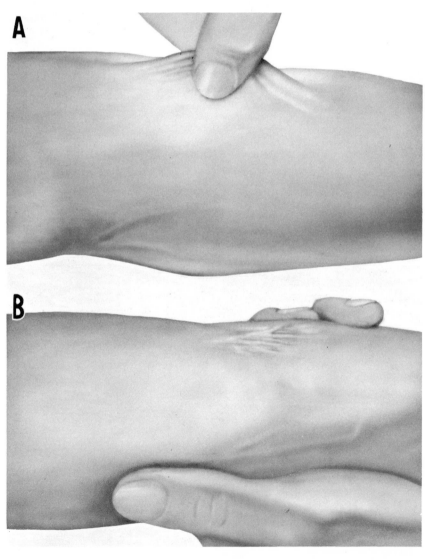

FIG. 32 (A & B). Poor skin turgor. (Moyer, C. A.: Fluid Balance, A Clinical Manual. p. 71. Chicago, Year Book Pub., 1952)

TABLE 8. SIGNIFICANCE OF SKIN AND MUCOUS MEMBRANE VARIATIONS

SYMPTOM	IMBALANCE INDICATED BY SYMPTOM
Poor skin turgor	Fluid volume deficit
Pallor of skin	Protein deficit Interstitial fluid-to-plasma shift Plasma-to-interstitial fluid shift
Flushed, dry skin	Sodium excess Diabetic acidosis
Cold, clammy skin	Sodium deficit Plasma-to-interstitial fluid shift
Pitting edema	Fluid volume excess
Fingerprinting on sternum	Sodium deficit
Dry mucous membranes with longitudinal wrinkles on tongue	Fluid volume deficit
Dry, sticky mucous membranes with rough, red, dry, tongue	Sodium excess

TABLE 9. SIGNIFICANCE OF SPEECH CHANGES

SYMPTOM	IMBALANCE INDICATED BY SYMPTOM
Difficulty in forming words without first moistening mouth	Sodium excess Fluid volume deficit
Hoarseness	Fluid volume excess
Hyperactivity of speech with tendency to irrelevancy	Potassium deficit
Difficulty in speaking due to muscular weakness or paralysis	Severe potassium deficit Severe potassium excess

is a young man with moderately severe extracellular fluid volume deficit.

A dry mouth may be due to a fluid volume deficit or may be due to mouth breathing. When in doubt, the nurse should run her finger along the oral cavity and feel the mucous membrane where the cheek and gum meet; dryness in this area indicates a true fluid volume deficit.

See Table 8 for possible implications of skin and mucous membrane variations.

Phonation

Speech variations can be significant in the evaluation of the patient's state of water and electrolyte balance. The nurse should observe for the presence of subtle changes in quality, content and formation of speech.

Hoarseness may indicate extracellular fluid volume excess. Irrelevant, hyperactive speech may be indicative of potassium deficit. Difficulty in forming words can be secondary to dry mucous membranes, or it may be due to a generalized muscular weakness. See Table 9 for possible implications of speech changes.

Behavior

Behavior changes may be indicative of water and electrolyte disturbances. See Table 10 for possible implications of behavior changes.

These changes are subtle at first and often the patient's family is the first to notice them. The attitude of the patient toward his illness is significant; a severely depleted patient is usually aware that he is seriously ill. Aged patients are particularly prone to develop personality changes and impaired mental function with fluid imbalances, because their homeostatic mechanisms are not as functional as those of younger persons.

Fatigue Threshold

Many factors contribute to a low fatigue threshold. Those related to fluid balance may include: extracellular fluid volume deficit and protein deficit. The nurse should compare the patient's activities and fatigue level with that of previous days to note significant changes. Episodes of muscular weakness, fatigability, and diminution of stamina and endurance should be noted. The latter symptoms are particularly descriptive of potassium deficit.

TABLE 10. SIGNIFICANCE OF BEHAVIOR CHANGES

SYMPTOM	IMBALANCE INDICATED BY SYMPTOMS
Lassitude	Fluid volume deficit
Emotional depression	Protein deficit
Impaired mental function	Potassium deficit Protein deficit
Apprehension and giddiness	Sodium deficit
Apprehension	Plasma-to-interstitial fluid shift
Irritability, apprehension, and extreme restlessness	Potassium excess
Excitement (may become maniacal)	Sodium excess
Disorientation	Respiratory acidosis Severe potassium deficit Magnesium deficit
Hallucinations (particularly auditory or visual)	Magnesium deficit
Stupor	Metabolic acidosis Potassium excess
Unconsciousness	Profound alkalosis Profound acidosis Profound shock
Carphologia (picking at bedclothes)	Potassium deficit Magnesium deficit

TABLE 11. SIGNIFICANCE OF SKELETAL MUSCLE CHANGES

SYMPTOM	IMBALANCE INDICATED BY SYMPTOM
Hypotonus	Potassium deficit Calcium excess
Flabbiness	Potassium deficit Protein deficit
Flaccid paralysis	Potassium deficit (severe) Potassium excess (severe)
Hypertonus: a. Chvostek's sign* may be positive	Calcium deficit
b. Tremors in mild deficit	Alkalosis (decreased calcium ionization)
c. Convulsions in severe deficit	Magnesium deficit
Cramping of exercised muscles	Calcium deficit
Muscle rigidity (particularly in limbs and abdominal wall)	Calcium deficit
Carpopedal spasm	Calcium deficit

*Chvostek's sign is a local spasm following a tap on the side of the face.

11 for possible implications of symptoms related to skeletal muscles.

Facial Appearance

A patient with a severe extracellular fluid volume deficit has a drawn facial expression; the eyes are sunken and feel much less firm than normal.

A patient with an excess of extracellular fluid may have puffy eyelids and the cheeks may appear fuller than usual.

Skeletal Muscles

Usually the condition of skeletal muscles is readily observable by the nurse. Subjective complaints from the patient, such as weakness or cramping, should be noted. See Table

Sensation

Patients with water and electrolyte imbalances frequently report changes in sensation. Some of the more common sensation changes are listed in Table 12.

Desire For Food and Water

Anorexia

The patient's interest in food and water is useful in evaluating his body fluid status. Anorexia is common in potassium deficit and in protein deficit. Many fluid imbalances are accompanied by nausea, vomiting, and anorexia.

TABLE 12. SIGNIFICANCE OF SENSATION
CHANGES

SYMPTOM	IMBALANCE INDICATED BY SYMPTOM
Tingling of ends of fingers and toes; circumoral paresthesia	Calcium deficit Alkalosis (decreased calcium ionization) Potassium excess
Light-headedness	Respiratory alkalosis
Abdominal cramps	Sodium deficit Calcium deficit Potassium excess
Muscle cramps	Calcium deficit
Numb, dead feeling—particularly in extremities (precedes flaccid paralysis)	Potassium deficit
Numbness of extremities	Calcium deficit
Nausea	Potassium excess
Deep bony pain	Calcium excess
Flank pain	Calcium excess
Tinnitus	Respiratory alkalosis
Abnormal sensitivity to sound	Magnesium deficit

Thirst

Thirst is a subjective sensory symptom. It has been defined as an awareness of the desire to drink.

The desire to drink can be initiated by cellular dehydration. Cellular dehydration may accompany (1) a decreased extracellular fluid volume or (2) a hypertonic extracellular fluid such as occurs with intravenous administration of excessive amounts of hypertonic salt solution, with or without extracellular fluid volume excess.

Cellular dehydration will occur when the body's water needs are not met. Gamble has estimated the daily water requirement of the adult at rest as 1,500 ml. Butler and his associates cite a somewhat higher figure, 1,500 ml. per square meter of body surface per day. These figures are minimal. The average active adult, not ill, requires from 2,000 to 3,000 ml. of water per day, including 1,000 to 1,500 ml. for insensible perspira-

TABLE 13. CALCULATION OF DAILY WATER
REQUIREMENTS

	CC. AVERAGE VARIATION
Uncomplicated Cases:	
For vaporization	1,000 – 1,500
For urine	1,000 – 1,500
	2,000 – 3,000
Complicated Cases (sepsis, elevation of temperature, humid weather, renal disease):	
For vaporization	2,000 – 2,500
For urine	1,000 – 1,500
	3,000 – 4,000
Seriously Ill Patients With Drainage:	
For vaporization	2,000
For urine	1,000
For replacement of body fluid losses:	
1,000 ml. bile	1,000
3,000 ml. Wangensteen	3,000
	7,000

Wohl, M., and Goodhart, R.: Modern Nutrition in Health and Disease. ed. 3, p. 1055. Philadelphia, Lea and Febiger, 1964.

tion and 1,000 to 1,500 ml. for urine excretion. Among the conditions that can increase the requirement for water are:

- Fever
- Excessive perspiration
- Abnormal loss of fluids from vomiting, diarrhea, intestinal suction, and fistulas
- Hyperthyroidism or any other cause of increased metabolic rate
- Diminished renal concentrating ability, such as occurs in old age

Of interest in this connection is the comparison of the water needs in patients with no complications with those of patients with increased water loss, as shown in Table 13.

The nurse should constantly remember how important it is to meet the daily water requirement of the patient. Water is the most important of all nutrients. The human can live for days, weeks, or months when deprived of other nutrients. If deprived of water, he lives only a few miserable days. The nurse can best assure meeting the patient's water requirement by keeping accurate records of his intake and output, and by carefully observing the patient for signs of water deficit.

Thirst is often caused by dryness of the

TABLE 14. SIGNIFICANCE OF CHANGES IN
DESIRE FOR FOOD AND WATER

SYMPTOM	IMBALANCE INDICATED BY SYMPTOM
Anorexia	Potassium deficit Protein deficit
Thirst	Fluid volume deficit Sodium excess (hypertonic extra-cellular fluid) Blood volume deficit due to hemorrhage Blood volume deficit due to acute heart failure
Absence of thirst	Sodium deficit (hypotonic extra-cellular fluid)

The specific gravity of urine is its weight compared with the weight of an equal volume of distilled water; it indicates the amount of dissolved solids in the urine. The specific gravity of distilled water is 1.000; the specific gravity of urine, in health, ranges from 1.003 to 1.030. The higher the solute content of urine, the higher the specific gravity.

The chief urinary solutes are nitrogenous end-products (urea), sodium and chloride; others include potassium, phosphate, sulfate and ammonia. Urinary solutes are mainly derived from ingested foods and from metab-

mouth resulting from decreased salivary flow, which can be caused by extracellular fluid volume deficit. In this case, true thirst exists. Decreased salivary flow can also be caused by administration of atropine, in which case, there is a desire to relieve the unpleasant dry sensation, but no true thirst.

Thirst is not always a reliable indicator of need and should not be the sole factor influencing fluid intake. The aged patient may be thirsty, but too weak to reach for a glass of water. Yet, thirst does not always indicate a need for water, as shown by the fact that patients with sodium excess and edema frequently thirst. The nurse must use caution in allowing patients to ingest as much water as they desire. Seriously burned patients experience great thirst; if allowed to drink all the water they desire, serious sodium deficit will develop. Thirst in the burned patient should be met with specially prepared oral electrolyte solutions.

See Table 14 for implications of changes in desire for food and water.

Character and Volume of Urine

Specific Gravity of Urine

To maintain fluid and osmolar balance, the kidneys must be able to dilute and concentrate urine. The specific gravity test is a convenient and simple method for evaluation of the kidney's ability to perform this function.

FIG. 33. Urinometer.

olism of endogenous protein and other substances. Diet, then, influences specific gravity of the urine. The usual diet supplies approximately 50 Gm. of urinary solutes in 24 hours. Patients on low sodium or low protein diets cannot concentrate urine to high levels because they are ingesting an inadequate amount of solute. The inability of the patient eating a normal diet to concentrate urine is an indication of renal disease.

The patient's state of hydration can be assessed by measuring specific gravity, provided the kidneys are healthy. A highly concentrated urine implies water deficit; a dilute urine implies adequate hydration or possibly over-hydration.

Urine specific gravity measurement can help differentiate between the scanty urinary output of acute renal failure and that of water deficit. In acute renal failure, the specific gravity is fixed at a low level (1.010 to 1.012); in water deficit, the specific gravity is high.

The nurse may be asked to measure the urinary specific gravity of patients with burns, renal disease, cardiovascular disease, febrile conditions and general surgical conditions. She should keep the following points in mind:

1. The nurse should be familiar with the equipment used to test the specific gravity of urine:

    a. The apparatus used for the test consists of two parts—the cylinder to contain the urine, and the urinometer. (See Fig. 33.)

    b. Note that the urinometer is calibrated in units of .001, beginning with 1.000 at the top and progressing downward to 1.060. A urinometer is read from top to bottom. (See Fig. 34)

    c. New urinometers should be checked for accuracy against distilled water before use, and rechecked from time to time thereafter—even a slight discrepancy can be significant.

2. The urine sample must be fresh.
3. The urine sample must be well mixed —remember, the specific gravity test measures solute concentration and a uniform solution must be used to yield an accurate reading.

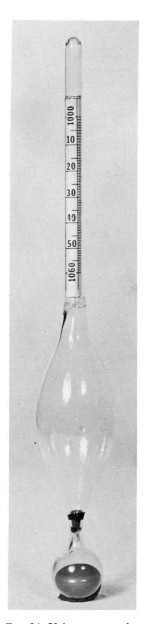

FIG. 34. Urinometer scale.

4. The cylinder should be filled ¾ of the way with urine.
5. After the urinometer is placed in the cylinder, it is given a gentle spin with the thumb and forefinger to prevent it from adhering to the cylinder's sides. (See Fig. 33.)
6. Should there be an insufficient amount of urine to float the urinometer, the reading cannot be made. In such an event, *q.n.s.* (quantity not sufficient) is charted.

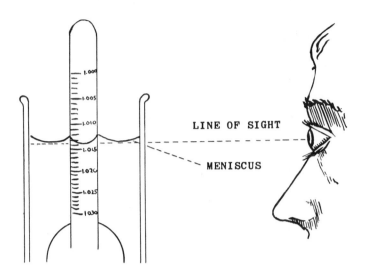

FIG. 35. Reading the urinometer. (Bredow, M.: The Medical Assistant. p. 342. New York, McGraw-Hill, 1964)

LINE OF SIGHT

MENISCUS

7. To read specific gravity, it is necessary that the urinometer be at eye level. It is read by imagining a line where the lower portion of the meniscus crosses the scale on the urinometer. (See Fig. 35.)

The results of specific gravity tests are evaluated in relation to other clinical signs shown by the patient. See Table 15 for conditions that may cause low or high specific gravity of urine.

pH of Urine

The kidneys play a major role in maintaining the acid-base balance in the body. They accomplish this by excreting electrolytes that are not required and by retaining those that are needed by the body. When an acid factor is in excess, the kidneys excrete hydrogen ions and conserve basic ions; when an alkaline factor is in excess, the kidneys excrete basic ions and retain hydrogen ions.

Urinary pH tests measure the hydrogen ion concentration in urine. Because the excreted electrolytes vary according to the body's need, the urinary pH can range widely (from 4.5 to 8.0) and still be within normal limits. However, the pooled daily urine output averages around 6. Several factors may cause normal fluctuations in urinary pH.

1. Sleep causes urine to become highly acid. Respiration is depressed during sleep and a mild state of respiratory acidosis is induced. (Shallow respiration favors retention of carbon dioxide, and an increase in the acid side of the carbonic acid:base bicarbonate ratio.) Note the low pH during the night hours in Figure 36. A rise in pH usually occurs upon awakening.

TABLE 15. CONDITIONS ASSOCIATED WITH PERSISTENTLY LOW OR HIGH URINARY SPECIFIC GRAVITY

Low Specific Gravity (1.010 or less)	Sodium deficit: Drinking large quantities of water Excessive parenteral administration of electrolyte-free solutions Severely restricted dietary intake of sodium chloride Diuresis from potent diuretics Diabetes insipidus (deficiency of antidiuretic hormone) Renal disease: Acute renal failure Pyelonephritis Hydronephrosis Severe potassium deficiency Calcium excess
High Specific Gravity (1.030 or higher)	Sodium excess: Decreased water intake Excessive loss of water Excessive ingestion of sodium chloride Glycosuria

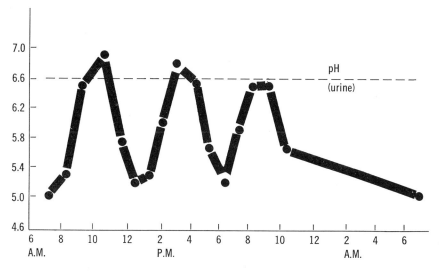

FIG. 36. Daily fluctuations of urinary pH. (Pictoclinic, 9:6, No. 6, Ames Co., Elkhart, Indiana, 1962)

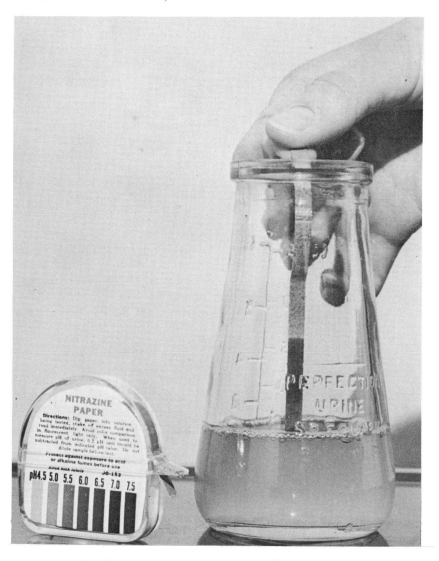

FIG. 37. Measuring urinary pH with Nitrazine paper.

TABLE 16. CLINICAL CONDITIONS ASSOCIATED
WITH PERSISTENTLY ACID OR
ALKALINE URINE

SYMPTOM	IMBALANCE INDICATED BY SYMPTOM
Acid Urine	Metabolic acidosis: Diabetic acidosis Ketosis of starvation Severe diarrhea Respiratory acidosis: Emphysema Asthma Metabolic alkalosis accompanied by severe potassium deficit
Alkaline Urine	Metabolic alkalosis: Excessive ingestion of alkalis Severe vomiting Respiratory alkalosis: Oxygen lack Fever with its hyperpnea Primary hyperaldosteronism Acidosis accompanied by the following clinical conditions: *Chronic renal infection,* in which the infecting organism converts urea in newly-formed urine to ammonia *Milkman's syndrome,* a severe chronic acidosis apparently secondary to renal tubular dysfunction *Fanconi's syndrome,* a form of chronic acidosis secondary to renal tubular dysfunction *Sulfanilamide intoxication* secondary to renal tubular dysfunction *Pharmacologic alkalinuria* produced by a carbonic anhydrase inhibitor (such as Diamox or Diuril) *Persistent acidosis* secondary to renal tubular dysfunction in infants

2. A rise in pH usually occurs following meals. Meals stimulate the production of hydrochloric acid, a process causing hydrogen ions to be extracted from the blood. The type of food ingested affects pH. See Table 27 in Chapter 10 for the acid-base reactions of various foods. Note the rise in pH following meals in Figure 36.

3. Certain drugs significantly alter urinary pH. Drugs that cause urine to become more acid include ammonium chloride, Mandelamine, or sodium acid phosphate. Drugs that can cause urine to become alkaline include alkaline salts, such as sodium bicarbonate or potassium citrate.

In spite of the variables that influence urinary pH, most random urine samples show a pH of less than 6.6.

The nurse may be asked to perform urinary pH tests at the bedside for patients with a variety of metabolic disorders. Table 16 lists some conditions in which urine is persistently acid or alkaline.

Several simple methods may be used by the nurse to measure urinary pH:

1. *Squibb Nitrazine Paper*: Nitrazine paper consists of a chemical (sodium dinitrophenolazonaphthol disulfonate) impregnated in cellulose. When Nitrazine paper is dipped into urine, a chemical change takes place that causes the paper to change color. The color can vary from yellow to blue and is matched against the scale on the paper dispenser. The color changes correspond to specific pH levels ranging from 4.5 to 7.5. (See Fig. 37) The nurse should keep the following points in mind while performing this test:

A. Only fresh urine should be used. (When urine is allowed to set for a time, urea breaks down into ammonia and the pH becomes more alkaline.)

B. The paper should be well moistened with urine but should not be left in the urine more than a few seconds—excessive fluid can wash away the chemicals from the paper.

C. After the paper has been dipped into the urine, the excess urine should be shaken off and the reading made immediately.

D. The color comparison between the Nitrazine paper and the color scale on the dispenser should be made in a good light—avoid color comparison in pure fluorescent light.

2. *Ames Combistix Dip Sticks*: Combistix is a dip-and-read combination test for urine

protein, glucose and pH. Barriers are impregnated in the dipstick to separate the three areas; otherwise, the chemicals from each portion would run together when moistened. The pH portion of the reagent strip is impregnated with methyl red and bromthymol blue. When dipped into urine, a color change takes place. The color varies from orange to blue and represents a pH range of from 5 to 9. The nurse should keep the following points in mind while performing this test:

A. Only fresh urine should be used.

B. Care should be taken to prevent excessive urine from washing chemicals from the other portions of the reagent strip onto the pH portion.

3. *Litmus Paper*: An acid turns blue litmus paper red; a base turns red litmus paper blue. This test is of little or no clinical value because it gives only a crude indication of urinary pH.

Regardless of the type of test used, it is important that the nurse read the manufacturer's directions carefully. Accurate results can be expected only when instructions are followed.

Changes in Urinary Volume

Generally speaking, urinary output can safely range from 25 to 500 ml. per hour. The nurse should report hourly output below 25 ml. or above 500 ml. She should also report an output of less than 500 ml. in a 24-hour period.

The expected urinary volume varies with each patient and is influenced by many factors. Nursing observations of urinary output are more meaningful when the nurse understands some of these factors.

Urine volume is dependent on:

1. The amount of fluid intake
2. Water needs of the lungs, skin, and gastrointestinal tract
3. The amount of waste products to be excreted by the kidneys
4. The ability of the kidneys to concentrate urine
5. Blood volume
6. Hormonal influences
7. Age

TABLE 17. 24-HOUR AVERAGE INTAKE AND OUTPUT OF WATER IN AN ADULT

INTAKE		OUTPUT	
Oral liquids ..	1,300 ml.	Urine	1,500 ml.
Water in food	1,000 ml.	Stool	200 ml.
Water of oxidation ..	300 ml.	Insensible:	
		Lungs ..	300 ml.
		Skin ...	600 ml.
Total ...	2,600 ml.	Total	2,600 ml.

Bland, J.: Clinical Metabolism of Body Water and Electrolytes. p. 48. Philadelphia, Saunders, 1963.

FLUID INTAKE

1. In health, urinary volume is approximately equal to the volume of liquids taken into the body—this rule does not hold true in illness. (See Table 17)

2. A large intake of liquids causes a large urinary output; a small intake causes a small urinary output.

3. Adults usually pass between 1,000 to 1,500 ml. of urine in 24 hours. (Most persons void 5 to 10 times during the waking hours; each voiding is usually between 100 to 300 ml.)

WATER NEEDS OF THE LUNGS, THE SKIN, AND THE GASTROINTESTINAL TRACT

1. Water is available for urine formation only after the needs of the skin, the lungs and the gastrointestinal tract have been met.

2. Excessive sweating causes a decreased urinary volume—daily urinary volume is several hundred ml. less in the summer.

3. Increased water loss from the lungs occurs with hyperpnea—this loss can cause a reduction in the urinary volume.

4. Excessive losses of fluid in vomiting and diarrhea can also cause a decreased urinary volume.

AMOUNT OF WASTE PRODUCTS TO BE EXCRETED

1. Under most circumstances, urine volume varies directly with the urinary solute load—a solute excess causes an increased need for water excretion.

2. Excessive fluid loss may occur as the

result of the increased solute loads found in diabetes mellitus, thyrotoxicosis, fever and response to stress.

3. A decreased solute load causes a decreased urinary volume.

ABILITY OF THE KIDNEYS TO CONCENTRATE URINE

1. Kidneys able to concentrate urine normally have less need for water than damaged kidneys—a normal individual with a urinary specific gravity of 1.029 to 0.032 requires 15 ml. of water to excrete 1 Gm. of solute; an individual with nephritis, and a urinary specific gravity of 1.010 to 1.015, requires 40 ml. of water to excrete 1 Gm. of solute.

2. Low concentrating ability of the kidneys results in large urinary output.

3. Provided renal concentration is normal, the least amount of urine needed for excretion of daily metabolic wastes is 400 to 500 ml.

4. An acutely ill patient, or one with poor kidney function, may need to excrete as much as 3,000 ml. of urine daily to rid the body of waste products.

BLOOD VOLUME

1. A decreased blood volume causes decreased urinary output primarily due to changes in arterial pressure and pressure in the glomeruli. (This phenomenon explains the oliguria or anuria of profound shock.)

2. An increased blood volume causes increased urinary output, again primarily due to changes in arterial pressure and pressure in the glomeruli.

HORMONAL INFLUENCES

1. An increased secretion of antidiuretic hormone occurs when the blood volume is decreased—the kidneys increase water reabsorption, and the urinary volume is decreased.

2. An increased secretion of aldosterone occurs when the blood volume is decreased —the kidneys increase sodium reabsorption, and the urine volume is decreased.

3. A decreased secretion of antidiuretic

TABLE 18. SIGNIFICANCE OF URINARY VOLUME CHANGES

SYMPTOM	IMBALANCE INDICATED BY SYMPTOM
Oliguria	Fluid volume deficit Sodium deficit Potassium excess Severe sodium excess Renal calcification due to calcium excess Shock Renal insufficiency (late in disease)
Polyuria	Interstitial fluid-to-plasma shift Diabetes insipidus Increased renal solute load: 　Diabetes mellitus 　Infection 　Calcium excess 　Hyperthyroidism Renal insufficiency (early) "Salt-losing" nephritis

hormone occurs when the blood volume is increased—the kidneys decrease water reabsorption, and the urinary volume is increased.

4. A decreased secretion of aldosterone occurs when the blood volume is increased—the kidneys excrete more sodium and the urinary volume is increased.

AGE

1. Data presented by Behnke indicates that the aged have a smaller urinary output (0.8 ml./minute) than do younger adults (1.0 ml./minute).

2. The decreased urinary volume in the aged is related to a decreased renal blood flow, secondary to vascular changes—the narrowed vessels decrease plasma filtration and cause less urine to be formed.

3. The decreased urinary volume in the aged may also be related to diet—most aged persons consume much more carbohydrate than protein. (Carbohydrate presents less of a solute load than the nitrogenous end-products of protein.)

4. The aged tend to drink less than younger adults.

5. The aged have a decreased concentrating power. It is important for the nurse to

remember that when an increased solute load is presented to such patients, a large urinary volume will result. Such patients require a larger water intake when the renal solute load is high. See Table 18 for conditions associated with urinary volume changes.

Measuring and Recording Fluid Intake and Output

Intake-Output Records. A workable intake-output record has appropriate columns for all avenues of fluid gains and losses. The volumes and types of fluid taken into the body are entered on the left side of the record, and the volumes and types of fluids lost from the body are entered on the right. The intake side of most records provides a column for oral intake and another column for parenteral fluids or other avenues of fluid gain. The output side usually provides a column for urine output and another column for gastrointestinal fluid losses or other routes of fluid loss. The record should be sufficiently simple so that the method of its use is self-evident. Necessary instructions should be incorporated in the record.

It is easy to become confused with intake-output records because they vary from hospital to hospital and even within the same hospital. For example, a burn unit requires a different intake-output record from that required in a general surgical unit.

The type of intake-output record used often depends on the patient's condition. A patient with a severe fluid balance problem may require an hourly summary of his fluid gains and losses, so that the physician can plan treatment according to immediate needs. Figure 38 depicts a bedside record suitable for an hourly fluid gain and loss summary. Many patients require only 8-hour summaries of their fluid gains and losses. Figure 39 depicts a bedside record suitable for this purpose. Both of these records provide for a 24-hour total. Some hospitals use a small intake-output slip at the bedside; at the end of each shift, the total is transferred to a summary sheet on the patient's chart. Completed intake-output records are attached to the patient's chart and kept as permanent records.

The use of the bedside intake-output record is facilitated when the chart is kept on a clipboard with an attached pen.

Indications for Intake-Output Measurement. Physicians often indicate which patients are to have records kept of their daily fluid intake and output. However, the failure of the physician to request intake-output measurement is no reason to omit it when the patient has a real or potential water and electrolyte balance problem. Many physicians assume that the nurse will initiate intake-output measurement when necessary, without a written order. Patients with the following conditions should automatically be placed on the fluid intake-output measurement list:

- Following major surgery
- Thermal burns or other injuries
- Suspected or known electrolyte imbalance
- Acute renal failure
- Oliguria
- Congestive heart failure
- Abnormal losses of body fluids
- Lower nephron nephrosis
- Diuretic therapy
- Corticoid therapy
- Inadequate food and fluid intake

Need for Accurate Intake-Output Records. The nurse should bear in mind that most fluid imbalances result from discrepancies between gains and losses of body fluids. These discrepancies can be detected when an accurate record is kept of the total fluid intake-output. The content of the gained and lost fluids is as important as their volume. Because the electrolytic content of the individual body fluids varies widely, the amount of each fluid lost should be designated on the intake-output record. The amounts and kinds of fluids taken into the body should also be recorded. All of this information is necessary to evaluate the body's gains of water and electrolytes in relation to its losses of water and electrolytes.

Ideally, the physician should be able to use the nursing intake-output records as a major tool in diagnosis, as well as in the formulation of fluid replacement therapy. However, most physicians regard the usual intake-output record with the proverbial grain of salt. They are justified in complain-

LIQUID INTAKE AND OUTPUT RECORD

Patient's Last Name   First Name

History Number

Location   Service   Date

Time A.M. or P.M.	INTAKE (in cc.)					OUTPUT (Measured or estimated in cc.)					
	Oral or tube		Parenteral		Running Total	Sweat + to ++++	Urine	Other (feces, vomitus, etc.)		Running Total	
	Type	Amount	Composition	Amount				Type	Amount		

FIG. 38. Liquid intake and output record suitable for hourly measurement. (Bland, J.: Clinical Metabolism of Body Water. p. 215. Philadelphia, Saunders, 1963)

ing that an accurate account of a patient's intake-output is extremely difficult to obtain in the average hospital.

CAUSES OF INACCURATE INTAKE-OUTPUT RECORDS. Neglect in keeping accurate nursing intake-output records is widespread and

Decatur and Macon County Hospital

24-HOUR INTAKE AND OUTPUT RECORD

7 A.M. — 7 A.M.

LIQUID MEASUREMENTS (Average)
Jello .... 90cc   Fruit Juice Glass.....100cc
Ice Cream.... 90cc   Reg. Drinking Glass ..200cc
Cup .... 90cc   Squat Tray Glass 150cc
Soup Bowl ...100cc   Bedside Water Pitcher 900cc
Coffee Pot ...180cc

RECORD OUTPUT
TIME: Check ☐

Directions: Enter amount ON LINE in square. When time of act is significant, write time in top corner of square and circle it. When recording a series, enter time in top square only. A new form must be put at bedside when 24-Hour Record is removed for totalling.

ORAL INTAKE (Include Tube Feedings)

	7 — 3	3 — 11	11 — 7

8-HOUR ORAL TOTALS ....

PARENTERAL FLUID INTAKE (Blood, Plasma, I.V., Sub. Fluids) RECORD TIME STARTED

	7 — 3	3 — 11	11 — 7

8-HOUR PARENTERAL TOTALS

8-HR. TOTAL INTAKE 7-3 ____ + 3-11 ____ + 11-7 ____ = TOTAL 24-HOUR INTAKE

NOTE: Record amount of Parenteral Fluid started. Make entry and minus sign if not taken. Subtract when totalling.

URINE OUTPUT (Record Urethral Catheter—C; Ureteral—U)

Describe urine if significant

	7 — 3	3 — 11	11 — 7

8 - HOUR URINE OUTPUT TOTALS ....

ALL OTHER OUTPUT (Emesis, Gastric Suction, Bile, Liquid Stool)

Record

	7 — 3	3 — 11	11 — 7

Diaphoresis {M—Moderate P—Profuse

8-HOUR OUTPUT (All Except Urine) TOTALS ....

8-HR. TOTAL OUTPUT 7-3 ____ + 3-11 ____ + 11-7 ____ = TOTAL 24-HOUR OUTPUT

Form No. 9314

FIG. 39. Twenty-four hour intake-output record. (Decatur and Macon County Hospital, Decatur, Ill.)

causative factors are extremely difficult to pinpoint. However, the difficulty seems to be related to a combination of the following factors:

- Failure to comprehend the value of accurate intake-output records
- Understaffed patient-care units
- Lethargic and improperly motivated personnel
- Lax supervision
- Unqualified personnel giving direct care to seriously ill patients
- Inadequate in-service education programs for all levels of personnel

- Failure to devise or implement a workable intake-output record

ACHIEVING ACCURATE INTAKE-OUTPUT RECORDS. It is not technically difficult to measure fluid intake and output or to record the measurements. Yet, persistent effort is required if one is to achieve an accurate account of gains and losses of fluids.

There are innumerable possibilities for error in the measurement and recording of fluid gains and losses; however, some errors occur much more frequently than others.

Common errors and suggestions on how to overcome them are presented below:

OVERCOMING COMMON ERRORS

COMMON ERRORS	SUGGESTIONS
Errors Involving Both Intake and Output:	
1. Failure to communicate to the entire staff those patients requiring intake-output measurement (**Body** fluids are often discarded without being measured, and oral fluids are not recorded, merely because staff members are not aware of the patients on intake-output)	a. A "measure intake-output" sign should be attached to the patient's bed to serve as a reminder (see Fig. 40) b. A list of all patients requiring intake-output measurement should be posted in a convenient work area for quick reference c. Also for quick reference, the cardex should contain a list of all patients requiring intake-output measurement d. An adequate patient report should be given to all personnel
2. Failure to explain intake-output to the patient and his family (Most patients will cooperate *if* they know what is expected of them)	a. Both the patient and his family should receive a simple explanation of why intake-output measurement is necessary b. Careful instructions are necessary to acquaint the patient and his family with their role in helping to achieve an accurate intake-output record
3. Well meaning intentions to record a drink of water or an emptied urinal at a later, more convenient time are often forgotten	a. Measurements should be recorded at the time they are obtained
4. Failure to measure fluids that can be directly measured because it takes less time to guess at their amounts	a. Measure *all* fluids amenable to direct measurement—guesses should be reserved for fluids that cannot be measured directly
Errors Related to Intake:	
5. Failure to designate the specific volume of glasses, cups, bowls and other fluid containers used in the hospital (Each person may ascribe a different volume to the same glass of water)	a. The bedside record should list the volumes of glasses, cups, bowls and other fluid containers used in the hospital (see Fig. 39)

CHART—(*Continued*)

COMMON ERRORS	SUGGESTIONS
6. Failure to obtain an adequate measuring device for small amounts of oral fluids (Patients frequently drink small quantities of fluids; the amounts must be estimated unless a calibrated cup is available—frequent estimates increase the margin of error)	a. Small calibrated paper cups should be kept at the bedside for such a purpose
7. The amount of fluid taken as ice chips is frequently under-estimated	a. The nurse should consider that a full glass of ice chips is approximately one-half of a glass of water when melted; for example: a 200 ml. glass filled with ice chips will contain approximately 100 ml. of water after the ice is melted (see Fig. 41)
8. Failure to consider the volume of fluid displaced by ice in iced drinks frequently causes an overstatement of ingested oral fluids	a. Only small amounts of ice should be used for iced drinks so that the accurate amount of fluid ingested can be recorded
9. Assuming that the contents of empty containers were drunk by the patient (Patients sometimes give their coffee or juice to a visiting relative or to other patients in the room; they may forget to tell the person checking the tray)	a. The patient should be asked what fluids he drank
10. Failure to detect that a patient has exaggerated his fluid intake, perhaps to avoid unwanted oral fluids or a parenteral infusion	a. Patients who frequently try to convey the idea that they will drink fluids after the nurse has left the room should be suspected
11. Failure to accurately record the amount of parenteral fluid administered on each shift (Because it takes less time, there is a tendency to record the total infusion volume at the time it is started or when it is discontinued)	a. The actual amount of parenteral fluid run in on each shift should be recorded b. The amount of solution left in the bottle at the end of a shift should be noted, in pencil, on the bedside record—this makes it easier for the next shift to determine the amount run in on their time
12. Failure to note inadequate intake of solid foods (It is frequently forgotten that solid foods are mainly water, and failure to eat solids causes an increased need for liquids)	a. Notations concerning inadequate food intake should be made in the appropriate place on the patient's chart

Errors Related to Output:

13. Failure to estimate fluid lost as perspiration (Many nurses fail to recognize perspiration as a major source of fluid loss)	a. An attempt should be made to describe the amount of clothing and bed linen saturated with perspiration—it has been estimated that one necessary bed change represents at least 1 L. of lost fluid b. Some intake-output records require the nurse to estimate perspiration as +, ++, +++, or ++++ (+ represents sweating that is just visible, and ++++ represents profuse sweating)

CHART—(*Continued*)

COMMON ERRORS	SUGGESTIONS
14. Failure to estimate "uncaught" vomitus (Frequently, "uncaught" emesis is recorded merely as a lost specimen)	a. The amount of fluid lost as vomitus should be estimated, and recorded as an estimate—it is better to make a guess than to give no indication at all as to the amount
15. Failure to estimate the amount of incontinent urine (Intake-output records often indicate the number of incontinent voidings but give no indication of the amounts; obviously, such records are of little value)	a. The amount of incontinent urine should be estimated—it is helpful to note the amount of clothing and bed linen saturated with urine
16. Failure to estimate fluid lost as liquid feces	a. The patient should be encouraged to use the bedpan rather than the toilet so that the fluid loss can be directly measured
	b. The amount of fluid lost in incontinent liquid stools should be estimated
17. Failure to estimate fluid lost as wound exudate	a. The amount of drainage on a dressing should be measured and charted—this can be done by measuring the width of the stained area and determining the thickness of the dressing
	b. If extreme measures are necessary, the dressing can be weighed before application and again when removed
18. Failure to check a urinary catheter for patency when there is decreased drainage of urine (It is sometimes too quickly assumed that decreased drainage from a catheter is due to renal failure or inadequate fluid intake)	a. Decreased drainage from a urinary catheter is an indication to irrigate it and check for patency before charting the absence of, or decrease in, urinary output
19. Failure to obtain an adequate measuring device for hourly or more frequent checks on urinary output (An error of even 10 ml. could be significant when dealing with small amounts of urine)	a. A handy device for frequent volume checks on urinary output is the Davol Uri-meter (see Fig. 42). This device is calibrated to measure small amounts of urine—after the hourly amount has been measured, the petcock can be opened and the urine drained into a bottle
	b. Another very convenient method for precise hourly urinary measuring is the Kurze Automatic Urinometer—this electrical device automatically measures output for a 12-hour period. (See Fig. 43.) A clock-like device automatically rotates the container so that a different segment is under the catheter each hour. Each pie-shaped segment holds up to 200 ml.; small quantities of urine are easily measured
20. Failure to record the amount of solution used to irrigate tubes and the amount of fluid withdrawn during the irrigation	a. One method for dealing with this problem is to add the amount of irrigating solution to the intake column, and to add the amount of fluid withdrawn to the output column

CHART—(*Continued*)

COMMON ERRORS	SUGGESTIONS
	b. Another method is to compare the amount of irrigating solution used and the amount of fluid withdrawn during the irrigation—if more fluid was put in than was taken out, the excess is added to the intake column; if more fluid was taken out than was put in, the excess is added to the output column

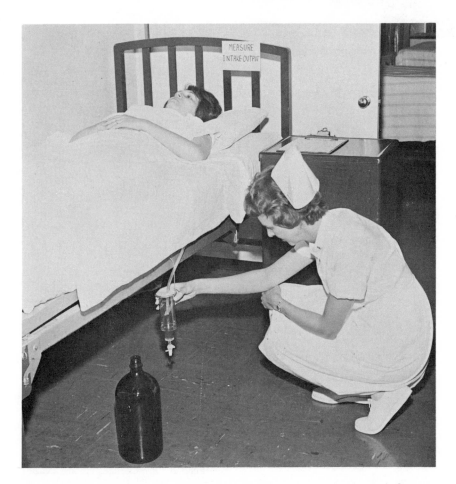

FIG. 40. Use of "Measure Intake-Output" bed sign as a simple reminder.

FIG. 41. Liquid volume of a glass of ice chips.

FIG. 42. Davol Uri-meter. (Davol Rubber Co., Providence, Rhode Island)

FIG. 43. Kurze Urinometer. (Zimmer Co., Warsaw, Indiana)

Body Weight

The daily weighing of patients with potential or actual fluid balance problems is of great clinical value because: (1) accurate body weight measurements are much easier to obtain than accurate intake-output measurements, and (2) rapid variations in weight closely reflect changes in fluid volume. A loss of body weight will occur when the total fluid intake is less than the total fluid output; conversely, a gain in body weight will occur when the total fluid intake is greater than the total fluid output. However, the nurse should recall that fluids can be lost to the body in the pooling that occurs, for example, with intestinal obstruction. Such losses, which can cause a serious fluid volume deficit, are not reflected by weight changes.

Daily weight measurement may be indicated in the same conditions listed earlier as indications for fluid intake-output measurement. At the minimum, all patients should be weighed on admittance, so that a baseline can be established for later comparison. Ambulatory patients may be weighed on

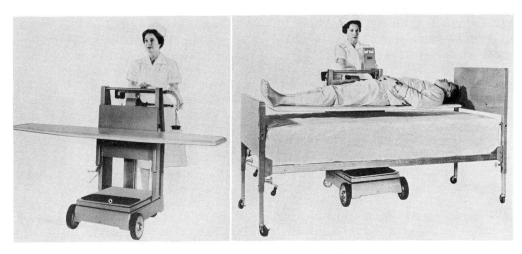

FIG. 44. (*Left*) In-bed Scale. (Acme Scale Co., Oakland, California)
FIG. 45. (*Right*) In-bed Scale in use. (Acme Scale Co., Oakland, California)

small portable scales; it is important that the same scale be used for repeated measurements, since any two portable scales seldom give the same reading. The daily variations in weight should reflect true body weight changes rather than variations between scales.

Seriously ill patients confined to bed can be weighed with a bed scale. (See Figs. 44, 45) The weighing procedure can be performed with a minimum of effort for both the patient and the nurse. The patient is turned on one side, making room for the scale board on the mattress. The scale is rolled under the bed, automatically positioning the weighing board over the mattress. The board is lowered until it rests on the mattress. The patient is turned onto the scale board with his body weight evenly distributed; the arms should be folded over the chest, if possible, to prevent them from hanging off the side of the board. The board is raised hydraulically a few inches above the mattress and the patient is weighed. Then the board is lowered to the mattress; the patient is moved off the board and the scale is removed. The In-Bed scale is particularly safe, since the patient remains within the confines of the bed during the entire process.

It is useless to weigh the patient daily if the procedure is not performed the same way each day. The nurse should strive for accurate weight measurements, because the physician often bases the administration of fluids and diuretics on the recorded weight changes. The following practices should be followed:

- The same scales should be used each time.
- The weight should be measured in the morning before breakfast.
- The patient should empty his bladder before each weight measurement.
- The same or similar clothing should be worn each time (the clothing should be dry).
- The patient may be weighed wearing his glasses and wrist watch, if desired— if so, they should be worn during each weight measurement.
- A summary of all of the above points

should be written on the cardex or the nursing care plan, so that a uniform weighing procedure is followed.

Brookline Metabolic Scale

The Brookline Instrument Company has designed a scale to make highly accurate, continual weight measurements of patients in bed. Its extreme sensitivity allows a determination to be made automatically of the rate of insensible water loss over a period as short as 30 minutes.

The Under-Bed Model of the Brookline Metabolic Scale is pictured in Figure 46. This scale has a platform that is designed to fit directly under a full-sized hospital bed or a crib without interfering with operation of the bed or normal patient care. The patient weight range is 0 to 110 Kg. and can be extended to 200 Kg. with an accessory weight. In addition to measuring the total body weight, changes in patient weight are shown on a console meter. An accessory strip recorder can be used to provide a continual record of weight changes.

The scale is balanced before the patient is put to bed; this eliminates from consideration the weight of the bed and bedclothes when the patient is weighed. The weight indicated on the scale is thus the true weight of the patient. Pillows, linens, and other equipment can be added or removed whenever necessary. The weight is checked *prior* to their addition or removal; then the scale is readjusted to this reading after the equipment has been removed or added. Position changes of the patient do not affect the reading. The scale has an automatic self-centering device which allows jolting of the bed without adverse effect on the instrument or even a change in the reading.

Usually fluid lost from the patient's skin into the bedding will not cause a significant error in weight measurement. When the patient's fluid loss is not excessive, the evaporation from the bedding to the room occurs as rapidly as water lost from the patient to the bedding. When the fluid loss is excessive, two techniques may be used to reduce errors. For insensible weight loss studies, the patient may be placed on a nylon net supported on top of the bed. This allows evap-

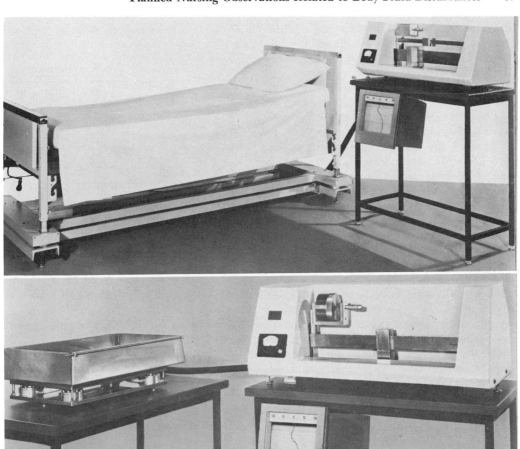

Fig. 46. (*Top*) Brookline Metabolic Scale, Model 100. (Brookline Instrument Co., White Plains, New York)

Fig. 47. (*Bottom*) Brookline Metabolic Scale, Model 80. (Brookline Instrument Co., White Plains, New York)

oration to take place from all surfaces of the body and eliminates absorption by the bedding. Or, absorbent pads can be placed under the patient and changed at suitable intervals. Since the pads used in most hospitals are obtainable from American Hospi-

tal Supply Company and are standardized in weight, the amount of water absorbed on the pads is easily measured when they are changed.

When only evaporative water loss is being measured, all intravenous and catheter drainage apparatus are mounted on the bed. In this way, a change in weight reflects only evaporative water loss. On the other hand, if I.V. therapy is being controlled to maintain the patient's weight at a specific level, the I.V. bottles and urine bottles are kept off the bed. In this way, intake can be balanced against output.

Some of the clinical applications of the Brookline Metabolic Scale include the control of intravenous therapy and the management of patients with burns, cardiac failure, diabetic acidosis, open-heart surgery and hemodialysis.

A pediatric model of the Brookline Metabolic Scale is also available for continuous monitoring of an infant's weight. (See Figure 47.) This scale has a weighing platform which is designed to be mounted inside an incubator or on a table. Total patient weight up to 11 Kg. is given on the balance or mechanism to the nearest $1/4$ Gm. This scale also provides a continuous record of weight changes when an accessory chart recorder is used.

TABLE 19. SIGNIFICANCE OF WEIGHT CHANGES

SYMPTOM	IMBALANCE INDICATED BY SYMPTOM
Acute weight gain (in excess of 5%)	Fluid volume excess
Acute weight loss (in excess of 5%)	Fluid volume deficit
Chronic weight loss	Protein deficit

TABLE 20. SIGNIFICANCE OF STOOL CHANGES

SYMPTOM	IMBALANCE INDICATED BY SYMPTOM
Hard fecal mass	Fluid volume deficit
Abdominal cramping with diarrhea	Sodium deficit Potassium excess
Ileus, abdominal distention (little or no stool or flatus passed)	Potassium deficit

See Table 19 for possible implications of body weight changes.

Frequency and Character of Stools

The nurse should record bowel movements, and any significant facts related to them, on the chart. The consistency of the stool (solid or liquid) and the frequency of evacuation should be noted.

Abnormal fecal losses and their causal relationship to fluid imbalances are discussed in a preceding section of this chapter.

Table 20 lists some of the fluid imbalances accompanied by changes in the character and the frequency of bowel movements.

Conclusion

The preceding discussion of planned nursing observations is intentionally general in nature. The reader is encouraged to further explore pertinent nursing observations (in context with appropriate nursing actions) in the chapters dealing with specific conditions.

Chapter 9

The Elements of Nutrition

Materials essential for nutrition can be divided into the "bulk" elements, which include protein, carbohydrate and fat; the vitamins; the minerals; and water.

The "Bulk" Elements

Protein, carbohydrate and fat make up the solid physical bulk of the diet. They are broken down and converted in the course of digestion, absorption and metabolism.

Protein. Proteins have been defined as *organic compounds containing the element nitrogen.* Together with the carbohydrates and fats, they constitute the principal part of the solids of living matter. The name *protein* comes to us from a Greek word *proteios,* meaning *first,* coined by the Dutch chemist Mulder in 1839, reflecting his conviction of the importance of protein. Proteins are used principally for body building and maintenance rather than for energy purposes. Although protein foods are derived both from plants and animals, proteins from animal sources appear to predominate in the average American diet. Proteins are the distinguishing constituents of many important foods, such as meat, fish, poultry, eggs, dairy products, beans, peas and peanuts. Although milk contains protein, it is an exceedingly dilute source that also contributes large amounts of fat and carbohydrates.

Proteins have many essential functions. For example, through their drawing power for liquids (oncotic pressure), they help prevent blood from leaking from the blood vessels. The amino acids of which proteins are composed are the building blocks for the growth of new tissue. When protein foods, such as meat, eggs, cheese, fish and fowl, are eaten, the proteins of which they largely consist are broken down in the digestive tract and absorbed into the blood as amino acids. In the liver and other manufacturing centers of the body, amino acids are reassembled into specific proteins to meet the diverse needs of the body.

Protein is required for the elaboration of enzymes, for the fabrication of those blood-borne messengers we call hormones, and even for the manufacture of some vitamins. Protein is essential for the body's defenses against infection. It deserves the term *keystone nutrient.*

The factors that can cause a protein deficit include decreased intake, increased loss, or imperfect utilization of protein. Bleeding, whether severe, repeated, or of long duration, drains the protein stores of the body, sooner or later causing a deficit. Infection has a destructive effect on our protein supplies. Starvation causes wasting and the internal cannibalization of the body tissues. Burns, fractures and surgical operations help to deplete the protein stores of the body through the destruction of tissues and apparently purposeless wastage called *toxic destruction of protein.* Diseases that affect the digestive tract interfere with the intake of protein by the body and cause protein poverty.

Symptoms of protein deficit include loss of weight and wasting of the muscles; body tissues become flabby and soft. The patient complains that he is always tired. He is chronically depressed. His poor appetite becomes still poorer, and he may vomit repeatedly. If he is injured, his wounds refuse to heal. His recuperative powers are greatly decreased; he may experience one infection right after another. Any patient with a disturbance of the body fluids is a candidate for protein deficit, particularly if he has been ill for a long time, since the sort of events that cause body fluid disturbances can also cause protein deficit.

Carbohydrates. The word carbohydrate means hydrated carbon—that is, the water and carbon combined. The hydrogen and oxygen atoms of carbohydrates are usually present in the same proportion as in water (HOH), so that the general formula of most carbohydrates can be expressed $C_n (HOH)_n$. The values for n can range from 2 to many thousands.

About 70 per cent by weight of the food in the average diet consists of carbohydrates. They are the distinguishing constituents of cereals, bakery products, confections, sugar, syrups, starch and fermentation products. They serve to provide calories for immediate use or, through the mechanism of storage, for delayed use. Carbohydrates not immediately used by the body for energy purposes are stored as fat.

Fat. The term fat suggests such familiar substances as butter, lard, tallow, olive oil, cottonseed oil, cream and oleomargarine. In nature, fats exist in less obvious and less easily characterized combinations. Because of the complexity and variability of fats, no satisfactory classification exists. Many protein foods, such as meat, fish and eggs, as well as dairy products, contain considerable quantities of fat. Carbohydrate foods are usually low in fat, if they contain any. The chief function of fat in the diet is to provide calories for energy.

The Calorie

In addition to being the unit of measure for heat, the calorie is also the unit of measure for energy, since heat can be converted into energy. Heat and energy are interchangeable, and the calorie measures both. The calorie employed in nutrition is the large or *great calorie*. It represents the quantity of heat needed to raise the temperature of 1 L. of water 1° C. Most adults expend about 70 calories per hour while resting; 105 calories per hour while standing; and several hundreds of calories per hour while exercising vigorously.

We use the calorie to express food values. A gram (about 1/28 of an ounce) of pure protein supplies 4 calories. A gram of carbohydrate supplies 4 calories. A gram of alcohol supplies about 7 calories, and a gram of fat, 9.

Most adults lose weight on a diet providing 1,600 calories per day. All adults lose weight on a diet of 1,200 calories or less. Most office workers require upwards of 2,500 calories per day to maintain weight. Heat loss increases the caloric needs, so that an Eskimo requires more calories than a south sea islander, assuming that their activities are equal.

The human body is not indifferent to the nature of the food from which it derives its energy. For best health, it appears that about 15 to 20 per cent of the total calories should be derived from protein; 35 to 50 per cent from starch or carbohydrate; and about 35 to 50 per cent from fat foods. Some persons, who have been dubbed "carboholics," appear to have an inordinate tendency to transform the carbohydrate of the diet into body fat. Diets quite high in protein, limited to not more than 50 to 60 Gm. of carbohydrate a day, have been recommended for such persons.

When a person fails to receive his required quota of calories, he begins, unconsciously but literally, to consume himself, since the internal chemical reactions of the body begin to metabolize body fat stores to generate needed calories. After the fat stores have been used up, the body converts solid tissues —chiefly muscles—into their constituent elements in order to obtain the desperately needed calories. When one is receiving an inadequate caloric intake, food entering the body is consumed for caloric purposes rather than being employed to repair damaged tissues or to provide new tissues for growth.

We see the ominous effect of inadequate caloric intake in illness and injuries in the young. Tissue repair cannot proceed until the caloric intake is more than just adequate. This principle is especially important in the growing individual, since growth will not occur unless the caloric intake is adequate. Naturally, the availability of generous quantities of fat helps ward off the evil day when the patient begins to cannibalize his own tissues. But that day inevitably comes sooner or later, unless one's daily demand for calories is met.

The symptoms of caloric deficit are easily recognized. The obvious one is hunger. Mental depression, apprehension and jitteriness occur. There is a loss of weight; fatigue results from slight effort. There are more subtle and less obvious symptoms, such as a shortness of breath, especially on exertion.

Insidiously, as caloric deficit persists, the baleful symptoms of protein deficit have their onset. Under such circumstances, dietary proteins are consumed for energy rather than for tissue synthesis.

Vitamins

Since vitamins differ from each other in composition, it is impossible to define them in terms of their chemical structure. However, vitamins can be defined from the physiologic standpoint as organic compounds that are essential constituents of the diet, yet are required only in minute amounts for the normal functioning of the body, since the role of vitamins in the chemistry of life processes is that of a catalyst.

The last of the basic nutritional essentials to be discovered, vitamins were at first believed to be amines. It was for this reason that they were designated as the *vital amines,* a term later shortened to vitamines, and still later to vitamins. We now know that vitamins differ widely from one another in their chemical nature and that they are not necessarily amines.

Vitamins cannot be manufactured within the body, at least in quantities sufficient to meet the daily requirement. When they are ingested in excess of the need, they are usually excreted; more than enough does not appear to be better than enough. Vitamins are amazingly safe. Apparently only two vitamins, vitamins A and D, can cause harm, and these only in doses far in excess of the daily requirement. When the vitamin intake is inadequate, deficiency disease occurs. Governmental and industrial application of the new knowledge of vitamins has made vitamin deficiencies, almost universal

a few years ago, now so unusual that many physicians have never seen them. Yet, in the developing areas of the world and in countries at war, vitamin deficiency disease still abounds.

Vitamin deficits arise not only from a decreased intake of vitamins, but from diseases of the digestive tract that impair the use of vitamins by the body. Infectious diseases, burns, or injuries can help to bring on vitamin deficits by increasing the use of vitamins by the body. Deficiencies of the B vitamins, for example, are prone to occur in alcoholics.

Each vitamin deficit has its own characteristic clinical picture. Vitamin A deficit may be indicated by the inability to see in a dim light. Signs of deficits of B vitamins include cracking at the mouth corners, beefy red tongue, diarrhea, anemia, dermatitis, anorexia, nervous disorders, loss of coordination and even mental disease. Vitamin C deficit may be revealed by bleeding gums, bleeding under the fibrous covering of the bones, impaired wound healing and wound dehiscence. Clues to vitamin D deficit include bowed legs, prominences of the bony bosses of the head, growth failure, flabbiness of the muscles, and impairment in the use of calcium by the body. Vitamin B_{12} deficit, stemming from internal metabolic factors rather than inadequate intake, causes pernicious anemia.

Vitamin deficits are usually remedied by administering the appropriate commercial vitamin preparations by mouth, or by giving a concentrated natural source of vitamins, such as lemon juice or orange juice for vitamin C. More and more physicians are becoming convinced of the value of giving patients under the stress of illness, infectious disease, surgery, burns, injury and during convalescence, generous quantities of vitamins by means of a carefully formulated supplement.

Minerals

Minerals are also called inorganic or ash elements. They are the chemical elements, exclusive of carbon, that remain wholly or partly in the ash when a food is burned. When minerals are dissolved in water, they develop electrical charges and are designated electrolytes. All minerals develop such charges when placed in an aqueous solution, except when they are part of a complex organic compound. The minerals usually listed in any table giving the mineral contents of foods include:

- Sodium
- Potassium
- Calcium
- Magnesium
- Iron
- Phosphorus
- Sulfur
- Chlorine

These minerals occur in important quantities in foods and have long been studied with respect to their functions in the body. During the past few years, additional chemical elements have been discovered in minute amounts in plant and animal materials. Some of these, including cobalt, copper, manganese, zinc and iodine, may play roles as important in animal nutrition as those elements that occur in larger quantities. Other minerals of common occurrence, but whose dietary properties have not been assessed, include aluminum, arsenic, bromine and fluorine. The latter has been found to be of definite value in preventing dental caries. Other chemical elements, including boron, molybdenum and silicon, have been found necessary for plants.

Clinical deficiencies of the following minerals have been observed:

- Sodium
- Potassium
- Calcium
- Magnesium
- Iron
- Copper
- Iodine

Findings of deficits of the first four were covered in the chapter on "Changes in Composition of Extracellular Fluid." Deficiency of iron or of copper is associated with anemia. Deficiency of iodine results in endemic goiter. There is no specific deficit of fluorine.

Water

Water is perhaps the most essential of all nutrients. One can live for fairly long periods without bulk nutrients, minerals, or vitamins; the person without any water lives only a few miserable days. Water possesses such unique chemical and physical characteristics that there is no substitute for it in the living cycle. It is the closest approach known to a universal solvent. The adult body is from 60 to 70 per cent water. In a real sense, each one of us is a bag of more or less solid materials dissolved in water. Water is required for the countless chemical reactions of the body. No major physiologic function can proceed without it. Although a generous intake of water is essential for health, and although water is usually regarded as completely innocuous, only seven times the usual daily intake of water can be harmful because it causes loss of the electrolytes from the body. For this reason, the syndrome resulting from excessive intake of water is called *water intoxication*. In reality, it is brought about by the dilution of the extracellular fluid and sodium deficit.

Sources of Information

The National Research Council has set up Recommended Dietary Allowances for calories, protein, calcium, iron, vitamin A, thiamine, riboflavin, niacin, ascorbic acid and vitamin D (presented in the *Recommended Dietary Allowances,* revised in 1958, Publication No. 589, National Academy of Sciences and National Research Council, 1958). The allowances are intakes designed for the maintenance of good nutrition in normal, healthy persons living in a temperate climate. The values are designed to allow for the normal ranges of individual needs under the usual conditions of life, plus a moderate additional safety factor. They are *not* intended to cover the special requirements that may be created by illness, unusual exertion, or other stress.

The United States Food and Drug Administration has promulgated Minimum Daily Requirements in connection with the

Federal Food, Drug, and Cosmetic Act. These requirements represent basic intakes deemed necessary for the actual prevention of deficiencies. The values are lower, in most instances, than the Recommended Dietary Allowances of the National Research Council.

For information and protection of consumers, the labels of special dietary foods and diet supplements are required to show the proportion of the Minimum Daily Requirement supplied by each nutrient listed. In case a Minimum Daily Requirement has not yet been set for a nutrient, or if the nutrient concerned has not been officially classified by the Food and Drug Administration as essential, this too should be stated on the label. In medical and dietetic literature, the Minimum Daily Requirements are referred to less frequently than are the Recommended Dietary Allowances.

An extremely helpful source for the evaluation of nutritional contributions of food portions is the book *Food Values of Portions Commonly Used* by A. Bowes and C. Church (edition 9, revised by Charles Frederick Church and Helen Nichols Church, Philadelphia and Montreal, J. B. Lippincott Company). It is invaluable for the food and diet planner.

Conclusion

It is indeed difficult to over-estimate the importance of nutrition. The Germans have a saying *Das Essen macht den Mann* ("Eating makes the man"). We are, in more than a figurative sense, *what we eat*. This applies, of course, to sick as well as to healthy persons; eating in the broader sense includes not only the usual foods, but materials administered by nasogastric tube, rectal tube, or by the parenteral route.

Chapter 10

The Nurse's Role in Preventing Imbalances of Water, Electrolytes, and Other Nutrients

INTRODUCTION

It is better to prevent disturbances of water, electrolytes and other nutrients than to have to treat them after they have developed. Any patient can develop a serious nutritional disturbance if his needs for nutrients are not considered and met. The practical application of the principles of nutrition is as much a part of nursing as is the administration of medications. Examples of common clinical events that can lead to nutritional disturbances include:

1. Inadequate intake
2. Excessive losses from such conditions as
   A. Fever
   B. Excessive perspiration
   C. Vomiting
   D. Gastric or intestinal suction
   E. Diarrhea
3. Medical therapy, such as the prolonged use of diuretics, laxatives, enemas, or steroids
4. Catabolic effects, such as those induced by
   A. Immobilization
   B. Draining decubitus ulcers
   C. Surgery (hemorrhage)
   D. Trauma

When one considers how frequently the nurse encounters situations such as these in her daily practice, the need for a carefully considered plan of action on her part becomes evident. Such a plan must include meticulous observation of the patient.

Compared to other healing disciplines, the profession of nursing is unique in that its ministrations are applied continuously to the hospitalized patient. The nursing staff is responsible for the intelligent execution of orders for solid foods and liquids during the entire 24-hour period. Far more is required than a rote performance of duties. Initiative is mandatory on the part of the nurse if the prescribed therapy is to produce optimal results.

In assuring the patient's nutritional welfare, the nurse functions in the framework formulated by the physician. At no time should she deviate from this framework without first consulting him. Nevertheless, much is left to her discretion. For example, the order "diet as tolerated" is frequently written on surgical services. The physician assumes that the nursing staff understands the patient's condition so as to execute properly such a diet order. Indeed, it would be impossible for the physician to detail step-by-step exactly what should be done for every patient, even when the diet order is relatively specific. When the nurse knows the general purpose and scope of the diet, she can exercise her judgment in accordance with the individual patient's needs.

The nurse should be constantly aware of

the problems that may be posed by medication. Suppose a thiazide diuretic has been ordered. Since the nurse knows that this medication will, in all probability, increase the patient's need for potassium, she can encourage the ingestion of high potassium foods and, in addition, alert the physician to the possible need for a potassium supplement.

In instances such as those cited above, the nurse can often institute action to meet the new situation. On other occasions, she must report her findings to the physician and seek his direction. Among the valuable resource personnel available to the nurse for consultation is the dietitian, who can frequently provide helpful suggestions if she is given background information based on careful nursing observations. The wise nurse consults other members of the health team when confronted by problems that tax her knowledge. Obviously, the patient benefits from such coordination.

The busy physician can easily miss notations in the nursing notes concerning a patient's inadequate intake of food and liquids. Sometimes such notations are not made because of laxity in checking the patient's tray after meals, or in recording the findings on the patient's chart, which should always contain a meaningful summary by the members of the nursing staff of the patient's food and fluid intake.

The importance of accurate nursing observations is revealed by questions commonly asked by physicians when they evaluate the state of the patient's water and electrolytes balance.

1. Has the patient been eating and drinking normally? If not, for how long?

2. Have abnormal losses of body fluids occurred, as perspiration; vomiting; gastric or intestinal suction; drainage from enterostomy, colostomy, or fistulas; liquid stools; wound or burn exudate?

3. Has there been an acute loss of weight? An acute gain in weight?

4. Have therapeutic fluids been given by tube, rectum, or parenterally (if patient has been under treatment by another physician)?

5. Has the patient been on a restrictive diet (if patient has been under treatment by another physician)?

6. Has the patient been given medications that might cause body fluid disturbances?

Obviously, conditions that cause disturbances of water and electrolytes can also cause deficits of other nutrients, such as protein, carbohydrate, fat, or vitamins.

INADEQUATE INTAKE

Intake Via the Gastrointestinal Route

Oral Route

The oral route for intake of water, electrolytes, vitamins, and other nutrients has long been preferred for the prevention of deficits and the correction of mild deficits already present. It offers several advantages:

1. Because it allows gradual absorption, the oral route provides far greater efficiency in the utilization of administered nutrients.

2. Large quantities of water, electrolytes and other nutrients can be ingested over a short period without upsetting water and electrolyte balance.

3. The oral route is far less expensive.

4. The oral route appeals to the patient as being more natural.

Naturally, the gastrointestinal tract must be functional if the oral route is to be used.

The ingestion of nutrients is so commonplace that its significance is frequently overlooked. Perhaps this is because the oral route lacks the dramatic impact of parenteral or nasogastric feedings. Yet, oral administration can frequently prevent serious disturbances of the body fluids.

Since the oral route is the normal way to obtain nutrients, it possesses a distinct psychologic appeal. A patient frequently feels he is quite ill simply because he is denied food by the oral route.

Nursing Measures to Promote Eating

Illness or imposed dietary restrictions may greatly decrease the desire to eat. Offering an adequate diet does not guarantee that the patient will accept it. The real test of nursing skill is not to order and serve a diet; rather, it lies in getting the patient to eat it. The dietitian must usually individualize the diet if she is to motivate the patient to eat

it. In some institutions, the patient can receive individual attention from the dietitian; unfortunately, this is frequently not
possible. In such instances, it is especially
important that the nurse study the patient's
eating habits, his food likes and dislikes, as
well as the cultural and religious beliefs that
influence his eating habits.

Whenever possible, the patient should be
permitted choices, since this will increase the
acceptability of the diet. The nurse must
remember that dietary restrictions are often
difficult for the patient. Unless steps are
taken to make the restrictions tolerable, the
patient will either cease eating or fail to
adhere to the diet. The patient will be more
likely to follow the diet if the nurse explains
why it has been ordered.

The nurse can help the patient accept his
diet if she displays a sincere interest and
makes it clear that she understands how difficult it is to be placed on a restricted diet
after years of freely choosing foods. A force-
ful, goading, or heckling approach may turn
the patient against the diet.

A pleasant environment encourages eating, but the establishment of such an environment is not always easy. The wise nurse
makes every effort to eliminate unpleasant
sights and odors. Naturally, this cannot be
done in ward rooms with seriously ill patients; but, at least, unpleasant sights such
as drainage bottles and parenteral infusion
apparatus can be screened. Soiled dressings
can be changed before meals. Ileostomy bags
can be changed or emptied. Ambulatory
patients can eat their meals outside the ward.

Since strong emotions affect both appetite
and digestive processes unfavorably, the
nurse should attempt to minimize such feelings. Emotional comfort is as important as
physical comfort, but it is often more difficult to achieve. Incidents that irritate the
patient should be noted on the nursing care
plan and avoided, if possible, in the future.
Unpleasant procedures can be avoided in
the vicinity of mealtime. What may appear
minor to the nurse may be quite irritating
to the seriously ill patient. Sometimes the
presence of a member of the family may
help to relax the patient at mealtime; sometimes he may prefer to eat alone.

Many patients like to have their hands
and face washed before each meal. Patients
having unpleasant mouth tastes such as occur with oral surgery or bronchiectasis can
be given a mouthwash before mealtime.

Since unpleasant symptoms, such as pain
and nausea, greatly decrease the patient's
interest in eating, every possible nursing
measure should be taken to alleviate these
and similar sources of discomfort. If simple
comfort measures fail, it may be wise to
administer p.r.n. medications in preparation
for the meal.

A patient in need of a cleansing enema or
a bladder catheterization is not apt to eat
or drink well. Thus, these problems should
be relieved prior to serving meals or forcing
fluids.

Nothing should interfere with the patient's eating his food while it is still warm.
The tray should be kept neat and attractive;
spilled liquids decrease the appeal of food,
hence deter the patient's appetite.

The nurse should give any assistance required to prepare the food for eating or to
arrange the eating utensils for easy access.

The patient should be placed in a comfortable position. All too frequently, the tray
is placed unthinkingly out of reach, or no
provision is made to help the patient cut
his food or pour his coffee. If the patient
must be fed, it should be done in a con-
siderate and unhurried manner. The patient who might be embarrassed by his eating habits (for example, the patient who
drools because of a stroke) should be tact-
fully provided with privacy.

The size of the servings should be appropriate for the patient's appetite. A patient
with a small appetite can be repelled by
large portions of food. Serving the meal in
courses may help such persons eat more.

Unnecessary interruptions during meals
can be avoided. The not-too-eager appetite
can be easily discouraged by the poor planning of nursing activities. Sufficient time
should be allowed for eating; the patient
should never be rushed. Frequently, a patient will stop eating when he sees other
trays in the ward being removed or when he
is asked repeatedly if he is finished. The
patient should be convinced that he can eat
at his own pace—*careful explanation is frequently required to accomplish this.* Above

all, the nursing staff should not become so wrapped up in routine that they unthinkingly subject the patient to time stress.

Every effort should be made to prevent nausea and vomiting after meals. Thus, the patient should not be turned quickly or subjected to excessive physical activity. On the other hand, mild exercise should not be condemned, for it may aid digestion. If nausea should occur, appropriate medication may be given in accord with medical orders. In the absence of a p.r.n. order for nausea, the nurse might seek a medical order. The cause of the nausea can be sought and noted on the chart.

Although the points just enumerated are well-known to most nurses, *we are convinced that they cannot be overemphasized.* One does well to remember that any program of diet therapy is worthless if the patient does not eat! Conversely, any measure capable of promoting food and liquid intake contributes to the patient's welfare. The nurse should impress the importance of these facts on the auxiliary staff members, who are frequently charged with important responsibilities associated with feeding the patients.

Nasogastric Tube Feedings

Indications for Tube Feedings

Oral intake might be impossible, even though adequate gastrointestinal function is present, in such situations as:

1. Semiconsciousness or unconsciousness
2. Oral surgery
3. Extreme anorexia
4. Swallowing problems
5. Weakness caused by chronic debilitating conditions
6. Disorientation
7. Serious mental diseases, such as major psychoses

The nurse must be aware of these conditions and report inadequate intake when any of them are present. The patient should not be permitted to develop malnutrition before another route for intake of nutrients is adopted. One solution to the problems posed by such patients is the use of nasogastric tube feedings. Such feedings have many advantages, especially when the prob-

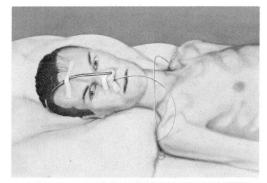

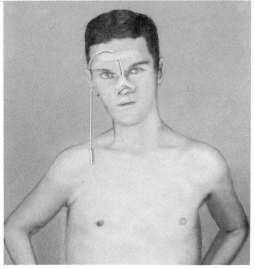

Fig. 48. Improvement in nutritional status as a result of tube feedings. (Barron, J.: Tube feeding of postoperative patients. Surg. Clin. N. Am., p. 1489, December, 1959)

lems requiring them are likely to be of long duration.

When oral intake is inadequate, tube feedings are used to administer the protein and calories necessary for tissue healing in such conditions as fractures, decubitus ulcers and burns. An intake of at least 1,600 to 2,000 calories must be provided if the protein is to be used for tissue repair; otherwise, it will be used to meet energy needs.

Disorders of the gastrointestinal tract, such as biliary or pancreatic fistulas, or delayed emptying of the stomach, may necessitate passing a feeding tube beyond the affected area in order to administer nutrients. One

TABLE 21.*

Type Feeding	Calories	Protein Gm.	Fat Gm.	CHO Gm.	Ca Gm.	Fe mg.	Vit. A I.U.	Ascorbic Acid mg.	Thiamine mg.	Riboflavin mg.	Niacin mg.
Sustagen 500 Gm. Water 1,000 Gm.	2,085	118	18	323	3.5	8	2,778	167	5.5	5.5	50
Whole Milk 1,000 Gm. Egg Yolks (4) Heavy Cream 40% 240 cc. Karo Syrup 100 Gm. Yeast: 2 cakes dissolved in 200 cc. hot water—mix altogether and cook in a double boiler. Cool, strain, and add orange juice 200 Gm. Cod Liver Oil 16 Gm.	2,321	54	158	183	1.5	7	7,270	110	0.9	2.9	10.2
Water 100 Gm. Powder Skim Milk 225 Gm. Powder Whole Milk 200 Gm.	1,798	132	56	193	4.8	3	2,890	28	1.4	7.3	2

* Above are recommended by the Commission on Nutrition of the Medical Society of the State of Pennsylvania. Goodhart, R., and Wohl, M.: Manual of Clinical Nutrition. pp. 92-93. Philadelphia, Lea & Febiger, 1964.

of the few contraindications for tube feedings is the complete obstruction of the lower gastrointestinal tract.

The provision of adequate nutrition by the nasogastric route may spell the difference between life and death. Pareira cited the example of a two-year-old child with a head injury, who had refused food with a resultant progressive drop in body weight:

The child became critically ill in spite of parenteral alimentation. His condition improved when tube feeding was instituted at the beginning of the third hospital week. Within one week the general condition was so much improved that a subdural hematoma could be successfully evacuated. Continued general improvement and weight gain followed, and two weeks later the tube was removed. The child ate well and was discharged from the hospital one week later.*

Even if the underlying disease process cannot be corrected, the patient can live more comfortably during the weeks and months remaining if he is adequately nourished. The incidence of trophic ulcers, wasting and debilitation is decreased by adequate nourishment.

Anorexia and malnutrition create a vicious cycle: anorexia leads to malnutrition; malnutrition promotes anorexia. The use of tube feedings for several weeks improves the patient's nutrition, as well as his appetite, thus interrupting the cycle. Many anorexic

* Pareira, M.: Therapeutic Nutrition With Tube Feedings. Springfield, Ill., Thomas, 1959.

patients request permission to "eat around the tube" after several weeks of tube feedings. Visual evidence of the general improvement brought about by tube feedings is presented in Figure 48.

Tube Feeding Mixtures

Any tube feeding mixture should provide all the required solid nutrients—protein, carbohydrate, fat, minerals and vitamins. It should incorporate generous quantities of water; however, additional water must be supplied if the daily requirement is to be met. It is especially necessary to provide adequate water for the elderly, the confused, the lethargic and the comatose, since these patients frequently do not experience or express normal thirst. The physician should prescribe the contents of the tube feeding and should designate the quantity and the times when it should be given.

A commercial feeding preparation, Sustagen, is easy to use since it requires only the addition of water. When supplemented by adequate water, Sustagen has maintained a state of adequate nutrition in comatose patients for years. It has also been found to be tolerated when administered directly into an enterostomy. (See Table 21.) Sustagen represents the end product of a long period of research at the Homer Phillips Hospital in St. Louis.

Also used for tube feedings are powdered

TABLE 22. COMPOSITION AND NUTRITIVE VALUE OF BLENDERIZED TUBE FEEDING MIXTURE

	AMOUNT	2,000 ML.*	1,000 ML.
Strained peas	Jars	1	½
Strained carrots	Jars	1	½
Strained beets	Jars	1	½
Strained applesauce	Jars	1	½
Strained beef	Jars	3	1½
Strained liver	Jars	1	½
Eggs	(Number)	2	1
Strained orange juice	ml.	200	100
18% cream	ml.	180	90
Milk	ml.	700	350
Glucose	Gm.	60	30
Salt	Gm.	5	2

* 2,000 ml. contain approximately 1,977 calories, 11 Gm. of sodium chloride, 120 Gm. protein, 89 Gm. fat and 174 Gm. of carbohydrate. Each 500 ml. would contain about 495 calories and 30 Gm. of protein.

Artz, C., and Hardy, J.: Complications in Surgery and Their Management. p. 352. Philadelphia, Saunders, 1961.

milk, and mixtures of milk, eggs, cream, syrup, yeast and other ingredients. (See Table 21.)

Whole foods can be liquefied in a blender and administered by means of a tube. Such mixtures provide the ingredients of a natural diet with all known and unknown dietary essentials, are relatively inexpensive, and may sometimes cause less diarrhea and other untoward symptoms than commercial preparations. The content of such mixtures is readily varied if diarrhea should occur. Commercial strained baby foods can be administered as tube feedings. (See Table 22.)

Tube Feeding Methods

Every nurse should thoroughly understand both the role and the method of tube feedings. Tube feedings can be administered by gravity flow or by a mechanical pump.

Many variations have been devised for administering tube feedings by gravity flow:

1. An **Asepto syringe** can serve as a funnel; it is frequently used to administer the feeding mixture. The syringe attaches directly to the nasogastric tube. The flow rate is regulated by the height at which the nurse holds the syringe. (See Fig. 49.)

Advantages of this method:

A. The equipment is simple and easy to care for.

B. The patient can be observed closely for untoward symptoms because the nurse is present during the entire feeding.

Disadvantages of this method:

A. The flow rate can be only crudely adjusted by raising or lowering the syringe.

B. The tube feeding mixture is often administered too rapidly because the nurse lacks sufficient time to remain at the bedside for a slow delivery of the feeding.

C. The syringe usually has to be refilled several times to give the desired amount of the feeding mixture.

2. Another commonly used apparatus consists of a **Murphy drip tube** used in conjunction with a Kelly flask or a Vitex Salvarsan tube (pictured), rubber tubing and a screw clamp. The flask or tube can be suspended from an I.V. standard. (See Fig. 50.)

Advantages of this method:

A. The flow rate can be regulated as desired by adjusting the clamp and counting the drip flow in the Murphy drip tube.

B. The nurse does not have to be constantly present during the feeding.

C. The reservoir is calibrated for easy measurement, and holds several hundred ml., depending on the type of flask used.

Disadvantages of this method:

A. Resterilized rubber tubing often cracks and can harbor pathogenic organisms.

B. The mixture is not in a closed container.

3. Some hospitals use **resterilized parenteral fluid bottles** and disposable intravenous tubing to administer tube feedings slowly by the drip method. The disposable tubing attaches directly to the nasogastric tube. The bottle is suspended from an I.V. standard. (See Fig. 51.)

Advantages of this method:

A. The flow rate can be adjusted as desired—when necessary, a large amount of the feeding mixture can be delivered over a long period of time.

B. The nurse does not have to be constantly present.

C. The plastic tubing is disposable; the bottle can be resterilized often.

D. The mixture is in a closed container.

Disadvantages of this method:

A. During prolonged administration, the mixture may be exposed to room temperature too long, causing bacterial multiplication in the mixture.

B. A thick mixture may clog the narrow tubing.

4. The **Davol disposable gastric feeding unit** consists of an 1,800 ml. graduated polyethylene bag, pet-cock shut-off for measurement of flow, drip chamber, wide plastic tubing, and a Sims connector for attachment to the gastric or the duodenal tube. The unit is suspended from an I.V. standard. (See Fig. 52.)

Advantages of this method:

A. The flow rate can be adjusted as desired—when necessary, a large amount

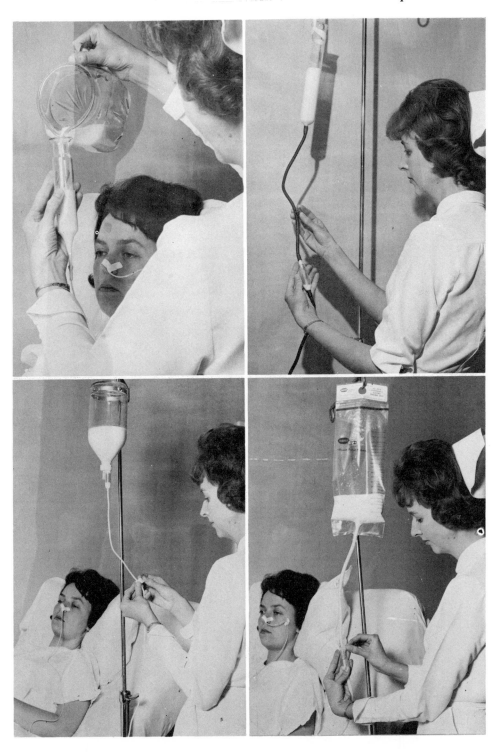

Fig. 49. (*Left, top*) Tube feeding with a syringe.

Fig. 50. (*Right, top*) Tube feeding with a flask and a Murphy-drip apparatus.

Fig. 51. (*Left, bottom*) Tube feeding with a resterilized I.V. bottle and disposable I.V. tubing.

Fig. 52. (*Right, bottom*) Tube feeding with the Davol Gastric Feeding Unit. (Davol Rubber Co., Providence, Rhode Island)

FIG. 53. Barron food pump. (Friedrich, H.: Oral feeding by food pump. Am. J. Nurs., p. 63, February, 1962)

of the feeding mixture can be delivered over a long period of time.

B. The apparatus will accommodate both light and heavy fluids; the flexible drip chamber may be used to assist the flow of viscous fluids.

C. The equipment is entirely disposable—it may be used more than once, as a one-patient item, if rinsed well after each feeding.

Disadvantages of this method:

A. During prolonged administration, the mixture may be exposed to room temperature too long, causing an increased bacterial count.

B. The cost to the patient can be a disadvantage if the set-up is used only once or twice.

5. The **mechanical pump method** is more dependable than the gravity drip method for slow constant delivery of tube feedings. Factors that may cause an uneven flow rate in the gravity drip method include:

A. A change in the patient's position after the flow rate has been adjusted; almost invariably the patient will desire to change his position during the feeding, especially when the mixture is given slowly.

B. Failure to adjust the flow rate as frequently as necessary; frequent checks are indicated to assure maintenance of the desired flow rate.

C. A viscous mixture may clog the tube, especially when the flow has been disrupted by a position change.

A food pump, on the other hand, assures a constant flow rate regardless of the patient's position.

An example of a commercial food pump is the Barron food pump. (See Fig. 53.) This device is the result of extensive work done by James Barron, M.D., of the Henry Ford Hospital, and the Engineering and Medical

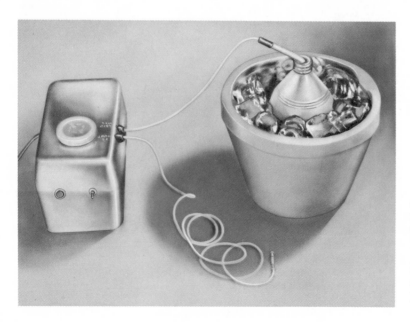

FIG. 54. Pump mechanism, food container, insulated ice container, and tubing of the Barron food pump. (Barron, J.: Tube feeding of postoperative patients. Surg. Clin. N. Am., p. 1488, December, 1959)

Departments of the Chrysler Corporation. The pump can be used to deliver intermittent or continuous feedings.

The equipment includes the pump mechanism, the food container, an outer insulated container for ice and the latex tubing. (See Fig. 54.) To prevent spoilage, the feeding solution is cooled by placing the food bottle in the non-drip insulated ice container.

The speed of the feeding, determined by the physician, is controlled by a pulley on the underside of the pump. (See Fig. 55.) There are four speeds for delivery of the solution:

1. First speed (low) — 43 ml./hr.
2. Second speed — 65 ml./hr.
3. Third speed — 113 ml./hr.
4. Fourth speed — 200 ml./hr.

The slowest speed is usually necessary when the patient is first started on tube feedings. Slow speeds minimize nausea, vomiting, cramping and diarrhea; the speed is gradually increased to the desired rate.

Figure 56 shows the type of pump arrangement used to refeed upper gastrointestinal body fluids in such conditions as delayed emptying of the stomach, biliary or duodenal fistulas, or pancreatic fistulas. Gastric

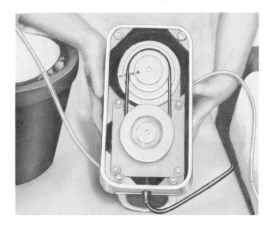

FIG. 55. Pully for regulating speed of Barron food pump. (Friedrich, H.: Oral feeding by food pump. Amer. J. Nurs., p. 63, February, 1962)

juice, bile and pancreatic juice can be removed by suction and then administered with the feeding mixture beyond the point of disturbance. The gastrointestinal fluids contain valuable electrolytes and enzymes and should be restored to the body when possible.

When used properly, food pumps conserve the nurse's time. The instructions accom-

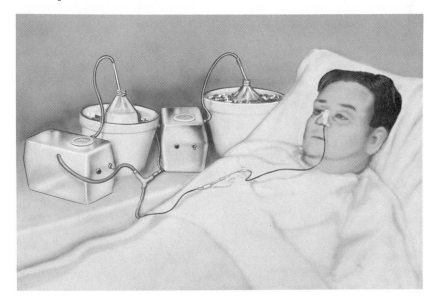

FIG. 56. Food pump arrangement for refeeding of upper gastrointestinal fluids. (Barron, J.: Tube feeding of postoperative patients. Surg. Clin. N. Amer., p. 1484, December, 1959)

panying the pump should be carefully studied before the feedings are started; otherwise the results will not be satisfactory.

Selection of the Feeding Method. When the tube feedings are ordered, the physician may indicate a specific method for administering the feeding solution. If he has no preference, the nurse may decide which method is best for the patient.

Factors to be considered in determining the best method to use include: (1) the patient's condition, (2) the viscosity of the feeding mixture, and (3) the type of equipment available.

The patient's condition is an important factor. For example, comatose patients must have a slow delivery of solution to prevent gastric distention and vomiting, with possible tracheal aspiration. A food pump set at a slow speed or a gravity drip method suitable for slow delivery of the mixture should be used. Patients receiving duodenal or upper jejunal feedings require a slow, constant feeding rate; best results are obtained with a mechanical food pump set at a low speed. All patients, however, do not require a constant, slow delivery of the feeding mixture. Many alert patients, free of gastrointestinal problems, can tolerate fairly rapid feedings if the amount given each time is small; any of the feeding methods described earlier can be adapted for their needs.

Failure to consider the viscosity of the feeding mixture can result in clogging the apparatus. A thick mixture is best given with a mechanical food pump, or with a gravity drip apparatus having wide diameter tubing.

The type of equipment available greatly influences the method chosen; most hospitals have their own routine set-ups for tube feedings.

Prevention of Tube Feeding Complications

Although tube feedings have proved to be of immense value, they can cause trouble if given incorrectly. Complications of tube feedings include:
1. Diarrhea
2. Nausea
3. Vomiting

4. Aspiration pneumonia
5. Inadequate provision for water requirements
6. Metabolic alkalosis (primary base bicarbonate excess)

In order to avoid untoward reactions from tube feedings, the nurse should keep the following in mind:

1. The feeding mixture and the apparatus used to administer it are excellent culture sites for bacteria. Proper precautions should be taken so that neither the tube feeding mixture nor the equipment used for administration will become contaminated.

A. Whatever the set-up used for administering tube feedings, it should be carefully cleaned prior to use. Glass receptacles should be washed in hot, soapy water and rinsed well following each feeding. Between feedings, equipment should be stored in a closed container or wrapped in a clean towel. Equipment should be resterilized often, even though tube feeding is not a sterile procedure. As mentioned earlier, disposable equipment may be used. One should always keep in mind possible sources for contamination of equipment. As an example, uncovered equipment stored at the bedside in the summer attracts flies, especially if it has not been thoroughly cleaned.

B. In order to discourage bacterial growth, the tube feeding mixture should be refrigerated until at least one hour before use. Diarrhea frequently occurs when the feeding mixture is improperly stored.

C. Only enough tube feeding mixture for a 24-hour period should be made up in advance.

D. From 20 to 50 ml. of lukewarm water should be administered through the tube after each feeding when the intermittent method is used. This will force the remaining mixture into the stomach and clean the tube.

E. When continuous feedings are necessary, the equipment should be changed often. Because of the danger of spoilage, the reservoir should not be filled to capacity and exposed to room temperature until emptied. Instead, small amounts of fresh solution should be added at regular intervals. Occasionally, when the gravity drip method is used, ice bags are wrapped around the mixture reservoir to retard spoilage.

F. As mentioned earlier, the Barron food pump has its own provision for cooling the mixture. When the food pump tube is to be disconnected for more than several minutes, the end of it should be placed in the food container and the motor turned on. This prevents spoilage of food and obstruction of the tube.

2. The tube feeding mixture should be given slowly and in small amounts in order to avoid distention, nausea and excessive peristalsis.

A. When the intermittent feeding method is used, the amount given at each feeding is determined by dividing the total 24-hour dose by the number of feedings. Frequently, 2,000 ml. is given over a 24-hour period. Divided feedings may be given at intervals of 2, 3, or 4 hours. Individual feedings frequently vary between 150 to 300 ml. The individual feeding should not exceed 400 ml. unless it is to be given quite slowly.

B. If the patient should experience difficulty, then the feeding can be diluted with water. Such diluted feedings are to be administered by slow drip or by a slow speed setting on the mechanical pump.

3. The tube feeding mixture should be neither too hot nor too cold, since such temperature extremes cause nausea and discomfort, especially if the feeding is given quickly.

A. Feedings should be warmed to body temperature—but not to exceed 100° F.—by placing the container in a pan of warm water. The mixture should not be overheated, however, since this would curdle the protein and clog the tubing.

B. The fact that the mixture fed by the Barron food pump is not warm presents no difficulty, since the amount entering the stomach over any given period is small.

4. Measures should be taken to prevent gastric distention due to the introduction of excessive amounts of air during the feeding.

A. The feeding mixture reservoir should not be allowed to empty completely before more mixture is added. When the last of the feeding is about to flow into the tube, a small amount of water should be added to the reservoir and the tube clamped off.

B. Small quantities of air cause no difficulty. If care is used during the feeding, excessive air will not enter.

5. Unpleasant stimuli can be minimized to prevent nausea.

A. The esthetic factors for patients taking food by mouth apply also to patients receiving nasogastric tube feedings. Unpleasant stimuli inhibit the flow of digestive juices needed for food utilization.

B. Even though the patient is not taking nourishment orally, one should respect his need for a clean mouth. Regurgitation can occur in patients receiving tube feedings. When it does, the patient should be given a mouthwash. Even the semi-alert patient can taste tube feedings. The nares should be cleaned and lubricated often in order to minimize the discomfort caused by the nasogastric tube.

6. If nausea should occur, the feeding should be stopped and the patient given a rest period until further medical orders are received. A p.r.n. medication for nausea may be necessary. After the nausea subsides, a small amount of the feeding can be given slowly while the nurse observes the patient's reaction. The following can be tried when nausea occurs:

A. Decrease the fat content of the mixture

B. Dilute the mixture

C. Administer the mixture more slowly

7. If diarrhea occurs, the feeding should be discontinued until further medical orders are received.

A. The order may involve a modification of the feeding, most frequently a decrease in its carbohydrate content.

B. Medication, such as Kaopectate or paregoric, can be ordered and given through the tube to relieve the diarrhea.

C. Addition of applesauce or of Kanana Banana Flakes to the mixture frequently controls the diarrhea.

8. Precautions should be taken to prevent the aspiration of gastric contents if vomiting or regurgitation occurs. Aspiration of the feeding mixture can cause pneumonia.

A. If possible, the patient should be in a sitting position when receiving nasogastric feedings. If this is not possible, the head of the bed should be elevated to a 45° angle, unless this position is contraindicated.

B. If vomiting occurs, the patient's head should be turned to the side and lowered to promote drainage of the vomitus.

C. A suction machine should be available when the patient is semiconscious, unconscious, or otherwise unable to control the expulsion of vomitus. When possible, a nurse should remain with such patients throughout the feeding in order to cope with vomiting or regurgitation.

9. The amount of the feeding taken should be recorded, as should the amount of water added before, between, and after feedings.

10. Urine output should be recorded. Unless abnormal fluid losses are occurring, the amount of water taken by mouth should roughly equal the urinary output.

11. The nurse will do well to watch for signs of inadequate water intake, particularly when the feedings are high in protein content. Otherwise, uremia may develop.

A. Often, tube feeding mixtures are rich in protein, which cannot be properly metabolized without generous quantities of water. Should insufficient water be provided, water will be drawn from the tissues to supply the needed volume for urinary excretion of the increased solute load. Eventually, dehydration (sodium excess) will occur, along with an accumulation of nitrogenous waste product in the blood stream.

B. The nurse should be alert for the untoward effects of excessive protein in relation to water. These include nausea, vomiting, diarrhea, and eventually, ileus. If the condition is allowed to go uncorrected, it will result in a high fever and accompanying disorientation. Laboratory tests will reveal an elevated blood urea nitrogen (BUN) level.

C. Malfunctioning kidneys require more water to excrete a given amount of solute than do normal kidneys. Because aged patients frequently have impaired renal function, they require more water than do the young. Ziffren maintained that an aged patient can ordinarily tolerate no more than 100 to 150 Gm. of protein per day without diarrhea.

D. Early in protein overloading, the urine volume is large even though the water intake is inadequate. The large urine volume can easily lead the staff to think that the water intake is adequate. In such instances, however, output actually exceeds intake. By the accurate recording of careful observations, the nurse can unmask the true situation.

E. Confused or unconscious patients should be observed carefully for inadequate water intake, since they are not aware of thirst.

12. A check commonly used to determine if the nasogastric tube is in the stomach is the withdrawal of a small quantity of gastric juice prior to each feeding. Gastric juice which has been withdrawn should be gently forced back into the stomach rather than discarded.

A. While it is essential to check the position of the tube before giving a feeding, aspiration of even small amounts of stomach juices before each feeding can add up to an important quantity over the course of 2 or 3 days' tube feeding therapy.

B. Metabolic alkalosis can easily result when small amounts of gastric juice are repeatedly removed over several days. Gastric juice is rich in potassium, chloride and hydrogen ions. The loss of chloride causes the bicarbonate of the body to rise in compensation. Loss of potassium further contributes to the alkalosis, since the kidneys of the potassium-deficient patient excrete hydrogen preferentially.

13. Measures should be taken to prevent nausea following the feeding.

A. Avoid movements that might contribute to nausea for 2 to 3 hours after the feeding.

B. Again, consider the esthetic factors discussed above.

14. Constipation may sometimes be a problem when liquefied natural foods are administered very slowly into the stomach. These measures can be taken to prevent constipation and fecal impactions:

A. The frequency of bowel movements and the character of the stools should be observed and charted so that constipation can be detected before a fecal impaction forms.

B. The nurse who is familiar with the symptoms of constipation and fecal impaction will report their presence to the physician. Thus, if the patient fails to have a bowel movement for 3 successive days, the physician can be notified. Some patients may require attention before 3 days; a few may normally have bowel movements no oftener than every 3 or 4 days. Other reportable signs include: dry, hard feces expelled with difficulty; watery stools following a prolonged period without a bowel movement. The nurse should recall that a fecal impaction can manifest itself with diarrhea, since the bowel may become irritated by the impacted fecal bolus and force liquid feces around the impaction and out the anus.

C. A change in the content of the feeding mixture may correct the constipation.

D. Laxatives may be added through the feeding tube to correct the constipation.

E. Adequate quantities of water are helpful.

Intake Via the Parenteral Route

The nurse's role in administering parenteral nutrients is discussed in Chapter 14.

MODIFYING THE DIET TO PREVENT OR MINIMIZE BODY FLUID DISTURBANCES

Fever

An increased metabolic rate accompanies fever. Each degree of Fahrenheit the temperature is elevated causes a 7 per cent increase in metabolic rate. Each degree of Centigrade elevation causes a 13 per cent increase. Prolonged fever, particularly if it is high, can easily lead to body fluid disturbances, especially when the body's requirements for water and electrolytes are neglected. Fever causes an increased loss of water and electrolytes from lungs, skin and kidneys. The increased metabolism that accompanies fever depletes the body stores of glycogen and causes an increased catabolism of protein. The increased solute load resulting from protein breakdown places an extra burden on the kidneys. Losses of sodium, chloride and potassium are increased.

The patient suffering from prolonged fever needs to have his intake of all nutrients augmented. Yet the feverish patient usually has anorexia. Moreover, there appears to be decreased intestinal motility and subnormal absorption of nutrients during fever. Catabolism of body tissues can easily lead to metabolic acidosis (primary base bicarbonate deficit).

The patient with prolonged fever requires increased water up to 3,000, 4,000 or more ml. daily. His intake of the bulk nutrients—protein, fat and carbohydrate—should be increased; so should his intake of the water soluble vitamins, including members of the B complex and C. Adequate electrolytes, too, should be provided, particularly sodium and potassium. The effort to increase the patient's nutritional intake should not, of course, overtax his ability to ingest and digest food. Small, frequent servings will help avoid overtaxing the gastrointestinal tract. If the patient is unable to ingest adequate nutrients by mouth, then feedings by nasogastric tube or by the parenteral route should be considered.

Sweet concentrated liquids can cause abdominal distention and loss of appetite. Carbonated beverages, on the other hand, are usually well tolerated, as are fruit juices, tea, coffee and water. The fat of fluid whole milk tends to slow down the emptying time of the stomach; skim milk is probably preferable for most patients.

Often a liquid diet is indicated for the acutely ill patient. Such a diet, providing 800 to 1,200 calories, will help meet the water needs and provide sufficient calories to prevent severe depletion. The patient should be returned to a full diet as soon as he is able to ingest it.

If possible, the daily intake of protein for the febrile patient should be 60 to 100 or more Gm. High protein drinks, such as powdered or liquid commercial protein concentrates, or eggnog, are frequently useful. Fats are an excellent source of calories and can be given in the form of egg yolk, milk, cream, ice cream, margarine and butter, provided they are tolerated. When fats are not tolerated, carbohydrates can be used to provide generous quantities of calories.

While the patient is convalescing from a febrile illness, a diet generous in all essentials should be administered in order to repair deficits.

Excessive Perspiration

Sensible perspiration, or sweat, is a hypotonic liquid containing sodium, potassium, chloride, and small amounts of ammonia and urea. Insensible perspiration consists of water only and is lost through evaporation from body surfaces, including the skin and the lungs.

High environmental temperatures can cause the loss of large quantities of body water and electrolytes. Workmen have been found to lose 8 to 10 L. of sweat a day. The bedfast patient must be given additional fluid if the environmental temperature is elevated.

Patients under heavy drapes in operating rooms that are not air conditioned can lose large volumes of fluid in the form of perspiration. Heatstroke and death have occurred in excessively hot operating rooms.

Perspiration losses can be recorded both on the intake-output sheet and on the nurse's notes. The saturation of pajamas and bed linen should be recorded. So should the

number of times it has been necessary to change them. Because it is difficult to estimate the amount of perspiration, some persons tend to ignore it altogether. Actually, it can be a major source of fluid loss and should never be ignored.

Insensible loss equals approximately 1,000 ml./sq.m. of body surface/day in the hospitalized patient. When respiration is hyperactive or fever is present, this loss may be greatly increased. Sweat losses (sensible perspiration) depend chiefly upon temperature, humidity, metabolic rate and fever. In disease, they may equal 1,000 or more ml./sq.m. of body surface/day. Sweat losses can be roughly measured by weight changes if one considers other gains and losses of fluids.

Liquids should be given freely to the heavily perspiring patient. They should contain both water and electrolytes. If sweat losses are replaced by water alone, sodium deficit (low sodium syndrome, hyponatremia, heat exhaustion) can easily occur. Among the sources of salt are the salt content of foods, salty broths, salt added at the table, and commercial salt tablets. Naturally, one should guard against producing a sodium excess by the administration of excessive quantities of sodium chloride. The patient on a low sodium diet often develops excellent sodium conservation. This applies only to patients not receiving diuretics, since diuretics counteract the body's sodium conserving action.

When the heavily perspiring patient is unable to take fluids by mouth, parenteral fluid orders should be requested from the physician.

Vomiting

One should know when to advise against oral intake, as well as when to encourage it. For example, the patient who is vomiting persistently should not drink water, since vomited water will carry with it gastric electrolytes.

Since persistent vomiting calls for parenteral administration of fluids, the nurse should report its presence to the physician. Untreated vomiting can lead to metabolic alkalosis and superimpose ketosis of starvation. Under such circumstances, alkalosis is more likely to occur than acidosis. One cannot depend upon them neutralizing each other.

When vomiting ceases or decreases in frequency, the patient can be given bland foods in small amounts. Toast, crackers, ginger ale and, in some instances, milk—especially skim milk—are tolerated well. Orange juice tends to increase peristalsis.

Recall that vomitus consists of water, hydrogen, chloride, sodium, potassium and other chemicals. As much as 6 L. of gastric secretion can be lost in a 24-hour period.

The reinstitution of a normal diet can repair mild deficits, particularly if the diet is supplemented with between-meal feedings of potassium-rich foods, such as meats, fruits, vegetables, milk and fruit juices. Excellent commercial potassium supplements are available and have the advantage that they can be given in doses containing known quantities of potassium. An example is the effervescent product K-Lyte.

Gastrointestinal Suction

The patient receiving gastrointestinal suction should never be given water or ice chips by mouth, since water washes electrolytes from the stomach, causing metabolic alkalosis. Statland cited a patient who was receiving suction and was permitted to ingest 21 L. of water. The water was drawn back from the suction tube, leaving the patient in profound alkalosis, which proved fatal. Ice chips made with appropriately constituted electrolyte solutions are permissible. A specific solution should be prescribed by the physician. A commercial oral electrolyte solution (Lytren) can be used to make chips for this purpose.

Sometimes the order is given to permit ice chips sparingly. The term "sparingly" can readily be stretched by well-meaning but ill-advised persons to the point where the intake of plain ice is excessive.

Diarrhea

Diarrhea results in the loss of water, electrolytes and partially digested nutrients. Prolonged diarrhea frequently results in potassium deficit, as well as in metabolic acido-sis. Prolonged watery diarrhea can result in sodium excess, since water is lost in excess of electrolytes. During the acute stage of diarrhea, the gastrointestinal tract is usually put at rest through parenteral alimentation. Food is given by mouth as soon as it can be tolerated. Some physicians institute oral feedings by the use of oral electrolyte solutions; others use skim milk. Some doctors employ tea and toast.

Liberal fluid intake should be encouraged with frequent, high caloric feedings. Such foods as puddings, custards and milk supply calories and protein and are well tolerated, provided the patient does not have a special sensitivity to them. The diet is gradually changed to normal.

MEDICAL THERAPY CAUSING NUTRITIONAL DISTURBANCES

Diuresis

The primary purpose of diuretics is to promote the excretion of sodium, chloride and water from the body. In varying degrees, diuretics—especially the thiazide diuretics and the mercurials—tend also to promote the excretion of potassium. (See Tables 23 and 24.) The amount of potassium excretion varies greatly from patient to patient. Particular attention should be devoted to the diet of the patient receiving a potent diuretic. The nurse should record the dietary intake. Although the usual diet provides potassium in amounts ranging from 75 to 125 mEq. per day, losses of potassium by patients receiving thiazide or mercurial diuretics can amount to several times this amount. Unfortunately, the body apparently has no mechanism for the conservation of potassium. For this reason, potassium deficit is prone to develop when the dietary intake is inadequate, when there are abnormal losses of potassium from the body, or when medical therapy causes important losses of potassium. Indeed, the patient dying of a potassium deficit may lose from 30 to 40 or more mEq. of potassium a day in the urine in spite of his dire need.

Determination of the daily urinary excretion of potassium through analysis of the potassium content of the 24-hour urine speci-

TABLE 23. THIAZIDE DIURETICS*

GENERIC NAME	TRADE NAME	AVERAGE DAILY DOSAGE
bendroflumethiazide	Naturetin	5–20 mg.
benzthiazide	NaClex	25–200 mg.
chlorothiazide	Diuril	500–1,000 mg.
cyclothiazide	Anhydron	2–8 mg.
flumethiazide	Ademol	25–200 mg.
hydrochlorothiazide	Esidrix	25–200 mg.
	HydroDiuril	
	Oretic	
methyclothiazide	Enduron	2.5–10 mg.
polythiazide	Renese	1–4 mg.
trichlormethiazide	Naqua	2–4 mg.

* All oral preparations
Grollman, A.: Diuretics. Am. J. Nursing, 65:84-89, (Jan.) 1965

men helps guide potassium replacement. A useful rule of thumb suggests that the patient receive a daily quota of potassium equal to his daily urinary excretion plus 10 per cent. Thus, if a patient was found to be excreting 160 mEq. of potassium in the urine each day, the total potassium intake for prevention of a deficit would be 176 mEq. daily. If the dietary intake of potassium was estimated at 75 mEq.—a frequent average intake—then one would administer about 100 mEq. of potassium as a supplement. The potassium contents of various foods are shown in Table 25. A pharmaceu-tical supplement such as K-Lyte provides 25 mEq. of potassium in each effervescent tablet.

An excellent source of the potassium content of foods, as well as of other dietary values, is Bowes, C., and Church, H.: *Food Values of Portions Commonly Used,* Philadelphia, J. B. Lippincott Co., 1966. This book is particularly helpful to the nurse, because food contents are expressed in terms of common servings rather than in portions of 100 Gm. If desired, the nurse can convert the value of potassium in mg. into mEq. simply by multiplying mg. of potassium

TABLE 24. MERCURIAL DIURETICS

GENERIC NAME	TRADE NAME	AVERAGE DAILY DOSE	METHOD OF ADMINISTRATION
chlormerodrin	Neohydrin	18.3 mg.	Oral
meralluride	Mercuhydrin Sodium	1 to 2 ml.	I.M., I.V., or subcutaneous
	Mercuhydrin with Ascorbic Acid	0.6 Gm.	Rectal suppository
mercaptomerin sodium	Thiomerin Sodium	0.5 to 2 ml.	Subcutaneous
mercumatilin	Cumertilin	1 to 2 ml.	I.M. or I.V.
		67 mg.	Oral
mercurophylline	Mercuzanthin	1 to 2 ml.	I.M.
		0.1 Gm.	Oral
merethoxylline procaine	Dicurin Procaine	0.5 ml.	I.M. or subcutaneous
mersalyl theophylline	Salyrgan-Theophylline	0.2 Gm.	Oral
		1 to 2 ml.	I.M. or I.V.

Grollman, A.: Diuretics. Am. J. Nursing, 65:84-89, (Jan.) 1965.

TABLE 25. POTASSIUM CONTENT OF VARIOUS
FOODS IN COMMON PORTIONS

FOOD, AMOUNT	MEQ./L. K
Beverages:	
Whole Milk, 240 ml.	9.11
Non-Fat or Skim Milk, 240 ml.	5.11
Instant Coffee, Folgers (2 Gm. in 240 ml. water)	6.14
Tomato Juice, ½ cup (canned)	7.29
Orange Juice, ½ cup (fresh)	5.68
Grapefruit Juice, ½ cup (canned)	4.41
Grape Juice, bottled, ½ cup	3.84
Apple Juice, ½ cup	3.20
Coca-Cola, 180 ml.	2.25
Pepsi-Cola, 240 ml.	0.18
Ginger-Ale, 240 ml.	0.03
Fruits:	
Banana, raw, 1 medium	16.12
Figs, dried, 7 small	19.96
Grapefruit, raw, ½ medium	10.24
Orange, 1 medium	9.21
Peaches, dried, uncooked, ½ cup	28.16
Raisins, dried seedless, 2 tbsp.	3.68
Cereals:	
Oatmeal, cooked, 1 cup	3.32
Corn Flakes, 1 cup	1.02
Meats and Meat Substitutes	
Canadian Bacon, cooked, 1 slice	2.32
Frankfurter, cooked, 1 average	2.72
Ham, cooked, 2 slices	13.31
Hamburger, cooked, 1 patty	9.77
Rib Steak, cooked, 1 serving (½ lb. raw)	9.93
Pink Salmon, ½ cup (canned)	7.42
Cheese, American Cheddar, 1 piece (2×2×1)	2.96
Egg, whole, 1 medium	1.23
Others:	
Brazil Nuts, shelled, ⅓ cup	17.15
Bre'r Rabbit Syrup, 1 tbsp.	6.91
Bar Candy, chocolate covered, average 10¢ size, 2½ oz.	14.84

Adapted from Bowes, C., and Church, H.: Food
Values of Portions Commonly Used. Philadelphia,
Lippincott, 1966.

times .0256. For example, 240 ml. of whole
milk provides 356 mg. of potassium or 9.11
mEq. of potassium (.0256 × 356).

The need for potassium supplementation
of the diet of patients receiving diuretics
becomes more pronounced when the diuretic
has been taken for a long period.

Frequently, the sodium intake of patients
receiving diuretics is restricted. This measure
reduces the need for large doses of potentially harmful diuretics. Usually, the sodium
restriction will not involve less than 1,000
mg. of sodium a day. The use of low sodium
diets containing lower levels of sodium in
patients receiving diuretics can cause acute
sodium deficit.

Low sodium diets and diuretics may be
used to treat a variety of conditions, such as
congestive heart failure, nephrosis, hepatic
cirrhosis and toxemia of pregnancy. Because
low sodium diets are commonly used, the
nurse should know what constitutes such
diets and be able to instruct patients in their
use.

An average daily diet not restricted in
sodium contains approximately 5,000 mg. of
sodium. Low sodium diets can range from a
mild restriction to as low as 200 mg. of sodium a day, depending on the patient's
needs. The American Heart Association has
prepared booklets describing mild, moderate
and strict sodium-restricted diets. The moderate sodium-restricted diet allows 1,000 mg.
of sodium daily; the strict diet allows only
500 mg. of sodium daily. The booklets are
available to patients on request of their
physicians.

Patients requiring only a mild sodium
restriction have a great deal of freedom in
planning their meals. They may salt most
foods lightly (about half as much as usual)
during preparation. Because most canned
and processed foods are already salted, no
additional salt should be added. Salt should
not be used at the table. (One level teaspoon
of salt contains about 2,300 mg. of sodium!)
Foods high in sodium content should be
avoided. Examples of such foods include:

- Sauerkraut and other vegetables prepared in brine
- Bacon
- Luncheon meats
- Frankfurters
- Ham
- Kosher meats
- Sausage
- Salt pork
- Sardines
- Processed cheese
- Bouillon cubes
- Peanut butter
- Catsup
- Mustard
- Olives
- Pickles

- Relish
- Horseradish
- Potato chips
- Pretzels

Low sodium diets must be planned to include all of the nutrients required by the body. The following is a sample of a 400 mg. sodium diet supplying approximately 1,800 calories. It lists foods to include in the daily diet, special instructions for the patient and sample menus. Lonalac is an important part of this diet; it supplies a high protein intake yet is low in sodium and almost free of cholesterol. It helps the patient receive adequate nutrition, particularly protein, while on a sodium-restricted diet. A daily vitamin supplement is included to provide generous amounts of vitamins. The substitution of unsalted ("sweet") butter will reduce the sodium content of this diet to 200 mg. daily.

Strict Low Sodium Diet (400 mg.) Include in each day's diet:

Liquid Lonalac	2½ cups (20 oz.)
Egg	1 medium
Meat	3 oz., raw weight
Bread, low sodium	4 slices
Cereal	1 serving
Potato	1 small
Vegetables (one green or yellow)	4 servings
Fruits (one citrus)	3 servings
Commercial butter	4 level teaspoons
Sugar, jam or jelly	3 level teaspoons
Dessert	1 serving
Deca-Vi-Sol chewable vitamin tablet	1 tablet

(If additional food is needed to make the total intake satisfying, extra Lonalac foods, cereals, breads, sugar, vegetables and fruits from the lists below may be chosen. Do not use more egg, meat or butter.)

Foods Which May Be Used:

Lonalac—Lonalac is similar to whole cow's milk, except that it is virtually sodium-free. It should be used in the diet just as one would use milk.

Meat: Fresh or frozen beef, lamb, veal, pork, rabbit, chicken, duck, turkey, quail, fish (other than shellfish) and fresh oysters. Do not eat clams, lobster, shrimp, or frozen fillets of fish.

Bread: Low sodium bread or rolls (available at some bakeries or may be baked at home); plain matzoth; thin tea matzoth.

Cereals: Barley, pearled; corn meal; cracked wheat; plain farina; macaroni; oatmeal (rolled oats); rice; spaghetti.

Vegetables: Any fresh or frozen vegetable that does not cause discomfort, with the exception of celery, beets, beet greens, dandelion, kale, mustard greens, spinach, sauerkraut and frozen peas.

Fruits: Any fresh (raw or cooked), frozen, canned or dried fruits and juices (unless label states that salt or sodium benzoate has been added).

Salads: When vegetables and fruits are used in salads, vinegar, lemon juice, salad oils or any of the seasonings below may be used. Use plain gelatin in preparing salads, not flavored gelatin mixtures.

Condiments and Flavorings: Allspice, caraway, cinnamon, curry powder, garlic, ginger, lemon extract, lemon juice, mace, mustard powder (not prepared mustard), nutmeg, paprika, black pepper, red pepper, white pepper, peppermint extract, poultry seasoning, sage, white sugar, thyme, tumeric, vanilla extract, vinegar, walnut extract.

Desserts: Fruit and gelatin desserts (use plain gelatin). In preparing desserts calling for milk and eggs, use only egg yolks (not egg whites) and replace milk with Lonalac.

Beverages: Liquid Lonalac (plain or flavored); fruit juices; chocolate made with liquid Lonalac; Coca Cola; cocoa, made with Hershey's cocoa and liquid Lonalac (avoid "Dutch process" cocoa); coffee; ginger ale; Postum; tea.

SPECIAL INSTRUCTIONS: *Use no salt at the table or in the cooking or preparation of food. Do not use:*

1. Commercially processed foods which contain added salt or sodium benzoate in the manufacture. (Read all labels carefully.)

2. Smoked, salt-cured and other processed meats, such as ham, bacon, salt pork, sausages, corned beef, salt fish, canned meats and fish; bouillon cubes and meat extracts; cheese; pickled and spiced products, such as olives, pickles, catsup, sauces, salad dressings and prepared mustard; canned vegetables, soups, meats and fish; salted butter, margarine or other salted fats (except the amount specified in this diet)—unsalted fats, such as lard and unsalted vegetable fats, may be used; ordinary bakery goods and crackers; many prepared cereals; and all other salted foods, such as pretzels, potato chips, salted popcorn and nuts, and most candies and candy bars.

3. "Soda" products, such as baking soda (so-

SAMPLE MENUS

MENU I		MENU II	
Breakfast:		*Breakfast:*	
Orange juice	½ cup	Grapefruit	½
Oatmeal	½ cup	Cooked rice	½ cup
(with ½ cup Lonalac)		(with ½ cup Lonalac and sugar and cinnamon	
Low sodium bread	1 slice	if desired)	
Butter		Low sodium bread, toast	1 slice
Peach	2 halves	Butter	
Lonalac beverage*	1 cup	Stewed prunes	3 medium
(4 level teaspoons butter and 3 teaspoons		Lonalac beverage*	1 cup
sugar, jam or jelly daily for use at table and		(4 level teaspoons butter and 3 teaspoons	
in preparing food)		sugar, jam or jelly daily for use at table and	
Lunch:		in preparing food)	
Scrambled egg	1	*Lunch:*	
Asparagus	½ cup	Creamed egg (using Lonalac)	1
Carrots	½ cup	Low sodium bread, toast	1 slice
Apple sauce	½ cup	Green beans	½ cup
Low sodium bread	1 slice	Cauliflower	⅔ cup
Lonalac beverage*	1 cup	Salad: pineapple	
Dinner:		on lettuce leaf	1 slice
Lean roast beef	3 oz., raw weight	Tapioca pudding	½ cup
Baked potato	1 small	Beverage	
Fresh peas	½ cup	*Dinner:*	
Salad: lettuce and cucumber	1 serving	Baked chicken	3 oz., raw weight
Low sodium bread	2 slices	Baked sweet potato	½ medium
Lonalac custard	½ cup	Brussels sprouts	6 average
Beverage		Salad: lettuce and tomato	1 serving
		Low sodium bread	2 slices
		Pear	2 halves
		Lonalac beverage*	1 cup

* Lonalac beverage—it is best to prepare liquid Lonalac beverage a day ahead and keep it in the refrigerator over night. Cocoa is an excellent drink to make with Lonalac, or sugar and vanilla may be added as desired to cold liquid Lonalac, or a few drops of lemon juice may be added to the cold liquid Lonalac.

dium bicarbonate) and self-rising flours, including pancake, biscuit, muffin and cake mixes.

4. Medicines without first consulting the physician. Certain medicines contain sodium, sometimes enough to interfere with the desired sodium intake. Some of the medicines that may contain sodium include:

- "Alkalizers" for indigestion (such as baking soda—one level teaspoon of baking soda contains about 1,000 mg. of sodium)
- Laxatives
- Pain relievers
- Sedatives
- Cough medicines
- Antibiotics

5. Water treated in water-softening equipment.

Tooth pastes, tooth powders, and mouth washes may be high in sodium content. Patients on sodium restricted diets should be instructed not to swallow these products and to rinse their mouths well with water after their use.

Prolonged Use of Laxatives and Enemas

The abuse of laxatives and enemas in our society is appalling. One reason for their widespread use is misunderstanding of the term constipation, which really refers to a hard, dry stool, difficult to evacuate. Even though the patient may not have a bowel movement for several days, *he is not constipated unless his stools are hard, dry and difficult to evacuate.* Some persons normally have bowel movements every day; others may have them every 3, 4, or 5 days. If the latter individuals have soft stools, they are not regarded as constipated.

It is the compulsion to have a daily evacuation that has led to the frequent use of laxatives and enemas! Many patients feel they must be "cleaned out" daily or their health will be impaired. These misconceptions should be corrected by the nurse at every opportunity; otherwise, patients, will continue to use laxatives and enemas unnecessarily. Reliance on laxatives and enemas decreases the natural reflex activity of the colon; hence, *stronger* laxatives and *more* enemas are required.

The repeated administration of plain water enemas causes electrolytes to be drawn into the bowel, since the body always tries to make any collection of fluid isotonic with extracellular fluid. When the enema is evacuated, it carries not only water, but electrolytes with it. Sodium deficit, potassium deficit, or both can be produced by repeated water enemas.

Should the patient actually be constipated, he should be provided a diet with these characteristics:

1. Generous quantities of fruits, vegetables, and bran cereals
2. Increased water intake
3. Regular meal hours

Stool softeners, such as Colace (dioctyl sodium sulfosuccinate) are useful physiologic tools for increasing the softness of the stools. A glass of warm water or hot coffee first thing in the morning can stimulate the evacuation reflex.

Roughage is useful. C. H. and J. A. Ross have suggested the following dried fruit recipe, which provides a supply for several breakfasts and does not necessarily require added sugar:

> ½ lb. dried apricots
> ½ lb. dried figs
> ½ lb. dried prunes
> ½ lb. dried raisins

Soak overnight in 2 pints of water. Bring to a boil in the morning. Reduce heat and simmer 45 minutes. Do not boil the fruit bodies out of shape. Cool and refrigerate. Serve 2 ounces for breakfast covered with a fruit juice different from day to day.

This is an ideal way to obtain roughage.

Adrenocorticosteroids

Administration of adrenocorticosteroids causes retention of sodium and excretion of potassium, particularly when prolonged, high doses are employed. For patients on such doses, the potassium intake should be increased and the sodium intake restricted. Prolonged doses of cortisone also encourage negative nitrogen balance. Dietary treatment includes a generous intake of protein, a potassium supplement, and an adequate caloric intake to prevent weight loss. The use of cortisone can also cause decreased tolerance to carbohydrate, with hyperglycemia and glycosuria.

The effect of adrenocorticosteroids on fat metabolism is not clearly understood. Prolonged administration tends to deposit fat in the subcutaneous tissues, producing the "moon face" and "buffalo hump" associated with steroid therapy. The hydrochloric acid and pepsin contents of the stomach are increased. This fact may be related to the occurrence of ulcers in patients on steroid therapy.

CATABOLIC EFFECTS CAUSING NUTRITIONAL DISTURBANCES

Immobilization

All patients subjected to long periods of bedrest develop metabolic disturbances. One of these is the increased excretion of calcium. As pointed out by Kottke and Blanchard,

The long bones of the lower extremities are designed to bear weight, and as long as weight is being borne by them, the calcium is maintained in the matrix of the bones. When the stresses of weight bearing have been removed, the calcium is very soon mobilized and enters the blood stream with the resulting increased concentration of circulating calcium in the blood. This increased calcium is filtered out through the kidneys, where it is deposited as calcium salts to form kidney and bladder stones.*

Pathologic fractures can occur due to bone rarefaction. Increased calcium excretion begins in the first week of immobilization and continues for a period of 4 to 8 weeks. After

* Kottke, F., and Blanchard, R.: Bedrest Begets Bedrest. Nursing Forum, 3:71, No. 3, 1964.

TABLE 26. ACID-BASE REACTION OF FOODS

POTENTIALLY ACID OR ACID ASH FOODS	POTENTIALLY BASIC OR ALKALINE ASH FOODS
Breads, all types	Fruits, all types (except cranberries, plums, and prunes)
Cakes and cookies, plain	
Cereals and crackers	Jams and jellies, honey
Cheese, all types	Milk, cream, and buttermilk
Eggs	Molasses
Fish and shellfish	Nuts: almonds, coconut, chestnuts
Fruits: cranberries, plums, and prunes	Vegetables, all types except corn and lentils
Macaroni, spaghetti, noodles	
Meats and poultry	
Nuts: Brazil, filberts, peanuts, walnuts	
Vegetables: corn and lentils	

NEUTRAL FOODS

Butter or margarine	Syrups
Candy, plain	Starches, corn and arrowroot
Cooking fats and oils	Sugars

Cooper, L., *et al.*: Nutrition in Health and Disease. ed. 14, p. 542. Philadelphia, Lippincott, 1963.

this period, the calcium drops back to normal or subnormal levels.

The nurse can help to prevent the development of stones in the urinary system by encouraging a fluid intake of 3,000 ml. or more, in order to increase urinary volume. The generous fluid intake keeps the urine dilute. Nursing preventive measures include turning the patient frequently, elevating the head of the bed, having the patient sit up, if possible, to prevent stasis of urine, plus frequent active and passive exercises.

Some feel that adjusting the pH of the urine can help prevent stone formation. An acid urine increases the solubility of calcium and magnesium phosphates and carbonates. The commonly occurring calcium phosphate stone, apatite, will not form when the urine pH is below 6.6. The use of cranberry juice, ale, beer and meat have been recommended to help acidify the urine. Urine acidifying drugs, such as ammonium chloride or Mandelamine, are commonly used in conjunction with dietary modifications. Table 26 shows how the diet can be modified to yield an acid or alkaline ash. Causes of urinary pH elevation in stone-forming patients include excessive intake of milk, alkali, or vitamin D (immense doses), and infection with urea-splitting organisms.

Some authorities feel that when calcium is being lost from the body, the intake should be increased over normal. Others believe

that only the amount of calcium required for maintenance of body stores should be permitted.

Ordering the diet modification lies within the province of the physician. The nurse should consult him before making any modifications other than water intake. When calcium is restricted, the patient is permitted only one pint of milk a day. Of course, other foods high in calcium, such as cheese and salmon, should be excluded from the diet. In addition to losing calcium, the immobilized patient loses nitrogen and may develop negative nitrogen balance unless his intake of protein and of calories is adequate.

Decubitus Ulcers

A draining decubitus ulcer can quadruple the body's need for protein. The ulcer exudate is high in protein content. The fact that most patients with decubiti are immobilized further contributes to the increased protein need.

It is often difficult for the patient to consume sufficient protein, since his appetite is usually poor. The nurse must use all her ingenuity to find foods rich in protein but acceptable to the patient. Usual food sources of protein can be supplemented by commercial high protein supplements or by skim milk powder. Both can be added to food without changing the bulk or flavor appreciably. Two tablespoons of dry skim milk powder supplies 6 Gm. of protein. It can be added to cereal, scrambled eggs, pudding, soup, hamburger and other foods.

The increased protein need must be considered as important as turning the patient often and keeping the skin clean and dry.

Hemorrhage

The well-nourished person can usually regenerate red blood cells following one episode of hemorrhage. Chronic blood loss, however, depletes the red cell stores and results in anemia. The body compensates for the decrease in circulating blood volume that accompanies hemorrhage by drawing fluid from the tissue spaces into the vascular compartment—an interstitial fluid-to-plasma shift of water and electrolytes. The total extracellular fluid volume is unchanged; only the distribution of the fluid is affected.

The patient who has suffered chronic hemorrhage should be provided a diet rich in protein, iron and vitamin C. Up to 100 Gm. of protein a day should be given. Excellent sources of protein are meat, eggs, cheese and fish. Protein supplements can also be employed, between meals or at bedtime or both. Iron can be supplied as meat, liver, prunes, apples, grapes, spinach, beans, enriched cereals and eggs. In addition, it is well to give an additional source of iron, preferably ferrous sulfate by mouth. Vitamin C intake can be increased by generous servings of citrus fruits. The fluid intake should be generous.

Trauma

Trauma, such as burns, fractures, wounds and crushing injuries, causes loss of protein through direct destruction of tissues. It contributes further to the loss through the so-called toxic destruction of protein, an increased catabolism brought on mysteriously by the trauma. It also promotes the accumulation of protein-rich fluid at the site of the injury, which contributes further to possible protein depletion. Immobilization made necessary by the injury also causes losses of protein and, in addition, of electrolytes.

Because of these losses and because of the requirements for optimal healing, the protein, electrolyte and vitamin C intake of the injured patient should be increased; as much as 150 Gm. of protein daily is frequently administered. The diet should be high in calories to prevent ingested protein from being consumed for energy purposes.

Chapter 11

Help from the Lab

For some years there hung on the wall of the office of a friend, Dr. Alex Steigman (then Professor of Pediatrics at the University of Louisville School of Medicine), an editorial which told of a pilot who was bringing his airplane to a landing in a fog. Unknown to the pilot, the airplane's instruments, by which he was attempting to land the plane, were out of kilter. The instrument readings, therefore, conflicted with what his senses told him. He was faced with an awesome choice: believe the instruments, or believe his own God-given faculties. He chose to place his faith in the instruments; the plane plunged into the water, and all were killed. The moral that the editor drew from the tragedy was this: modern mechanistic aids are wonderful, and they frequently give us invaluable help; but now and then we must choose between believing the robot and believing what our own ears and eyes and judgment tell us.

Certainly this lesson applies to the use of laboratory findings in body fluid disturbances. We must always direct our attention to the recovery of the patient, rather than to the manipulation of his biochemical findings. The famous pediatrician, Dr. Edward Park, used to tell of the nurse whose grief over the death of an infant with diarrhea was considerably eased by the fact that, before the baby died, he had had a "beautiful stool." The "beautiful stool" was no more satisfaction to the baby than the correction of an abnormal biochemical finding would be to the patient who does not live to enjoy it. We must view the clinical picture as being of primary importance; we must regard the laboratory findings as confirmatory rather than diagnostic; we must always treat *pa-*

tients rather than *biochemical findings*. In short, we must place the clinical Dobbin before the biochemical cart, which is, of course, where he belongs. Dr. Robert E. Cook stated the matter well when he said: "Regardless of the multiplicity of laboratory determinations, proper interpretation and therapy depend nonetheless upon frequent and accurate clinical evaluation."

Limitations of the Laboratory

Now, what are some of the limitations of laboratory help? First of all, many of the usual test procedures have difficulties inherent in them that make consistently accurate results difficult to attain, even though the tests are performed by highly-skilled technicians. Moreover, physicians do not always know the "normal" laboratory values for ill persons, since our tables of values are based on those found in healthy persons. It may sometimes be undesirable—even dangerous—to attempt to restore the "abnormal" value of a patient to "normal," since what we regard as an abnormal value may be the result of a defensive action on the part of the body. For example, in primary carbonic acid deficit (respiratory alkalosis), caused by the blowing off of carbonic acid through the lungs in the form of carbon dioxide, the body lowers the level of base bicarbonate in order to maintain the carbonic acid:base bicarbonate balance. The plasma level of base bicarbonate is, therefore, lower than normal; but the normal referred to is the normal for health, not for this particular imbalance. The normal level of base bicarbonate for carbonic acid deficit is much lower than the level for health. To bring this properly low base bicarbonate level up to the normal level for health by the injection of base bicarbonate into the blood would be unfortunate. It would make the disturbance worse and might well kill the patient.

We can cite many other examples showing why we must take the laboratory reading with the proverbial grain of salt. For example, the level of potassium in the plasma is only one indication of the cellular stores of potassium, which are far more important than that shown by the plasma level. The plasma level may be elevated in the face of a cellular deficit, or it may be depressed in the face of a cellular excess; it may be normal in either case, for the cellular stores of potassium are only one of the factors that determine the plasma level of potassium. All that the plasma level shows is potassium in transport.

The urine is ordinarily acid in acidosis, but it may be alkaline even though acidosis is present. This fact is demonstrated in several clinical conditions, such as chronic renal disease, in which the infecting organism converts urea in newly-formed urine to ammonia. And, although the urine is usually alkaline in alkalosis, we may find an acid urine when alkalosis is accompanied by a severe potassium deficit. Nevertheless, the physician can almost always do a better job of diagnosing and treating the patient with disturbances of the body fluids when he has laboratory aids available. The problem is how to use the aids intelligently. What are these laboratory aids?

Laboratory Aids Available

In addition to the chemical methods for determining the plasma levels of calcium, chloride, phosphorus, proteinate, albumin, bicarbonate, non-protein nitrogen and urea, the *flame photometer* has been immensely useful in determining the level of sodium and potassium in the body fluids. The flame photometer reading depends upon the color of the flame given out when the electrolyte in question is burned.

The *electrocardiograph* is useful in diagnosing potassium deficit, potassium excess, calcium deficit and calcium excess, although,

like other laboratory tests, it is confirmatory rather than primarily diagnostic. The *x-ray*, too, is a useful diagnostic aid, helping to diagnose certain imbalances in the calcium level. An important development in laboratory techniques is the number of tests that can be performed on a tiny quantity—for example, a few drops of blood. These *microchemical determinations* are particularly useful in the case of the small baby, who does not have much blood to spare for laboratory tests. The use of *radioisotopes* is becoming more and more important in medicine. These fruits of the atomic age may soon be of value to the practicing physician as he diagnoses abnormalities of the body fluid. In addition to laboratory tests that require complex equipment, there are many tests that physicians can do in their offices, including tests to determine the acidity or specific gravity of the urine, the hemoglobin level of the blood, the red blood cell count, and the packed cell volume.

There are other measurements which are not strictly laboratory tests but which are extremely valuable, including the determination of body weight and measurements of fluid intake and fluid output. Indeed, a careful measurement both of the kind and quantity of fluids going into and passing from the patient is of utmost importance for the proper treatment of disturbances of the body fluids. Since the nursing staff has the responsibility for the 24-hour supervision of the patient, the important duty of measuring the intake and output falls to them. Knowledge of the basis for body fluid disturbances and for their treatment makes it apparent to nurses that accurate intake-output records are often, quite literally, worth their weight in gold to the patient. There is usually no substitute for them. They are often the chief basis for accurate diagnosis and effective treatment. Knowledge of the intake-output figures greatly simplifies the problem of the physician who is treating a patient with an imbalance of the body fluids.

Evaluation of Laboratory Test Results

Variations in laboratory values for individuals of different ages are important considerations when evaluating the results of

Table 27. Laboratory Values

I. Normal Ranges

*A. Blood Formed Elements**

	Birth	3 mo.	1 yr.	5 yr.	12 yr.	Women	Men
RBC—million/cu. mm.	4.1-5.7	3.1-4.7	3.9-4.7	4.0-4.8	4.3-5.1	4.2-5.0	4.8-6.0
Hemoglobin—Gm./100 ml.	14-20	9-13	11-12.5	12-14.7	13.4-15.8	13-16	15-18
Hematocrit—% Vol. of packed RBC/100 ml.	43-63	28-40	32-40	36-44	39-47	39-47	44-52

B. Plasma Chemical Constituents

Plasma Na^+	137-147 mEq./L.
Plasma K^+	4.0-5.6 mEq./L.
Plasma Ca^{++}	4.5-5.8 mEq./L.
Plasma Cl^-	98-106 mEq./L.
Plasma Protein	6-8 Gm./100 ml.
Plasma HCO_3^-	Adults: 25-29 mEq./L.
	Children: 20-25 mEq./L.
Plasma Cl^- plus Plasma HCO_3^-	123-135 mEq./L.
Plasma pH	7.35-7.45
Plasma HPO_4^-	1.7-2.6 mEq./L.

C. Urine Values

Urine pH	4.5-8.2
Urine specific gravity	1.010-1.030

* Covers 94% of normal population.

II. Average Values in Health

A. Blood Formed Elements

	Birth	3 mo.	1 yr.	5 yr.	12 yr.	Women	Men
RBC—million/cu. mm.	4.9	3.9	4.3	4.4	4.7	4.6	5.4
Hemoglobin—Gm./100 ml.	17.1	11.1	11.7	13.3	14.5	14.5	16.5
Hematocrit—% Vol. of packed RBC/100 ml.	53	43	36	40	43	43	48

B. Plasma Chemical Constituents

Plasma Na^+	142 mEq./L.
Plasma K^+	5 mEq./L.
Plasma Ca^{++}	5 mEq./L.
Plasma Cl^-	103 mEq./L.
Plasma Protein	7.0 Gm./100 ml. (16 mEq./L.)
Plasma HCO_3^-	Adults: 27 mEq./L.
	Children: 23 mEq./L.
Plasma pH	7.4
Plasma HPO_4^-	2 mEq./L.

C. Urine Values

Urine pH	6.0
Urine specific gravity	1.015

laboratory tests. The normal values for the red cell count, hemoglobin, packed cell volume and plasma bicarbonate differ in infants, children and adults. Moreover, not only *average values*, but *normal ranges* should be considered. Both are presented in the preceding Table. Plasma levels are best reported as milliequivalents per liter (mEq./L.). When they are reported as milligrams (mg.), they can be quickly converted by reference to the conversion table.

A reasonable minimal daily program for

laboratory surveillance of the patient with imbalances of the body fluids should include, if facilities are available, plasma sodium, plasma potassium, plasma bicarbonate, and plasma chloride. Initially, the hemoglobin, urinary pH and urinary specific gravity are useful. The plasma pH is always helpful if facilities are available for its determination. When tests are abnormal, they should be repeated daily until they return to normal. Although body weight and fluid intake-output measurements are not strictly laboratory procedures, they do provide important objective information, which helps to guard against the gross over-provision of water and electrolytes. If possible, these measurements should be performed daily until fluid balance is achieved.

The ancient Hebrews must have been interested in something akin to modern laboratory diagnosis, since they had a proverb that states: "The causes of all diseases are to be found in the blood." Today, the examination of the blood, particularly of its constituent the plasma, and of other body fluids is invaluable in the management of the patient with body fluid disturbances. But while medicine is a science, it is not an exact science—it has a great deal of art woven into its scientific fabric. Help from the laboratory is not to be decried, but frequently it is upon the skill, ability and judgment of the patient's professional attendants—physician and nurse alike—that the patient's destiny must largely rest. Although "blood will tell," it frequently will not tell all.

Normal ranges of laboratory values are presented in Table 27(I); average values in health, in Table 27 (II).

Chapter 12

Gauges for Dosage

Among the most beautiful passages in the medical literature are these from the clinical reports of early physicians who used parenteral fluid therapy. Latta, of Leith, England, thus described the effect of an intravenous solution administered to a patient suffering from cholera in 1832:

. . . Like the effects of magic, instead of the pallid aspect of one whom death had sealed as his own, the vital tide was restored and life and vivacity returned . . .

Cantini, who practiced in Naples, Italy, and died in 1893, wrote as follows:

The cold, cyanotic, dehydrated, comatose patients, lying pulseless and almost lifeless, became animated after the subcutaneous infusion of warm salt water. Remarkably their pulse and voice often returned in a few minutes and they are even able to sit alone in bed . . .

Neither Dr. Latta nor Dr. Cantini felt much need for precise knowledge of parenteral fluid dosage, nor was a great need experienced for many decades to come. So long as the parenteral injection of water and electrolytes remained an emergency measure, to be performed only as a last resort, the clinical response of the patient—if respond he did—was regarded as gauge enough for proper dosage. Now, with the striking advances in the knowledge of clinical fluid disturbances that we have seen during the past three decades, there has been a great extension in the use of parenteral fluids. The medical profession has, therefore, felt a mounting need for simple, widely applicable dosage gauges suitable for assisting the physician in determining the volume and the rate of administration of parenteral fluids.

The gauges for dosage most frequently used have been body weight related to age, and body surface area. Caloric requirement has been employed to a lesser extent. Some authorities feel that body weight related to age possesses an important shortcoming: requirements for water and electrolytes determined on the basis of body weight are different for patients of different ages. However, body surface area possesses no such shortcoming. Expressed in terms of square meters of body surface per day, requirements for water and electrolytes are approximately the same for patients of all age groups, as shown in the tables for approximate water requirement and for approximate sodium requirement.

Body surface area is proportional to many essential physiologic processes, including heat loss, blood volume, glomerular filtration rate, organ size, respiration, blood pressure and nitrogen requirement. Alan Butler and his co-workers at the Massachusetts General Hospital were the first to emphasize that the basic water and electrolyte requirements are also proportional to body surface area, regardless of the age or size of the patient. They pointed out that, since body surface area provides a quantitative index of our total metabolic activity, it also provides us with a remarkably useful gauge for determining doses of water and electrolytes in fluid therapy. At the same time, it provides us with an easy technique for determining the proper rate of administration of parenteral fluids. In addition to these two uses, body surface area can provide nurses with a simple, rapid method of checking the correctness of parenteral fluid orders, especially in regard to volume and rate of administration. It can also be used to determine if orders for

APPROXIMATE WATER REQUIREMENT

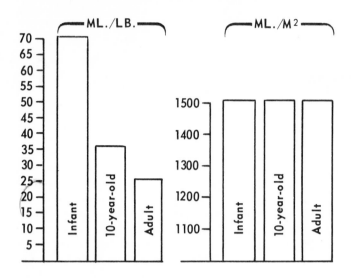

Fig. 57. We can use the same values for water and sodium requirements for persons of all ages if we use body surface area, rather than weight, as the dosage criterion.

APPROXIMATE SODIUM REQUIREMENT

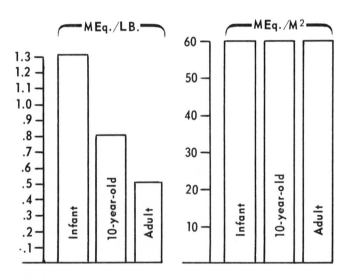

sodium and potassium in parenteral solutions are within the realm of safety. These matters will be discussed, with appropriate examples, in the next Chapter.

There are various methods of measuring body surface area, including the covering method, geometric method, skinning method, and other investigational methods. Clinicians employ simple nomograms that enable one to rapidly estimate body surface area from height and body weight. Actually, one can quickly obtain the approximate surface area from weight alone, as shown in the following tabulation:

CHART FOR CONVERTING WEIGHT TO
SURFACE AREA

(Figures are approximate and apply only to individuals of average build.)

Pounds	Surface Area in Square Meters
4	.15
6	.20
10	.27
15	.36
20	.45
30	.60
40	.72
50	.87
60	.97
70	1.10
80	1.21
90	1.33
100	1.4
125	1.6
150	1.75
175	2.0
200	2.2
250	2.7

The chart is extremely simple to use. An infant weighing 10 lbs. would have an approximate surface area of .27 sq. m.; a child weighing 50 lbs. would have an approximate surface area of .87 sq. m.; an adult weighing 150 lbs. would have an approximate surface area of 1.75 sq. m.

The body surface areas arrived at by use of the weight chart are approximate only, and apply to individuals of average body build. In general, obese or stocky individuals have less surface area than tall lanky persons. (Just as a long, low one-story ranch house has more external surface than a two- or three-story house of equal floor space.) For example, our 10-lb. infant would have a surface area of .2 sq. m. if he were only 16 inches tall; but he would have .3 sq. m. of surface area if he were 28 inches in height. Our 50-lb. child would have .68 sq. m. of surface area if he were 2 feet, 10 inches tall; .84 sq. m. if his height were 3 feet, 10 inches. Our 150-lb. adult would have 1.47 sq. m. of surface area if he were only 4 feet, 4 inches tall; 1.86 sq. m. if he had a height of 6 feet.

Chapter 13

The Treatment of Body Fluid Disturbances

THE GOALS OF FLUID THERAPY

In managing the illness of a patient with an actual or potential disturbance of the body fluids, the physician keeps three goals in mind in his day-to-day planning of treatment:

1. Any pre-existing deficits of water and electrolytes must be repaired. *In terms of a person's day-to-day problems of living, this is similar to paying one's debts.*

2. Water and electrolytes must be provided to meet the patient's maintenance requirements. *This corresponds to meeting one's living expenses.*

3. Continuing abnormal losses of water and electrolytes through such routes as vomiting, diarrhea, tubal drainage, wound drainage, burn drainage, diuresis, and the like, must be replaced. *This is similar to meeting unplanned expenditures, such as loss of money through gambling or theft.*

There are various, widely different methods for achieving these goals. Rather than describe several methods, we will present one simple method that has worked out well in practice, that will help give the nurse a basic understanding of the principles involved in fluid therapy. From the standpoint of clinical results, this method is no better than other methods of fluid therapy. Certainly it has its drawbacks and limitations—we have chosen it for pedagogical reasons. The method that we shall briefly describe is that developed by Butler and his co-workers at the Massachusetts General Hospital. It has, since that time, been used with great success in many parts of the world.

PRELIMINARY TESTING

Before the physician can proceed with the correction of pre-existing deficits, meeting maintenance needs and counteracting continuing abnormal losses, he must consider the status of the kidneys. Various types of solutions, particularly those containing potassium, can be hazardous if renal function is not adequate. Many patients with a body fluid imbalance have oliguria or even anuria. Before administering fluid therapy, it is necessary to determine if the suppression of urination is due simply to an extracellular fluid volume deficit, or whether it is due to serious renal impairment. If the urinary suppression is caused simply by volume deficit, the therapeutic test will reveal that fact by re-establishing urinary flow. This result of the test makes it safe to proceed with the fluid therapy program, including the administration of potassium-containing solutions. The therapeutic test for functional renal depression is carried out if any of the following criteria exist:

1. If the specific gravity of the urine is above 1.030

2. If there have been less than 3 voidings in 24 hours

3. If there is no urine in the bladder

4. If there has been a massive acute loss of extracellular fluid, such as is seen in fulminating infantile diarrhea

In any of these instances, a special solution,

frequently called an initial hydrating solution or a pump-priming solution, is administered. Such a solution often provides sodium, 51 mEq./L.; chloride, 51 mEq./L., and glucose, 5 Gm./L. It actually represents a solution containing one part of isotonic solution of sodium chloride in 5 per cent glucose, and two parts of 5 per cent glucose in water. The solution is administered at the rate of 8 ml./sq. m. of body surface/minute for 45 minutes. When the kidneys begin to function, as shown by the restoration of the flow of urine, then the initial hydrating solution is discontinued and therapy is started with other types of solutions, as described below. If the urinary flow is not restored, then the physician reduces the rate of infusion to 2 ml./sq. m. of body surface/minute, continuing it for another hour. If urination has not occurred at the end of this period, the physician assumes he is dealing with renal impairment rather than functional depression. Such impairment demands a battery of laboratory tests plus careful management of the renal problem.

ADMINISTERING FLUID THERAPY

If the patient's kidneys have been shown to be functional, then the physician proceeds to repair pre-existing deficits and to provide water and electrolytes for maintenance. To accomplish these goals, the physician can use a single solution of the type devised by Butler. Such a solution is so designed that *when used to meet the patient's fluid volume requirement, it supplies electrolytes in quantities balanced between the minimal needs and the maximal tolerances of the patient.* The Butler-type solution is actually one-third to one-half as concentrated as plasma. It thus provides free water for urinary formation and metabolic activities. It provides both cellular and extracellular electrolytes. It incorporates 5 or 10 per cent of carbohydrate to minimize tissue destruction, reduce ketosis and spare protein. The Butler-type solution utilizes the body homeostatic mechanisms, which select the electrolytes that are required and reject those that are not needed. The Butler-type solution, when used properly, has a great margin of safety.

The patient's needs for maintenance can be met by the administration of 1,500 ml. of a Butler-type solution/sq. m. of body surface/day. If the patient should have a moderate pre-existing deficit, then one can both correct this deficit and meet the maintenance requirement by giving 2,400 ml./sq. m. of body surface/day. If the patient has a severe pre-existing deficit, then one can correct the deficit and provide maintenance by giving 3,000 ml. of a Butler-type solution/sq. m. of body surface/day.

A moderate fluid volume deficit is indicated by weight loss up to 5 per cent in a child or adult, up to 10 per cent in an infant, and by symptoms moderate in degree. A severe fluid volume deficit is indicated by an acute weight loss of over 5 per cent in a child or adult, and over 10 per cent in an infant, with symptoms and laboratory findings severe in degree. The Butler-type solution is given intravenously, by mouth, or by nasogastric tube, but *not subcutaneously.* The dose should be calculated carefully, regardless of what route is used. Various modifications of the Butler-type solution are made available by manufacturers of parenteral solutions. The usual Butler solution for older children and adults contains 75 mEq. of total cation (and hence of total anion). The solution usually used for infants and small children contains 48 mEq. of total cation (and hence of total anion). Manufacturers gladly provide information concerning available solutions and their proper use. In giving the solution intravenously, the usual rate of administration is 3 ml./sq. m. of body surface/minute.

For correcting abnormal losses from vomiting, drainage from an intestinal tube or fistula, or severe diarrhea, the physician employs replacement solutions with a composition resembling the body fluid lost. Thus, to replace gastric juice, the physician administers a gastric replacement solution intravenously. To replace intestinal or duodenal juices, he uses an intestinal replacement solution intravenously. To replace diarrheal fluid or excessive perspiration loss, he uses the Butler-type solution, since this is fairly close in composition to the secretions lost. The rate of administration for replacement solutions is usually 3 ml./sq. m. of body surface/minute.

This simple plan of therapy can be used for treating body fluid disturbances that result from imbalances between intake and output, which include the following disturbances:

- Extracellular fluid volume deficit
- Sodium excess of extracellular fluid
- Potassium deficit of extracellular fluid
- Base bicarbonate deficit of extracellular fluid
- Base bicarbonate excess of extracellular fluid
- Carbonic acid deficit of extracellular fluid
- Carbonic acid excess of extracellular fluid

Calculating Dosage

The body surface area gauge for dosage is especially useful for checking the correctness of water and electrolytes ordered for patients with body fluid disturbances. Remember the following rules:

1. For maintenance, administer 1,500 ml./sq. m. of body surface/day.

2. For correction of a moderate deficit in extracellular fluid volume, administer 2,400 ml./sq. m. of body surface/day.

3. For correction of a severe deficit in extracellular fluid volume, administer 3,000 ml./sq. m. of body surface/day.

4. Rate of administration should be 3 ml./sq. m. of body surface/minute, except when giving initial hydrating solution.

By applying these rules, the nurse can quickly check the correctness of an order for fluid therapy. Let us suppose that the physician has written an order for a liter of solution to be given over a 24-hour period to an infant weighing 20 lbs. The baby has a moderate fluid volume deficit. A quick check of the conversion chart shows that a 20-lb. baby would have .45 sq. m. of body surface; the volume of fluid for correction of a moderate fluid volume deficit in such

a baby should be .45 times 2,400 ml., or 1,080 ml., approximately the correct dose.

Let us suppose, on the other hand, that a large man with a severe fluid volume deficit is to receive 3 L. of solution for the first 24 hours. Reference to the conversion chart shows that a 175-lb. man would have a body surface area of 2.0 sq. m.; 2.0 times 3,000 ml., the requirement per sq. m. of body surface per day for a severe fluid volume deficit, gives a figure of 6 L., or 6,000 ml.; 3 L., therefore, is grossly inadequate.

Suppose that a 12-year-old boy with no fluid imbalance is to be given water and electrolytes for maintenance for a few days following abdominal surgery. The physician orders 3 L. of his favorite maintenance solution. The boy's body surface area is 1.33 sq. m. Maintenance should call for 1,500 ml. times 1.33, or 1,995 ml., approximately 2 L. of fluid. The extra liter ordered might embarrass the boy's homeostatic mechanisms, and the physician should appreciate having the order questioned. Of course, in the presence of fever or heavy sweating, the extra fluid might well be entirely proper.

Using the above information, the rate of administration for the infant with .45 sq. m. of body surface would be $.45 \times 3 \times 60 = 81$ ml./hr.; for the 2.0 sq. m. man, $2 \times 3 \times 60 = 360$ ml./hr.; for the 1.33 sq. m. boy, $1.33 \times 3 \times 60 = 240$ ml./hr.

The quantity of sodium or potassium being administered parenterally can quickly be checked by recalling that the average daily maintenance requirement for sodium is 50 to 70 mEq./sq. m. of body surface/day. The same figures hold for potassium. The minimal needs for each of these cations is 10 mEq./sq. m. of body surface/day, and the maximal tolerances, 250 mEq./sq. m. of body surface/day.

Specific Types of Therapy

There are several important imbalances that require therapy specifically tailored to the imbalance. These are as follows:

Sodium Deficit of Extracellular Fluid. In sodium deficit, the physician provides sodium chloride in such concentration as to restore the sodium level of the extracellular fluid to normal without causing a fluid volume excess. If the extracellular fluid volume is normal or excessive, the physician corrects the imbalance by administering a 3 or 5 per cent solution of sodium chloride. If there is a deficit in the volume of the extracellular fluid, then the physician will administer an isotonic solution of sodium chloride.

Calcium Deficit of Extracellular Fluid. In acute calcium deficit, calcium should be administered intravenously, employing a 10 per cent solution of calcium gluconate; this is particularly important if tetany or convulsions have occurred.

Calcium Excess of Extracellular Fluid. Treatment of calcium excess should be directed at the underlying condition. If other imbalances are present, only solutions free of calcium should be employed.

Extracellular Fluid Volume Excess. The object of therapy here is to reduce the extracellular fluid volume to normal without altering the electrolyte concentration of the fluid. It may be necessary to withhold all liquids for a period.

Potassium Excess of Extracellular Fluid. The treatment of an uncomplicated potassium excess with functional kidneys consists of avoiding additional potassium either orally or parenterally. If the kidneys are impaired, however, several methods may be employed, all aimed at removing excessive potassium from the extracellular fluid. These methods include carefully measured replacement therapy, supplying fats and carbohydrates but no protein materials; administration of insulin and dextrose; administration of carbonic anhydrase inhibitors; the use of ion exchange resins, use of peritoneal dialysis; or employment of the artificial kidney.

Plasma-to-Interstitial Fluid Shift. Such a shift can be restricted by relieving the condition causing it, and by the application of a binder for localized shifts. Plasma volume can be maintained or restored by the parenteral administration of plasma, dextran, or a plasma-like electrolyte solution.

Interstitial Fluid-to-Plasma Shift. When remobilization of edema fluid causes this shift, the physician may employ phlebotomy, or he may apply tourniquets. If the shift results from internal or external loss of whole blood, blood transfusions should be given.

Whole Blood Deficit. A whole blood deficit should be repaired by giving whole blood. If the extracellular fluid volume is excessive, red cells should be given alone.

Protein Deficit. Protein deficit should be corrected by the administration of high-protein foods or high-protein supplements, or by the intravenous administration of amino acids with provision of generous quantities of calories in the form of dextrose or alcohol or both. All three expedients may be required.

Complex Combined Imbalances. The severe burn is an excellent example of a complex combination of body fluid imbalances. Therapy of this condition requires knowledge of the hazardous aftermaths of the burn, which include losses of body fluid, shock, renal depression and remobilization of edema fluid. Carefully controlled therapy must be directed at the correction of the imbalances secondary to these aftermaths.

Many Types of Solutions

Solutions vary greatly from hospital to hospital. The nurse is urged to become familiar with the solutions employed in the hospital in which she works. This familiarity can be gained by talking with knowledgeable physicians and by carefully reading the excellent literature provided by the pharmaceutical company that supplies the parenteral solutions for the hospital.

Chapter 14

Parenteral Fluid Administration— Nursing Implications

INTRODUCTION

The nurse plays a major role in the administration of parenteral fluids. Her exact responsibilities are not uniformly defined and vary with geographical areas and individual hospitals. For example, the nurse in a large medical center does not usually start intravenous fluids; the nurse in a small hospital starts them routinely because resident physicians are not available. However, regardless of who starts the fluids, the nurse shares in the responsibility of assuring their safe and therapeutic administration. To ably assume this responsibility, she must understand basic principles of safe fluid administration. She must also become familiar with parenteral fluids. If intelligent observations are to be made during their infusion, the purposes, contraindications and complications associated with their use must be known.

ROUTES AND TECHNIQUES OF PARENTERAL FLUID ADMINISTRATION

Intravenous

Indications for Use

Veins provide an excellent route for the quick administration of water, electrolytes and other nutrients. Fluids administered intravenously at the proper rate and in the proper dose pass directly into the extracellular fluid. They are rapidly acted upon by the body homeostatic mechanisms and hence do not, in proper doses, produce abnormal changes in volume or electrolyte concentration of extracellular fluid. The intravenous route is essential when nutrients are needed in a hurry, such as glucose in severe hypoglycemia, 5 per cent sodium chloride in severe sodium deficit, or calcium gluconate in acute calcium deficit. Relatively large volumes of fluids can be given by the intravenous route, provided due care is exercised.

General Psychological Considerations

Few persons are without some fear or dread of a needle being introduced into their vein, and normal fears are exaggerated in illness. Many patients associate intravenous fluids with critical illnesses and are disturbed when such therapy is employed. It is the nurse's responsibility to explain away as much of the fear as possible. She can point out that I.V. fluids are commonly used until oral intake is again possible.

Because all patients are individuals, the nurse must plan her approach on an individual basis. Some patients feel less singled out if they are allowed to observe others on the ward receiving I.V. fluids. A detailed explanation of why and how the fluids are given is indicated for some; others want only a brief account. The patient should *never* be approached with no explanation at all; the fear of not knowing what is to happen can be worse than the most painful venipuncture. Some patients will not ask questions for fear of learning something too unpleasant to accept; yet, their imaginations may run wild during the infusion. Some patients have heard of fatalities during an intravenous infusion; for example, due to an air embolus. The nurse must always re-

member that although I.V. therapy is commonplace to her, it is far from routine to the patient.

Only persons capable of skillful venipuncture should start fluids on anxious patients;

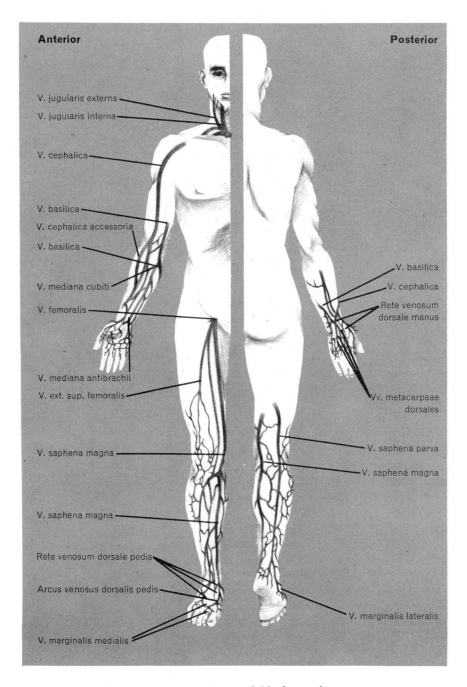

FIG. 58. Superficial veins available for venipuncture.

just one traumatic experience may make I.V. therapy totally unacceptable to them. The nurse starting fluids must always appear confident—patients sense insecurity and are understandably upset by it.

Not only must the nurse dispel the patient's fears, she must also dispel the fears of the family. It is not uncommon for a relaxed patient to become upset after observing the obvious anxiety of his relatives. The need for intravenous therapy should be explained to the family and any misconceptions cleared up.

Selection of Site

Suitable Superficial Veins. A number of superficial veins are available for venipuncture. (See Fig. 58.) Those most commonly used include:

- Veins in and around the cubital fossa (antecubital, basilic, and cephalic veins)
- Veins in the forearm (basilic and cephalic veins)
- Veins in the radial area of the wrist
- Veins in the hand (metacarpal and dorsal venous plexus)
- Femoral and saphenous veins in the thigh
- Veins in the foot (dorsal venous plexus, medial and lateral marginal veins)
- Scalp veins in infants and the aged

Criteria for Selection. Selection of a vein depends upon a number of factors:

- Availability of sites (depends upon condition of veins)
- Size of needle to be used
- Type of fluids to be infused
- Volume, rate and length of infusion
- Degree of mobility desired
- Skill of operator

The most common sites for venipuncture are the veins in and around the cubital fossa. These veins are large and easily accessible. They can accommodate large needles, large volumes of fluids, and all but the most irritating intravenous solutions. A great deal of skill is not necessary to perform a venipuncture in these veins because, in addition to being large, they are kept from rolling and sliding by surrounding tissues. In most patients these veins are readily palpated. (See Fig. 59.)

Arteries in the antecubital area, though usually more deeply located, lie in close proximity to veins. It is easy to mistake an artery for a vein in this area. Aberrant arteries are not uncommon in the cubital fossa. (These arteries, more superficially located than usual, are found in 1 out of 10 persons.) Injection of fluids into an artery usually causes the patient to complain of sudden severe pain in the arm and hand. The pain is caused by arteriospasm and is an indication to stop the infusion immediately.

When frequent blood specimens are necessary, it is wise to save the veins in the antecubital area for this purpose; large quantities of blood can be obtained from them. It is extremely difficult to get sufficient blood from small veins.

A disadvantage in using veins in the antecubital area is the restriction of elbow flexion during the infusion. When long-term infusions are anticipated or the patient is uncooperative, it is best to use the veins in the forearm, because the patient can be moved and ambulated with less danger of

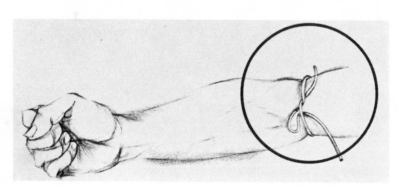

FIG. 59. Veins in the cubital fossa. (Abbott Laboratories: Parenteral Administration. p. 9. North Chicago, Ill., 1965)

dislodging the needle. A right-handed person has more freedom if the infusion is given in the left arm; however, the need for multiple venipunctures is an indication to employ alternate sites in both arms.

Veins in the back of the hand appear prominent, but they are difficult to enter because they roll and slide easily, due to the lack of supportive tissue. Because of their small diameter, they do not accommodate large needles. Small veins cannot accept large volumes or rapid administrations of fluids. An irritating solution is more traumatic in small veins because less blood is present to dilute it. Once such a vein is entered, it is difficult to anchor the needle securely for long-term therapy. Blood extravasates into the surrounding tissues when the needle is removed. These small peripheral veins collapse sooner in the presence of shock than do more centrally located veins.

Veins in the dorsum of the foot are sometimes used when other veins are not available or desirable. Venipuncture in this area, as in the hand, is difficult because the veins tend to roll and slide. Larger veins are found in the ankle; however, the use of these can be dangerous. Thrombus formation at the venipuncture site occurs to some degree in *all* venipunctures, but when ankle veins are used, the thrombus can extend to deeper veins and may result in pulmonary embolism. When feasible, it is best to use veins in the upper part of the body. When multiple punctures are anticipated, it is best to make the first venipuncture distally and work proximally with subsequent punctures.

Temporal scalp veins are prominent in infants and are frequently used for fluid administration. Other sites utilized in infants are the jugular vein and the superior sagittal sinus. Infusion into the superior sagittal sinus is dangerous; it should be utilized only as a last resort.

Venipuncture should not be performed on a varicose vein or at a site below a varicosity. Such veins do not readily transport fluids into the general circulation, and they may cause a pooling of fluid in veins around the injection site. Varicose veins are easily traumatized. Moreover, they are difficult to enter because they tend to roll, and the blood flow in them is frequently reversed.

Methods for Venous Entry

Methods. Fluids may be introduced into a vein by means of:

- A metal needle
- A plastic needle (see Fig. 60)
- A plastic catheter threaded through a metal needle (see Fig. 61)
- A plastic catheter introduced by means of a cut-down (minor surgical procedure)

Selection of Methods. Short-term infusions are usually given through metal needles. The size of the needle to be used depends on the vein as well as on the type of solution. Most commonly used are 19 or 20 gauge, one or one-and-a-half inch needles; an 18 gauge needle is indicated for blood administration. (The smaller the gauge number, the larger the internal diameter of the needle.)

Plastic needles or catheters are used for therapy lasting longer than 12 hours; they allow the patient more freedom of motion

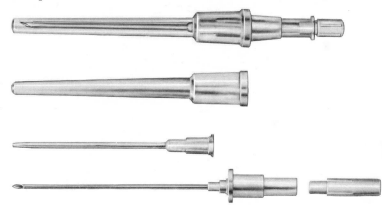

FIG. 60. Intravenous cannula placement unit. (Deseret Angiocath.) (C. R. Bard, Inc., Murray Hill, New Jersey)

FIG. 61. Intravenous catheter placement unit. (Deseret Intracath 1600 Series.) (C. R. Bard, Inc., Murray Hill, New Jersey)

than is possible when a metal needle is used.

A cut-down involves an incision in the skin and slitting the vein; the catheter is introduced through the slit in the vein and secured with a suture. This method is employed when veins are difficult to find and long-term fluid therapy is anticipated. Obese patients, infants, or those in or near shock frequently require cut-downs. This procedure is performed only by physicians.

Techniques of Insertion

Venipuncture With a Metal Needle. After a suitable site has been located, the next step is to distend the vein. A tourniquet will usually accomplish this (see Fig. 59); it also helps to steady the vein when it is placed no higher than 2 inches above the site of injection. Occasionally, other methods are necessary to distend the vein, such as placing the part in a dependent position for several minutes, or applying heat by means of a warm towel. (See Fig. 62.) Other methods for heat application include immersion in warm water, or the use of an electric hair dryer or an electric blanket. Heat does little good if it is applied only to the immediate area of the injection site—the entire extremity must be warmed. Sometimes a light flap over the proposed site of venipuncture helps; so does exercising the muscles distal to the site of puncture. However,

exercising should not be done when blood is being drawn for determination of serum electrolytes, since a false reading may result. The tourniquet should be applied lightly and should restrict only outflow. It is a common error to apply the tourniquet too tightly.

A large gauge needle always causes pain; its insertion may be preceded by locally injecting a small amount of 1 per cent procaine. This should be done only by order of the physician; also the patient should be questioned about a possible allergy to procaine. The injection of procaine tends to obscure landmarks. It should be done intradermally, and only an extremely small amount of procaine should be employed. Sometimes it is advantageous to insert the procaine above the proposed site for venipuncture since distal anesthesia occurs after a short wait. Frequently, the operator does not wait a sufficient time for the full anesthetic effect of the procaine, which results in a tendency to use larger amounts of procaine than are necessary.

Usually only alcohol is used to prepare the site for insertion of the needle, but sometimes the area is cleaned with PhisoHex or another detergent prior to the use of alcohol. If heat has been applied to the site, the alcohol sponge should be at room temperature—a cold solution causes vessels to contract. If the injection site is hairy, the

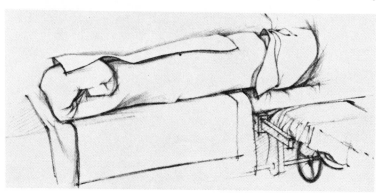

FIG. 62. Use of a warm towel to distend veins prior to venipuncture. (Abbott Laboratories: Parenteral Administration. p. 7, North Chicago, Ill., 1965)

FIG. 63. Needle bevel position for venipuncture. (Pfizer Laboratories: Intravenous technique. Spectrum, September-October, 1961)

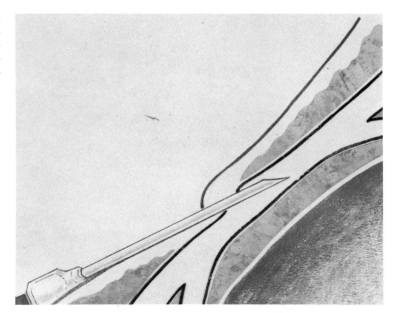

area should be shaved, taking care to prevent nicks. Shaving eliminates much of the discomfort associated with the removal of adhesive tape after the infusion.

Generally, the bevel of the needle should be facing upward during insertion. (See Fig. 63.) However, the introduction of a large needle into a small vein may require the bevel to face downward; otherwise, the needle would pierce the posterior wall of the vein when the tourniquet is removed.

With the tourniquet in place, the needle should pierce the skin to one side of, and approximately one half to one inch below, the point where the needle will enter the vein. As the needle enters the skin it should be at about a 45° angle; after the skin is entered, the needle angle is decreased. Although it seems more logical to enter the vein from above, there seems to be less flattening of the vein when a lateral approach is used. The free hand is used to palpate the vein while the needle is being introduced. An experienced operator can feel a snap as the needle enters the vein; after this, less resistance is offered to the needle. At this point, one should proceed very slowly with the insertion of the needle. It is threaded into the lumen approximately one-half to three-fourths of an inch. The tourniquet is released. Frequently a thin stream of blood is seen in the tubing when

the needle enters the vein. To be sure the needle is in the vein, the infusion bottle can be lowered below the site of injection; the negative pressure causes blood to enter the tubing.

The next step involves anchoring the needle comfortably and safely. A sterile cotton ball or a small gauze pad should be placed under the hub of the needle and fixed in place with adhesive tape. Another strip of tape should be placed over the needle to help hold it steady. A loop should be made in the tubing and taped in place; this allows some slack in the tubing and minimizes pull on the needle when the patient moves. (See Fig. 64.) The fluid should be allowed to run in and the proper flow rate established. One will do well to start with a rate slightly above that of the desired rate, since the rate of most intravenous infusions slows 25 to 50 per cent during the first 3 to 5 minutes. The area should be observed for swelling; its presence indicates that the needle is not in the vein and fluid is entering the subcutaneous area. The infusion should be discontinued immediately when swelling is noted; a venipuncture must then be made in another area.

Plastic Needle. The basic principles of venipuncture described above are also employed in the insertion of a plastic needle. A plastic needle is usually not used near a

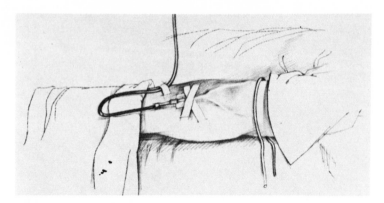

FIG. 64. Loop in I.V. tubing to prevent traction on the needle. (Abbott Laboratories: Parenteral Administration. p. 13. North Chicago, Ill., 1965)

joint, because flexion could obstruct its flow or possibly cause it to break.

Plastic Catheter. The basic principles of venipuncture are again employed in the insertion of the plastic catheter.

Temperature of Solution

The temperature of fluids for intravenous administration is rarely of significance. Few fluids require refrigeration and most are stored at room temperature; those requiring refrigeration include Lipomul and blood. Cold solutions are quickly warmed as they mix with blood during usual administration rates. Rapid massive replacement of cold blood has caused cardiac arrest. When it is deemed necessary to warm blood before administration, heat exchange coils may be used. (See Fig. 65.) The blood is warmed by immersing the coiled tubing in a warm water bath and allowing the blood to flow through the coil. The adult coil warms approximately 150 ml./minute. (A single pediatric coil is available and warms approximately 50 ml./minute.)

Hypodermoclysis

Hypodermoclysis, the administration of a solution subcutaneously, compares unfavorably with the intravenous route and is used less and less. It presents many problems.

The types of fluids that can be given sub-

FIG. 65. Heat exchange coil to warm blood. (Cutter Laboratories, Berkeley, California.)

cutaneously are few, since they must closely resemble the electrolyte content and tonicity of extracellular fluid if they are to be absorbed. Some of the fluids generally considered reasonably safe for subcutaneous administration include:

- Isotonic saline (0.9%)
- Half-isotonic saline (0.45%) with $2\frac{1}{2}\%$ dextrose
- Ringer's solution
- Half-strength Ringer's with $2\frac{1}{2}\%$ dextrose
- Lactated Ringer's solution
- Half-strength lactated Ringer's with $2\frac{1}{2}\%$ dextrose
- Darrow's solution

Fluids that are contraindicated for subcutaneous administration include electrolyte-free solutions, hypertonic solutions, alcohol, amino acids, fat emulsions, and solutions that differ significantly from body pH (such as the gastric replacement solutions). Orders for the subcutaneous administration of any of these solutions should be questioned.

The subcutaneous administration of a 5 per cent dextrose in water solution attracts electrolytes from the surrounding tissues and from the plasma, which enter the pool created at the infusion site. The decreased plasma volume can cause hypotension and even shock. If the patient is already suffering from sodium deficit, the ultimate result can be death.

Probably the only advantage hypodermoclysis has over the intravenous route is that it is easier to start. It is most often used for obese patients, infants, and the aged (because intravenous fluids are difficult to start). Suitable sites include the subcutaneous tissues in the lateral aspect of the thigh or abdomen. Infections are not uncommon with hypodermoclysis. Infection is usually

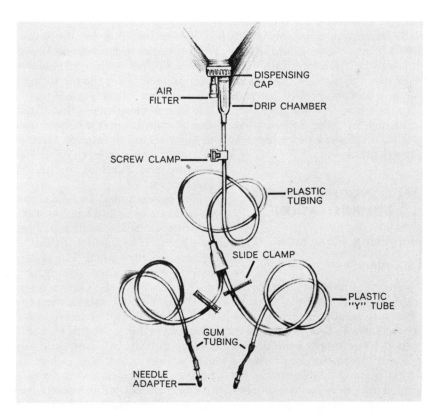

Fig. 66. Hypodermoclysis setup. (Abbott Laboratories: Parenteral Administration, Cly-Q-Pak. p. 34. North Chicago, Ill., 1965)

proportionate to the distention that occurs (because of tissue ischemia) and to the length of time required for the infusion.

Most often, two needles are used and the fluid is infused into two sites at once. The inverted Y-tubing from the solution bottle separates and goes to two sites. (See Fig. 66.) The rate of infusion depends upon how well the fluid is absorbed from the injection site. When the fluid is absorbed well, 250 to 500 ml. can be given at one site in 1 hour to an adult. To hasten absorption, an enzyme, Wydase, may be injected into the tissues at the injection site. The patient must be checked often when this route is used; a large amount of swelling can develop unless the flow rate is adjusted carefully. A small sterile gauze pad should be placed under the needle hub and another should cover the injection site. Following the removal of the needles, a light sterile dressing should be applied. Edematous injection sites are fertile fields for infections.

Much discomfort is usually associated with hypodermoclysis. This route is undependable, especially when large amounts of fluids are needed in a hurry; as mentioned above, the fluids that can be given safely are quite limited. Ironically, the patients for which hypodermoclysis is most often used (infants, the aged, and the obese) are the ones most prone to be harmed by them. Some authorities feel that a cut-down carries less risk than does hypodermoclysis.

GENERAL CONSIDERATIONS IN FLUID ADMINISTRATION

Determining Flow Rate

Physician's Orders

Ideally, when the physician writes an order for intravenous fluids he also designates how fast they should be given; however, very few actually do this. Physicians in university hospitals are more prone to give the desired rate of flow than those practicing in non-teaching hospitals. Most merely list on the order sheet the type and the amount of fluids to be given. The nurse should encourage the physician to write more specific orders; it is highly desirable that he deter-

mine infusion rates because of his deeper understanding of the patient's condition as well as of the fluids to be administered. Unfortunately, attempts to obtain specific orders from the physician are not always fruitful. Although poorly prepared to do so, the nurse is often left with the task of deciding how fast to give fluids. If the nurse is to intelligently assume this responsibility, she must learn more about parenteral fluids and their safe administration.

Factors Influencing the Desired Rate of Administration

Factors considered in determining the best flow rate for the infusion include:

• Type of fluid
• Need for fluids
• Cardiac and renal status
• Body size
• Age
• Patient's reaction during the infusion
• Size of the vein

The desired rate for the infusion varies with the type of fluids used. For example, a 5 per cent dextrose in water solution can be administered faster than a 10 per cent dextrose in water solution or a 5 per cent alcohol solution. Although the other variables must also be considered, it is helpful for the nurse to know the usual infusion rates for various solutions. They are given in the descriptions of parenteral fluids in the next section of this chapter.

The patient's need for fluids influences the desired rate of administration. For example, a patient in hypovolemic shock needs fluids in a hurry. The infusion in this instance is much faster than usual. The presence of cardiac or renal damage can greatly alter the desired infusion rate. The heart and kidneys both play a major role in the utilization of fluids introduced intravenously. If the pumping action of the heart is inadequate, a rapid infusion of fluids could cause a dangerous fluid excess. The failure of the kidneys to excrete unneeded water and electrolytes can also result in excessive amounts of these substances in the body.

Body surface area is an important criterion for fluid infusion rate. As mentioned in

TABLE 28. VARIATION IN SIZE OF DROP IN COMMERCIAL ADMINISTRATION SETS

Company	APPROX. NO. OF DROPS TO DELIVER 1 ML.		
	"Special" Set	"Regular" Set	"Pediatric" Set
Baxter Labs		10	50
American Sterilizer		10	60
Don Baxter		13	52
Abbott	10 (Blood)	13-15	60
Cutter	12 (Blood)	20	60
Fenwal	17 (Blood)		
Upjohn	20 (Lipomul)		

Weisberg, H.: Water, Electrolyte and Acid-Base Balance. ed. 2, p. 286. Baltimore, Williams & Wilkins, 1962.

Chapter 12, the usual flow rate is 3 ml./sq.m. of body surface/minute. This rate does not apply to all types of fluids and must at times be altered. Generally speaking, however, it is logical that a large individual can tolerate a greater amount of fluid per minute than a smaller individual, if other factors are equal.

The aged almost always have some degree of cardiac and renal impairment; therefore, fluids are administered more slowly to them than to younger adults.

One of the best guides to safe flow rate is the patient's reaction to the infusion. The fact that individuals respond differently to parenteral fluid infusions, just as they do to other medications, must never be forgotten. For this reason, the patient should be checked at least every 15 minutes during an infusion. The nurse should be aware of symptoms associated with the improper administration of various solutions so that she can know what to look for. Reactions associated with different parenteral fluids are described later in the chapter.

Variations of Drop Size With Different Commercial Sets

Most nurses think in terms of "drops per minute" when considering rate of fluid flow. It must be remembered that commercial parenteral administration sets vary in the number of drops delivering 1 ml. (See Table 28.) Unless one knows which administration set is to be used, it is more practical to consider the number of milliliters to be infused in 1 minute. From this figure, the number of drops per minute can be computed when the drop size of the administration set is learned.

Formula:

Drop Factor × ml./min. = drops/min.

For example, to deliver 3 ml./minute using a set with 10 drops to 1 ml., a flow rate of 30 drops/minute would be necessary. To administer the same amount using a set with 15 drops to 1 ml., a flow rate of 45 drops/minute would be necessary.

Calculation of Flow Rate

If the nurse knows the amount of fluid to be given in a prescribed time interval, plus the drop factor of the administration set to be used, she can easily compute the desired number of drops/minute. The following formula is used:

$$\text{Drops/min.} = \frac{\text{Total volume infused} \times \text{Drop factor (drops/ml.)}}{\text{Total time of infusion in minutes}}$$

Sample Problem:

Infuse 1,000 ml. of 5% D/W in 2 hours (Assume an administration set with 10 drops to 1 ml. is to be used)
Total volume = 1,000 ml.

Drops/ml. = 10
Total time of infusion in minutes = 120

$$\frac{1,000 \times 10}{120} = \text{approximately 80 drops/min.}$$

To save the nurse time, some handy calculators* have been devised by manufacturers of parenteral fluids to determine the desired flow rate when the above factors are known. Directions for their use are included with them.

Mechanical Factors Influencing Flow Rate

After the desired flow rate has been regulated, there are several mechanical factors that may alter it:
• Change in needle position (needle lumen may be lodged against venous wall)
• Because infusions flow in by gravity, a change in the height of the infusion bottle or bed can increase or decrease the rate (the greater the distance between the patient and the bottle, the faster the rate)
• Patency of needle (a small clot may occlude the needle lumen and decrease the flow rate—when released, the rate increases)
• Limb movement or exercise

PARENTERAL FLUIDS—SPECIAL CONSIDERATIONS

Parenteral Nutrition

Parenteral nutrition is frequently lifesaving. As Dr. Robert Elman said, "Parenteral alimentation does not compete with oral alimentation; it competes only with death." Substances that can be given intravenously include:

> • Carbohydrates
> • Protein hydrolysates
> • Fat emulsions
> • Alcohol
> • Vitamins
> • Water
> • Electrolytes

Provision of nutrients intravenously is indicated when it is desired to put the gastrointestinal tract at relative rest, as in the

* Abbott Laboratories (Flow Rate Calculator for Abbott Blood or Solution Infusion Sets)
    AMSCO Laboratories (Parenteral Solutions Administration and Fluid Requirements in Burns Charts)
    Baxter Laboratories (Minislide Calculator)
    Cutter Laboratories (Cutter Guide to Flow Rates)

presence of nausea, vomiting, diarrhea, peritonitis, ileus, or fistulas. Intravenous nutrition is also indicated when the patient cannot take nutrients by an enteral route. In considering the nutritional needs of the patient exclusively on parenteral feedings, it should be borne in mind that the recommended energy need of an adult at bedrest is 1,600 calories. This is a basal figure and does not allow for fever, high environmental temperatures, or other causes of increased metabolism. Although it is difficult to restore the nutritionally depleted patient by the intravenous route, it is possible to maintain the state of nutrition fairly well for limited periods.

Nevertheless, the goal of parenteral nutrition is chiefly to pinch-hit until the patient can again take nutrients by mouth. Every effort should be made to restore a patient receiving parenteral feedings to the oral or tube route as soon as possible. The nurse can contribute to this restoration by reporting signs of improvement, such as the absence of nausea and vomiting, and by encouraging the patient to take materials by mouth as soon as permissible. Another indication for parenteral alimentation is the urgent need for a nutrient, such as glucose in severe hypoglycemia, 5 per cent sodium chloride in severe sodium deficit, or calcium gluconate in acute calcium deficit. In such instances, the use of the intravenous route is essential.

Carbohydrates

Carbohydrates that can be administered and absorbed intravenously include glucose, fructose and invert sugar. These are all monosaccharides, therefore they are ready for utilization by the body cells. Disaccharides and polysaccharides cannot be utilized when given by the intravenous route. Table 29 presents an analysis of various parenteral carbohydrate solutions.

To provide the patient with sufficient calories through the administration of carbohydrate alone would necessitate giving a large quantity of a dilute solution, or a smaller quantity of a concentrated solution. To supply 1,600 calories with a 5 per cent dextrose solution would require 9 L. This volume of fluid would exceed the volume

TABLE 29. PARENTERAL CARBOHYDRATE SOLUTIONS

TYPES OF SOLUTIONS	CALORIES/L.	TONICITY
Dextrose		
5% Dextrose in water	170	Isotonic
5% Dextrose in saline	170	Hypertonic
10% Dextrose in water	340	Hypertonic
10% Dextrose in saline	340	Hypertonic
20% Dextrose in water	680	Hypertonic
50% Dextrose in water	1,700	Hypertonic
Fructose		
5% Fructose in water	187.5	Isotonic
10% Fructose in water or saline	375	Hypertonic
Invert Sugar		
5% Invert sugar in water	187.5	Isotonic
5% Invert sugar in saline	187.5	Hypertonic
10% Invert sugar in water or saline	375	Hypertonic

tolerance of most patients. Mixtures of carbohydrate and alcohol are useful because of their rich caloric contribution and limited bulk.

Concentrated solutions, such as 20 per cent or 50 per cent dextrose, are useful for supplying calories for individuals with renal insufficiency or who for other reasons are unable to tolerate large volumes. In order that the glucose be utilized, concentrated solutions must be administered slowly and intermittently. When administered rapidly, such solutions act as a diuretic and pull interstitial fluid into the plasma for subsequent renal excretion. Such hypertonic solutions damage veins in direct proportion to their tonicity. When used, they should be injected into large functioning veins so that they will be diluted by the relatively large blood volume. A functioning vein is soft to the touch. Moreover, it fills when compressed proximally—that is, on the side toward the heart. However, the site of injection should be alternated to avoid repeated irritation of one vein.

Carbohydrate is often administered parenterally to minimize the ketosis of starvation. When ingestion of carbohydrate and fats is inadequate, the body burns its own fats to supply caloric needs. As a result of this process, ketone bodies are formed. Since these are acids, they neutralize bicarbonate and produce metabolic acidosis (primary base bicarbonate deficit). Ketones require water for renal excretion and thus cause an increased demand for renal water expenditure. Administration of 100 Gm. of carbohydrate daily can prevent the ketosis of starvation by supplying readily accessible carbohydrate.

One advantage of carbohydrate as a source of calories lies in the fact that, following its utilization, there remains only water and carbon dioxide to be used by the body or excreted. Nevertheless, when solutions of carbohydrate are administered too rapidly, the body cannot utilize all the carbohydrate and part of it is excreted in the urine. The body receives no benefit from the excreted glucose. On the other hand, the glucose may carry with it other important nutrients. If a hypertonic carbohydrate solution is infused too rapidly, hyperinsulinism may occur. The pancreas secretes extra insulin to metabolize the infused carbohydrate; discontinuance of the administration may leave an excess of insulin in the body. Symptoms include nervousness, sweating and weakness. It is not uncommon for small amounts of isotonic carbohydrate solution to be given after hypertonic solutions to "cover" for the extra insulin and allow the return to normal secretion. The nurse, therefore, should be familiar with the usual rates of administration of carbohydrate solutions.

Rates of Administration. The maximal speed for administration of glucose to normal adults without producing glycosuria is approximately 0.5 Gm./Kg./hr. At this rate, it would take 3 hours for the injection of 1 L. of 10 per cent dextrose. Some workers maintain that fructose can be administered more rapidly than glucose, and that invert sugar's optimal rate of administration lies somewhat between the two. Whether fructose and invert sugar offer real advantages from the standpoint of rate of administration appears open to question.

It is, of course, the province of the physician to specify the rate of administration of parenteral fluids. Factors unknown to the nurse could well alter average infusion rates

TABLE 30.

MAXIMAL RATES OF INFUSIONS FOR CARBO-
HYDRATE AND WATER SOLUTIONS

Dextrose 5% 1,000 ml.	1½ hours
Dextrose 10% 1,000 ml.	3 hours
Dextrose 20% 1,000 ml.	6 hours
Invert Sugar 5% 1,000 ml.	1½ hours
Invert Sugar 10% 1,000 ml.	2 hours
Fructose 10% 1,000 ml.	1½ hours

in the case of a particular patient. Nevertheless, it is wise for the nurse to keep infusion rates in mind as guidelines for what is usually safe. (See Table 30.)

Protein Hydrolysates*

Protein is necessary for cellular repair, wound healing, growth, and for the synthesis of certain enzymes and vitamins. One cannot supply enough carbohydrate parenterally to prevent burning of some body protein for energy purposes. Hence, one should supply the minimal requirements for protein by parenteral administration of protein hydrolysate solutions, if the patient is to be maintained exclusively on parenteral nutrition for more than a limited period of time. Protein hydrolysates are usually given in conjunction with other substances, such as glucose or alcohol, or both, in order to supply sufficient calories so that the protein will be used for tissue repair rather than for caloric purposes. (See Table 31.)

Starvation causes a breakdown of protoplasm. Since protoplasm is largely a protein substance, and since protein contains nitrogen, there is an increased excretion of nitrogen. In starvation, there is little or no intake of nitrogen; therefore, more nitrogen is lost than is taken in—hence, the patient is said to be in *negative nitrogen balance*. It has become customary to use the measure-

* *Amigen*—Baxter Laboratories, Inc.
Aminosol—Abbott Laboratories
Stuart Amino Acids—The Stuart Company
Travamin—Travenol Laboratories, Inc.

ment of nitrogen balance as an indication of the state of protein metabolism of the patient, just as water balance is used to measure the degree of water exchange. Approximately 1 Gm. of nitrogen is contained in 6.25 Gm. of protein.

Postive nitrogen balance can be achieved by supplying protein, or the elements of protein, plus sufficient calories to prevent protoplasmic breakdown. A healthy adult requires approximately 1 Gm. of protein/Kg. (2.2 pounds) of body weight daily to replace normal protein losses. Nitrogen balance can be maintained either by vegetable or animal protein. Animal proteins, in general, are far more efficient sources of protein nutrition for the human body than are vegetable proteins. Nevertheless, some vegetable proteins, such as soybean, peanut and yeast, closely approach animal protein in nutritional value. Clinically, protein hydrolysates are useful for a wide variety of patients who are unable to ingest sufficient food to maintain positive nitrogen balance.

Before a protein hydrolysate is administered to the patient, he should be asked if he has any allergies. For the patient allergic to milk products, a hydrolysate of beef protein would appear advisable. For the patient allergic to beef, one might well choose a hy-

TABLE 31. PARENTERAL AMINO ACID
SOLUTIONS

TYPE OF SOLUTION	CALORIES/L.	TONICITY
5% Amino Acids	175	Isotonic
5% Amino Acids 5% Glucose	345	Hypertonic
5% Amino Acids 5% Fructose	362.5	Hypertonic
5% Amino Acids 10% Glucose	515	Hypertonic
5% Amino Acids 10% Fructose	550	Hypertonic
5% Amino Acids 5% Glucose 5% Alcohol	625	Hypertonic
5% Amino Acids 12.5% Fructose 2.4% Alcohol	778	Hypertonic

Adapted from Weisberg, H.: Water, Electrolyte, and Acid Base Balance. ed. 2, p. 297. Baltimore, Williams & Wilkins, 1962.

drolysate of casein. Actually, there have been so few authenticated cases of allergic sensitivity to protein hydrolysates as to render this hazard almost nonexistent.

Rates of Administration. The first few milliliters of the protein hydrolysate should be given slowly, since some patients have what might be termed as *pharmacologic sensitivity* to certain amino acids. If any untoward symptoms occur, the infusion should be stopped.

Sometimes excessively rapid administration causes nausea, a feeling of warmth and flushing of the face. Vomiting may occur. These symptoms usually disappear when the rate of administration is retarded. Other patients experience unpleasant effects, such as peculiar sensations of taste and smell.

If complications do not occur, a reasonable administration time for 1 L. of a 5 per cent protein hydrolysate solution is one and one half to two and one half hours. Individual variation in rate tolerance is great; the patient's reaction to the infusion should be checked often.

Protein hydrolysate solutions have a high NH_4^+ level and should be administered with especial care to patients with hepatic insufficiency or emaciation. A rate slower than usual for other I.V. solutions should be employed. Seriously impaired renal function constitutes a contraindication to the administration of protein hydrolysate or amino acid solutions, since the seriously impaired kidney cannot normally excrete nitrogenous wastes.

Especially important in the administration of protein hydrolysate solutions is the employment of disposable tubing. Every protein hydrolysate solution should be examined carefully before it is infused into the patient. Either particulate matter or cloudiness should call for discarding the solution. *Once a bottle is opened, it should be administered at once. It should never be placed in a refrigerator for later use.* Deaths have occurred from this unwise practice.

Fat Emulsions*

Fats supply more than twice the calories of proteins or carbohydrates, since 1 Gm. of

* Lipomul.

fat yields 9 calories, while a gram of protein or a gram of carbohydrate yields only 4 calories. Each 100 ml. of Lipomul furnishes 160 calories. For this reason, fat emulsions have long been regarded as ideal sources of calories for parenteral infusion. They have been recommended for patients whose gastrointestinal tracts are nonfunctional. They have also been employed in the management of patients with burns and of those with severe renal disease, who require calories with a maximal nitrogen sparing effect. Ideal though they appear from the theoretical standpoint, fat emulsions have many disadvantages. Immediate reactions to them include chills, fever, back or chest pain, dyspnea, severe flushing, urticaria, nausea, vomiting, headache, dizziness and variations in blood pressure and pulse. The incidence of untoward symptoms with fat emulsions appears to be highly variable. When they are employed, both nurse and physician should read the manufacturer's instructions with great care.

General precautions the nurse should keep in mind when administering Lipomul are:

• Avoid mixing Lipomul with any other infusion fluid or medicine

• Do not administer any other substance simultaneously through the same tubing.

• Give slowly and increase the rate as the patient's reaction allows

The suggested maximum rates of infusion for adults are approximately:

first 5 minutes — 10 drops/min.
next 25 minutes — 40 drops/min.
then   — 60 drops/min.
(Use only special Lipomul set—approximately 20 drops/ml.)

• Patients having high fever, severe liver disease, bleeding tendency, acidosis, or thromboembolic or other cardiovascular disease, should be observed very closely during the infusion

Alcohol Solutions

One Gm. of absolute ethyl alcohol yields 6 to 8 calories. Obviously an excellent source of calories, alcohol has been combined with carbohydrate and with both carbohydrate

TABLE 32. PARENTERAL ALCOHOL
SOLUTIONS

SOLUTION	CALORIES/L.	TONICITY
Alcohol 5% Dextrose 5%	450	Hypertonic
Amino Acids 5% Dextrose 5% Alcohol 5%	625	Hypertonic
Amino Acids 5% Fructose 12.5% Alcohol 2.4%	778	Hypertonic

and protein hydrolysates to provide a high calorie repair solution. When alcohol is infused with carbohydrate, it is apparently burned preferentially, thus permitting the glucose to be stored as glycogen. Alcohol spares body protein by providing readily accessible calories. Its sedating effect is highly desirable for patients with pain. *Sedation can be achieved in the average adult without symptoms of intoxication by giving 200 to 300 ml. of a 5 per cent solution per hour.*

The nurse should be aware of the physiologic and psychologic effects of alcohol parenterally administered. These include dulling of memory, loss of ability to concentrate and an improved sense of well-being. Respiration and pulse are increased; vasodilation occurs. Alcohol solutions should *not* be employed in shock, impending shock, epilepsy, severe liver disease, or in patients with coronary thrombosis. Nausea and vomiting do not occur as frequently when alcohol is given parenterally as when a comparable amount is taken orally. However, whenever the rate of administration of alcohol given parenterally exceeds its metabolic destruction by the body, restlessness, inebriation and coma can occur. The lethal dose of alcohol is approximately 500 ml. of pure alcohol. The amount of alcohol contained in a liter of 5 per cent alcohol solution, 50 ml., is thus quite safe. The rate at which alcohol solutions are administered obviously influences the patient's reaction to the alcohol.

The parenteral administration of alcohol, particularly of hypertonic solutions, can cause phlebitis. Tissue necrosis can occur if the needle accidentally leaves the vein and permits solution to perfuse the surrounding tissue spaces. Table 32 shows the caloric values and the tonicity of various solutions of alcohol.

Parenteral Vitamins

Vitamins should be administered parenterally when there is inadequate oral intake or when parenteral therapy is necessary for longer than 2 or 3 days. Although not food in themselves, vitamins are essential for the utilization of other nutrients. The need for vitamins is increased during periods of stress, such as acute illness, infection, surgery, burns, injury and convalescence. Some parenteral fluids have vitamins incorporated. Special vitamin preparations designed for injection with parenteral fluids are also available.

The vitamins most frequently needed in parenteral alimentation are vitamin C and members of the B complex. These vitamins are water soluble and are not stored by the body in large amounts; they serve as coenzymes in the essential metabolic processes of the cells. Vitamin deficiency has been observed after only one week of parenteral administration of glucose and water alone. Since most patients are on parenteral therapy for only limited periods, they do not require the fat soluble vitamins A and D.

Because there is some waste of parenterally infused vitamins through urinary excretion, it is necessary to administer generous amounts to assure an adequate intake. Hence, the patient who is on exclusive parenteral alimentation is usually given more than the daily vitamin requirement. The depleted patient may require as much as ten times the minimal requirement. A basic formula of parenteral vitamins is as follows:

Thiamine	10 mg.
Riboflavin	5 mg.
Niacinamide	50 mg.
Calcium Pantothenate ...	20 mg.
Pyridoxine Hydrochloride	20 mg.
Folic Acid	5 mg.
Vitamin B_{12}	15 μg.
Vitamin C	up to 1 Gm. as indicated

Vitamin C is particularly important in surgical patients to promote wound healing. The B complex vitamins provide factors to aid carbohydrate metabolism and the maintenance of normal gastrointestinal function. An occasional patient may show extreme sensitivity to the B complex vitamins. Sometimes vitamin K is given; flushing, sweating, and a constricted feeling in the chest may follow the intravenous injection of vitamin K.

Water

The patient on parenteral fluids exclusively can be provided with water by means of solutions of carbohydrate or electrolytes or both. Probably the most common solution used for this purpose is 5 per cent dextrose in water. Also useful are the various types of Butler solutions, which supply glucose or fructose, electrolytes and water in a hypotonic solution. Isotonic solution of sodium chloride has the same tonicity as body fluid. Therefore, when administered to the patient requiring water, it provides no water at all—it merely *expands* the extracellular fluid volume. The administration of isotonic solution of sodium chloride to the patient requiring water ignores the patient's requirements for water for renal excretion, for insensible loss, and for the several metabolic needs of the body. It should never be used for this purpose.

Electrolyte Solutions

A wide variety of electrolyte solutions are available for parenteral administration. Some of the more common solutions are listed in Table 33 for quick reference. Included in the table are the following:

- Electrolyte content
- Trade marks (brand names)
- Precautions for administration
- Usual rate of administration

Administration of Potassium Solutions. Potassium may be given in the form of commercially prepared electrolyte solutions, or a potassium salt may be added as a supplement to an intravenous fluid, such as 5 or 10 per cent dextrose in water.

The nurse should keep the following facts in mind when potassium-containing solutions are administered (see Table 33):

1. As a general rule, no more than 30 mEq. of potassium should be infused in 1 hour.

2. Potassium solutions should never be allowed to run with the flow valve wide open or be given under pressure; high concentrations of potassium in the bloodstream can result in cardiac arrest.

3. Small ampules containing concentrated solutions of potassium salts for addition to I.V. fluids are meant to be mixed with at least 1 L. of solution. They should never be directly administered in concentrated form through the tubing or needle. The danger is, again, cardiac arrest.

4. It is wise to limit the potassium concentration in 1 L. of fluid to 40 mEq. No more than 80 mEq. should ever be contained in 1 L.; an accidental rapid infusion rate is less dangerous when the potassium content of the solution is moderate.

5. Potassium should be administered intravenously only after adequate urine flow has been established. The presence of oliguria or anuria is an indication to withhold potassium until initial hydrating or pump-priming solutions (such as 5 per cent D/W or 0.45 per cent saline) have demonstrated adequate renal function. It should be remembered that potassium is mainly excreted by way of the kidneys; when the kidneys are non-functional, a high potassium level builds up in the bloodstream. An exception to this rule may be the occasional administration of lactated Ringer's solution in the presence of oliguria; the potassium content of this solution is low and is probably not harmful unless anuria is present.

6. A solution containing sizable amounts of potassium (30 to 40 mEq./L.) is sometimes associated with pain in the vein it is entering; slowing the rate usually relieves this sensation. Infiltration of a potassium solution into the subcutaneous tissues is painful. Rarely, potassium is administered by means of hypodermoclysis; when it is, the concentration should be no higher than 10 mEq./L. to avoid local pain.

Incompatible Combinations of Additives and Parenteral Fluids

The nurse is frequently required to add medications to parenteral fluids. She should take precautions to prevent the administra-

TABLE 33. ELECTROLYTE SOLUTIONS

SOLUTION	TONICITY	pH	Na+	K+	Ca++	Mg++	NH4+	Cl-	LACTATE	HCO3-	HPO4-	BRAND NAMES	REASONS FOR USE	COMMENTS
			mEq./L.											
Sodium chloride 0.45% (One-half isotonic saline)	Hypotonic	4.5-7	77					77					Supply daily salt requirements — Supply water for excretory purposes	Available commercially with varying concentrations of carbohydrates
Sodium chloride 0.9% (Isotonic saline)	Isotonic	4.5-7	154					154					Replace Na+ and Cl- losses — Expand extracellular fluid volume when fluid deficit is present — Correct alkalosis	Widely used as a routine electrolyte replacement solution even though it supplies *only* Na+ and Cl- (Many feel its routine use should be replaced by a solution that more closely resembles extracellular fluid, such as Lactated Ringer's) — Does *not* supply free water for excretory purposes — Cl- is supplied in excess of normal plasma Cl- level—excessive use of isotonic saline can cause the Cl- to replace the basic HCO_3^- — Sometimes erroneously referred to as "normal saline" or "physiologic saline" — Available commercially with varying concentrations of carbohydrates.

Solution	Tonicity	pH	Na	K	Ca	Cl	Lactate	Uses	Comments
Sodium chloride 3%	Hypertonic	4.5-7	513			513		Rapid correction of severe low-salt syndrome	Contraindicated unless severe salt depletion is present.
Sodium chloride 5%	Hypertonic	4.5-7	855			855			Usually only small amounts are used (200-300 ml.)—not more than 400 ml. of 5% saline should be infused in one day. Rate of administration should be *slow*—usually not more than 100 ml./hr. (check with physician).
Lactated Ringer's (Hartmann's)	Isotonic	6-7.5	130	4	3	109	28	Routine electrolyte maintenance solution	Electrolyte concentration closely resembles extracellular fluid
								Correct metabolic acidosis	Same precautions as for any K-containing solution*
								Replace fluid lost as bile, diarrhea, and in burns	(It is permissible to use Lactated Ringer's in burns since the amount of K+ is so small as to be inconsequential) (May at times be administered cautiously in the presence of decreased urinary output.)

Ordinarily given at a rate of 400-500 ml./hr.—may be given much faster in special instances (check with physician).

TABLE 33. ELECTROLYTE SOLUTIONS—(Continued)

SOLUTION	TONICITY	pH	Na+	K+	Ca++	Mg++	NH4+	Cl-	LACTATE	HCO3-	HPO4-	BRAND NAMES	REASONS FOR USE	COMMENTS
			MEQ./L.											
Gastric (Cooke and Crowley)	Isotonic	3.3-3.7	63	17			70	150				Electrolyte No. 3 Baxter Lab. Cutter Lab.	Replace gastric fluid lost in vomiting and gastric suction	Available commercially with varying concentrations of carbohydrates. Should not be used as a routine maintenance solution.
												Electrolyte C Amsco Hosp. Liq.		pH of solution is acid; similar to that of gastric juice.
												Ionosol G Abbott Lab.		Contraindicated in hepatic insufficiency
												Isolyte G McGaw		Same precautions as for any K-containing solution.*
Duodenal	Isotonic		138	12				100		50		Ionosol D Abbott Lab.	Replace duodenal fluid loss	Available commercially with varying concentrations of carbohydrates. Same precautions as for any K-containing solution.* Can be given at a rate up to 500 ml./hr. (check with physician).
													Correct mild acidosis	Rate should not exceed 660 ml./hr. (check with physician).
Duodenal (modified)			80	36	4.6	2.8		63		60		Electrolyte No. 1 Baxter Lab. McGaw	Replace pancreatic and duodenal fluid losses	Same precautions as for any K-containing solution (K+ content is high).*

	Tonicity	pH				Trade names	Uses	Nursing considerations / Contraindications
(Alkalinizing Solution) Sodium lactate ⅙M	Isotonic	6-7.3	167	167	167	Electrolyte A Amsco Hosp. Liq. — Ionosol D (modified) Abbott Lab. — Ion-O-Trate Abbott Lab.	Supply water for excretory needs — Correct deficits of K^+, Ca^{++}, Mg^{++}, Na^+ and HCO_3^- — Relieve hyperpnea of severe acidosis	Contraindicated in liver disease, shock, and right-sided heart failure (lactate ions are improperly metabolized in these conditions). — Contraindicated in respiratory alkalosis. — Can be given at a rate of 250-400 ml./hr. (check with physician).
(Acidifying Solutions) Ammonium chloride 0.9%	Isotonic		168	168		Ion-O-Trate Abbott Lab.	Severe metabolic alkalosis in children	Contraindicated in disturbed hepatic function, renal failure, or any condition with a high NH_4^+ level.
Ammonium chloride 2.14%	Hypertonic		400	400			Severe metabolic alkalosis in adults	Excessive amounts of this solution can cause metabolic acidosis with • drowsiness • hyperpnea • nausea and vomiting • confusion • disorientation • coma Give *slowly*—check with physician (rate should not

[129]

TABLE 33. ELECTROLYTE SOLUTIONS—(Continued)

SOLUTION	TONICITY	pH	Na+	K+	Ca++	Mg++	NH₄+	Cl-	LACTATE	HCO₃-	HPO₄-	BRAND NAMES	REASONS FOR USE	COMMENTS
														exceed 300 ml./hr. in an adult).
Balanced electrolyte (Fox)	Isotonic		140	10	5	3		103		55		Equivisol Amsco Hosp. Liq.	Replace gastrointestinal losses of: •small intestinal juice •bile •diarrhea	Electrolyte content similar to plasma except that it has twice as much K+ (K+ content similar to that of intestinal juice).
												Plasma-lyte Baxter Lab.	Burn treatment	Same precautions as for any K-containing solution.*
												Polysal Cutter Lab.	Postoperative fluid replacement	
												Isolyte E McGaw	Correct Na+ deficit	Should not be given at a rate faster than 1 L. in 1½ hours (check with physician).
Darrow's (K-lactate)	Isotonic	6.5-7.5	121	35				103		55		Ionosol Abbott Lab.	Correct K+ deficit	Same precautions as for any K-containing solution* (K+ content is high).
												KNL Cutter Lab.		
												"Lactated potassic saline" Baxter Lab. Don Baxter, Inc. McGaw		When given I.V. to children it should be diluted with 2 or 3 parts of equal volumes of 5% D in 1/3 isotonic saline.
														Administer at a slow rate.

MEQ./L.

Solution	Tonicity	pH							Equivalent products	Use	Precautions
Electrolyte No. 88 (Butler)	Hypotonic	7.4	55	23	5	45	26	12	Electrolyte No. 2 Cutter Lab.	Supply water	Best for repairing past deficits and providing water and electrolytes for maintenance.
	Hypotonic	7.4	57	25	5-6	49-50	25	13	Electrolyte No. 2 Baxter Lab. McGaw	Supply maintenance needs of Na+, K+, and Cl−	Same precautions as for any K-containing solution.*
									Electrolyte B Amsco Hosp. Liq.	Replace fluid lost from the large intestine	
									Ionosol B Abbott Lab.		Should not be given at a rate faster than 500 ml./hr. in adults (check with physician).
Electrolyte No. 48 (modified Butler)	Hypotonic		25	20	3	22	23	3	Electrolyte No. 48 Baxter Lab. Cutter Lab.	Supply water	Same precautions as for any K-containing solution.*
									Electrolyte F Amsco Hosp. Liq.	Used in pediatrics to treat dehydration of acidosis, diarrhea, and burns	Should not be given at a rate faster than 250 ml./hr. in adults.
									Ionosol MB Abbott Lab.		
									Isolyte P McGaw		

TABLE 33. ELECTROLYTE SOLUTIONS—(*Concluded*)

SOLUTION	TONICITY	pH	Na+	K+	Ca++	Mg++	NH4+	Cl-	LACTATE	HCO3-	HPO4-	BRAND NAMES	REASONS FOR USE	COMMENTS
						mEQ./L.								
Electrolyte No. 75 (Talbot)	Hypotonic		40	35				40		20	15	Electrolyte No. 75 Baxter Lab. Don Baxter, Inc. Cutter Lab.	General maintenance solution	Same precautions as for any K-containing solution.*
												Ionosol T Abbott Lab.	Pediatric maintenance solution	
	Hypotonic		40	16	5	3		40		24		Electrolyte D Amsco Hosp. Liq.		
												Polysal M Cutter Lab.		Should not be given at a rate faster than 500 ml./hr. in adults.

* K-containing solutions should be infused with caution and are contraindicated when these conditions are present:
• oliguria or anuria
• potassium excess
• renal damage
• Addison's disease
(See section on K-solutions)

tion of incompatible combinations. The formation of a precipitate when a medication is added to an intravenous fluid is an indication to discard the solution (unless directions accompanying the medicine state otherwise). When in doubt as to the safety of mixing certain medicines and parenteral fluids, the nurse should consult with the physician, the pharmacist, or both. Abbott Laboratories has available a table (*Compatibility Studies of Parenteral Admixtures*) showing the reaction of specific medications with Abbott parenteral solutions.

Administration of Levophed

Levophed, levarterenol bitartrate, is a potent vasopressor used in the treatment of hypotension or shock caused by such conditions as surgical procedures, myocardial infarction, hemorrhage, trauma and septicemia. Because it causes vasoconstriction, Levophed increases blood pressure and promotes an adequate blood flow through vital areas, such as the brain, the heart and the kidneys. After an adequate blood pressure has been established, more specific treatment for shock can be given. For example, blood replacement is necessary if shock was caused by blood loss.

Levophed is supplied in a 4 ml. ampule as a 0.2 per cent solution; it must be suitably diluted before use. Either 5 per cent dextrose in water or 5 per cent dextrose in saline is used to administer Levophed. Plain saline causes it to oxidize rapidly.

A mixture of 4 ml. of Levophed in 1 L. of fluid contains 4 μg. (microgram) of Levophed/ml. Levophed may be mixed with only 250 ml. of fluid if it is necessary to limit fluid volume; such a mixture contains 16 μg. of Levophed/ml.

Great caution must be exercised during Levophed administration. It is mandatory that blood pressure be checked every 5 or 10 minutes, or oftener if indicated; the flow rate is speeded or slowed in order to maintain blood pressure at a low normotensive level. *The usual rate of administration is 2 to 4 μg. of Levophed/minute.*

If the solution's concentration is 4 μg. of Levophed/ml. (4 ml. of Levophed in 1 L. of solution) the desired rate would be 0.5 to

1.0 ml./minute. The number of drops necessary to deliver 0.5 to 1.0 ml./minute depends upon the drop size of the administration set to be used.

For example: (Drop Factor $\times$ ml./min. = drops/min.)
Using a set
delivering: Desired rate is:
10 drops/ml.—5 to 10 drops/min.
15 drops/ml.—7 and 8 to 15 drops/min.
50 drops/ml.—25 to 50 drops/min.
60 drops/ml.—30 to 60 drops/min.

If the solution's concentration is 16 μg./ml. (4 ml. of Levophed in 250 ml. of solution), the desired rate would be .125 to .250 ml./minute. Again, the number of drops necessary to deliver this amount depends on the drop size of the administration set. A constant rate pump may be useful for such critical infusions.

For example:
Using a set
delivering: Desired rate is:
10 drops/ml.—1 to 3 drops/min.
50 drops/ml.—6 to 13 drops/min.
60 drops/ml.—8 to 15 drops/min.

The flow rate can be more accurately regulated when an administration set with a small drop size is used, such as Abbott's Microdrip and Baxter's Minimeter. When a regular administration set is used, the desired number of drops per minute is so small that accurate regulation is extremely difficult.

The patient receiving Levophed should be constantly attended. If the flow rate is closely observed, the chance of administering a highly excessive volume is remote. The nurse should realize that factors other than the flow regulating clamp may alter the flow rate. For example, a flow rate established while the needle lumen was pressed against the venous wall, or partially occluded with a small clot, would greatly increase if the lumen were cleared. Lowering the patient's bed level or elevating the I.V. pole can also cause an increased flow rate. Failure to quickly note the increased flow rate could result in a large overdose of Levophed. An overdosage causes dangerous hypertension. To help prevent a large overdosage, Levophed is sometimes administered in small containers, such as Baxter's Pedatrol set, and Abbott's Soluset set.

The pliable plastic Pedatrol set is divided into 5 aliquots of 10 ml. each. (See Fig. 87, Chap. 24.) By simply moving a hemostat's position on the set, the maximum amount of solution to be infused can be limited to 10, 20, 30, 40 or 50 ml. When empty, the set can easily be refilled from the solution bottle above.

The rigid plastic Soluset cylinder is calibrated, in units of 5 ml., from 0 to 100. (See Fig. 86, Chap. 24.) The cylinder can be filled to any level up to 100 ml.; the maximum amount of solution that can be infused is limited to the amount in the cylinder. A hinged valve abruptly seals off the cylinder when the fluid level reaches the O mark. More solution can be given by simply refilling the cylinder.

Use of sets such as those described above provides additional patient protection against a highly excessive overdosage of Levophed. However, the use of such sets does not exclude the need to observe the flow rate carefully. Even though the maximum amount of solution that can be infused is limited to a relatively small volume, it must be remembered that this small amount is meant to be infused over a long period. For example, to infuse the concentrated Levophed solution (4 ml. of Levophed in 250 ml. of fluid) at the usual rate for 24 hours would require a volume of only 180 to 360 ml. Administration of a solution containing 4 μg. of Levophed/ml. at the usual rate for 24 hours would require a volume of 720 to 1,440 ml. The usual administration rate described in the above discussion is only a general guide. The need to check the blood pressure often and regulate the flow accordingly cannot be overemphasized.

Great care should be taken to avoid extravasation of Levophed into tissues around the injection site, because it causes serious and extensive tissue slough. Five or ten mg. of phentolamine may be diluted in 10 to 15 ml. of saline and injected into the area of infiltration to minimize slough. Some physicians prefer to add 5 or 10 mg. of phentolamine to the Levophed solution to prevent serious

tissue damage if the solution should accidentally infiltrate into surrounding tissues.

There is less chance of infiltration when the solution is given through a plastic catheter rather than a needle. Veins in the hands or legs of patients with peripheral vascular disease should be avoided. The nurse should check the site of infusion *frequently* when Levophed is given.

SPECIAL EQUIPMENT FOR INFUSIONS

Drop Size Reduction

When potent medications are added to intravenous solutions, extreme precautions must be taken to prevent too rapid administration. Manufacturers of parenteral solutions have recognized this need. Abbott Laboratories has developed the Microdrip for precision drop control. Approximately 60 drops from the Microdrip deliver 1 ml.

Baxter Laboratories has developed the M-50 Minimeter for reduction of drop size to 1/50 ml. in parenteral solution infusions (delivers 50 drops/ml.). The Minimeter tubing is inserted through the plug-in and drip tube of a Baxter administration set. (See Fig. 67.)

Don Baxter, Inc. has developed an administration set that delivers approximately 52 drops/ml. Cutter Laboratories has developed a set that delivers approximately 60 drops/ml. (Pediatric sets are described in Chap. 24.)

Bottle Arrangements

A simple intravenous infusion involves a setup such as the one illustrated in Figure 68.

A series hookup is sometimes used to add more fluid or to change fluids while an infusion continues. If the solution in the secondary bottle has a higher specific gravity than the first, most of it will infuse first. If the solutions are of equal specific gravity, they will infuse simultaneously. The secondary container always empties first. (See Fig. 69.)

A parallel hookup may be used to admin-

FIG. 67. Minimeter drop adaptor. (Baxter Laboratories, Morton Grove, Ill.)

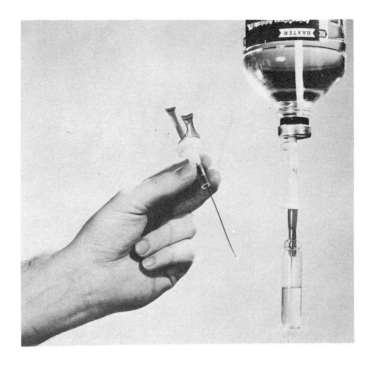

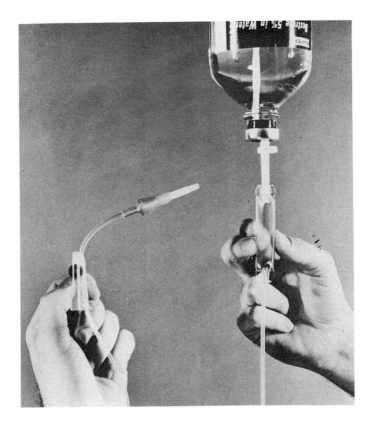

FIG. 68. Simple intravenous infusion set. (Baxter Laboratories, Morton Grove, Ill.)

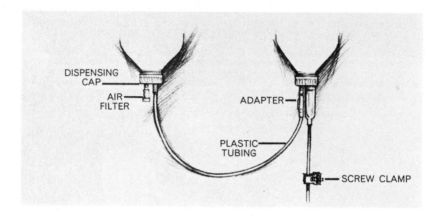

FIG. 69. Bottles connected in series (secondary hookup). (Abbott Laboratories: Parenteral Administration, Secondary Venopak. p. 25. North Chicago, Ill., 1965)

ister two solutions alternately or simultaneously. (See Fig. 70.) This type of hookup is more dangerous than a series hookup. If either of the bottles empty completely and its clamp closure is not complete, air will leak in by way of the empty bottle and form air bubbles in the infusion tubing. The nurse must exercise great care when using a Y-type set; complete clamp closure should be made when there is still a little fluid in

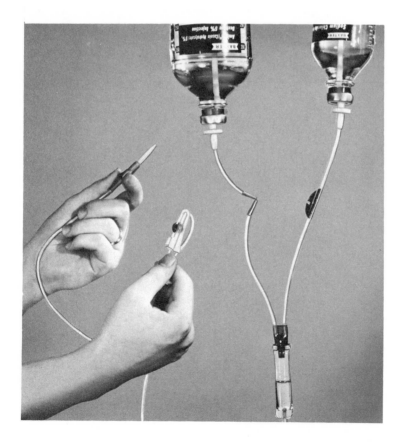

FIG. 70. Bottles connected in parallel (Y-type setup). (Baxter Laboratories, Morton Grove, Ill.)

the bottle. Well meant intentions to administer every drop in the bottle are not warranted.

COMPLICATIONS OF INTRAVENOUS FLUID ADMINISTRATION

Patients receiving parenteral fluids should be observed often to detect the early appearance of complications. The nurse should periodically check the rate of flow, the amount of solution in the bottle, the appearance of the injection site and the patient's general response to the infusion.

Complications sometimes occurring with intravenous infusions include:

- Pyrogenic reactions
- Local infiltration
- Circulatory overload
- Thrombophlebitis
- Air embolism
- Speed shock

Pyrogenic Reactions

The presence of pyrogenic substances in either the infusion solution or the administration setup can induce a febrile reaction. (Pyrogens are foreign proteins capable of producing fever.) Such a reaction is characterized by:

- An abrupt temperature elevation (from 100 to 106° F.) accompanied by severe chills; the reaction usually begins about 30 minutes after the start of the infusion
  - Backache
  - Headache
  - General malaise
  - Nausea and vomiting
- Vascular collapse with hypotension and cyanosis may occur when the reaction is severe

The severity of the reaction depends upon the amount of pyrogens infused, the rate of flow and the patient's susceptibility. Patients having fever or liver disease are more susceptible than others.

If these symptoms occur the nurse should stop the infusion at once, check the vital signs and notify the physician. The solution should be saved so that it can be cultured if necessary.

The wide use of commercially prepared solutions and administration sets has dramatically decreased the number of pyrogenic reactions. It must be remembered, however, that contaminants can enter the solution flask after the seal is broken. A solution should be used immediately once the seal is broken or else be discarded. Any evidence of cloudiness in a normally clear solution is an indication to discard it. Unless the nurse uses the most careful technique, organisms can be introduced when medications are added to the infusion fluid.

Local Infiltration

The dislodging of a needle and the local infiltration of solution into the subcutaneous tissues is not uncommon, especially when a small, thin-walled vein is used and the patient is active. Infiltration is characterized by:

- Edema at the site of injection
- Failure to get blood return into tubing when the bottle is lowered below the needle
- Discomfort in the area of the injection (the degree of discomfort depends on the type of solution)
- Significant decrease in the rate of infusion, or a complete stop in the flow of the fluid

Hypertonic carbohydrate solutions cause local pain. Solutions with a pH varying greatly from that of the body (such as protein hydrolysates, sixth molar sodium lactate, or ammonium chloride) often cause great pain if they infiltrate into the subcutaneous tissues. Potassium solutions are also quite painful when deposited in subcutaneous tissues. Tissue slough may result from the local irritation, especially when norepinephrine (Levophed) is the offending solution.

The infusion should be immediately discontinued when infiltration is apparent.

Circulatory Overload

Overloading the circulatory system with excessive intravenous fluids may cause the following symptoms:

- Increased venous pressure
- Venous distention
- Increased blood pressure
- Coughing
- Shortness of breath, increased respiratory rate
- Pulmonary edema with severe dyspnea and cyanosis

The nurse should be particularly alert for this reaction in patients with cardiac decompensation. If the above symptoms occur, the infusion should be stopped and the physician notified immediately. The patient can be raised to a sitting position to facilitate breathing.

Thrombophlebitis

Thrombophlebitis is a condition associated with clot formation in an inflamed vein. Although some degree of venous irritation accompanies all intravenous infusions, it is usually of significance only in infusions kept going in the same site for more than 12 hours. Thrombophlebitis at an infusion site may be manifested by:

- Pain along the course of the vein
- Redness and edema at the injection site
- If severe, systemic reactions to the infection may occur (tachycardia, fever and general malaise)

Irritating solutions, such as alcohol, can be instrumental in causing thrombophlebitis. Hypertonic solutions are often associated with venous irritation; carbohydrate solutions in excess of 10 per cent almost always produce this reaction. Solutions with an alkaline or acid pH are more frequently associated with thrombophlebitis than are the solutions that approximate body pH.

Once thrombophlebitis is detected, the infusion is stopped. Consideration should be given at this time to obtaining a change in the order for the infusion; otherwise, more veins may be lost. The infusion may be started in another site to allow the traumatized vein to heal. Usually, cold compresses are applied to the thrombophlebitic site. Later, warm moist compresses can be employed to relieve discomfort and promote healing.

Air Embolism

The danger of air embolism is present in *all* intravenous infusions, even though it usually occurs when blood is given under pressure. Small amounts of air are not always harmful, yet as little as 10 ml. may be fatal in some patients.

The nurse should take these measures to prevent the occurrence of air embolism:

1. Discontinue an infusion before the bottle and tubing are completely emptied, otherwise air from the bottle will enter the vein.

2. The needle and any other attachments should be tightly fitted to the infusion tubing to prevent the entrance of air.

3. The first bottle to empty in a Y-type set (parallel hookup) should be completely clamped off; otherwise, air will be drawn into the vein from the empty bottle.

4. Instructions for use of blood pumping apparatus should be carefully followed when blood or, indeed, any fluid is given under pressure. (See section on blood administration.)

5. *Kerr has pointed out that the extremity receiving the infusion should not be elevated above the level of the heart since this results in venous collapse and negative venous pressure.* Negative pressure in the vein receiving the infusion draws in large amounts of air if there are any defects in the apparatus.

6. *The clamp used to regulate fluid flow-rate should be kept at a low level; preferably no higher than the level of the heart,* certainly no higher than 4 to 11 cm. above the heart. Venous pressure normally causes a column of water to rise 4 to 11 cm. above the level of the heart. If the flow regulating clamp is placed above this height, a negative pressure will result in the tubing below. The negative pressure can be great enough to draw in sizable amounts of air if there are any defects in the apparatus.

7. Permitting the infusion tubing to drop below the level of the extremity may help prevent air entering the vein if the infusion

flask empties unobserved. There is nothing wrong with enlisting the patient's help in observing the infusion bottle and notifying the nurse when the infusion is about to run out. A tape can be placed on the side of the infusion flask showing the level at which the patient should buzz the nurse.

The presence of an air embolism is manifested by sudden vascular collapse, with the following symptoms:

- Cyanosis
- Hypotension
- Weak rapid pulse
- Venous pressure rise
- Loss of consciousness

The occurrence of these symptoms in the patient receiving an infusion should lead one to suspect air embolism.

If an air embolism occurs, some physicians place the patient on his left side with his head down, on the theory that this allows the air to rise into the right atrium and permits some blood to empty from the right ventricle into the left side of the heart. Oxygen should be administered.

Speed Shock

Too rapid administration of solutions containing drugs may induce a systemic reaction called *speed shock*. The bloodstream is flooded with the drug and toxic concentrations are supplied to organs such as the heart and brain, which have a rich blood supply. Syncope and shock may occur. Symptoms, of course, vary with the offending drug. The nurse should check the flow rate often and reduce it if untoward symptoms develop.

ADMINISTRATION OF BLOOD, PLASMA AND DEXTRAN

Blood

Whole blood is preserved with a solution of sodium citrate, citric acid and glucose. Sodium citrate acts as an anticoagulant by combining with ionized calcium and thus interrupting the clotting mechanism. Glucose prolongs the viability of red blood cells.

Blood preserved with acid-citrate-dextrose (A.C.D.) solution can be kept safe for use up to 21 days after collection from the donor, if stored at 4° C. (39° F.).

Blood Transfusion Reactions

Whole blood transfusions are indicated in the presence of a significantly decreased blood volume. Blood replacement therapy is often lifesaving. However, without careful attention to its hazards, it may also be lethal. Because the nurse shares a large responsibility in assuring safe blood administration, she should be familiar with complications associated with its use.

Stored Blood and Potassium Excess. Continual destruction of red blood cells occurs when blood is stored; at the end of 21 days only 70 to 80 per cent of the original number of cells remain. The longer the blood ages, the higher its plasma potassium level becomes. Not only is potassium released from the destroyed red blood cells, but there is also a transfer of potassium from the intact cells into the surrounding plasma.

Aged blood should not be given to patients with oliguria or anuria, since there is great danger of causing potassium excess. Potassium excess may be recognized by the following symptoms:

- Gastrointestinal hyperactivity (nausea, intestinal colic and diarrhea)
- Vague muscular weakness, first in the extremities, later extending to the trunk
- Paresthesia of hands, feet, tongue and face
- Flaccid paralysis (involving respiratory muscles last)
- Apprehension
- Slowed pulse rate (may also be irregular)
- Cardiac arrest and death when plasma potassium level reaches 10 to 15 mEq./L. (due to marked dilation and flaccidity of the heart)

According to LeVeen, the high incidence of cardiac arrest during surgery is correlated with the rapid infusion of large quantities of aged blood.

Citrated Blood and Calcium Deficit. Calcium deficit can be caused by the rapid administration of large volumes of citrated blood. It should be recalled that A.C.D. solution contains citrate in excess of that needed to combine with the calcium in the blood collected. The binding of blood calcium will be the more serious if a partial flask of blood is withdrawn from the donor. If citrate ions (furnished by sodium citrate) are infused too rapidly, the liver is unable to remove them and they combine with ionized calcium in the bloodstream. The reduced level of circulating calcium ions may cause these signs of neuromuscular irritability:

- Tingling of the fingers and the circumoral region
- Muscular cramps
- Hyperactive muscular reflexes
- Carpopedal attitude of hands
- Convulsions
- Laryngeal stridor
- Cardiac arrest

Calcium deficit due to excessive administration of citrated blood is more prone to occur in patients with liver damage. Blood should be given slowly to such patients to eliminate this hazard.

Circulatory Overload. Circulatory overload is discussed earlier in the chapter as a possible complication of all intravenous infusions. It is particularly likely to occur in massive blood replacement for hypovolemia or when blood is given to a patient with normal blood volume. In addition to inducing pulmonary edema, the increased blood volume may cause hemorrhage into the lungs and the gastrointestinal tract.

To guard against the occurrence of circulatory overload, many physicians monitor venous pressure during the rapid replacement of large volumes of blood. (The procedure is discussed in the last section of the chapter.) Aged patients and patients with cardiac damage should be closely observed for circulatory overload even when small volumes of blood are given. Venous pressure monitoring is frequently used to protect such patients from overload.

Administration of packed red blood cells, obtained by centrifuging whole blood and drawing off the plasma, is sometimes necessary when a patient with congestive heart failure or fluid volume excess requires blood. Packed cells are administered in a minimal amount of fluid and are thus less prone to overload the circulatory system.

Allergic Reactions. Prospective donors with known food and drug allergies are rejected in order to decrease the incidence of allergic reactions following blood transfusions. Blood from a donor with hypersensitivities may cause urticaria, asthma, or anaphylactic shock. Appearance of any of these conditions is an indication to immediately stop the transfusion. Antihistamines, such as Benadryl or Pyribenzamine, usually relieve mild symptoms. Severe reactions require treatment with an injection of 0.5 ml. of 1:1000 solution of Adrenalin, or with steroids.

Serum Homologous Hepatitis. No methods have been developed to eliminate the hazard of transmitting serum homologous hepatitis by means of blood transfusions. Persons known to have had hepatitis are not allowed to give blood. Nonetheless, not all patients with hepatitis have had the condition diagnosed; therefore, the danger always exists. One person out of every several hundred has had serum hepatitis. Before blood bank blood is given out for use, its bilirubin content can be checked; if elevated, the blood is discarded. Elevated bilirubin content may be indicative of liver disease, which could have been caused by serum homologous hepatitis. The incubation period for serum hepatitis is from 2 to 6 months.

Bacterial Contamination. Blood should be inspected before use for signs of bacterial growth, such as discoloration or gas bubbles. If these are present the blood should be discarded. If blood used for transfusion is grossly contaminated, the recipient usually develops symptoms of shock. Treatment may consist of vasopressors, steroids and antibiotics.

Hypothermia. When large volumes of cold blood are rapidly transfused the patient may develop hypothermia and cardiac arrest. To prevent this hazard, blood should be warmed by means of a long coil of tubing immersed in warm water (see Fig. 67).

Pyrogenic Reactions. A pyrogenic reaction has been described earlier in the chapter as a possible complication of all intravenous infusions. It is sometimes confused with an incompatible blood reaction. A pyrogenic reaction to blood tends to occur toward the end of a transfusion or even after it is completed. The most predominant symptoms are fever and chills; back pain, characteristic of incompatible blood reaction, is often absent. The onset of malarial chills can also be confused with a pyrogenic reaction but this, of course, is more of a problem in tropical and semitropical climates.

Incompatible Blood Reaction. The most dreaded reaction to blood transfusion is that caused by incompatible blood, most often caused by the careless administration of the wrong blood. A transfusion of incompatible blood causes hemolysis of the red blood cells with the liberation of hemoglobin into the plasma. Symptoms of a hemolytic reaction may occur within the first 10 to 15 minutes of the transfusion and include:

- Lumbar pain
- Feeling of coldness
- Feeling of fullness in the head
- Feeling of constriction in the chest
- Urge to defecate or urinate
- Fever and severe shaking chills
- Later, hemoglobinuria and acute renal tubular necrosis may occur

Because an acute hemolytic reaction becomes evident during transfusion of the first 50 to 100 ml. of blood, it is highly desirable that the patient be carefully observed during this part of the infusion. If the transfusion is stopped early, acute renal tubular necrosis and death rarely occur; if more than several hundred ml. are infused, renal shutdown and death are common.

The blood transfusion should be discontinued immediately when a hemolytic reaction is evident. The blood bottle and set should be refrigerated so that further compatibility tests may be made. All urine should be saved and observed for discoloration; urine is sent to the laboratory for evaluation of hemoglobin content. The onset of a hemolytic reaction may be delayed when factors of less moment than the ABO system are involved. For example, a patient who has received multiple transfusions in the past may have become sensitized to Rh

or to the minor factors. His hemolytic reaction might have a delayed onset.

Hemolytic reactions are more prone to occur in patients who have had past transfusions. They tend to be proportionate to the number of such transfusions, regardless of when given.

Treatment of an incompatible blood reaction usually consists of rapid administration of dilute fluids to promote diuresis. Alkaline fluids, such as sixth molar sodium lactate, increase the solubility of hemoglobin and aid in its excretion. An osmotic diuretic may be given intravenously; further treatment is dependent upon the amount of renal damage present. It is impossible to overstress the need to check and recheck all labels for both donor and patient. Errors in relation to labeling still constitute a frequent cause of reaction.

Safe Blood Administration

To help assure that blood transfusions be as safe as possible the nurse should keep the following points in mind:

1. Be aware of the complications associated with blood administration; keep their descriptions in mind while observing the patient.

2. *Give the right blood to the right patient.*

A. Read the labels identifying the blood and check them carefully with the patient's full name. The patient's name can be obtained from the bed card and preferably from the wrist identification band.

B. The patient should be called by name and his response observed; this practice in itself is not foolproof because some patients respond to any name!

C. Location of the patient should not be relied upon as the sole means of identification; patients are moved frequently in most hospitals.

D. Particular precautions are necessary when the patient has a common name; many errors have been made by not checking further than the last name and first initial. This is not to imply that two patients with the same uncommon name cannot be confused; it *has* happened.

3. Blood sent to nursing divisions should be stored in the refrigerator unless it is to be used immediately. Rapid deterioration of red blood cells occurs after blood has been exposed to room temperature for more than two hours. The best storage temperature is 4° C.; care should be taken to prevent freezing the blood because this renders it unsuitable for use.

4. The patient's temperature should be taken before the transfusion to serve as a baseline for later temperature comparisons. An elevated temperature during a transfusion may indicate either a pyrogenic or an incompatible blood reaction. For this reason the temperature should be checked hourly during the blood administration and for several hours afterwards.

5. The blood should be inspected before use for discoloration or gas bubbles; if present, the blood is probably contaminated and must be discarded.

6. Blood should always be given through a filter to remove the particulate matter formed during storage. Care should be taken to keep the filter unclogged. A clean filter should be used with each unit of blood.

7. Do not start whole blood with 5 per cent dextrose in water, or hook whole blood in series or in parallel with it. Even though 5 per cent dextrose in water is an isotonic solution, it contains no electrolytes and can cause hemolysis of red blood cells when allowed to mix with blood. (This reaction does not occur when 5 per cent dextrose in water is given into the bloodstream, because it is rapidly diluted.) Isotonic saline is quite compatible with blood and is usually used to start blood.

8. Do not use a calcium-containing solu-

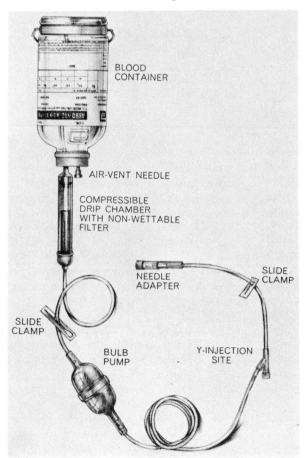

BLOOD CONTAINER

AIR-VENT NEEDLE

COMPRESSIBLE DRIP CHAMBER WITH NON-WETTABLE FILTER

NEEDLE ADAPTER

SLIDE CLAMP

SLIDE CLAMP

BULB PUMP

Y-INJECTION SITE

FIG. 71. Blood pump administration set. (Abbott Laboratories: The Use of Blood. p. 59. North Chicago, Ill., 1965)

FIG. 72. Plastic drip chamber used to pump blood. (Baxter Laboratories, Morton Grove, Ill.)

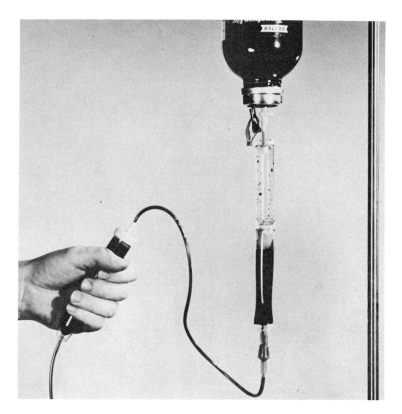

tion to start citrated blood or hook it in series or parallel with citrated blood. Calcium ions may cause the blood to clot and clog the infusion apparatus.

9. If it is necessary to warm blood before administration, a heat exchange coil can be used, as described earlier. Hot water should never be used to heat blood because excess heat destroys red blood cells.

10. The first 50 ml. of blood should be delivered slowly over a 30-minute period. The patient should be continually observed during the first 15 minutes and frequently thereafter. If no adverse reactions occur, the rate may be increased as ordered.

11. Unless the patient has severe hypovolemia, blood transfusions should be given no faster than 500 ml. every 30 minutes. The presence of factors such as cardiac, renal, or liver damage may necessitate much slower rates. A patient with normal blood volume should receive blood at a slow rate to prevent circulatory overload.

12. Blood under pressure must be administered with great caution.

The fluid level in the bottle should be closely watched so that air is not accidentally pumped into the vein. Figure 71 shows a pump set used with a glass container for rapid administration of blood. The bulb is compressed to pump in blood; when released, the flow rate returns to its original speed.

Another set makes use of a specially designed plastic drip chamber to pump blood. (See Fig. 72.) The drip chamber contains a floating ball valve that seals intake to the bottle when the chamber is filled with blood. The blood is then pumped downward through the set; when the chamber is released it refills with blood. This set cannot pump air from the bottle. Normal gravity flow can be resumed at any time.

Because plastic blood containers do not contain air, the danger of air embolism originating from the blood container is

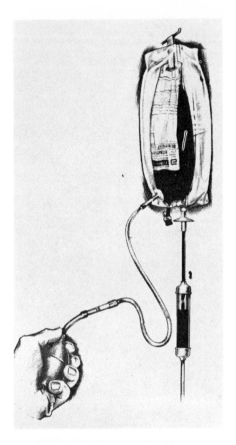

FIG. 73. Plastic blood bag with pressure cuff. (Abbott Laboratories: The Use of Blood. p. 60. North Chicago, Ill., 1965)

eliminated. Blood can be given under pressure by squeezing the sides of the bag or by applying the special pressure unit designed for this program. (See Fig. 73.)

Plasma

Plasma is the liquid component left after blood has been centrifuged and the red blood cells removed. It is prepared commercially from citrated whole blood and dispensed as liquid, frozen, or dried plasma.

Storage of plasma is much less of a problem than blood storage. Liquid plasma stored between 15 to 30° C. (59 to 86° F.) can be used for 2 years after date of manufacture. Frozen plasma is stored at −18° C. and can be used for 5 years after date of manufacture. Dried plasma is stored at room temperature and has a 5-year expiration date.

Because plasma is readily available, it is often used in emergency situations to restore blood volume until whole blood can be obtained. Plasma does not require typing and cross-matching (with the exception of fresh frozen liquid plasma).

Serum homologous hepatitis is more commonly spread by means of plasma than by means of blood. Pooled plasma is prepared from the blood of at least 8 donors, and thus the likelihood of contamination with the virus is considerably greater. (Storage of liquid plasma at a room temperature of 88 to 90° F. for 6 months is helpful in reducing the spread of serum homologous hepatitis.)

Dextran

Dextran is a polymer of glucose having a large molecular weight. It is often used for emergency treatment of hypovolemic shock.

When infused into the bloodstream, the large dextran molecules increase intravascular osmotic pressure and draw in interstitial fluid to restore blood volume. When blood loss is not severe, dextran may serve as the total replacement fluid. If blood loss is severe, dextran should be followed by whole blood when available.

Dextran does not require special storage. Because it is prepared synthetically rather than from blood, there is no danger of serum homologous hepatitis.

Dextran 6 per cent is available in isotonic saline or in 5 per cent dextrose in water. The latter is used for patients requiring a low sodium intake. Dextran is for intravenous use only. The usual dose is 500 ml. More than this amount can be given but is not recommended, since dextran is not broken down rapidly and will expand the intravascular space for many days. By so doing, it limits the rapidity of red blood cell replacement.

Reactions to dextran are uncommon, but may include:

- Mild urticaria
- Chest tightness
- Wheezing
- Hypotension

If any of these symptoms appear, the infusion should be stopped; Adrenalin may be necessary to control severe symptoms.

Particular caution is necessary when dextran is administered to patients with heart disease or renal shutdown, because of the danger of congestive heart failure and pulmonary edema.

The physician should indicate the desired flow rate. The first few milliliters should be given slowly and the patient's reaction observed. If no reaction is evident, the definitive rate can be attained. Dextran can be given at a rate of 20 to 40 ml./minute (at this rate it would take from 15 to 30 minutes to infuse 500 ml.).

If more than 1,000 ml. of dextran is given, a prolonged bleeding time may occur.

VENOUS PRESSURE MEASUREMENT DURING INFUSIONS

Venous pressure is sometimes measured frequently during rapid intravenous fluid replacement in hypovolemic patients to warn of impending circulatory overload. It is the best single sign for determining the adequacy of fluid replacement. The nurse may be called upon to measure and record venous pressure, and therefore should have an understanding of the basic principles involved.

Venous pressure can be measured in peripheral veins (as in the arm) or in cannulated central veins in either the inferior or superior caval systems. Central venous pressure measurement is the more accurate of the two, but the procedure is more complicated. Peripheral venous pressure reflects central pressure fairly well if the limb in which it is measured is not acutely compressed between the manometer and the heart.

When venous blood return into the right atrium is in physiologic balance with blood flow from the right atrium, venous pressure is 4 to 11 cm. of water (40 to 110 mm. of water). A decreased blood volume causes a decreased venous blood return into the right atrium and thus a decreased venous pressure. An increased blood volume causes an increased venous blood return and thus an elevated venous pressure.

In an individual with normal cardiac function:

- A normal venous pressure indicates an adequate circulating blood volume.
- A decreased venous pressure indicates an inadequate circulating blood volume and the need to increase fluid flow rate
- An increased venous pressure indicates an excessive circulating blood volume and the need to decrease fluid flow rate

In an individual with cardiac disease and acute failure, increased venous pressure is present because there is an inadequate blood flow out of the right atrium, due to the ineffective pumping action of the heart. Venous pressure measurement is particularly helpful in guiding the treatment of patients with cardiac damage and blood volume changes, such as in the postoperative management of open-heart surgical patients.

Equipment used to measure venous pressure during intravenous fluid administration is simple. A glass water manometer may be used in conjunction with a three-way stopcock to connect to the needle or catheter and to the infusion setup.

Commercial sets have been devised to further simplify the procedure of venous pressure measurement. One such set is the Bardic Anpro Venometer. This set consists of a water manometer graduated, in units of 10 mm., from −30 to 300 mm. (Negative readings are found only in profound shock.) A T-connector attaches the manometer to the infusion setup and to the needle or catheter in the vein. (See Fig. 74.) The set is a one-patient item. It is easy to use and can be set up in minimal time. The manufacturer's directions for its use are as follows:

1. Attach Venometer to I.V. stand.
2. Connect setup (normal saline or dextrose and water) to side arm of "T" connector at base of manometer.
3. Fill manometer tube to 250 mark.
4. Place "O" mark of manometer at same level as patient's atrium by sliding the manometer up or down the I.V. pole.
5. Remove cap from end of connecting tube and allow fluid in manometer tube to displace air in connecting tube. Proceed with normal venipuncture using I.V. catheter or needle. Attach connecting tube from man-

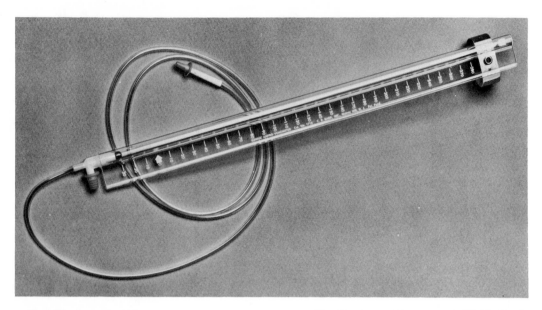

FIG. 74. Apparatus for venous pressure measurement. (Bardic Anpro Venometer.) (C. R. Bard, Inc., Murray Hill, New Jersey)

ometer. The level of solution in the manometer tube will continue to fall until the hydrostatic pressure in the manometer is equalized with the venous pressure. The venous pressure may then be read directly from the scale on the manometer in millimeters of solution.

6. FLOW RATE: A rate of 5 drops per minute will provide sufficient flow for constant venous pressure monitoring. A more rapid flow rate will necessitate compensating for the pressure increase in the system. If a higher flow rate is desired, the following steps should be carried out:

   a. Set the flow of the infusion at the desired rate and note the level of the fluid in the manometer.

   b. Clamp the infusion administration set and note the level to which the fluid in the manometer falls. This is the actual venous pressure.

   c. Reset the flow of the infusion to the desired rate.

   d. Move the manometer up the I.V. pole until the level of the fluid in the manometer is at the level of the actual venous pressure as just determined. As long as the rate of infusion remains constant, the level of the fluid in the manometer will accurately represent the venous pressure. The level will rise or fall with changes in the venous pressure.

Chapter 15

Fluid Balance in the Surgical Patient

THE BODY'S RESPONSE TO SURGICAL TRAUMA

Although a surgical procedure may be lifesaving, the body responds to it as trauma. Postoperative responses bear a direct relationship to nursing care.

Endocrine Response (Stress Reaction)

Period of Fluid Retention and Catabolism. The stress reaction described by Selye, representing a response to surgical trauma, is present for the first 2 to 5 days. The intensity of the changes depends on the severity and duration of the trauma. Thus, a pelvic evisceration produces a more severe reaction than a simple herniorrhaphy. Postoperative apprehension and pain enhance the stress reaction. Extreme preoperative apprehension can initiate the stress reaction *before* surgery.

The endocrine responses may be briefly outlined at follows:

1. Increased ACTH (adrenocorticotropic hormone secretion from the anterior pituitary)

2. Increased mineralcorticoid and glucocorticoid secretion from the adrenal cortex (in response to stimulation by ACTH)

  A. Mineralcorticoids (desoxycorticosterone [DOCA] and aldosterone) cause:
    a. Na+ retention
    b. Cl− retention
    c. K+ excretion

  B. Glucocorticoids (mainly hydrocortisone) cause:
    a. Na+ retention
    b. Cl− retention
    c. K+ excretion
    d. Catabolism
      (1) protein breakdown
      (2) gluconeogenesis and elevated blood sugar
    e. Fat mobilization
    f. Drop in eosinophil count

3. Increased ADH (antidiuretic hormone) secretion from posterior pituitary causes decreased urinary output

4. Vasopressor substances (epinephrine and norepinephrine) are secreted from the adrenal medulla to help maintain blood pressure; this response is stimulated by fear, pain, hypoxia and hemorrhage

The body's response to stress appears purposeful. For example, sodium retention, chloride retention, potassium loss and increased ADH secretion help to maintain blood volume. Sodium and chloride retention cause water retention; cellular potassium loss releases cellular water into the extracellular space, and ADH secretion causes decreased fluid excretion by way of the kidneys. Glucocorticoids cause protein breakdown and make amino acids available for healing at the site of trauma. Glucocorticoids also cause conversion of protein and fat to glucose (gluconeogenesis), creating a ready supply of glucose for use during the stress period. (The elevated blood sugar may be mistaken for diabetes mellitus.)

Laboratory findings during the stress period include a reduced eosinophil count and an elevated level of serum 17-hydroxycorticosteroid hormones; both indicate increased adrenal activity.

The changes described above are *normal* responses to trauma and do not require corrective measures; in fact, "correction" can be harmful. For example, a high water intake may erroneously be thought necessary to increase the low urinary output of the first few postoperative days. If fluids are forced, the output remains low due to the water-retaining effects of increased ADH secretion and sodium retention; the extra water is retained by the kidneys, and symptoms of water excess may appear. The changes evoked by stress must be understood so that their effects are not misinterpreted. Although aware of the effects of stress, the physician should, nevertheless, institute a careful investigation if the output seems unduly low, particularly if the low output is prolonged.

Periods of Diuresis and Anabolism. After the second to fifth postoperative days, adrenal activity is decreased and a mild water and sodium diuresis occurs. The body also begins to retain potassium. Following an uncomplicated abdominal operation, it is not uncommon for a normal adult male to lose from 4 to 9 lbs. during the first postoperative days.

Anabolism, the building up of body protein, usually begins by the seventh to the tenth postoperative day. The renal excretion of nitrogen no longer exceeds the nitrogen intake from protein foods. The patient begins to gain weight, provided oral intake is adequate.

Tissue Injury

The operative site is edematous for the first few days after surgery. The fluid closely resembles plasma; its volume is roughly proportionate to the amount of tissue trauma. While the amount of fluid lost in edema is not in itself significant, it may enhance the extracellular fluid volume deficit created by peritonitis, hemorrhage, or other complications. The edema fluid is reabsorbed and excreted during the diuretic phase of the stress reaction.

Immobilization

Usually a patient remains in bed during the first postoperative days. Immobilization favors increased renal nitrogen and calcium excretion and negative nitrogen balance. Most surgical patients are not immobilized long enough to significantly affect metabolism. (For nursing implications of prolonged immobilization, see Chap. 10.)

Starvation Effect

Most patients eat inadequately, or not at all, during the first few postoperative days; thus, a starvation effect is induced. Accompanying starvation is a daily weight loss of about one-half lb., reflecting a decrease in lean and fatty tissue mass. Renal nitrogen excretion is increased as a result of lean tissue catabolism.

Starvation favors both water and sodium retention, especially the former. This retention often masks actual tissue loss during the early phase of a drastically reduced caloric diet, a fact well-known to low-calorie dieters. The weight loss following surgery is generally constant, however, as revealed by accurate weighing procedures and recording the findings on a weight chart.

PREVENTION OF POSTOPERATIVE COMPLICATIONS BY CAREFUL PREOPERATIVE PREPARATION

Nutrition

A patient in good nutritional condition preoperatively withstands postoperative negative nitrogen balance and early starvation without serious effects. On the other hand, the nutritionally depleted patient goes to surgery under a serious handicap. He has a poor tolerance for operative stress. Increased susceptibility to infection results from the diminished ability to form antibodies, and from the superficial atrophy in the mucous membrane linings of the respiratory and gastrointestinal tracts that often accompanies malnutrition. Hypoproteinemia follows prolonged negative nitrogen balance and increases susceptibility to shock from hemorrhage. The body gives top priority for nutrients to the incision site and good wound healing is seen in some nutritionally depleted patients; in others, wounds fail to heal. Diminished supplies of protein and vitamin C retard wound healing.

When surgery is elective, the patient with a real or potential fluid balance problem is hospitalized early for preoperative evaluation and buildup. Weisberg advocates baseline electrolyte studies for all infants, adults over 50, and any patient subjected to an exploratory laparotomy or gastrointestinal surgery. During this time the patient is given a well-balanced diet to provide the body with substances to make its own repairs and to help the patient weather the impending surgical trauma. Specific oral or parenteral medications may be deemed necessary after evaluation of clinical and laboratory findings.

A primary nursing responsibility in the preoperative period is getting the patient to eat. This is sometimes difficult, especially when the patient's illness is such that his appetite is diminished. Fear and depression, common before surgery, may also deter the patient's desire to eat. (For nursing measures to promote eating see Chap. 10.) The benefits of activity are sometimes overlooked in the preoperative period; activity stimulates appetite and sleep, as well as general well-being.

Another important nursing responsibility is reporting inadequate oral intake, as when all efforts fail to promote eating. Nasogastric tube or parenteral feedings may then have to be given. (For nursing responsibilities in administering tube feedings see Chap. 10.) Anorexia accompanies malnutrition; correction of malnutrition with tube feedings often restores the patient's appetite. (For nursing responsibilities in parenteral nutrition see Chap. 14.)

Emotional Response

The patient's attitudes toward surgery may significantly affect his postoperative course. Some fear of surgery is natural; undue fear and apprehension, however, may initiate the adrenocortical stress reaction and thus produce changes in electrolyte metabolism. Most nurses can recall more than one postponement of surgery because the patient was not emotionally ready for the experience.

The nurse has an ideal opportunity to observe the patient's behavior and to detect signs of apprehension or severe depression that may be missed by the busy surgeon. Patients display fear in different ways: some refuse to discuss the oncoming surgical event, others can talk of nothing else. Significant behavior observations should be discussed with the physician.

No nursing function is more important than providing emotional support for the surgical patient. The most effective support comes from persons who have a sincere interest in the patient's welfare and a respect for his feelings. Thoughtful explanations before new procedures and experiences do much to relieve fear. Inspiring confidence by performing all nursing functions with skill and confidence is also a form of emotional support. Willingness to listen when the patient feels like talking helps; many patients find it easier to verbalize fears to an understanding nurse than to a relative or close friend. This is understandable when one considers the patient's desire to spare his loved ones additional worry. Some patients regard fear of surgery as a weakness and prefer to hide such fears from those close to them.

Body Weight

All surgical patients should have an admission weight recorded on the chart. The preoperative body weight serves as a baseline for comparison with subsequent body weight measurements. Obtaining the weight of an ambulatory patient presents no problem; the patient confined to bed can be weighed on a bed scale. (For procedures in weighing the patient see Chap. 8.)

Intake-Output

Patients requiring preoperative electrolyte studies are placed on the nursing intake-output measurement list. An accurate record of fluids gained and lost from the body is of great importance in detecting inadequate intake and abnormalities in renal function and fluid balance. (For nursing responsibilities in measurement of fluid intake and output see Chap. 8.) The nurse should be alert for inadequate urinary output in all preoperative patients even when intake-output measurement is not required. (For factors influencing urine volume see Chap. 8.)

Medications

Steroids. Some physicians routinely ask all surgical patients if they have recently taken cortisone or any other steroid preparation. Steroid preparations are widely used for a variety of illnesses for which surgical therapy may be needed. When a patient is on steroid therapy there is less need for adrenal secretion and the glands tend to atrophy from disuse. After withdrawal of steroid therapy, the adrenals gradually resume their function. However, if steroids are suddenly withdrawn and the patient is subjected to massive trauma, such as a major surgical procedure, the atrophied adrenals may be unable to respond to the stress signal. *Adrenocortical failure* may follow cessation of adrenocortical substitution therapy. Symptoms include fall in blood pressure, a pronounced elevation in body temperature, rapid pulse, disorientation and, eventually, coma. The reaction usually occurs within the first 24 hours and is treated with intravenous cortisone. Patients who have been on steroids preoperatively are given extra cortisone during surgery to prevent this complication.

Today, due to medical specialization, one patient may have two or three physicians prescribing medications at the same time. The fact that the patient may have received steroids recently is often overlooked. Many patients do not know what medicines they have taken; if this is the case, the nurse can ask for a description of the medication and why it was given. Frequently one can obtain information in this way, but when in doubt, the physician in charge can check with those who prescribed medications for the patient.

Drug Allergies or Idiosyncrasies. The physician or the nurse should always ask the prospective surgical patient if he knows of any drug allergies, sensitivities, or idiosyncrasies he may have. If the patient does not understand the question, typical symptoms of sensitivity, such as urticaria, asthma and the like, can be mentioned. One can also ask the patient if a physician has ever cautioned him to avoid a specific medication because of an unusual reaction to it. In questioning the newly admitted patient, the nurse will do well to remember that he is often upset and may have difficulty remembering.

Some patients assume that their physician remembers any drug allergies from office interviews prior to hospital admission, and unless specifically asked, they may not volunteer information. Allergies must be discovered before the patient is sedated or anesthetized; it is too late to ask when he is unconscious or semi-reactive after surgery, since most medications are ordered in the immediate postoperative period. Failure to ascertain the presence of allergies may be disastrous. The most dreaded allergic reaction is anaphylactic shock; other less dangerous reactions include skin eruptions and asthma.

Idiosyncratic reactions to drugs deserve consideration. For example, a narcotic may cause more depression in one patient than in another of equal weight and age. A dose creating the desired effect in one patient may overwhelm the patient who is unusually reactive to the drug. The aged are particularly sensitive to narcotics and should be given much smaller doses than younger adults; this is particularly important in aged surgical patients.

Pulmonary Ventilation

Inadequate pulmonary ventilation is common after operation and can lead to respiratory acidosis (primary carbonic acid excess) or atelectasis. During the preoperative period, the nurse should teach the patient how to deep-breathe and cough postoperatively. She should explain that these activities are excellent preventives against lung complications. Once the patient is properly motivated and knows what is expected of him, the nurse will have greater success in carrying through the common postoperative order to "have the patient cough and deep-breathe every hour."

Intermittent positive pressure treatments are sometimes used preoperatively and postoperatively to improve pulmonary ventilation in patients with chronic pulmonary conditions, such as emphysema.

Chronic Illnesses. Certain chronic illnesses greatly increase the hazard of postoperative water and electrolyte imbalances. Such illnesses include:

- Diabetes mellitus
- Addison's disease
- Renal disorders
- Cardiac disorders
- Hepatic disorders
- Thyroid disorders
- Pulmonary disorders

The presence of any of the above conditions requires careful preoperative preparation so that postoperative disturbances can be kept at a minimum.

The physician does a careful history and physical examination before surgery to detect pre-existing illness. However, the patient may forget an important item and mention it later to the nurse. Such information should be brought immediately to the physician's attention. The nurse should also be alert for symptoms of chronic illness.

Special Considerations in the Aged

Conscientious preoperative preparation often means the difference between success or failure of surgery in the aged. The decreased body homeostatic adaptability of these patients predisposes to difficulty when they are exposed to stress.

These facts apply to the aged:

1. Malnutrition is more common in the aged than in younger adults.

2. Thirst is not as accurate a gauge of fluid needs as it is in younger adults.

3. Moderate fluid volume deficit and decreased circulating blood volume are not uncommon in the aged *before* operation.

4. Changes in pH are less well tolerated in the aged. Anemia, with its decreased hemoglobin, depletes one of the major buffer systems; emphysema is not uncommon in the aged and disrupts pH control.

5. Hypoxia is not well tolerated in the aged; for this reason local or spinal anesthetics are preferable to inhalation anesthetics.

6. Hypotension is poorly tolerated by the aged, and unless correctly quickly, is frequently complicated by renal damage, stroke or myocardial infarct. (Shock becomes irreversible earlier than in younger patients.)

Preoperative dietary management is particularly important; optimal nutrition helps the aged patient withstand the electrolyte deficits and pH changes occurring after surgery. Electrolyte solutions may be given intravenously prior to surgery to supplement dietary intake; deficits of potassium and sodium especially should be corrected.

Small, frequent blood transfusions are sometimes used to restore blood volume and to correct anemia. Ambulation and activity improve appetite and sleep. An accurate account should be kept of the patient's urinary output. Renal function tests and an ECG may be indicated. A conservative dose of preoperative medication is used to help avoid respiratory depression and hypoxia.

Immediate Preoperative Preparation

Enemas. A cleansing enema may be ordered either the night before or on the morning of abdominal or rectal surgery. Occasionally one still sees an order for "tap water enemas until returned clear"; fortunately, it is seen less and less. As many as 5 to 10 enemas may be needed before the solution is "returned clear"; large amounts of sodium and potassium are lost with the enema return, thus depleting the patient of valuable electrolytes when he can ill afford to lose them. Most surgeons feel that 1 cleansing enema, properly given, suffices.

Withholding Fluids. A few years ago one commonly saw the order "nothing by mouth after midnight" for all surgical patients, whether the patient was scheduled for surgery at 7:00 A.M. or 12:00 NOON. Recently emphasis has been placed on allowing fluids up to 6 hours before surgery. The goal, of course, is to allow the patient to take needed fluids as long as possible and still prevent the complications resulting from a full stomach during anesthesia.

Vital Signs. All vital signs should be checked before the preoperative medication is given. An elevated temperature should be reported immediately; postponement of surgery may be necessary until the source of the fever is disclosed. An unusually rapid pulse and respiratory rate may indicate undue apprehension and should be reported.

A more accurate appraisal of the patient's blood pressure may be obtained by checking it both the evening before and the morning of surgery, and after sedative medication has been given. For example, a blood pressure of 140/80 would be of no significance for the normotensive patient, but it might indicate approaching shock for the patient whose blood pressure prior to sedation was 180/100. Postoperative blood pressure findings must be compared with the patient's usual blood pressure if they are to be evaluated correctly. For example, some patients normally have a systolic pressure of 90; unless this reading is established as the patient's norm, it may be inaccurately interpreted as a symptom of early shock.

POSTOPERATIVE GAINS AND LOSSES OF WATER, ELECTROLYTES AND OTHER NUTRIENTS

Need for Intake-Output Measurement

Surgery often brings into play abnormal routes of fluid loss, such as gastric or intestinal suction, vomiting, or drainage from an ileostomy or colostomy. Failure to measure the amounts and kinds of fluids lost makes adequate replacement therapy almost impossible. Without an accurate account of gains and losses, the early discovery of water and electrolyte imbalances is unlikely. It behooves the nurse, then, to automatically place postoperative patients on the intake-output list and to make a conscientious effort to keep the intake-output record accurate.

The 8-hour and 24-hour totals are significant in assessing fluid balance in general; it is equally important to know the types and amounts of fluids making up the total. For example, to state that a patient has lost a total of 3,000 ml. of fluid in 24 hours is not as revealing as an itemized analysis of the loss:

- 1,000 ml. urine
- 800 ml. gastric suction
- 200 ml. bile from T-tube drainage
- 1,000 ml. estimated perspiration

The aim of fluid replacement therapy is to restore to the body the quantities of water and electrolytes lost. Special parenteral fluids are available to replace losses of gastric juice, intestinal juice, bile, and others.

(Chapter 8 tabulates the electrolyte content of most of the body fluids of concern in postoperative care plus imbalances to be expected with large losses of each fluid. The reader is encouraged to review this section because of its importance for the formulation of intelligent postoperative care.)

Urinary Output

In health, the daily urinary output is roughly equal to the volume of liquids taken into the body. However, during the postoperative stress reaction the urine volume may tend to be low regardless of the amount of fluids taken in. Following a major surgical procedure, the 24-hour urine output may be only 600 to 700 ml. for the first few postoperative days. Unless the stress reaction's influence on urinary output is understood, the low volume and high specific gravity may be confused with fluid volume deficit. As mentioned earlier, attempts to increase urine volume by forcing fluids fail; forced fluids are retained by the body and may cause several complications. Among these are (1) water excess (sodium deficit), if the extra fluids were primarily 5 per cent glucose in water; (2) pulmonary edema; and (3) increased edema at the operative site. In intestinal surgery, the increased edema may be sufficient to cause partial or complete obstruction.

Fluid Intake

The usual daily fluid intake during the stress reaction should be about 1,500 to 2,000 ml., varying with the patient's need for replacement.

Parenteral Fluids. Nausea, gastrointestinal surgery and gastrointestinal suction contraindicate oral fluids. A parenteral route, almost always the intravenous, is then relied on to furnish the body with needed substances.

As little as 100 Gm. of carbohydrate given daily can reduce protein breakdown (catabolism) by as much as one-half. This amount is contained in 2 L. of 5 per cent glucose solution or 1 L. of a 10 per cent glucose solution.

Five per cent glucose in water or in hypotonic (quarter strength isotonic) saline is often given intravenously during the first few postoperative days. The physician may choose saline in instances in which sodium has been lost incident to the surgical procedure, and in which there is no indication of sodium retention.

After adequate renal function has been established, potassium is given daily to prevent potassium deficit, if the patient is not yet eating. Forty mEq. per day suffices unless large volumes of gastrointestinal fluids, rich in potassium, are being lost by vomiting, suction, or fistulas. (Nursing responsibilities in administering potassium solutions are discussed in Chap. 14.) As a general rule, a solution containing 40 mEq. of potassium per L. may be given at a rate of 500 ml. per hour to normal adults; this is equivalent to 20 mEq. of potassium (suitably diluted) per hour. In older patients, it is best to give potassium solutions at a slower rate, preferably no faster than 20 to 30 mEq. over a 3 to 4 hour period.

After the fluid retention of stress has subsided, a larger amount of fluid is given. If oral intake is still prohibited, an attempt must be made to supply body needs solely with parenteral fluids. Magnesium replacement may be necessary when parenteral fluid administration is prolonged. Magnesium deficit is not as rare as was once thought; prolonged administration of magnesium-free fluids dilutes the plasma magnesium level and may produce symptoms of deficit, particularly when magnesium loss has resulted from gastric suction. Parenteral vitamin preparations of the B complex group and vitamin C should be given daily when parenteral therapy is necessary for more than 2 days.

Amino acid preparations (protein hydrolysates), or intact protein preparations such as Sustagen, are beneficial after the catabolic phase has passed and the body is again able to build tissues. Many authorities feel it is useless to give amino acids during the catabolic phase, because the body is unable to use them and they are excreted in the urine. Others believe they are helpful in decreasing the extent of the negative nitrogen balance. The increased solute load of amino acid preparations can be harmful in the aged patient whose kidneys are already overtaxed.

Other sources of parenteral calories include alcohol solutions and fat emulsions. Alcohol can serve a dual postoperative function because it supplies calories and reduces pain. (Nursing responsibilities in the administration of carbohydrate solutions, electrolyte solutions, alcohol, protein hydrolysates and fat emulsions are discussed in Chap. 14.)

Oral Intake. Many physicians prefer that patients undergoing gastrointestinal suction receive nothing by mouth; others allow "ice chips sparingly" to relieve thirst. The term "sparingly" is open to interpretation by the staff, and more ice chips may be given than was intended by the physician, because of a thirsty patient's constant plea for more ice.

Drinking plain water causes a movement of electrolytes into the stomach to make the solution isotonic; before the water and electrolytes can be absorbed they are removed by the suction apparatus. This process can deplete the body of valuable electrolytes, primarily sodium, chloride and potassium. Profound states of metabolic alkalosis or of sodium deficit have been caused by the unwise practice of giving plain water to a patient undergoing gastric suction. *If ice chips are to be given, they should be made from isotonic saline or a balanced electrolyte solution indicated by the physician,* Lytren, for example.

When oral feedings are allowed, the nurse should encourage the patient to eat those foods most likely to replace his probable deficits. For example, a patient with an ileostomy should receive high potassium foods; a patient with a cholecystectomy and bile drainage should receive high sodium foods. Contraindications to high potassium intake (such as renal disease) and to high sodium intake (such as cardiac disease) should, of course, be considered. The patient should be returned to a full diet as early as possible, because good nutrition decreases both the duration and the complications of convalescence.

POSTOPERATIVE PROBLEMS IN WATER AND ELECTROLYTE BALANCE

Water Excess

Water excess (sodium deficit) is also referred to as water intoxication or hyponatremia. This imbalance is most likely to occur in the first 1 or 2 postoperative days while the water retention effect of stress is still present. Excessive administration of water-yielding fluids, such as 5 per cent glucose in water, predisposes to this condition. Symptoms of water excess (sodium deficit) include:

1. Behavior changes
   A. Inattentiveness
   B. Confusion
   C. Hallucinations
   D. Shouting and delirium
   E. Drowsiness
2. Acute weight gain
3. Overbreathing
4. Normal or elevated blood pressure
5. Skin color normal, or pinker than usual
6. Neuromuscular changes
   A. Weakness
   B. Twitching
   C. Incoordination
   D. Convulsions
   E. Hemiplegia

The nurse should suspect water excess (sodium deficit) when several of these symptoms occur in the early postoperative period. Behavior changes are usually noticed first. The aged and the very young are particularly susceptible to this imbalance.

Prevention of body fluid disturbances demands the study of daily accurate body weight measurements; a sudden weight gain in the early postoperative period is an indication to decrease fluid intake. Fluid intake during the water-retention of stress should not exceed body fluid losses; a reasonable 24-hour intake for most patients is about 1,500 to 2,000 ml. Here again, much depends upon how accurately the nurse performs body weight and intake-output measurements.

Mild water excess can be corrected by prohibiting further water intake; however, serious illness or death may supervene if the condition is allowed to go untreated.

Respiratory Acidosis

Normally carbon dioxide is given off by the lungs during exhalation. Respiratory acidosis (primary carbonic acid excess) occurs when the lungs retain carbon dioxide, because of decreased respiration depth or blockage of oxygen-carbon dioxide exchange at the alveolar level. Breathing excessive amounts of carbon dioxide will also produce this imbalance. The surgical patient may develop respiratory acidosis for one or several reasons:

1. Depression of respiration by anesthesia
2. Blockage of oxygen-carbon dioxide exchange in the lungs due to atelectasis, pneumonia, or bronchial obstruction
3. Depression of respiration with too frequent or too large doses of narcotics
4. Shallow respiration due to abdominal distention and crowding of the diaphragm
5. Excessive breathing of carbon dioxide during anesthesia
6. Shallow respiration due to pain in the operative site or large cumbersome dressings

A threat to postoperative ventilation is posed by surgical procedures involving the diaphragm, such as hiatus hernia repair. Also, patients having thoracic or high abdominal incisions are particularly prone to develop ventilatory problems.

The indiscriminate use of oxygen in the postoperative period increases the chances of overlooking respiratory acidosis. Cyanosis is usually the chief criterion for detecting inadequate ventilation; oxygen therapy may prevent cyanosis and keep the skin color pink even though respiratory acidosis is progressing. When oxygen is necessary, it is usually given by nasal catheter rather than by tent. (Some physicians feel that an oxygen tent predisposes to respiratory disorders, since excessive amounts of carbon dioxide can be inhaled in a tent from which carbon dioxide is not adequately absorbed.)

The nurse can help prevent respiratory acidosis by encouraging the patient to cough and breathe deeply at regular intervals, unless contraindicated by the type of surgery. Even when coughing is to be avoided in neurological or eye surgery the patient can be encouraged to breathe deeply. Administration of narcotics requires good nursing judgment. Enough medication should be given to make coughing tolerable, yet not enough to produce shallow respiration.

The nurse should remember that seemingly small doses of barbiturates or narcotics may produce respiratory depression and acidosis in the aged patient. If the ordered dose appears inadequate, or produces adverse effects, the nurse should report her observations to the physician and seek new orders. Conscientious physicians welcome such nursing observations; they realize that what may be a therapeutic dose in one patient may be ineffective or harmful to another. Observations made by the nurse take on added weight because she spends more time with the patient than does the physician. Turning the patient at regular intervals helps prevent pneumonia and atelectasis and thus discourages respiratory acidosis.

Gastric Dilatation

Gastric dilatation can occur within the first few postoperative days; before peristalsis returns, liters of fluid can be trapped in the stomach. The extracellular fluid volume may be significantly decreased and these symptoms of shock may develop:

- Dyspnea
- Cyanosis
- Rapid thready pulse
- Cold extremities

Additional symptoms include regurgitation of blood-tinged fluid, effortless vomiting and epigastric discomfort. Symptoms of metabolic alkalosis (primary base bicarbonate excess) may result from the pooling of stomach secretions in the massively distended viscus.

Treatment includes gastric suction, water and electrolyte replacement therapy, and, in some instances, blood transfusion. Gastric dilatation can often be prevented by instituting gastrointestinal suction until peristalsis returns.

Ileus

Ileus in some degree is prone to occur in all patients having abdominal surgery. Large amounts of water and electrolytes may be sequestered into the bowel. The amount of fluid "lost" in this manner is not revealed by body weight change or measured output. Clinical signs of fluid volume deficit, decreased urinary volume and specific gravity, and increased thirst help indicate the amount of fluid sequestered. (See the discussion of bowel obstruction in Chap. 17.)

Use of Plain Water as Irrigating Fluid for Suction Tubes

Plain water should never be used to irrigate suction tubes because it depletes the body of valuable electrolytes. The mechanism is the same as that operating when plain water is drunk while gastrointestinal suction is being used. (See Chap. 10 for a discussion of this subject.) Isotonic solution of sodium chloride largely eliminates the hazard and should be used unless the physician requests a specific fluid, such as an oral electrolyte mixture.

Imbalances Associated With Specific Body Fluid Losses

Metabolic alkalosis is most commonly seen in surgical patients as a result of the loss of large amounts of gastric secretions, either through vomiting or gastric suction. It is closely associated with potassium deficit, produced by the excessive loss of potassium-rich intestinal secretions or by prolonged parenteral therapy without potassium replacement. Potassium deficit is enhanced by the stress reaction in the early postoperative period.

Metabolic acidosis (primary base bicarbonate deficit) follows the excessive loss of alkaline intestinal secretions, bile and pancreatic juice.

(The reader is referred to Chap. 8 for a more thorough discussion of imbalances prone to occur with specific body fluid losses.)

Hemorrhage and Shock

Severe hemorrhage and hypovolemic shock are dreaded complications of surgery. The nurse should be alert for, and report, symptoms of hemorrhage and hypovolemic shock such as:

- Apprehension
- Restlessness
- Rise, then rapid fall in blood pressure
- Visual evidence of bleeding at the site of operation or elsewhere
- Pallor
- Cold extremities
- Loss of consciousness

Prompt correction of the cause of hemorrhage and replacement of fluids are mandatory to prevent irreversible shock. Blood is the fluid of first choice, but dextran, plasma or electrolyte solutions may be used until it is available. Sometimes Levophed, levarterenol, is used to maintain adequate blood pressure. (See Chap. 14 for principles of Levophed administration.)

The period of hypotension must be kept at a minimum, because it results in decreased blood flow and damage to vital organs, primarily the brain, the heart and the kidneys. Hypotension in a patient with arteriosclerosis is particularly dangerous because of the high incidence of thrombosis, resulting in either cerebral vascular accident or myocardial infarct. Acute renal insufficiency may follow prolonged hypotension, particularly in the aged.

Acute Renal Insufficiency

Acute renal insufficiency not uncommonly complicates surgery. Usually it is secondary to reduction of renal blood flow (as in shock) or to a hemolytic blood transfusion reaction. The aged patient has a higher incidence of acute renal insufficiency.

In acute renal insufficiency the urinary output is greatly decreased and may be less than 100 ml. in 24 hours. Metabolic acidosis, less frequently sodium deficit, may be present. The specific gravity is fixed at a low level.

Only enough fluids should be given to replace insensible losses and abnormal losses from suction tubes or fistulas. Extremely accurate intake-output records and body weight measurements are mandatory. Alkaline solutions, such as sodium lactate or sodium bicarbonate, or Butler-type solutions can be given to correct the acidosis. The plasma potassium level rises if anuria persists; peritoneal dialysis helps meet this problem. (Nursing reponsibilities in peritoneal dialysis are discussed in Chap. 18.)

Spontaneous diuresis occurs within 1 to 2 weeks in many patients with acute renal insufficiency, provided appropriate treatment has been given. Yet months may pass before renal function returns to normal.

The nurse can help prevent acute renal insufficiency by being alert to, and reporting, *early* symptoms of shock. Prompt correction of shock prevents a pronounced reduction in renal blood flow. (Nursing responsibilities in preventing hemolytic blood transfusion reactions are discussed in Chap. 14.)

Chapter 16

Fluid Balance in the Badly Burned Patient

INTRODUCTION

Burns cause a series of major water and electrolyte changes. The purpose of this chapter is to explore these changes and their implications for nursing care. A background discussion of physiologic changes accompanying burns precedes the discussion of treatment and nursing care.

EVALUATION OF BURN SEVERITY

The severity of water and electrolyte changes is largely dependent on the *burn depth* and the *percentage of body surface* involved.

Burn Depth

Burns are classified as first, second, or third degree, according to the depth of skin damage. Factors considered in determining burn depth include:

• Amount of sensation remaining (pin-prick test may be done to denote the degree of sensation)
• Appearance of the burned surface
• Nature of burning agent plus length of exposure to it
(See Fig. 75.)

In a first-degree burn, vasodilation is the only important change. A second-degree burn is characterized by damaged capillaries and the appearance of blebs containing fluid. Third-degree burns result in thrombosed capillaries and the formation of an eschar (dead tissue). Each percent of a third-degree burn is about twice as severe as each percent of a second-degree burn.

Percentage of Surface Involved

The "rule of nines" is commonly used to estimate the severity of burns in adults. It divides the body surface into areas of 9 per cent or its multiples:

Head	= 9%
Each arm	= 9%
Each leg	= 18%
Front of torso	= 18%
Back of torso	= 18%
Genitalia	= 1%

Unless used cautiously, this method can result in dangerously high estimates. A more detailed breakdown is beneficial. (See Fig. 76.)

After the percentage of second- and third-degree burns is estimated, the therapeutic approach is planned. Burns may be classified as critical, moderate, or minor. (See Table 34.)

In general, burns that cover 20 per cent of the body surface may endanger life; burns that cover 30 per cent of the body surface may be fatal unless adequate treatment is established; and burns of over 50 per cent may be fatal even with adequate treatment.

Age as a Factor in Burn Severity

The mortality rate in burns increases with age. To illustrate the effect of advanced age

Fig. 75. Diagnosis of Burn Depth

	Degree	Nature of Burn	Symptoms	Appearance	Course
Epidermis	First	Sunburn	Tingling	Reddened; blanches with pressure	Complete recovery within a week
		Low-intensity Flash	Hyperesthesia	Minimal or no edema	Peeling
			Painful		
			Soothed by cooling		
Dermis	Second	Scalds	Painful	Blistered, mottled red base, broken epidermis, weeping surface	Recovery in 2 to 3 weeks
		Flash flame	Hypesthesia		
			Sensitive to cold air		Some scarring and depigmentation
				Edema	Infection may convert to third degree
Subcutaneous Tissues	Third	Fire	Painless	Dry; pale white or charred	Eschar sloughs
			Symptoms of shock		Grafting necessary
				Broken skin with fat exposed	
			Hematuria and hemolysis of blood likely	Edema	Scarring and loss of contour and function

Sako, Y.: Emergency management of the acutely burned patient. Hospital Medicine, p. 7, Wallace Laboratories, New York, October, 1964.

Table 34. Classification of Burn Severity

Critical Burns	Moderate Burns	Minor Burns
2° burns of over 30%	2° of 15-30%	2° of less than 15%
3° burns of face, hands, feet, or over 10%	3° of less than 10% (except hands, face, feet)	3° of less than 2%
Burns complicated by: Respiratory tract injury Fractures Major soft tissue injury		

Artz, C., and Reiss, E.: The Treatment of Burns. Philadelphia, Saunders, 1957.

on burn mortality, compare these statistics: a burn covering 15 to 24 per cent of the body surface carries a mortality of 6 per cent in persons from 15 to 44 years old, whereas an equal burn in persons 65 years and older carries an 80 per cent mortality. Even minor burns present a serious threat to the aged. They frequently have pre-existent cardiovascular-renal damage and cannot respond to stress as well as their younger counterparts.

WATER AND ELECTROLYTE CHANGES IN BURNS

Loss of Body Fluids in Burns

Body fluids are lost in severe burns as:

• Plasma leaves the intravascular space and becomes trapped as edema fluid
• Plasma and interstitial fluid are lost as exudate

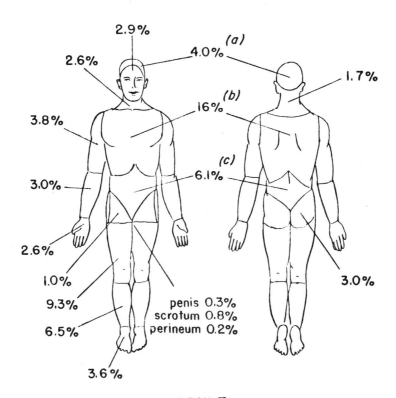

ADULT

Surface areas of the parts of the body (%)
(a) Entire scalp
(b) Entire upper trunk, front and back
(c) Entire lower trunk, front and back

FIG. 76. Surface diagram constructed from Meeh's data. Persons aged eight or up, except for the very obese. (Moyer, C.: Treatment of large burns. Arch. Surg., *90*:856, June 1965)

• Water vapor is lost from the denuded burn site

• Blood leaks from the damaged capillaries

Plasma-to-Interstitial Fluid Shift. Intravascular water, electrolytes and protein are lost through damaged capillaries at the burn site. Clinically, the shift results in edema; the magnitude of this shift depends upon the burn depth and the percentage of surface area involved. Consider a specific example: An adult with a body surface of 1.75 sq. m. has about 10.5 L. of extracellular fluid. If he sustains a 50 per cent burn, the volume of edema fluid formed during the first day or two would approximate 5.25 L. This quantity exceeds the total plasma volume of the patient. Obviously all of the edema fluid is not derived from plasma; some of it comes from the body cells and some from administered fluids.

Proportionately greater amounts of water and electrolytes than of protein are lost from the plasma. (Protein molecules are larger and thus fewer escape through the damaged capillaries.) As a result, the circulating plasma protein becomes more concentrated; the increased osmotic pressure draws fluid from undamaged tissues in all parts of the body. Generalized tissue dehydration results. It is sometimes difficult to visualize the presence of severe dehydration in a patient so obviously edematous; one must remember that the edema represents trapped fluids unavailable for body use.

Burn Exudate. A protein-rich fluid is lost through the leakage of approximately equal parts of plasma and interstitial fluid from the burned surface. Visible fluid loss by way of the surface is mostly limited to second-degree burns. The amount of fluid lost in this manner is proportional to the percentage of second-degree burns; such losses do not increase appreciably in burns involving 50 per cent or more of the body. Burn exudate has approximately two-thirds as much protein as plasma.

Water Vapor. The intact skin serves as a barrier against the loss of water. When skin is destroyed by a burn, increased water loss results. The larger the burned surface, the larger the water vapor loss. The amount lost in this manner can be great. Applying a dressing to the burned skin helps prevent evaporative losses, but it may increase exudative losses through the capillary action of the dressing. Skin grafting should be done as soon as possible. The application of oleic acid and other emollients to burns has been used to restore the water barrier; however, these measures are unsatisfactory because they favor bacterial growth.

Other Effects. Fever contributes to fluid loss by increasing the metabolic rate. Infection is dreaded in burns; its presence may cause the rectal temperature to rise to 104-107° F. and extend the tissue damage unless adequate antibiotic therapy is employed.

Vomiting is frequently observed in severely burned patients; it may be a sign of circulatory collapse, acute gastric dilatation, or paralytic ileus.

WATER AND ELECTROLYTE CHANGES IN MAJOR BURN PHASES

The nurse should be aware of the water and electrolyte changes occurring in burns so that she can recognize significant changes in the patient. Observations are more meaningful when one has at least some idea what to look for. An outline of expected water and electrolyte changes is presented in Table 35. The reader is referred to earlier chapters for detailed descriptions of these imbalances. Planned nursing observations are discussed in Chap. 8.

Physiologic Basis for Treatment and Nursing Care During the Fluid Accumulation Phase

The adequacy of early burn treatment largely depends upon the physician's and the nurse's understanding of physiologic derangements caused by burns, the organization of equipment, and the ability to act quickly and skillfully.

Need for Early Treatment

The shift of fluid from plasma to the interstitial space is rapid and well underway by the end of the first hour. The maximal speed of edema formation is reached by the

TABLE 35. WATER AND ELECTROLYTE CHANGES IN DIFFERENT BURN PHASES

PHASE	WATER AND ELECTROLYTE CHANGES	COMMENTS
Fluid Accumulation Phase (Shock Phase)	Plasma-to-Interstitial Fluid Shift (edema at burn site)	Plasma leaks out through the damaged capillaries at the burn site—edema forms
First 48 hours	Generalized Dehydration	Undamaged tissues give up fluids to help increase plasma volume—part of it leaks through the damaged capillaries and helps form edema
	Contraction of Blood Volume	Loss of plasma causes a decreased circulatory volume
	Decreased Urinary Output	Secondary to: • Decreased renal blood flow • Increased secretion of ADH (antidiuretic hormone) • Sodium and water retention caused by stress (increased adrenocortical activity) • Severe burns may cause hemolysis of red blood cells; the ruptured cells release Hb and it is excreted by the kidneys (hemoglobinuria can cause severe renal damage)
	Potassium Excess	Massive cellular trauma causes the release of K^+ into the extracellular fluid (recall that most of the body's K^+ is located *inside* the cells; only small amounts are tolerated in plasma)
	Sodium Deficit	Large amounts of Na^+ are lost in the trapped edema fluid and in the exudate (recall that Na^+ is the chief extracellular ion and large amounts are lost when extracellular fluid is lost)
		Research work done under the direction of C. A. Moyer indicates sodium deficit in unburned tissues is closely linked with burn shock—partial correction of Na^+ deficit relieved burn shock symptoms in some patients even though a substantially decreased blood volume persisted
	Metabolic Acidosis (base bicarbonate deficit)	Loss of bicarbonate ions accompanies sodium loss
	Hemoconcentration (elevated hematocrit)	Relatively greater loss of liquid blood components in relation to blood cell loss
Fluid Remobilization Phase	Interstitial Fluid-to-Plasma Shift	Edema fluid shifts back into the intravascular compartments

TABLE 35. WATER AND ELECTROLYTE CHANGES IN DIFFERENT BURN PHASES—(*Continued*)

PHASE	WATER AND ELECTROLYTE CHANGES	COMMENTS
(Stage of diuresis) starts 48 hours post-burn	Hemodilution (hematocrit decreased)	The blood cell concentration is diluted as fluid enters the vascular compartment—also, at this time a decrease in the number of cells becomes evident (destruction of red blood cells at the burn site causes anemia—as much as 10% of the total number of RBC's may be destroyed)
	Increased Urinary Output	Fluid shift into the intravascular compartment increases renal blood flow and causes increased urine formation
	Sodium Deficit	Sodium is lost with water when diuresis occurs
	Potassium Deficit (may occasionally occur in this phase) Metabolic Acidosis	Beginning about the fourth or fifth post-burn day, K^+ shifts from the extracellular fluid into the cells
Convalescent Phase	Calcium Deficit	Since calcium may be immobilized at the burn site in the slough and early granulation phase of burns, symptoms of calcium deficit may occur
		(Recall that for some unknown reason calcium rushes to damaged tissues)
	Potassium Deficit	Extracellular K^+ moves into the cells, leaving a deficit of K^+ in the extracellular fluid
	Negative Nitrogen Balance (present for several weeks following burns)	Secondary to: · Stress reaction · Immobilization · Inadequate protein intake · Protein losses in exudate · Direct destruction of protein at the burn site
	Sodium Deficit	

end of the first 8 to 10 hours; the shift continues until the 36th to the 48th hour. (By this time, the capillaries have healed sufficiently to prevent further fluid loss.) The decreased plasma volume can lead to hypovolemic shock and renal depression (due to decreased renal blood flow) unless quickly corrected by fluid replacement therapy. Oliguria or anuria are particularly threatening during this phase because of the excessive amounts of potassium flooding the extracellular fluid. Remember that potassium is mainly excreted in urine; decreased urinary output causes a dangerous excess to build up in the bloodstream. The sodium deficit requires prompt attention, as does the acidosis so frequently present.

Emergency Room Setup. Hospitals that accept burned patients should have a burn cart setup with necessary equipment so that precious time is not wasted gathering it after the patient arrives. Such a cart should contain at least the following articles:

1. Parenteral solutions:
    * Lactated Ringer's
    * Isotonic saline

- 5% dextrose in water or saline
- Plasma

2. I.V. tray:
   - Needles and syringes
   - Tourniquet
   - Tape, gauze, arm board
3. Cut-down tray
4. Tracheotomy tray
5. Catheterization tray, indwelling catheters, drainage apparatus
6. Device to measure small volumes of urine
7. Sterile linen, gowns, gloves
8. Sterile gauze and dressings
9. Sterile swabs and culture tubes
10. Sodium chloride and sodium bicarbonate in liter bottles

The cart should be checked at regular intervals so that its equipment can be resterilized when necessary. A burn cart is of no value if its contents are not safe for use.

Initial Patient Evaluation

Ideally a burn team made up of physicians and nurses skilled in the care of burn patients is on hand to treat burn emergencies. Most hospitals do not have a burn team; when at all possible, patients should be transferred to a hospital having such a team. Fortunately, burned patients withstand travel fairly well.

Some hospital emergency rooms are staffed with at least one house physician. Unfortunately, however, *many* emergency rooms are staffed only with R.N.s and "on-call" physicians. While the nurse in this situation cannot initiate therapy without medical orders, she can obtain valuable information to expedite treatment when the physician arrives. Pertinent questions include:

1. When did the burn occur?
   (The degree of fluid shift is related to the length of time the burn has been present.)
2. What was the nature of the burning agent?
   (Notice in Fig. 75 that burns are classified in relation to burning agents frequently associated with them.)
3. What was the length of exposure to the burning agent?
   (Questions 2 and 3 are intended to help the physician establish the burn depth—appearance of the burns on admission is often misleading.)
4. Were any medications given prior to hospital admission?
   (Sometimes narcotics are given at the scene of the accident; it is important to avoid repeating drugs too soon, especially if respiratory tract burns or shock are present.)
5. Was the burn sustained in an enclosed area where heat and fumes were inhaled?
   (This question is highly significant in establishing the likelihood of respiratory burns.)
6. Are there any pre-existent illnesses, such as cardiac or renal damage or diabetes, that will require therapy in addition to burn treatment?
   (Failure to ascertain the presence of such illnesses is not uncommon in the initial rush.)
7. What is the normal pre-burn weight?
   (The pre-burn weight is a baseline for comparison for later weight changes; the weight is also instrumental in determining drug doses.)
8. Is pain present? If so, how severe?
   (It should be remembered that severe pain can cause a drop in blood pressure and further complicate the patient's condition.)
9. Is the patient known to have any drug allergies?

While asking these questions, the nurse can be busy with other activities, such as readying fluid equipment, removing loose clothing not stuck to the burns, and removing constrictive jewelry before edema becomes severe. The unit that is to receive the patient after initial treatment should be notified so that necessary preparations can be made. The patient should be placed on sterile sheets; reverse isolation is indicated to minimize infection. Burned areas should be handled only with sterile gloves; no matter how dirty a wound appears, further contamination must be prevented.

Observing for Burn Shock

The nurse should be particularly alert for symptoms of burn shock:

- Extreme thirst (due to generalized cellular dehydration)
- Restlessness (initially the patient is active and does not appear seriously ill)
- Tachycardia (heart beats faster to compensate for decreased blood volume)
- Pallor, cold perspiration (however, the skin *may* be pink, warm or dry)
- Disorientation may occur (due to central nervous system depression)
- Oliguria
- Vomiting blood
- Sleepiness may occur

The blood pressure can vary considerably in burn shock; it may be normal, decreased, or increased. If possible the blood pressure should be checked at least once an hour. The body surface may be too extensively burned to permit the application of a blood pressure cuff. Temperature, pulse and respiration should be checked hourly (or more often if indicated).

The patient should be observed carefully for changes in behavior. Restlessness and disorientation may indicate the onset of burn shock.

Initial Urine Observations

An indwelling urinary catheter is usually inserted when burns involve 20 per cent or more of the body surface. If the patient voids before the catheter is inserted, the urine should be measured and saved. It should be observed for discoloration due to blood; if present, the patient probably has severe third degree burns. Hemolysis of red blood cells at the burn site (due to trauma) causes the release of hemoglobin and consequently, hemoglobinuria.

Initial Observations of Respiratory Tract

The nurse should observe the patient closely for symptoms of respiratory burns. These include:

- Singed nasal hair
- Hoarseness
- Red painful throat
- Dry cough
- Moist rales and dyspnea

Such symptoms should be reported promptly. Burns about the face and neck can cause edema and pressure around the trachea. Difficulty in breathing should, of course, be reported immediately.

Initial Treatment

After the initial evaluation, the most pressing problems are dealt with first. More than one person should attend the patient so that all serious problems can be dealt with simultaneously—time is a vital factor.

Intravenous fluids are started *immediately* when moderate or severe burns are present. Blood is drawn for determination of electrolytes, hemoglobin, hematocrit and urea nitrogen. The blood is also typed and cross-matched. Cut-downs are indicated in adults with over 20 per cent of body surface burned. Physicians are of varied opinions about intravenous fluids to be used. Those commonly used initially include:

- Lactated Ringer's
- Isotonic saline
- Plasma
- Dextran
- Blood
- 5% dextrose in water or saline

The aim of early fluid therapy is to give the least amount of fluids necessary to maintain the desired urinary output and keep the patient relatively free of burn shock symptoms.

(See Chap. 14 for the contents of parenteral fluids, precautions for their administration, and complications of intravenous fluid therapy.) Lactated Ringer's is used to correct sodium deficit and acidosis. Although potassium is contraindicated in early burn treatment, the small amount in lactated Ringer's can usually be disregarded. Isotonic saline can be used to correct sodium deficit, but it has the disadvantage of supplying an excessive amount of chloride ions which contribute to the acidosis rather than correcting it. Blood is contraindicated when the hematocrit is 60 per cent or higher. Both blood and plasma can transmit viral hepatitis.

Whenever parenteral fluids are given there is a danger of giving too much or not enough; both hazards are always present in burn therapy. To serve as a guide for the amount and types of fluids to be given early to burned patients, several formulas have been devised. These include the *Evan's formula* and the *Brook's formula*.

1. Evan's Formula
   A. First 24 hours:
      a. 2 L. of non-electrolyte solution (5% D/W to meet water needs)
      b. Colloid and electrolyte solutions in equal parts according to this formula:

      ml. replacement fluid = 2 ml.
      $\times$ Kg. $\times$ % burn

      (One-half the total amount is given in the first eight hours and the rest in the remaining 16 hours)
   B. Second day:
      a. 2 L. of non-electrolyte solution for hydration
      b. Half the amount of colloid and electrolyte solution

2. The Brook's formula is similar; the total volume is the same but the ratio of electrolyte to colloid is 3 to 1. There is a growing tendency to use less colloids and more electrolyte solutions. Moreover, it is doubtful that 2 L. of non-electrolyte solution is sufficient to meet water needs. The importance of water vapor loss through the burned surface is sometimes overlooked. When both colloids and electrolyte solutions are given, no more than 10 L. are usually considered safe in a 24-hour period. Recent work by Carl Moyer has shown that much larger volumes of electrolyte solutions (primarily modified lactated Ringer's) can safely be infused when colloids are not given. (See Patient Care Study.)

The nurse must be alert for symptoms of inadequate or excessive fluid administration. Inadequate fluid therapy in burned patients is indicated by:

- Decreased urinary output (see Table 36.)
- Thirst
- Collapsed veins
- Restlessness and disorientation
- Poor skin turgor
- Hypotension and increased pulse rate

Circulatory overload is indicated by:

- Venous distention
- Shortness of breath
- Moist rales
- Increased blood pressure
- Increased venous pressure (as measured on manometer)

Measurement of venous pressure is useful in determining the amount of parenteral fluids that can be safely infused. Clinically, the patient with hypovolemia due primarily to plasma depletion (as in burns) may have good venous filling and pink warm skin. Such a patient needs parenteral fluids to correct hypovolemia, yet there is a danger of giving too much. Frequent checks of venous pressure allow more aggressive fluid replacement therapy without the risk of circulatory overload. Normal venous pressure is from 4 to 11 cm. of water. A level of 15 to 20 cm. represents a significant elevation. When venous pressure becomes elevated above a point designated by the physician, the fluid infusion rate is curtailed. Venous pressure may be checked as often as indicated, usually every 30 minutes. It is a simple procedure and readings may be made by either physician or nurse. (The reader is referred to the section on venous pressure in Chap. 14.)

If possible, the patient should be weighed daily, for at least the first week, to get an indication of the amount of fluid retention present. Sudden weight gains indicate fluid retention. Loss of weight accompanies the stage of diuresis and indicates loss of edema fluid. An in-bed scale may be used if the patient is immobilized. (See Chap. 8.)

Observations of Urinary Output as a Basis for Therapy

Urinary output is the best single index of the adequacy of fluid replacement therapy; the nurse should take measures to assure its accurate meaurement.

The output may be measured every one-half hour or hour as a guide to fluid replacement therapy. Commercial devices available for urine volume measurement include the Davol Uri-Meter and Kurze Urinometer; their use is described in Chapter 8. Any clear cylinder with small calibrations may be used.

When dealing with small volumes any error can be significant.

Absent or decreased urinary output can be due to:

- Inadequate fluid replacement
- Gastric dilatation
- Renal failure

Remember that a clogged catheter may falsely indicate oliguria.

If the urinary output has been inadequate for 3 hours or more, a test can be performed to differentiate between the oliguria of inadequate fluid therapy and that of renal failure. One can carry out this test by infusing a solution composed of 5 per cent dextrose in 0.2 per cent sodium chloride or in 0.33 per cent sodium chloride over a period of 40 to 60 minutes. If the oliguria is due to inadequate fluid therapy, the urinary volume will increase; if it is due to renal failure, the output will remain small. Fortunately, renal failure in burns is uncommon.

Haste may cause a clogged catheter to be overlooked; to prevent this, the catheter should be irrigated at regular intervals with a carefully measured amount of solution. The volume of irrigating solution used should be noted; if less than this amount is withdrawn, the deficit should be noted and subtracted from the hourly urine volume. Conversely, if more fluid is withdrawn than was put in, the excess should be added to the hourly urine volume. Obviously, failure to record an irrigation correctly could lead to a false high or low urinary volume.

Gastric dilatation is not uncommon in burned patients. When it is present, fluids taken orally become trapped in the distended stomach. Thus, even though oral fluids are swallowed, they are not available for body use and urine formation. Gastric distention can be detected by effortless vomiting, nausea, epigastric distress and grunting respiration. If vomiting occurs, a Levine tube is inserted to prevent aspiration of the vomitus. Additional parenteral fluids are needed to make up for the fluid lost in gastric suction. A gastric replacement solution is preferred. The severe stress imposed by a serious burn may produce a Curling's ulcer in the stomach with resultant hematemesis.

The physician usually indicates the de-

TABLE 36. DESIRED URINARY OUTPUT

AGE GROUP	DESIRED URINE FLOW (ML./HR.)
Adult:	
Male	30-50
Female	25-45
Child:	
1-10	10-25
1 or under	5-10

Weisberg, H.: Water, Electrolyte and Acid-Base Balance. ed. 2, p. 386. Baltimore, Williams & Wilkins, Co., 1962.

sired urinary volume plus the variations in either direction to be reported. (See Table 36 for desired hourly urine volumes.)

The desired urinary volume should be realistic and approach the minimum, not the maximum. Attempts to increase fluid input sufficiently to cause large urine volumes in the aged or the very young are dangerous; the kidneys will not excrete excessive fluids because of the body's reaction to stress (increased retention of sodium and water, plus increased secretion of the antidiuretic hormone).

Specific gravity tests are performed on urine: a low reading indicates adequate hydration, a high reading indicates inadequate hydration. (See Chap. 8.)

An accurate intake-output record is a necessity. A record suitable for a burn patient is shown in Figure 81. (See Patient Care Study.)

Treatment of Respiratory Tract Burns

A tracheotomy is indicated in all but very mild respiratory tract burns. Massive involvement of respiratory tissue is nearly always fatal, even when tracheotomy is performed.

Fluid should be suctioned frequently from the respiratory tract to prevent its accumulation. Humidifiers are used to loosen secretions. Oxygen is administered to decrease anoxia. Prophylactic antibiotics are given to prevent infection of the lungs and consequent increased edema. Parenteral fluids are administered cautiously to avoid overloading the circulatory system and causing pulmonary edema. (The desired urinary volume is slightly less when respiratory tract burns are present.)

Heat Loss

Abnormal loss of body heat occurs from the burn site. (Recall that the skin plays a key role in regulating body temperature.) Room temperature should be kept between 72 to 80° F.; electric heaters can be used to blow heat on burned patients. Dressings may help conserve body heat. Immersion in a temperature-controlled tank of Locke's solution (an electrolyte solution) has been used to decrease water vapor loss and maintain body temperature. (See Patient Care Study.) Infants may be placed in heat-controlled incubators.

Oral Electrolyte Solutions

Oral salt solution therapy is effective in combating burn shock. It may be the sole source of fluids for the patient with minor burns and may be used in conjunction with intravenous fluids in more seriously burned patients. (Early, only potassium-free solutions should be used.) Oral electrolyte solutions should not, of course, be administered if gastric dilatation is present.

Thirst is an early symptom following burns. The patient permitted unlimited quantities of plain water is in danger of developing water intoxication (sodium deficit) because of simple dilution. It is characterized clinically by:

- Headache
- Depression
- Apprehension
- Tremors
- Muscle twitching
- Blurring of vision
- Vomiting
- Diarrhea
- Disorientation
- Excessive salivation
- Mania
- Generalized convulsions

The nurse must explain to the seriously burned patient that plain water should be taken only in limited amounts, if at all. (It is usually not allowed until the second or third postburn day.) The demand for oral liquids should be met with the oral electrolyte solution prescribed by the physician. The exact contents and proportions desired vary among physicians. A commonly used solution consists of 1 teaspoon of sodium chloride and 3 teaspoons of sodium bicarbonate in 1 L. of chilled water. Occasionally isotonic saline or sixth molar sodium lactate is used.

The solution should be carefully prepared; errors between teaspoons and tablespoons can be serious. Oral electrolyte solutions have a definite taste and some patients find them difficult to accept. However, the patient with intense thirst usually welcomes any type of oral liquid. Measures which help to make the solution more palatable include chilling it, making ice chips from it, flavoring it with lemon, or disguising it in juices (when allowed). Orange juice and other potassium-containing fluids (see Table 25, Chap. 10) should be withheld until renal function is established and the physician approves their use. They are usually allowed by the third or fourth day. (Potassium is contraindicated in the first 2 days after burns because of the likelihood of potassium excess; see Table 35.)

Oral electrolyte solutions are not given in the presence of:

1. Acute gastric dilatation
2. Frequent vomiting
3. Sodium excess (Sodium excess may occur during hot summer months when water vapor loss is particularly high. It is characterized by dry, sticky mucous membranes, rising temperature, and plasma sodium above 142 mEq./L. Water may be necessary within 36 hours after burning during hot summer months.)
4. Peripheral vascular collapse
5. Mental confusion (There is danger of aspirating fluid into the lungs.)

Control of Pain

The amount of pain present varies with the depth of the burn, the extent of surface area involved, and the patient's pain threshold. Third degree burns are painless because the nerve endings are destroyed. Pain is experienced around the periphery of third degree burns where first degree and second degree burns are present.

Severe pain can cause hypotension (because of neurogenic shock). While it is best to use only barbiturates, morphine may occasionally be needed. Morphine causes depression of respiration and should not be used when respiratory burns have occurred.

The subcutaneous absorption of medications is frequently poor in the severely burned patient; sometimes a site is not available for subcutaneous injections. Whenever possible, intravenous administration is indicated. Serious consequences may result from the frequent injections of drugs into edematous subcutaneous tissues. The drugs are not well absorbed and accumulate in the area; when the stage of fluid remobilization occurs the drug is presented to the circulatory system in large amounts.

It is important not to confuse the restlessness of burn shock with pain. A patient thrashing about in bed, without complaints of pain, may well be in burn shock. In this case, a narcotic is contraindicated; the physician usually orders an increased rate of parenteral fluid administration.

Physiologic Basis for Treatment and Nursing Care During the Fluid Remobilization Phase

Remobilization of edema fluid represents an interstitial fluid-to-plasma shift which begins on the second or third day after the patient has been burned. Its usual duration is from 24 to 72 hours.

Observing Urinary Output

Reabsorption of edema fluid takes place about the second to fifth postburn day. The blood volume is greatly increased and large amounts of urine are excreted. The nurse should be alert for increasing urine volume and report its presence to the physician.

When diuresis does not occur as expected, the possibility of renal damage must be considered.

Observing for Pulmonary Edema

Fatal pulmonary edema may occur be-

cause the renocardiovascular system is not capable of handling the volume of water and electrolytes shifting from the interstitial fluid into the plasma. (Recall that the volume of edema fluid in a burn may equal the total normal plasma volume.)

The nurse should be alert for signs of circulatory overload and pulmonary edema:

- Venous distention
- Shortness of breath
- Moist rales
- Cyanosis
- Coughing of frothy fluid

Parenteral Fluid Therapy

Once the fluid remobilization phase is reached, parenteral fluids are sharply curtailed or discontinued. Infusion of large volumes of fluids could easily cause circulatory overload with pulmonary edema. Oral fluids and food may supply adequate fluid and nutrition during this phase if tolerated; if not, moderate quantities of intravenous fluids may be necessary to meet daily needs. If possible, a high protein and high caloric diet is started by the second or third day.

Physiologic Basis for Treatment and Nursing Care During the Convalescent Period

Diet

Good nutrition is of first importance for burned patients. They have great nutritional needs, several times those of the healthy person. Frequent oral feedings of foods or commercial mixtures high in protein, calories and vitamins should be started as soon as possible. Nutrament, available in several flavors, and Sustagen are excellent for this purpose. Vitamin preparations containing at least members of the B complex and vitamin C should be administered. If the patient refuses oral feedings, tube feedings may be employed. (Nursing responsibilities in administration of tube feedings are discussed in Chap. 8.) The nurse should be alert for gastric bleeding or other indications of a Curling's ulcer. Because the patient often has a poor appetite and psychologic depression, the nurse must take every opportunity to make food appealing to him. (Measures to promote eating are also described in Chap. 8.)

Oral electrolyte supplements may also be given, depending upon the electrolytes needed. Serum electrolytes should be determined daily.

While providing the patient with optimal nutrition pays rich dividends, failure to meet his nutritional needs may lead to what Blocker terms "burn decompensation." This state is characterized by chronic weight loss, decreased resistance to infection, anorexia, failure of skin grafts to take, cachexia and death.

Ambulation

Early ambulation, even in severely burned patients, improves appetite, helps to prevent contractures, helps correct negative nitrogen balance and sustains the patient's morale. Patients treated by the *closed* method (dressings) are more mobile than those treated by the *open* method (exposure).

Observing for Specific Electrolyte Imbalances

The convalescent phase is often complicated by inadequate electrolyte intake from the diet; if supplemental replacements are not given, the patient may insidiously develop deficits of potassium, sodium and calcium. The nurse should be alert for symptoms of these imbalances. (A thorough description of each is offered in Chap. 6. Observations to be made by the nurse are discussed in Chap. 8.)

Obviously, some of the major nursing problems have been omitted in the preceding discussion of burns, not because they are unimportant but because space does not allow.

PATIENT CARE STUDY

This section was prepared by P. Maxwell, R.N., Hartford Burn Unit, Barnes Hospital, St. Louis, Missouri.

"A man, aged 25 years, was burned at 10 P.M. on July 6, 1964, by the flame of exploding gas in a laundry room. His cotton shirt was ignited. The force of the explosion displaced a wall of the laundry room more than a foot.

"The deep burn covered 75 per cent of the body surface; 12 per cent was superficial partial-thickness (healed in 20 days), 35 per cent was full thickness, and 40 per cent was was deep partial-thickness burns. [See Fig. 77 for the percentage of body burns. The "rule of nines" is not used at the Hartford Burn Unit.]

"Shock was treated with 13,500 ml. of Ringer's solution with lactate and 500 ml. of blood. During the first 48 hours, 1,800 ml. of salt-containing fluids were taken orally. The original weight was 218 lbs.; this increased to 257 lbs. during the treatment of shock.

"All blistered and loose epidermis was removed before the 0.5 per cent $AgNO_3$ wet dressing was applied to the burned surface.

"The postburn course was complicated by tracheitis and bronchitis during the first three days and nights. This was treated with Isuprel and Alevaire inhalations every 6 hours. The second complication consisted of two massive hemorrhages from a Curling's ulcer of the duodenum.

"One [hemorrhage], on the 17th postburn day, stopped while 3,500 ml. of blood were transfused. Another hemorrhage on the 26th day did not stop during the transfusion of 5,000 ml. of blood; a partial gastric resection was performed while 1,000 ml. of blood were given. The incision was made through unhealed deep partial-thickness burns. No postoperative complications occurred, and the wound healed per primum. Body weight was 191 lbs. before the first hemorrhage, 190 lbs. before the second, and 167 lbs. when a regular select diet was resumed 13 days after the resection. Seven days later, the weight was 175 lbs., and there it remained until the patient was discharged.

"The third complication was a sinus tachycardia that at times attained 160 beats per minute. This began six days after the gastric resection. Because neither oligemia nor fever coexisted with the tachycardia, full digitalization was accomplished, and the tachycardia disappeared within two days.

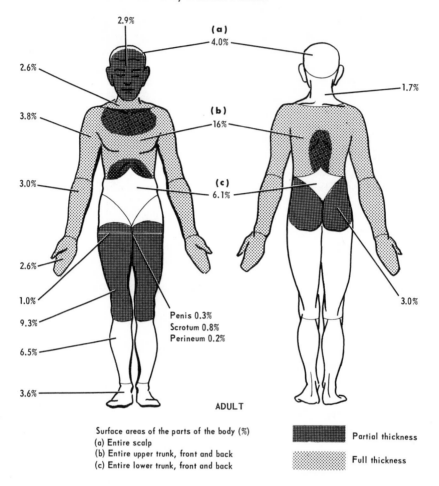

Surface areas of the parts of the body (%)
(a) Entire scalp
(b) Entire upper trunk, front and back
(c) Entire lower trunk, front and back

Partial thickness

Full thickness

FIG. 77. Percentage of body burns—case study. (Hartford Burn Unit, Barnes Hospital, St. Louis, Missouri)

"The patient was febrile (temperature above 37.6° C.) two days out of 99, and both of these days were those in which the gastrointestinal hemorrhages occurred.

"All the eschar had been removed by the 24th postburn day. Autographing of the arms, nose, and hands was begun on the 34th postburn day, having been delayed at least 12 days by the bleeding ulcer and gastric resection. The last grafts were performed on the 130th postburn day. Removal of the eschar and the skin grafting were done without a general anesthetic and without transfusion of blood.

"The hematocrit was 40 per cent just before the first gastrointestinal hemorrhage, and 25 per cent before the second. Seven days after gastric resection it was 44 per cent. The lowest level subsequently attained after seven grafting procedures during 32 days was 38 per cent. No blood was transfused after the gastric resection."*

Nursing Care

E. W. was received on the Hartford Burn Unit approximately 4 hours postburn. A urinary catheter was in place and functioning; a venous cutdown had been performed in the right ankle. Facial edema was immediately evident. Although the patient was coughing a large amount of mucus with a

* Moyer, C. *et al.*: Treatment of large burns. Arch. Surg., 90:847 (June) 1965.

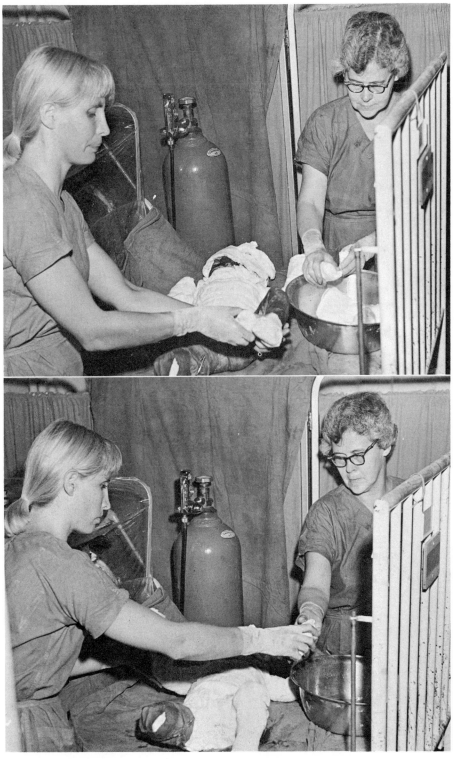

FIG. 78. Application of 0.5 per cent silver nitrate solution on dressings to control infection. (Hartford Burn Unit, Barnes Hospital, St. Louis, Missouri)

NAME _E. W. #1_   DATE _July 7, 1964_

DATE & TIME	Blood or Plasma	Type of IV	Amount Absorb.	Per Os	TOTAL	Urine	Sp.Gr.	Emesis	Stool	TOTAL	Wt. Hg. Hct.	Tank/Temp	T	P	R	B/R	Remarks and/or Meds.
ADM 3:30 A	Ringer's Lactate	2000	NPO	2000	150		50		200	218 PRIOR TO BURN	51		38 50	138	26		DRSG WET
4:30 A			700	1	700	30	1.022	1		30		56		38	130	24		QUIET
5:30 A			700	1	700	15		1		15				39	134	26		Dr SG WET
6 A			1300	1	1300	25		1		25				39	148	26		VERY RESTLESS
TOTAL @ 7 AM			(4700)	0	(4700)	(220)		(50)		(270)								
7:30 A			350	1	350	30				30				39	138	46		RESTLESS
8:30 A			650	30	680	45	1.028			45		58		38	130	24		RESTLESS
9:30 A			300	1	300	50	1.026			50				39	120	26		DOZING
10:30 A			400	1	400	86				80				38	112	26		DRSGS. WET
noon 12			300	1	300	40				40				38	114	26		DRSGS. WET
1 PM		5 D/W	350	1	350	15				15				39	120	26		DRSGS. WET
2 PM			150	1	150	12				12				39	6			DRSGS. WET
3 PM		Ringers Lactate	400	MOYER'S COCKTAIL	400	0		0		0								
7A–3P TOTAL			(2900)	(30)	(2930)	(272)		0		(272)		61						
4 PM	ONE UNIT WHOLE BLOOD		1	80	80	55				55					130	46		DRS GS. WET
5 PM				120	120	40				40				39		44		DRSGS. WET
6 PM				60	60	15				15				39	130	26		DRSGS. WET
7 PM	(500) BLOOD			60	60	25				25				39	133	26		DRSGS WET — BLOOD FINISHED

NAME __E.W.   #2__   DATE __July 7, 1964__

DATE & TIME	Blood or Plasma	Type of IV	Amount Absorb.	Per Os	TOTAL	Urine	Sp.Gr.	Emesis	Stool	TOTAL	Wt.	Hg.	Hct.	Tank Temp.	T	P	R	B/R	Remarks and / or Meds.
7-7 8PM		Ringer's Lactate		240	240	35									39	132	98		IPPB
9PM			1000	100	1100	30	1.032								39	128	98		DRSGS. WET
10PM 30			100	100	200	70	1.030						66		39	131	98		IPPB DRSG. WET
3-1 TOTAL	(500)		(1100)	(760)	(860)	(270)			0	(270)									DRSGS. WET
11PM 30			200	60	260	18									39	106	98		
20 TOTAL	(500)		(8600)	(850)	(9450)	(780)		(50)		(830)									
7-8 12 30A		Ringer's Lactate	225	60	285	30									39	128	98		IPPB DRSGS. WET
1 30A			200		200	30	1.030								39	130	98		DRSG. CHG.
2 30A			275	60	335	40									39	134	92		RESTLESS
3 30A			250	30	280	70	1.030								39	131	98		WET IPPB
4 30A			150	30	180	40									39	132	98		DRSG. WET
5 30A			100	30	130	30	1.032								39	130	98		WET
6 30A			100	30	130	40									39	130	98		LESS RESTLESS
12-7 TOTAL			(1300)	(240)	(1540)	(280)				(280)									

Fig. 79 (No. 1 and 2). Intake-output records for burned patient. (Hartford Burn Unit. Barnes Hospital, St. Louis, Missouri)   [173]

smoky odor, no respiratory difficulty was present.

The patient's wounds were cleansed of excess debris and damaged skin, and 0.5 per cent AgNO₃ dressings were applied. The patient had been placed on a Circ-O-Lectric bed on admission. Urinary output was maintained with large amounts of intravenous Ringer's lactate solution. (See Fig. 79.)

Both a nurse and a physician were needed almost constantly during the first 24 hours. E. W. became increasingly restless with hallucinations. Morphine sulfate was prescribed once. The nurse recorded the vital signs and urinary output hourly. In addition, she observed for symptoms of burn shock.

Small amounts of Moyer's Cocktail solution (4 Gm. of NaCl and 1.5 Gm. of NaHCO₃ in 1 L. of water) were given orally to relieve the patient's frequent complaints of thirst. E. W. continued coughing up copious amount of smoky sputum and was placed in an oxygen tent. Alevaire and Isuprel were given by means of a positive pressure breathing device every six hours.

During the 24th to 26th hour postburn, the patient complained of hunger. He then became disoriented and restless. His urine appeared blood-tinged. He also complained of sore throat and difficulty in swallowing, but no signs of respiratory distress were noted.

At the 32nd hour postburn, E. W. still had periods of mild confusion and restlessness. The nurse remained in constant attendance the first 72 hours, assisting the physician, observing the patient, and applying dressings and keeping them soaked with the AgNO₃ solution.

The edema slowly disappeared without any real respiratory complications occurring. E. W. was placed in a tub of Locke's solution for a few hours two or three times to facilitate the removal of eschar. (Patients are no longer soaked in this solution for comfort or prevention of fluid loss, and rarely for the removal of eschar. The rapid increase in the bacteria count that occurs is too hazardous.)

The burn wounds and the patient progressed satisfactorily until the 17th postburn day, when he complained of being "nervous." He coughed up a pint of bright red blood. The physician was notified; preparation was made to insert a nasogastric tube, and to start an intravenous infusion. The pulse rate increased and the patient became

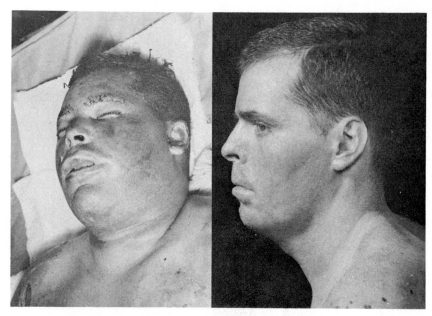

Fig. 80. (*Left*) Facial edema 12 hours postburn. (*Right*) Facial appearance on 90th postburn day. (Moyer, C.: Treatment of large burns. Arch. Surg., *90*:840, June, 1965)

disoriented. He passed a large liquid stool consisting of bright red blood. He was given 3,500 ml. of whole blood. Active bleeding ceased. The nurse observed closely for further hemorrhage. On the 23rd postburn day, he again hemorrhaged; a partial gastric resection was performed with the incision made through unhealed burned skin. The patient did well postoperatively.

Skin grafting was accomplished on the unit, and the patient received physical and occupational therapy, the nurse assisting with both types of therapy. All available resources were used—the chaplain, the social worker, the psychiatrist and the family. Once the patient was well enough for visits to his home (one month prior to discharge), his mental attitude improved tremendously.

E. W. follows closely the textbook picture of the severely burned patient. Any such patient represents a formidable challenge to the nurse's, as well as to the physician's, ability.

Chapter 17

Fluid Balance in the Patient With Digestive Tract Disease

CHARACTER OF GASTROINTESTINAL SECRETIONS

The average daily volume of gastrointestinal secretions is approximately 8,000 ml., as compared to a plasma volume of 3,500 ml. Most of these secretions are reabsorbed in the ileum and proximal colon; only about 150 ml. of relatively electrolyte-free fluid is excreted daily in the feces.

Gastrointestinal secretions consist of saliva, gastric juice, bile, pancreatic juice and intestinal secretions. Their average daily volume and pH are listed in Table 37. The electrolyte content of these secretions is presented in Table 38.

With the exception of saliva, the gastrointestinal secretions are isotonic with the extracellular fluid. In addition, material entering the gastrointestinal tract tends to become isotonic during the course of its absorption. Many liters of extracellular fluid pass into the gastrointestinal tract, and back again, as part of the normal digestive process. This movement of water and electrolytes is

TABLE 37. AVERAGE DAILY VOLUME OF GASTROINTESTINAL SECRETIONS AND THEIR USUAL pH

SECRETION	VOLUME (ML.)	pH
Saliva	1,500	6-7
Gastric juice	2,500	1-3
Pancreatic juice	700	8.0-8.3
Bile	500	7.8
Small Intestine	3,000	7.8-8.0

TABLE 38. ELECTROLYTE CONTENT OF GASTROINTESTINAL SECRETIONS EXPRESSED IN MILLIEQUIVALENTS PER LITER

SECRETION	NA^+	K^+	CL^-	HCO_3^-
Saliva	9	25.8	10	10-15
Gastric juice (fasting)	60.4	9.2	84	0-14
Pancreatic juice (fistula)	141.1	4.6	76.6	121
Bile (fistula)	148.9	4.98	100.6	40
Small intestine (suction)	111.3	4.6	104.2	31

Weisberg, H.: Water, Electrolytes, and Acid-Base Balance. ed. 2, p. 143. Baltimore, Williams & Wilkins, 1962.

sometimes referred to as the "gastrointestinal circulation."

FLUID IMBALANCES ASSOCIATED WITH THE LOSS OF GASTROINTESTINAL FLUIDS

Loss of gastrointestinal fluids is the most common cause of water and electrolyte disturbances. This fact becomes evident when one considers the large volume of fluids in the gastrointestinal tract and the many ways in which they can be lost from the body. Vomiting, gastrointestinal suction, diarrhea, fistulas and drainage tubes are some of the abnormal ways in which these fluids can be lost. Fluids trapped in the gastrointestinal tract, as in intestinal obstruction, are physiologically *outside* the body. Any condition that interferes with the absorption of fluids from the gastrointestinal tract can cause serious water and electrolyte disturbances.

Vomiting and Gastric Suction

Vomiting and gastric suction interfere with the absorption of gastric secretions and ingested fluids. To understand the imbalances likely to occur with these conditions, it is helpful to review the normal characteristics of gastric juice. Gastric juice is the most acid of the gastrointestinal secretions, with a pH of from 1 to 3. Occasionally the pH is higher than 3. The chief electrolytes in gastric juice are hydrogen, chloride, potassium and sodium. Imbalances most often associated with the loss of gastric juice include:

- Fluid volume deficit
- Metabolic alkalosis (base bicarbonate excess)
- Potassium deficit
- Sodium deficit

Fluid Volume Deficit

Fluid volume deficit results when a large volume of water and electrolytes is lost from the body. Note in Table 39 that 100 to 6,000 ml. may be lost in 24 hours from vomiting or suction. Since the gastric secretions are greatly reduced when the stomach is at rest, the patient should receive nothing by mouth during gastric suction or persistent vomiting.

If the suction or vomiting is prolonged, and fluid replacement therapy is inadequate, fluid volume deficit will result. The nurse should be alert for these symptoms indicating the presence of fluid volume deficit:

- Dry skin and mucous membranes
- Longitudinal wrinkling of the tongue
- Oliguria
- Acute weight loss—in excess of 5%
- Body temperature drop
- Exhaustion

Metabolic Alkalosis

Excessive loss of gastric juice by vomiting or gastric suction causes metabolic alkalosis, (primary base bicarbonate excess), because hydrogen and chloride ions are lost from the body. Loss of chloride ions causes a compensatory increase in bicarbonate ions. The base bicarbonate side of the carbonic acid:base bicarbonate ratio is increased and the pH becomes alkaline. The nurse should be alert for symptoms of metabolic alkalosis when the patient has sustained a prolonged loss of gastric juice by vomiting or gastric suction. These symptoms include:

- Slow, shallow respiration (compensatory respiratory reaction to retain CO_2 and to correct alkalosis)
- Muscle hypertonicity and tetany (due to decreased calcium ionization in alkalosis)
- Changes in sensorium
    Personality change may be first

TABLE 39. POSSIBLE ABNORMAL FLUID EXCHANGE OF ADULT IN 24-HOUR PERIOD

ENTRANCES	EXITS	WATER (ML.)	NACL (GM.)
G.I. Tract	G.I. Tract		
Gastric Gavage	Saliva	500- 1,500	2-8
Duodenal Gavage	Vomiting	100- 6,000	0.5-40
Enemas	Suction Drainage, Intubation or		
	Fistula	100- 6,000	0.5-40
	Diarrhea	500-17,000	2-80
	Rectal Mucorrhea ("Pseudodiarrhea")	350- 2,000	1-9
	Primary or Secondary Malabsorption Syndrome	100-14,000	0.5-75

Weisberg, H.: Water, Electrolyte and Acid-Base Balance. ed. 2, p. 140, Baltimore, Williams & Wilkins, 1962.

Previously placid patient may become irritable and uncooperative
May be disoriented

Potassium Deficit

Gastric juice is rich in potassium. A prolonged loss of this fluid frequently leads to potassium deficit, particularly if potassium replacement therapy is inadequate. The nurse should be alert for symptoms of potassium deficit. These include:

- Weakness
- Gaseous distention
- Soft, flabby muscles
- Tremors
- Paresthesia and flaccid paralysis of extremities
- Disorientation
- Heart block and cardiac arrest, as late symptoms

Sodium Deficit

The sodium content of gastric juice is relatively high. The nurse should be aware that gastric suction or prolonged vomiting can lead to sodium deficit, especially if plain water is drunk. Symptoms of sodium deficit include:

- Apprehension
- Abdominal cramps
- Hypotension
- Rapid thready pulse
- Oliguria
- Cold clammy skin
- Convulsions
- Fingerprinting on sternum

Other Imbalances

Prolonged vomiting or gastric suction can result in magnesium deficit. This imbalance is not as common as those listed above. The magnesium concentration in gastric juice is 1.4 mEq./L. In addition, the body conserves magnesium well. However, its continued loss by suction or vomiting, plus its dilution with magnesium-free replacement fluids, can result in symptoms of magnesium deficit. These include:

- Confusion and disorientation
- Gross tremors (may resemble the so-called hepatic flap)
- Hallucinations, usually visual
- Abnormal sensitivity to sound
- Hyperirritability and convulsions

Unless adequate parenteral nutrition is provided for the patient with prolonged vomiting or gastric suction, ketosis of starvation will occur. Due to the absence of carbohydrate, the body must use fat for energy purposes. As a result of increased fat utilization, ketone bodies accumulate in the blood. Because ketones are strong acids, they can convert metabolic alkalosis into metabolic acidosis. The odor of acetone on the breath indicates starvation ketosis. Other symptoms of metabolic acidosis include deep, rapid respiration and weakness.

Nursing Implications

The nurse should be alert for symptoms of the imbalances described above and report their occurrence to the physician. In addition, she should attempt to minimize the loss of water and electrolytes by vomiting and gastric suction. When the nurse is in charge of patients with vomiting, she should:

1. Discourage oral intake, particularly water, if vomiting is persistent and frequent. Ingested substances stimulate gastric secretions. If the substance is hypotonic, electrolytes will move from the extracellular fluid into the stomach. When the stomach is emptied by vomiting, water and electrolytes from the gastric secretions and extracellular fluid are lost. Obviously, oral intake in the face of persistent vomiting promotes water and electrolyte depletion.

2. Report vomiting early so that appropriate treatment can be started before water and electrolyte losses become serious. Medications to relieve nausea may prevent further vomiting. Nutrition by the parenteral route allows the stomach to rest.

3. Administer p.r.n. medications, as prescribed, to relieve nausea.

4. Measure or estimate as accurately as possible the amount of vomitus lost from the body so that lost water and electrolytes can be replaced by parenteral fluids. All fluids

lost and gained by the body should be recorded on the intake-output record. (Nursing responsibilities in measuring and recording fluid intake and output are discussed in Chap. 8.)

5. Measure body weight daily to detect significant changes in fluid balance. Daily weights are helpful in detecting fluid volume deficit, particularly if vomitus has not been measured. A patient on a starvation diet should lose about one-half pound a day. A loss in excess of this amount probably implies a fluid volume deficit. A weight gain implies fluid volume excess if the patient is on a starvation diet. (Nursing responsibilities in measuring daily weights are discussed in Chap. 8.)

6. Report substantial improvement in the patient's condition early so that he can be returned to oral intake as soon as tolerated. (Dietary considerations for the patient with vomiting are discussed in Chap. 10.)

Important nursing actions in the care of the patient with gastric suction are as follows:

1. Irrigate the tube with an isotonic electrolyte solution, such as isotonic solution of sodium chloride, or as prescribed by the physician. Lytren can be employed. Plain water or other electrolyte-free solutions, such as glucose and water, are unsuitable for irrigating solutions. Because they are hypotonic, such solutions cause gastric secretions to increase in order to render them isotonic. The irrigating solution is sucked out along with electrolytes from the gastric secretions and from the extracellular fluid.

2. Record the irrigating solution volume as intake, and whatever is recovered as output.

3. Prohibit intake of water or other electrolyte-free solutions, for the same reason as described under 1. Ice chips made from a suitable electrolyte solution, such as isotonic solution of sodium chloride or Lytren, may be administered if prescribed by the physician.

4. Measure and record the amount of fluid lost by suction, as well as all other fluid gains and losses.

5. Measure daily weight variations to help detect early fluid volume deficit or excess.

Diarrhea, Intestinal Suction and Ileostomy

Fluid Volume Deficit

Intestinal hypermotility shortens the opportunity for absorption of intestinal fluids and thus results in increased fluid loss in bowel movements. The hypermotility can be caused by a disease process, such as ulcerative colitis, or by the frequent use of an irritant cathartic. The liquid stools expelled as a result of hypermotility contain water and electrolytes derived from secretions, ingested food and fluids, and extracellular fluid brought into the bowel to render ingested substances isotonic. Note in Table 39 that as much as 17,000 ml. can be lost in 24 hours from diarrhea. Obviously, prolonged diarrhea is a serious threat to water and electrolyte balance. The amount of fluid lost in intestinal suction averages around 3,000 ml. daily. The nurse should be alert for symptoms of fluid volume deficit when the patient has sustained large fluid losses from the intestinal tract. (Symptoms of fluid volume deficit are listed in the discussion of gastric suction and vomiting.)

Metabolic Acidosis

Intestinal juice varies in composition according to the area of the intestine in which it was formed. However, the intestinal secretions are all alkaline, including pancreatic juice and bile, which are mixed with intestinal juices in the intestines. The chief electrolytes in intestinal juice include sodium, potassium, bicarbonate and chloride.

The intestinal secretions are alkaline because of the preponderance of bicarbonate ions. Loss of bicarbonate results in a compensatory increase in chloride ions. The base bicarbonate side of the carbonic acid:base bicarbonate ratio is lightened and the pH is decreased. Symptoms of metabolic acidosis (primary base bicarbonate deficit) include:

- Shortness of breath on exertion (mild deficit)
- Deep, rapid breathing (moderate or severe deficit)
- Weakness and general malaise
- Stupor progressing to coma

Sodium Deficit

Intestinal secretions have a high concentration of sodium. Excessive loss of these secretions results in sodium deficit. (Symptoms of sodium deficit are listed in the discussion of gastric suction and vomiting.)

Potassium Deficit

Relatively large amounts of potassium are contained in the intestinal fluid; therefore, potassium deficit occurs frequently with diarrhea and prolonged intestinal suction. Ileostomy fluid may have a potassium concentration as high as 70 mEq./L. (Symptoms of potassium deficit are listed in the discussion of gastric suction and vomiting.)

Nursing Implications

The nurse should be alert for symptoms of fluid imbalances likely to occur in the presence of diarrhea, ileostomy or intestinal suction.

Important nursing actions in the care of the patient with *diarrhea* include:

1. Discourage oral intake, particularly irritating foods apt to stimulate peristalsis. Less fluid is formed when the intestinal tract is at rest.

2. Report diarrhea early so that appropriate treatment can be started before water and electrolyte losses are severe. Medications to reduce peristalsis may relieve diarrhea. Nutrition by the parenteral route allows the intestinal tract to rest.

3. Administer p.r.n. medications as prescribed to prevent diarrhea.

4. Measure, or estimate as accurately as possible, the amount of liquid feces lost from the body so that lost water and electrolytes can be replaced by parenteral fluids. All fluids lost and gained by the body should be recorded on the intake-output record.

5. Measure body weight daily to detect significant changes in fluid balance. Daily weights are helpful in detecting fluid volume deficit, particularly if the liquid stools have not been measured.

6. Report substantial improvement in the patient's condition early so that he can return to oral intake as soon as tolerated.

(Dietary considerations for the patient with diarrhea are discussed in Chap. 10.)

Important nursing considerations and actions in the care of the patient with recent *ileostomy* include:

1. Measure and record the fluid lost by ileostomy, as well as other fluid losses and gains by the body.

2. Be alert for symptoms of water and electrolyte disturbances in the immediate postoperative period; potassium deficit is the most frequent imbalance. Other imbalances may include sodium deficit and fluid volume deficit. Patients with ileostomies are more likely to develop water and electrolyte disturbances when their stomas first begin to function, as shown by a comparison of the amount of water and electrolytes lost in a 24-hour period in the early postoperative period, with the amounts lost in a similar period after the ileostomy has adapted. Fluid loss from a recent ileostomy may be as high as 4,000 ml. in 24 hours. Each liter of the fluid may contain 130 mEq. of sodium and 12 mEq. of potassium. An adapted ileostomy usually loses no more than 500 ml. in 24 hours. Each liter of fluid may contain 46 mEq. of sodium and 3 mEq. of potassium.

Nursing responsibilities in the care of the patient with *intestinal suction* include:

1. Irrigate the tube with an isotonic or hypotonic electrolyte solution, or as instructed by the physician. Plain water should never be used to irrigate intestinal suction tubes, particularly those located low in the intestines, since plain water is injurious to the mucosa of the ileum. In addition, it promotes increased secretion of intestinal juice and causes electrolytes to be withdrawn from the extracellular fluid in an attempt to render it isotonic. The irrigating solution is sucked out with electrolytes from the intestinal juice and from the extracellular fluid.

2. Record the irrigating solution volume as intake and whatever is recovered as output.

3. Prohibit the intake of water or other electrolyte-free solutions in liquid or solid form, for the same reason as described in number 1. Ice chips made from a suitable electrolyte solution, such as isotonic solution of sodium chloride or Lytren, may be administered if prescribed by the physician.

4. Measure and record the amount of fluid lost by suction, as well as all fluid gains and losses by the body.

Prolonged Use of Laxatives and Enemas

The prolonged use of laxatives and enemas results in serious water and electrolyte disturbances, particularly potassium deficit. Other possible deficits include sodium deficit and fluid volume deficit.

Cathartics increase the water and electrolyte output through the fecal route, by hastening the excretion of fecal contents and thus reducing the absorption time. Irritant cathartics cause hypermotility of the bowel by irritating the bowel mucosa. Saline cathartics draw water from the extracellular fluid into the bowel. The distended bowel produces mechanical stimulation and the large amount of fluid is propelled out of the bowel. A large fluid volume deficit can result from continued use of saline cathartics, which interfere with electrolyte absorption from the intestines.

Enemas also deplete body water and electrolytes, particularly if plain water is used. Electrolytes from the extracellular fluid enter the bowel to make the water isotonic. Then the water and electrolytes are excreted by propulsive movements initiated by distension of the bowel with water.

The nurse should teach patients to avoid the repeated use of cathartics and enemas. When frequent bowel irrigations are indicated, an isotonic electrolyte solution should be used. (Measures to help patients overcome the habitual use of laxatives and enemas are described in Chap. 10.)

Fistulas and Drainage Tubes

Gastrointestinal fluids can also be lost through fistulas. Deficits of sodium, potassium, chloride, or bicarbonate may result, depending on the area in which the fistula is located.

An educated guess as to the content of the fluid and imbalances likely to accompany its loss can be made by reviewing the usual electrolyte content of the fluid in the region of the fistula. (See Table 38.) For example, fluid from a pancreatic fistula has a high sodium content—as much as 185 mEq./L. Thus, one would expect a sodium deficit to result unless adequate sodium replacement is carried out. Because pancreatic juice is alkaline, one would expect metabolic acidosis to accompany its loss from the body. When in doubt, the physician may choose to test the fluid's pH and electrolyte content.

In addition to pH changes, fistulas can cause a serious contraction of extracellular fluid volume. For example, a duodenal or jejunal fistula may drain 3 to 6 L. daily. A pancreatic fistula may drain 2 L. daily.

If possible, the nurse should attempt to measure the fluid lost by way of a fistula. If not, she should try to estimate the volume as accurately as possible. Statements as to how much of a dressing was saturated, as well as extent of gown and linen saturation, help the physician plan fluid replacement therapy.

A large volume of bile can be lost after cholecystectomy when a T-tube is inserted. The nurse should measure this drainage the same as she does drainage obtained by gastrointestinal suction. The physician has to know the amount lost from the body in order to replace the water and electrolyte losses with parenteral fluids. The nurse should be alert for symptoms of sodium deficit when large volumes of bile are lost, especially if sodium is also being lost by gastric suction. Bile has an alkaline pH, so one would anticipate metabolic acidosis if the bile loss is prolonged.

Trapped Gastrointestinal Fluids

Fluids trapped in an obstructed bowel, or in the peritoneal cavity, are "lost" because they are not available for use by the body. Yet, they cannot be directly measured as one measures fluid losses caused by vomiting or suction. Trapped fluids present a problem in planning fluid replacement therapy. Gastrointestinal conditions associated with fluid accumulation in the body include: gastrointestinal obstruction, peritonitis and cirrhosis of the liver.

Gastrointestinal Obstruction

Gastrointestinal obstruction is accompanied by serious imbalances in water and electrolytes, the nature of which depends on the site of the obstruction.

If the *pylorus* is obstructed, gastric contents cannot enter the intestines and are lost by vomiting. The patient may develop metabolic alkalosis. This imbalance occurs because excessive amounts of hydrogen and chloride ions are lost in vomiting. In addition, nutrition is impaired because the patient cannot eat. Metabolic acidosis (primary base bicarbonate deficit) produced by starvation ketosis can result unless parenteral nutrition is adequate.

If the *upper small intestine* is obstructed, the patient will vomit intestinal juices and gastric juice. The loss of acid and alkaline fluids may be approximately equal; this prevents serious disturbances in pH.

If the obstruction is in a *distal segment of the small intestine,* the patient may vomit larger quantities of alkaline fluids than of acid fluids. Recall that secretions below the pylorus are mainly alkaline. Thus metabolic acidosis can result from a low intestinal obstruction.

If the obstruction is *below the proximal colon,* most of the gastrointestinal fluids will have been absorbed before reaching the point of obstruction. Solid fecal material accumulates until symptoms of discomfort develop. Reverse peristalsis may cause vomiting of a fecal nature, which can be severe, late in bowel obstruction.

Small intestinal obstruction traps gastrointestinal fluids proximal to the obstruction. The mucosa of distended portions of bowel above the obstruction secretes large amounts of fluid into the bowel. As much as 10 L. of fluid can collect in the bowel, resulting in severe extracellular fluid volume deficit. The increased pressure within the distended bowel draws liquid from the extracellular fluid. Proteins are lost from the blood stream into the bowel wall and intestinal lumen. Plasma volume is substantially reduced, partly because of loss of blood into the peritoneal cavity.

Blood loss from a strangulated hernia may be great. The volume of blood sequestered into an infarcted bowel segment may be approximately 10 per cent of the total blood volume for every 24 hours of obstruction. A reduced circulating blood volume causes hypotension, rapid thready pulse and decreased renal blood flow with azotemia and oliguria. Death may result unless the blood volume is restored.

Nursing Implications. The nurse should frequently observe the vital signs of patients with gastrointestinal obstruction. A fall in blood pressure with an increased pulse rate indicates further contraction of the plasma volume and oncoming circulatory collapse. Such findings should be quickly reported to the physician. Fluid administration before surgery aims at stabilizing the vital signs sufficiently to withstand the stress of surgery. Isotonic saline, plasma and whole blood are frequently used replacement fluids. (Nursing responsibilities in parenteral therapy are described in Chap. 14.) The hourly urinary output should be observed; oliguria or anuria are indications of inadequate fluid replacement. Urinary specific gravity is high when fluid replacement is inadequate. When possible, the urinary output should be at least 50 ml. per hour before surgery.

Recall that the volume of fluid trapped in the intestine can only be estimated. Weight measurements are also valueless in detecting the amount of fluid trapped in the bowel. Thus, careful observation of vital signs, the patient's appearance, and urinary volume and specific gravity are especially significant.

Peritonitis

Peritonitis involves the loss of extracellular fluid into the peritoneal cavity as an inflammatory exudate, causing fluid volume deficit.

Calcium deficit can also occur in generalized peritonitis and acute pancreatitis, because large amounts of calcium are immobilized in the diseased tissues and exudates, for reasons unclear.

Cirrhosis of the Liver with Ascites

Liver disease is associated with retention of sodium and water, caused by increased portal pressure and increased aldosterone secretion. (Recall that aldosterone is an adrenocortical hormone exerting a potent sodium-retaining effect and potassium-excreting effect.) The use of aldosterone antagonists often promotes a sodium diuresis in patients with liver disease.

Although both sodium and water are retained in patients with liver damage, it appears that water is retained in excess of sodium. Why this occurs is not clear; antidiuretic hormone has been implicated as a contributing factor. Perhaps the damaged liver is unable to inactivate ADH normally; as a result, water is retained by the body. The plasma sodium level is low, even though the total body sodium content is increased, because water is retained in excess of sodium. The plasma sodium level may be further decreased by the prolonged use of potent diuretics and a low-sodium diet.

Potassium deficit can also occur; this imbalance may be caused by increased aldosterone secretion, prolonged use of potent diuretics, and poor intake due to anorexia. Severe potassium deficit is often a late manifestation of liver disease.

Ascites results from a combination of factors: (1) obstruction to venous outflow from the liver with resultant liver congestion, (2) increased capillary permeability, (3) reduced plasma osmotic pressure and (4) sodium and water retention.

The increased liver congestion causes protein rich fluid to leave the capillaries and pass into the abdominal cavity. Increased capillary permeability and hypoalbuminemia also accompany cirrhosis of the liver. The result is decreased plasma osmotic pressure. Albumin is lost into the ascitic fluid. The osmotic pressure of the fluid derived from plasma is greater than that of extracellular fluid; thus water is drawn into the ascitic fluid from other extracellular spaces. The plasma then has to replenish the loss of extracellular fluid; plasma volume is reduced, causing hormonal responses that decrease urinary loss.

Patients with ascites are treated with low-sodium diets and diuretics. Dietary restriction of sodium to less than 100 mg. daily prevents additional fluid retention in most patients with cirrhosis. Eventually patients with ascites become refractory to diuretics and require paracentesis to relieve symptoms of pressure or respiratory distress. As much as 20 L. of ascitic fluid may accumulate in one week. Unfortunately, its removal only causes more to form. Paracentesis further depletes the body of protein, sodium, and water. The patient should be observed for symptoms of circulatory collapse following the removal of a large volume of fluid by paracentesis since a rapid shift of fluid from the plasma to the ascitic fluid space may follow the procedure.

Chapter 18

Fluid Balance in the Patient With Urological Disease

INTRODUCTION

The kidneys excrete water, electrolytes and organic materials, and conserve whatever amounts of these substances the body requires. They act both autonomously and in response to blood-borne messengers, such as the mineralcorticoids and antidiuretic hormone. Failure of renal function causes a variety of water and electrolyte disturbances.

ACUTE RENAL FAILURE

Etiology

Acute renal failure implies a pronounced reduction in urine flow, lasting for days or weeks, in a previously healthy person. The condition can be of a type characterized by *degenerative and necrotic* changes in the renal tubules, or it can be of the *functional* type.

1. Degenerative Necrotic Type:
   - Crushing injuries
   - Burns
   - Hemolytic blood transfusion reaction
   - Accidental infusion of distilled water
2. Functional Type:
   - Heart failure
   - Severe fluid volume deficit
   - Severe infections
   - Toxins (such as lead, arsenic, and carbon tetrachloride)
   - Eclampsia
   - Nephrotic syndrome

Patients with these conditions should be observed for the possible development of acute renal failure. The nurse should measure the urinary output carefully, as well as all other fluid losses and gains. A reduced urinary output may be due to excessive fluid loss through another route, or to inadequate intake. Or, it may be due to acute renal failure. A urinary output under 400 ml. in the adult represents oliguria and should be reported.

Acute renal failure can be divided into two phases—oliguria and diuresis.

Oliguric Phase

Pathologic Physiology and Symptoms

The first manifestation of acute renal failure is decreased urinary output, usually appearing within a few hours after the causative event. Anuria is rare; instead, a 24-hour output of about 50 to 150 ml. is the rule for the first few days. After this time, the urine output gradually increases. The oliguric phase may last one day or several weeks; the average duration is 10 to 12 days in severe cases.

The nurse should be alert for symptoms of the major problems of this phase: they include potassium excess, fluid volume excess, metabolic acidosis (primary base bicarbonate deficit) and uremia. Other problems include calcium deficit, sodium deficit and anemia. Death is usually due to cardiac arrest caused by potassium excess or pulmonary edema caused by fluid volume excess.

Potassium Excess

Potassium excess usually, but not invariably, occurs in the oliguric phase. Recall that the kidneys normally excrete 80 per cent or more of the potassium lost daily from the body. When the kidneys are not functioning, potassium excretion is greatly reduced. If no protein or potassium is ingested, and if sufficient calories are supplied to prevent endogenous cellular catabolism, it is unlikely that serious potassium excess will develop during the first few weeks of oliguria. However, patients with massive crushing injuries or large quantities of necrotic tissues may have a rising plasma potassium concentration despite no intake of protein and potassium, since catabolized necrotic tissue releases potassium into the extracellular fluid.

Recall that the normal plasma potassium level is 5 mEq./L. When this level is doubled, death may occur, due to cardiac arrest. (Excessive potassium causes weakness and dilatation of heart muscle, and cardiac arrest in diastole.)

The nurse should be alert for the symptoms of potassium excess. They include:

- Anxiety and restlessness
- Muscular weakness progressing to flaccid paralysis (primarily affects limbs and respiratory muscles)
- Respiration decreased as a result of respiratory muscle weakness
- Decreased pulse rate, finally resulting in bradycardia
- Cardiac arrhythmias
- Falling arterial blood pressure
- Cardiac arrest and death

A plasma potassium concentration of 6 mEq./L. is a cause for concern; a concentration of 7 mEq./L. demands immediate treatment. (See discussion of treatment.)

Fluid Volume Excess

Fluid volume excess is a frequent problem during the oliguric phase. Symptoms include elevated venous pressure, distention of the neck veins, edema, puffy eyelids, bounding pulse, and shortness of breath. It is usually due to the excessive administration of fluids, either orally or intravenously. Hypertension, pulmonary edema and congestive heart failure are complications of fluid volume excess. Pulmonary edema is manifested by severe dyspnea, moist rales and frothy sputum.

Metabolic Acidosis

Metabolic acidosis is the result of the retention of acid metabolites normally excreted in the urine. Their accumulation in the blood stream causes the pH to drop. Decreased food intake causes increased utilization of body fats and the accumulation of ketonic acids in the blood stream. These acids further decrease the pH.

Metabolic acidosis causes a compensatory increase in pulmonary ventilation, which causes the elimination of large amounts of carbon dioxide from the lungs with a resultant decrease in the carbonic acid content of the blood. The pH is partially corrected by this mechanism. Anorexia, weakness, apathy and coma may also be symptoms of metabolic acidosis.

Vomiting commonly occurs with the development of uremia. If vomiting occurs at the time metabolic acidosis is developing, it is possible that the metabolic alkalosis (primary base bicarbonate excess) accompanying vomiting may help to counteract acidosis. However, because gastric hypoacidity frequently occurs with uremia, vomiting may not have a significant effect on the pH. Extensive diarrhea contributes to the development of metabolic acidosis.

Sodium Deficit

The plasma sodium concentration may be normal or below normal. Contributing to sodium deficit is the administration of excessive amounts of water, which dilutes the plasma sodium. It may also be due to a shift of sodium into the cells, particularly if acidosis is present. Occasionally sodium deficit becomes severe as a result of excessive loss of sodium in vomiting, diarrhea, or as a result of treatment with cation exchange resins. Symptoms of sodium deficit include:

- Apprehension
- Abdominal cramps

- Rapid thready pulse
- Hypotension
- Convulsions
- Cold, clammy skin

Calcium Deficit

The plasma calcium concentration may be below normal; calcium deficit may be related to the increased concentration of phosphorus in the blood stream. (Phosphorus is a constituent of one of the retained metabolic acids.) A reciprocal relation exists between calcium and phosphorus so that an increase in one causes a decrease in the other.

Calcium deficit does not usually present symptoms of tetany, probably because the decreased blood pH of metabolic acidosis favors calcium ionization. (Recall that calcium ionization increases in acidosis and decreases in alkalosis.) Chvostek's sign may be positive even though other symptoms of calcium deficit are not present. If metabolic alkalosis develops as a result of treatment with alkaline fluids, calcium deficit becomes manifest with the development of muscle twitching and convulsions.

The major significance of calcium deficit is that it enhances the toxic effects of potassium on the heart. (Recall that calcium and potassium have antagonistic actions on heart muscle.) Sodium deficit also enhances potassium toxicity because sodium is mildly antagonistic to potassium.

Anemia

Normochromic, normocytic anemia of unknown etiology usually occurs. It is possibly due to increased blood destruction and erythropoeisis. The hematocrit may fall below 20 per cent, and the hemoglobin below 7 Gm. The degree of anemia seems to be related to the level of azotemia.

Urine Changes

The urine is usually bloody for the first few days, becoming clear about the end of the oliguric phase. If renal failure is due to hemolytic blood transfusion reaction, the urine has a port wine color. A low specific gravity ranging from 1.002 to 1.010 characterizes the oliguric phase.

Uremia

If therapy fails to relieve oliguria and uremia progresses, nausea, vomiting, diarrhea, abdominal distention and mild ulcerations of the gastrointestinal tract may occur.

Treatment

Because acute renal failure is a self-limiting condition, treatment is aimed at maintaining life long enough for the injured renal tubules to heal and resume function.

Food and Fluid Intake

Carbohydrates. *At least* 100 Gm. of carbohydrate should be administered daily. This amount decreases endogenous protein catabolism by approximately one-half, and also helps prevent ketosis. Such catabolism is harmful, since it releases potassium and nitrogenous products into the extracellular fluid; plasma levels of these substances rise. Administered glucose forms glycogen, essential for restoration of cellular potassium stores.

Oral carbohydrate intake should be encouraged if nausea and vomiting are not present. Sometimes these symptoms can be relieved by Dramamine or Benadryl. Hard candy balls, syrup, and stick candy supply carbohydrates. High carbohydrate, low protein foods are occasionally added to the diet. Examples of such foods include rice, sweet or Irish potatoes, cornmeal and toast. High caloric intake decreases endogenous protein catabolism.

Intravenous carbohydrate administration is necessary if oral intake is impossible. A hypertonic carbohydrate solution must be used to supply the necessary amount of carbohydrate and to avoid excessive fluid administration. A 25 per cent glucose solution may be administered by slow drip over the 24-hour period. One liter of 10 per cent glucose in water can be used to supply 100 Gm. of carbohydrate if the patient requires as much as 1,000 ml. of water.

Insulin. Insulin may be added to the carbohydrate solution to increase its utilization and promote further removal of potassium from the extracellular fluid. The patient should be observed for signs of hypoglycemia after the administration of a concentrated carbohydrate solution, particularly if insulin has been added to it. The pancreas is stimulated to secrete insulin due to the high carbohydrate intake; sudden discontinuing of the infusion may result in an excessive supply of insulin; 200 or 300 ml. of a 5 per cent glucose solution may be administered following the concentrated solution to counteract this effect.

An emergency measure for the treatment of potassium excess is the administration of 50 ml. of 50 per cent dextrose with 20 units of regular insulin intravenously every 3 or 4 hours.

Restriction of Potassium and Protein Intake. High potassium foods should be excluded from the diet because the non-functioning kidneys are unable to excrete potassium. Foods to avoid include meats, legumes, nuts, milk, fresh fruits, fruit juices, tea and coffee.

The diet should be low in protein. Four Gm. of protein furnish 1 Gm. of urea, hence a high protein intake adds to the severity of the uremia. In addition to urea, protein foods provide potassium, sulfates, phosphates and water.

High Fat, High Caloric Diet. Fat provides less water of oxidation than carbohydrate or protein; thus it is least likely to cause an excessive fluid volume. Frozen butter balls, ranging in size from 5 to 15 Gm., are frequently administered to achieve a high caloric intake. Some are prepared with powdered sugar to further increase palatability and caloric value.

Tube feedings composed of Lipomul, glucose, vitamins and water have been administered to patients with acute renal failure to increase caloric intake. Use of tube feedings can be hazardous, however, when frank uremia is present, because of the possibility of producing gastric bleeding.

The aim of the diet in uremia is to give as many non-protein, non-electrolyte calories as possible.

Restriction of Fluid Intake. The amount of fluid administered must be carefully planned to suit the patient's needs, with the body considered as a closed-system. Excessive fluid intake should be avoided. The physician calculates a fluid dose that will just replace fluid losses from the body. Insensible losses are approximately 500 to 600 ml. The rest of the fluid dose matches the urinary output of the previous day and other losses, such as from vomiting or diarrhea. The nurse must keep an accurate account of fluid gains and losses. An inaccurate record could lead to a fluid overdose and fluid volume excess with its dangerous sequelae. (Nursing considerations in measuring and recording fluid intake and output are discussed in Chap. 8.)

Accurate daily body weight measurements are also necessary for determining the desired fluid dose. (Nursing considerations in obtaining accurate body weight measurements are discussed in Chap. 8.) With decreased food intake, the patient can be expected to lose from one-third to one-half lb. daily. Failure to lose this amount implies fluid retention. On the other hand, a loss in excess of this amount implies excessive loss of body fluid.

The nurse should check the fluid intake orders carefully and avoid administering an excessive amount. All routes of fluid gain should be considered when recording the daily fluid intake. For example, fluid retained from an enema counts as part of the daily intake.

Alkalinizing Fluids. Alkalinizing fluids, such as sodium bicarbonate or sodium lactate, are administered when acidosis is manifested by frank Kussmaul respiration, stupor, or coma. Indiscriminately used, these fluids may cause volume excess, congestive heart failure and pulmonary edema.

Sodium Administration. Sodium deficit is usually treated by limiting the water intake. Occasionally hypertonic solution of sodium chloride is administered to correct a severe sodium deficit produced by excessive vomiting or diarrhea. Hypertonic solution of sodium chloride should be administered with caution because it can easily result in fluid volume excess with congestive heart failure and pulmonary edema.

Calcium Administration. Calcium deficit can be treated with calcium gluconate by the oral or intravenous route—orally if nausea and vomiting are absent, otherwise intravenously. Ten ml. of a 10 per cent calcium gluconate solution is sometimes used to reduce the toxic effects of potassium excess on the heart. Calcium can cause pronounced improvement in electrocardiograph changes produced by potassium excess, even though the plasma potassium concentration is not changed.

Calcium may be indicated when alkalinizing fluids are given to treat acidosis, since symptoms of calcium deficit may be induced by an increase in blood pH. (Calcium ionization is decreased when alkalinity of the extracellular fluid increases.) Restoration of a normal pH may disclose a calcium deficit that was not evident when the plasma pH was below normal.

Blood Administration. Packed red blood cells may be administered if the hematocrit drops below 20 per cent, the hemoglobin drops below 7 Gm., or obvious blood loss occurs.

Digitalization. Although potassium excess makes the heart less susceptible to digitalis intoxication, potassium and digitalis can exert an additive effect upon the AV node, causing heart block. For this reason, digitalization should be approached with extreme caution in patients with potassium excess.

Pus Drainage and Debridement of Necrotic Tissue. If the patient has dirty wounds, undrained pus collections, or necrotic tissue, the plasma potassium concentration rises as a result of catabolism. To prevent severe potassium excess, it is important that necrotic tissue and pus be removed.

Cation Exchange Resins. Cation exchange resins may be used to increase potassium excretion from the bowel. The resins may be taken by mouth, if tolerated, or may be instilled as a retention enema. When the resin is administered orally, the solution in which it is suspended should be recorded as part of the daily fluid allowance. While the cation exchange resins are given to remove potassium ions from the intestinal tract, they also remove other cations, such as sodium, calcium and magnesium. It may be necessary to replace these ions if the resins are used for more than a few days. Kayexalate is a sodium polystyrene sulfonate cation exchange resin that has the advantage of removing less calcium and magnesium than do some of the other resins.

The enema vehicle administered with the cation exchange resins should be measured before instillation and after expulsion, with the amount absorbed by the bowel counted as part of the daily fluid allowance. The enema should be retained for 4 to 10 hours if possible. Cation exchange resins are of most value when used as a preventive rather than as an emergency measure to reduce severe potassium excess.

Diuretic Phase

Pathologic Physiology and Symptoms

The diuretic phase begins when the 24-hour urine volume approaches 1 L. a day, usually around the tenth day after onset. In some instances, it may not occur for 14 to 21 days. During this phase, the partially regenerated tubules are unable to concentrate urine, and the glomeruler filtrate is excreted virtually unchanged. Thus, the patient's condition does not improve in the first few days of the diuretic phase; indeed, uremia may be more severe during this period than at any other time. Convulsions, stupor, nausea, vomiting, hematemesis, bloody diarrhea, or hemorrhage may occur. The reason for the severity of the uremia lies in the rapid contraction of the total body fluid. For this reason, early and prompt replacement of fluid is needed until the blood urea nitrogen begins to fall. This replacement must be carried out, even though it may cause a persistence of edema and other untoward symptoms. The chief cause of death during the diuretic phase is infection, since the patient has extremely low resistance.

The amount of urinary output depends on the treatment the patient received during the oliguric phase. If fluid overloading was allowed, the urine volume may be more than 5,000 ml. daily. If the patient was well managed, the urine volume is not excessive.

Treatment

Treatment during this phase depends on

Fig. 81. Peritoneal dialysis setup.
(Abbott Laboratories: Inpersol. pp.
16-17. North Chicago, Ill., 1964)

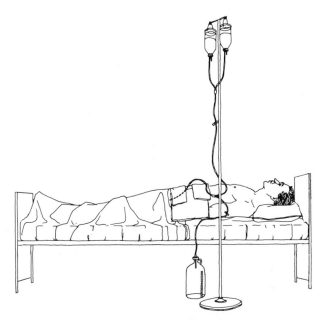

the amount of water and electrolytes excreted in the urine. The patient's body weight should be closely observed. If the body weight decreases at a moderate rate, oral fluids are not forced. If, however, it decreases too rapidly, water and electrolytes must be supplied in sufficient amounts to prevent deficits.

Alkalinizing fluids may be administered if acidosis is severe. Since excessive sodium loss may occur during diuresis, the daily plasma sodium level should be observed and replacement carried out if necessary. Potassium replacement may also be required.

If uremia is severe, as indicated by a high plasma potassium level, a high BUN, and pronounced symptoms, dialysis may be indicated.

Peritoneal Dialysis

Because of its large surface area, the peritoneum can be used as a dialyzing membrane for the removal of toxic substances, body wastes, water, and electrolytes. Peritoneal dialysis can be used in the treatment of acute renal failure from any cause. While it is only about one-fourth as effective as hemodialysis (artificial kidney), it is nevertheless an efficient method for treating renal failure. Its chief advantage is that it can be used in all hospitals, while the artificial kidney is usually available only in large medical centers. Moreover, no special training is necessary to perform peritoneal dialysis, as contrasted to the highly technical operation of the artificial kidney. The nurse may be asked to continue with peritoneal dialysis after the physician has initiated the procedure. Indications for peritoneal dialysis include high plasma levels of potassium and urea nitrogen, severe metabolic acidosis, pulmonary edema, and deterioration of the patient's general condition.

The dialyzing solution resembles plasma in electrolyte concentration and tonicity. It must be at least slightly hyperosmotic to plasma to prevent its absorption with development of fluid volume excess. Glucose in different concentrations is used to render the solution hyperosmotic. A slightly hyperosmotic fluid, such as Abbott's Impersol with dextrose 1.5 per cent, or Baxter's Dianeal with dextrose 1.5 per cent, is useful in removing abnormal plasma constituents, such as barbiturates, or excessive amounts of normal plasma constituents, such as potassium or calcium. A more hyperosmotic solution, such as Abbott's Impersol with dextrose 7 per cent, or Baxter's Dianeal with dextrose 7 per cent, is sometimes useful in removing edema fluid. Solutions are available with and without potassium, the latter for patients with potassium excess. Potassium-containing solutions are used for patients with normal plasma potassium concentration. Occasionally, varying concentrations of potassium are added to potassium-free solutions.

Prior to peritoneal dialysis, the bladder and colon should be emptied to avoid injury during insertion of the catheter. The patient's weight and vital signs should be checked prior to the procedure for later reference during dialysis.

After the abdomen is shaved and prepared, an abdominal paracentesis is performed and a catheter is inserted into the peritoneal cavity. Two liters of solution are allowed to enter the peritoneal cavity through the catheter in about 10 minutes. If the patient complains of discomfort when the fluid is instilled, the flow rate may need to be reduced. The fluid is left in for 1 to 2 hours and then drained into a bottle. Drainage of the fluid from the peritoneal cavity usually takes from 10 to 20 minutes. To facilitate drainage, it may be necessary to gently massage the abdomen or adjust the patient's position.

The dialyzing solution is instilled and drained at regular intervals until the patient shows definite improvement. Intermittent peritoneal dialysis is usually performed for 12 to 36 hours in the adult patient.

The nurse should use meticulous technique during peritoneal dialysis to prevent peritonitis. She should observe the vital signs for significant changes. The time each exchange begins and the amount of fluid instilled and removed should be recorded. If the amount instilled exceeds the amount removed by more than 500 ml., or if the amount withdrawn exceeds the amount instilled by more than 500 ml., the physician should be notified. A too vigorous use of dialysis can cause excessive fluid loss or excessive fluid absorption. Symptoms of fluid volume deficit or excess should be reported. Fluid intake and output from all routes should be measured and recorded. Body weight measurements are beneficial in detecting significant fluid losses and gains.

CHRONIC RENAL DISEASE

Etiology

Chronic renal disease can result from glomerulonephritis, pyelonephritis, polycystic kidneys, essential hypertension, and urinary obstruction.

Pathologic Physiology and Symptoms

Water and Electrolyte Changes

Chronic renal failure is characterized by progressive disease with loss of renal tissue. Eventually, renal blood flow and glomerular filtration decrease. The tubules lose their ability to form ammonia and to excrete nonprotein nitrogenous products. Renal control of water and electrolytes is impaired.

Plasma potassium concentrations in patients with chronic renal failure vary widely. Some have normal levels until oliguria and starvation occur. In some cases of chronic nephritis with polyuria, the plasma potassium may be low. Excessive dietary protein intake or the administration of stored blood may cause the potassium concentration to rise. High plasma potassium levels do not usually occur until late in chronic renal failure. Metabolic acidosis occurs as a result of the impaired renal excretion of acid metabolites and the inability of the tubules to form ammonia. The respiratory mechanism partially corrects the decreased blood pH.

Sodium is lost in the urine, but the plasma level usually remains near normal if the patient is not placed on a severely restricted low-sodium diet, or if excessive sodium loss does not occur with vomiting and diarrhea. Some patients retain sodium when it is given in average amounts. Fluid volume excess, hypertension, congestive heart failure and pulmonary edema may result from the excessive administration of salt to such patients. The plasma calcium concentration is decreased, and the phosphorus concentration is increased. Because acidosis is present, tetany is not common. Muscle twitching may occur due to calcium deficit, but convulsions in patients with chronic renal failure are usually of another origin.

Other Changes

Anemia occurs in chronic renal failure; its severity is related to the degree of azotemia. Mild anemia does not usually present symptoms. Severe anemia can contribute to the development of congestive heart failure. Anemia also predisposes to acidosis because of the decreased buffer action of the deficient red blood cells.

Mild bleeding, such as bruising or bleeding of gums, may occur early. Severe bleeding into the brain or lungs can develop late. The cause of the bleeding tendency in uremic patients is not known; it is thought to be related to the failure of a platelet factor. Other complications of chronic renal failure include pericarditis, pleurisy, hyperparathyroidism, osteomalacia, osteodystrophy and uremia. Pericarditis and pleurisy are usually late symptoms; they may be associated with myocarditis and pneumonitis. (Hyperparathyroidism is discussed in Chap. 20.) Osteomalacia may be revealed by the x-ray. Chronic negative calcium balance can produce osteodystrophy in the adult; symptoms include pain and stiffness of the limbs and joints.

Uremia is a toxic condition caused by failure of the kidneys to excrete urea, potassium, organic acids and other metabolic waste products. Symptoms of uremia include:

- Ammonia odor to the breath
- Uremic frost (urea crystals excreted through sweat glands, heaviest on nose, forehead, and neck)
- Pruritis
- Pale sallow skin (due to urochrome deposition in skin and to anemia)
- Increased bleeding tendency revealed by epistaxis, bleeding gums, easy bruising and conjunctival hemorrhage
- Alternating drowsiness and irritability
- Muscle twitching (due to calcium deficit)
- Cracked lips
- Deep respiration (respiratory compensatory mechanism to relieve metabolic acidosis)
- Chest discomfort (may be caused by pericarditis or pleurisy)
- Stupor and coma
- Convulsions

Treatment

Food and Fluids

Patients with symptoms of chronic renal failure should have their protein intake reduced. This measure alone may improve symptoms greatly. A caloric intake high enough to prevent endogenous protein catabolism is also indicated. Oral intake may be discouraged by the presence of nausea and vomiting and require medication, such as chlorpromazine. The nurse should seek such an order when necessary to relieve the patient's nausea. Attractive small frequent feedings may encourage eating. Encouraging activity may also stimulate appetite, provided congestive heart failure requiring bedrest is not present.

Sodium restriction may be necessary for some patients and harmful to others. Those retaining excessive sodium and water require a low-sodium diet. On the other hand, patients who excrete large quantities of sodium in the urine require a normal diet to prevent sodium deficit. The physician has to determine sodium needs according to test diets and clinical observations, such as excessive weight gain. (Low-sodium diets are described in Chap. 10.) If the plasma potassium level is elevated, foods containing potassium should be eliminated.

Patients with chronic renal failure should be urged to drink from 2,000 to 3,000 ml. of water daily to aid in the elimination of urinary waste products. If the patient is unable to excrete large volumes of water, however, fluid intake should be limited to his needs.

Diuretics

Patients with excessive salt and water retention may be helped by diuretics, such as the thiazides or the mercurials. The danger of toxicity from diuretics is reduced by giving them intermittently rather than daily. Patients who require frequent diuretic therapy can be protected from toxicity by alternating drugs every few days.

Alkalinizing Fluids

Severe metabolic acidosis may be treated with alkaline fluids such as sodium bicarbonate or sodium lactate, although the danger of giving a sodium salt to a patient with a tendency to sodium retention must be considered. Potassium citrate or potassium bicarbonate can be given to patients who are losing potassium because of excessive production of aldosterone. Daily weight measurements are valuable clues to the body's fluid volume status. Symptoms of increased fluid retention should be reported.

Treatment of Calcium Deficit

When the pH is increased due to the administration of alkalinizing fluids, it may be necessary to administer calcium to prevent tetany. Measures to reduce the high phosphorus level may cause an increased calcium level. Therefore, aluminum hydroxide is sometimes administered to combine with phosphate in the gastrointestinal tract.

Blood Transfusions

Low hematocrit and hemoglobin concentration may necessitate blood transfusion. Symptoms of low hemoglobin include weakness, shortness of breath and anorexia. Blood transfusion may relieve these symptoms if uremia is not present. Stored blood should not be used if potassium excess is a problem. (Recall that stored blood is high in potassium.)

Antibiotics

Patients with uremia have a low resistance to infection and commonly develop pneumonitis. Urinary tract infections may be the precipitating cause of renal failure. Although antibiotics are necessary to combat infection, all antibiotics cannot be used. Those that may have toxic effects on the kidneys, such as streptomycin, neomycin and kanamycin, should be avoided. Aqueous penicillin is frequently used because it is non-toxic.

Dialysis

Until recently, patients with chronic renal failure had limited access to dialysis. Frequent cannulation rendered blood vessels useless and prevented frequent hemodialysis. Frequent peritoneal punctures predisposed to peritonitis and made repeated peritoneal dialysis hazardous.

The recent development of a device to eliminate the need for cannulating blood vessels for each hemodialysis has made this measure more accessible to the patient with chronic renal failure. The device consists of two cannulae, one inserted into the radial artery and the other into a forearm vein. The two cannulae are joined by a connecting loop of Teflon between dialyses; this allows blood to circulate between the two and prevents clogging.

A prosthesis, developed to maintain an opening for peritoneal dialysis, has eliminated the need for multiple abdominal punctures in the patient with chronic renal failure in need of frequent dialysis. This device forms a fistula from the skin to the peritoneum that can be opened when dialysis is necessary, closed with an obturator and a screw collar when dialysis is completed. The device does not protrude far when closed and does not cause serious discomfort.

NEPHROTIC EDEMA

Patients with nephroses lose large amounts of albumin through the kidneys, thus decreasing the protein osmotic effect of the blood. Fluid is lost from the plasma (intravascular space) to the interstitial fluid.

Sodium retention is also a factor in nephrotic edema; it may be due to decreased glomerular filtration, increased tubular reabsorption, or both. Large quantities of aldosterone may be found in the urine when edema is present.

The administration of intravenous salt-free human albumin temporarily increases the protein osmotic effect of blood and draws the edema fluid into the intravascular space, increasing blood volume and stimulating sodium excretion. Unfortunately, the effects of albumin administration are only transient because the kidneys continue to lose albumin. A high protein diet will be of some benefit.

Sodium restriction helps relieve nephrotic

edema, as do mercurial diuretics. ACTH may be used to decrease proteinuria and increase urine output. Although it is thought that ACTH may affect glomerular permeability and inhibit the secretion of ADH, its exact actions in relieving edema are not known.

URETERAL TRANSPLANT INTO THE INTESTINAL TRACT

Electrolyte Imbalances

Ureteral transplants can be made into the sigmoid colon (ureterosigmoidostomy), terminal end of the ileum (ureteroileostomy), or into a segment of the ileum isolated from the intestinal tract (ileal-bladder). Patients with ureteral transplants into the intestinal tract may develop metabolic acidosis and eventually potassium deficit.

Metabolic acidosis occurs when urine is reabsorbed from the intestinal tract. Recall that urine is usually acid (average pH of 6) and has a high chloride content. Absorption of urinary chloride into the blood stream causes a compensatory decrease in bicarbonate. The decrease in the bicarbonate side of the carbonic acid:base bicarbonate balance causes the blood pH to drop.

Potassium deficit occurs, largely as the result of excessive renal chloride excretion. This can be explained in the following way. Urinary chloride is absorbed from the intestine into the blood stream and must eventually be re-excreted by the kidneys. A cation, such as potassium or sodium, is excreted with chloride. The continued absorption of urinary chloride by the intestine can deplete the body of potassium. Other factors contribute to potassium deficit. Patients with ureteral-intestinal transplants often have diarrhea, a common cause of potassium deficit. Also, it is possible that the dilute (hypotonic) urine stimulates intestinal secretions to achieve isotonicity. (Recall that all substances entering the gastrointestinal tract assume the tonicity of the area of the tract in which they are located, provided they remain there long enough.)

Intestinal secretions are rich in potassium; if the urine is excreted from the intestine before absorption can take place, the potassium of the intestinal secretions is lost with the urine, further depleting the body's potassium stores. In addition to pH decrease, potassium deficit, and perhaps mild sodium deficit, the blood urea nitrogen level is elevated, due to the absorption of urinary urea from the intestine into the blood stream. The patient with electrolyte disturbances following ureteral transplants may have weakness, intense fatigue, anorexia, nausea and vomiting. When acidosis is severe, hyperpnea is noted.

Factors Contributing to the Development of Electrolyte Imbalances. Electrolyte disturbances do not occur in all patients with ureteral-intestinal transplants. Persons with normal renal function can withstand the absorption of urine without changes in pH or electrolyte levels. Some degree of renal damage must be present for patients with such implants to develop electrolyte imbalances. Unfortunately, many patients with good kidney function develop renal damage as a result of urinary tract infections caused by intestinal organisms, and *then* begin to develop electrolyte imbalances.

Absorption of urine is increased when the urine remains in the intestine for a prolonged period. Thus, the likelihood of metabolic acidosis is greater in patients with ureteral-sigmoid transplants than in those with implants into the ileum since the sigmoid is larger than the ileum and can accommodate larger volumes of urine before peristalsis is initiated.

Prolonged periods of inactivity, as when the patient is bedfast during an illness, favor unsatisfactory urinary drainage. Stricture of the ileal-bladder stoma can also cause urinary retention. Since exposure of a large area of the intestinal mucosa is associated with a higher urinary absorption than is the exposure of a small area, it may sometimes be better to transplant the ureters into an ileal conduit or onto the abdominal wall.

Treatment

Treatment of the electrolyte disturbances usually consists of the administration of potassium and sodium, as gluconate, lactate, or citrate salts. Patients with ureteral transplants into the intact bowel may require the insertion of a rectal catheter to drain urine when they are confined to bed for a prolonged period. A low acid-ash diet may also be helpful. (See Chap. 10.) The success of treatment is inversely proportional to the degree of renal damage present.

Nursing Implications

To prevent or minimize electrolyte disturbances in patients with ureteral transplants into the intestine, the nurse should:

1. Encourage the patient to drink approximately 3,000 ml. of fluids daily, unless intake is restricted. This amount of fluids ensures frequent emptying of the intestine.

2. Encourage the patient to walk; activity favors emptying of the intestines.

3. Encourage the patient with ureteral transplant into the intact bowel to evacuate every few hours. This practice limits the absorption time of urine.

4. If the patient has an ileal-bladder, see that the ileostomy bag is emptied before it is completely full so that urine drainage will not be hindered or back up into the ureters; the patient should also be instructed on how to dilate his stoma and thus prevent poor urine drainage due to a stricture.

5. Look for and report symptoms of electrolyte disturbances, such as weakness, intestinal distention, soft flabby muscles, deep rapid respiration and disorientation.

Chapter 19

Fluid Balance in the Patient With Cardiac Disease

ALTERATIONS IN ELECTROLYTE CONCENTRATIONS: EFFECTS ON THE HEART

Electrolytes Affecting the Myocardium

Potassium, calcium, sodium, magnesium and hydrogen ions influence neuromuscular irritability; therefore, deficient or excessive quantities of these ions can alter heart contractions.

Potassium influences both impulse conduction and muscle contractility; alterations in its concentration may change myocardial irritability and rhythm. Potassium deficit may cause arrhythmias; a pronounced deficit may induce excessive myocardial irritability with cardiac arrest in systole. Potassium excess, on the other hand, has a depressant effect on heart muscle and causes the heart to become weak, flaccid and dilated. Elevation of the extracellular potassium level to two or three times the normal usually causes death through cardiac arrest during diastole.

The effects of calcium on the heart are almost opposite to those of potassium. Thus, calcium deficit depresses the heart in much the same way as does potassium excess. Because the actions of calcium and potassium are antagonistic, the two ions must be present in the proper ratio if normal heart action is to continue. For example, a deficit of calcium renders the myocardium more susceptible to potassium toxicity.

Sodium is also a physiologic antagonist to potassium. Sodium deficit decreases the strength of the heart contraction. Sodium excess, on the other hand, appears to have little or no effect on the myocardium.

Acid-base disturbances influence cardiac activity. High concentrations of carbon dioxide in the blood can cause cardiac arrhythmias, both auricular and ventricular.

Electrocardiograms

The electrocardiogram (ECG) reflects the sum of all ionic influences on the myocardium. Therefore, disturbances in the concentrations of electrolytes alter electrocardiographic tracings (See Table 40). The ECG renders important diagnostic help in detecting disturbances in electrolyte concentration, especially of potassium and calcium. It is most useful when studied in conjunction with serum electrolyte values.

Since ECG changes are usually parallel to alterations in electrolyte concentrations, it is important that the physician interpreting the ECG be familiar with the patient's history. Ideally, ECG tracings should be interpreted by the attending physician.

Nursing Implications

Frequently, the only information available to the physician interpreting the ECG is that appearing on the requisition filled out by the nurse. The nurse, therefore, should supply as much pertinent information as possible.

Although ECG request forms differ, the typical form has spaces for the following:

TABLE 40. EFFECTS OF POTASSIUM AND CALCIUM IMBALANCES ON THE ELECTROCARDIOGRAM

ELECTROLYTE ALTERATION	EFFECT ON ECG
Potassium deficit	Low, rounded, prolonged T waves Prolonged Q-T interval Depression of the S-T segment Negative T waves A-V block Premature contractions Paroxysmal tachycardia Auricular flutter Auricular fibrillation
Potassium excess	Elevation and peaking of T waves Depression of the S-T segment Widening of the QRS complex Disappearance of P waves Heart block
Calcium deficit	Prolonged Q-T interval Normal T wave
Calcium excess	Shortening of the Q-T interval (not diagnostic)

Adapted from Grace, W.: Practical Clinical Management of Electrolyte Disorders. p. 76. New York, Appleton-Century-Crofts, 1960; and Weisberg, H.: Water, Electrolyte and Acid-Base Balance. ed. 2, p. 203. Baltimore, Williams & Wilkins, 1962.

• Whether the patient is taking digitalis, quinidine, diuretics, or other drugs that influence electrolyte metabolism
  • The blood pressure reading
  • Reason for taking the ECG
  • Clinical diagnosis
  • Clinical comments

The nurse must understand the reasons behind the questions if she is to fill out the request correctly.

Medications That Can Affect the Electrocardiogram

Digitalis. Digitalis produces ECG changes since it shortens the heart's recovery time after excitation. Recall that digitalis is commonly employed to increase the strength of cardiac muscle contractions. Unless the physician reading the ECG knows that the patient is receiving digitalis, he may make an incorrect interpretation. For example, digitalis affects the Q-T interval, as does myocardial disease. Both digitalis and potassium depletion affect the T waves and depress the ST segment. Excessive doses of digitalis cause changes in the T wave. Similar changes are caused by myocardial ischemia, pericarditis, myocarditis, thyrotoxicosis and uremia.

These facts serve to emphasize the point that the physician reading the ECG must know if the patient is taking digitalis. Yet, carelessness in filling out the ECG requisition may result in this essential information being omitted.

Quinidine. It is important that the use of quinidine be recorded on the requisition. Quinidine produces ECG changes related to the fact that this drug lengthens the repolarization time of cardiac muscle. Recall that quinidine is used to treat cardiac arrhythmias because it depresses the excitability of cardiac muscle and prolongs both the conduction time and the effective refractory period.

Quinidine characteristically increases the Q-T interval, and flattens and broadens the T-wave. In high doses, it prolongs the P-R interval and widens the QRS complex.

Clinical Comments and Diagnosis

As emphasized above, the nurse filling out the ECG requisition should state the reason for the ECG and briefly describe the patient's clinical condition. If the patient has experienced chest pain, then the nature of the pain and its location should be briefly described. The presence of dyspnea or symptoms of "indigestion" should be recorded. So should the presence of electrolyte imbalances or suspected imbalances. Losses of electrolytes from vomiting, diarrhea, gastric suction, and so on should be noted. (Potassium deficit readily results from such body fluid losses.)

If the diagnosis has been established, it should be recorded. Frequently, the diagnosis may give hints as to the patient's electrolyte status. For example, acute renal failure or chronic nephritis cause potassium excess. Diabetic acidosis is often associated with potassium deficit. Acute pancreatitis or accidental removal of parathyroid tissue during thyroidectomy can cause calcium deficit.

CONGESTIVE HEART FAILURE

The nurse should have a basic understanding of the pathologic mechanisms involved in congestive heart failure so that she can base nursing care on sound physiologic principles.

Pathologic Mechanisms

It was once thought that the primary disturbance underlying congestive heart failure was the failure of the heart as a pump. Now it is recognized that congestive heart failure stems from many factors, including disturbances involving the following organs:

- Heart
- Adrenal cortex
- Central nervous system
- Kidneys
- Vascular network
- Liver

The Heart

The incomplete emptying of the heart causes an increase of venous blood volume at the expense of arterial blood volume. Decreased arterial volume apparently stimulates increased secretion of aldosterone. Aldosterone causes the retention of sodium and water, thus producing an increase in total blood volume. But because of cardiac weakness and the incomplete emptying of the heart, the venous blood volume increases more than the arterial blood volume. The increased hydrostatic pressure produced by the excessive venous blood volume causes a transudation of fluid from the capillaries to the tissues or edema.

The Adrenal Cortex

The secretion of aldosterone may increase to two or three times the normal value in patients with congestive heart failure. Because of the hormone's potent sodium-retaining action, much attention has been focused on it as one of the major causes of edema in congestive heart failure. In addition to promoting sodium retention, aldosterone causes excessive potassium excretion.

The Central Nervous System

Antidiuretic hormone (ADH) acts on the distal tubules of the kidneys, causing water retention. This secretion by the posterior pituitary gland is increased in most patients with congestive heart failure. Thus, such patients frequently retain water in excess of sodium.

Statland states that the increased ADH secretion stems from stimulation of the pituitary gland by the volume receptors in the left atrium and the great veins, as well as from the decreased cerebral blood flow caused by decreased cardiac output.

The Kidneys

Aldosterone acts on the renal tubules to cause increased retention of sodium and water. ADH acts on the distal tubules to cause increased water retention. Decreased cardiac output causes decreased renal blood flow; the kidneys respond by retaining sodium and water. Contributing to the decreased renal blood flow is the vasoconstriction described below.

The Vascular System

Widespread vascular spasm tends to compensate for the decreased circulating blood volume caused by weak heart action. The vasoconstriction affects both venous and arterial vessels and is probably due to sympathetic stimulation and the release of norepinephrine. The vascular spasms are particularly pronounced in the kidneys and cause a further reduction in renal blood flow.

The Liver

The increase in the venous blood volume may, in time, cause liver congestion or cirrhosis, with decreased hepatic function. Normally, aldosterone and ADH are inactivated by the liver. It is possible that the liver congestion of congestive heart failure contributes to edema by preventing the inactivation of these hormones.

TABLE 41. WATER AND ELECTROLYTE DISTURBANCES IN CHF

CAUSE	WATER AND ELECTROLYTE DISTURBANCE
Excessive aldosterone secretion Decreased renal blood flow secondary to cardiac failure and vasoconstriction	Increased retention of sodium and water by the kidneys resulting in: · Increase in total sodium content of body · Increase in total extracellular water volume
Excessive secretion of ADH causes increased retention of water	Relatively greater retention of water than sodium · May depress serum sodium to abnormally low levels, even though the total body sodium is above normal
Hydrostatic pressure is increased by the excessive venous blood volume	Shift of fluid from the intravascular compartment to the interstitial compartment with edema
Excessive aldosterone secretion promotes potassium excretion Excessive use of diuretics or prolonged loss of potassium by vomiting or diarrhea represent typical causes of potassium deficit	Potassium deficit · Primarily a cellular deficit · Sometimes the serum potassium level is not reduced substantially · Cellular acidosis may result as sodium and hydrogen ions enter the cell to replace the deficient potassium ions
Hypotonicity of the extracellular fluid causes water to enter the cells	Increased cellular water volume
Slowing of the circulation interferes with the excretion of metabolic acids and carbon dioxide Increased liberation of lactic acid from anoxic tissues and failure of the body to metabolize it rapidly	Mild metabolic acidosis
Pulmonary congestion interferes with the elimination of carbon dioxide from the lungs	Respiratory acidosis
Mercurial and thiazide diuretics cause a greater excretion of chloride ions than sodium ions; loss of chloride ions causes a compensatory increase in bicarbonate ions, hence alkalosis	Metabolic alkalosis if mercurial or thiazide diuretics are used extensively
Extensive use of potent diuretics plus severely restricted sodium intake Excessive loss of sodium from other routes, such as repeated paracentesis, vomiting, or diarrhea	Sodium deficit

Summary of Water and Electrolyte Disturbances Accompanying Congestive Heart Failure

A multitude of water and electrolyte disturbances are associated with congestive heart failure. The probable causes of these disturbances and the disturbances themselves are itemized in Table 41.

It is important that the nurse be aware of the water and electrolyte disturbances that can occur with congestive heart failure and with therapy. Such understanding is necessary for meaningful nursing observations.

Knowledge of which fluid imbalances may occur in treatment enables the physician to institute suitable preventive measures.

Symptoms of Congestive Heart Failure

Congestive heart failure can be caused by a variety of conditions, including myocardial infarction, disease of the valves, hypertension, arteriosclerosis and thyrotoxicosis. Although these conditions differ widely, they produce much the same clinical picture. Characteristic symptoms and their probable causes are listed in Table 42.

TABLE 42. SYMPTOMS OF CHF AND THEIR CAUSES

SYMPTOM	CAUSE
Fatigue with little exertion or at rest	Tissue anoxia due to decreased cardiac output
Troublesome cough producing non-characteristic sputum, although it may at times be brownish or blood-tinged	Transudation of serum into the alveoli causes pulmonary congestion
Dyspnea on exertion	Cardiac output is inadequate to provide for the increased oxygen required by exertion
Elevated venous pressure	Increase in total blood volume. Accumulation of blood in the venous system results from incomplete emptying of the heart
Decreased urinary output	Decreased cardiac output and renal blood flow. Sodium and water retention caused by excess aldosterone secretion. Increased water retention caused by excess ADH secretion
Visible distention of peripheral veins, most noticeable on face, neck and hands	Elevated venous pressure
Edema first appears in dependent parts	Hydrostatic pressure is greatest in dependent parts of the body
Edema later becomes generalized	Progressive cardiac failure causes substantial increase in hydrostatic pressure in all parts of the body
Fever	Complications accompanying congestive heart failure, such as bronchopneumonia, thrombophlebitis, or myocardial infarction. Fever may be present even in the absence of complications; Steel feels that the cutaneous vasoconstriction occurring with CHF interferes with normal heat loss from the skin
Tachycardia	Effort to compensate for decreased cardiac output

TABLE 42. SYMPTOMS OF CHF AND THEIR CAUSES—(*Continued*)

SYMPTOM	CAUSE
Engorgement of the liver and other organs	Decreased cardiac output causes damming of venous blood Increase in total blood volume and interstitial fluid volume
Nausea and vomiting	Edema of the liver and intestines Impulses arising from the dilated myocardium in acute CHF Digitalis toxicity
Anorexia	Potassium deficit Digitalis toxicity
Constipation	Poor nourishment and inadequate bulk in diet Lack of activity Depression of motor activity by hypoxia
Increased respiratory difficulty · Dyspnea even at rest · Orthopnea	Increased tissue hypoxia due to progressive failure of the heart as a pump
Cyanosis, particularly of lips and nail beds	Venous distention Inadequate oxygenation of blood
Pulmonary edema with severe dyspnea, coughing of pink frothy fluid, cyanosis, shock and death	Increased venous pressure may cause serum and blood cells to transude into the alveoli

Additional symptoms may be caused by the various water and electrolyte disturbances that may occur with congestive heart failure and its treatment; these disturbances may include sodium deficit, potassium deficit, respiratory acidosis (primary carbonic acid excess), metabolic alkalosis (primary base bicarbonate excess), metabolic acidosis (primary base bicarbonate deficit), and fluid volume excess. (Descriptions of these imbalances are given in Chaps. 5, 6 and 7.)

Clearly, congestive heart failure is a complex illness, demanding highly-skilled nursing care. Because fluid imbalances represent a major problem in congestive heart failure, the nurse must make meaningful observations relating to these disturbances. Such observations are of great help to the physician as he plans therapy. The major areas of concern to the nurse are pointed out in the following section, which deals with the treatment of congestive heart failure.

Treatment of Congestive Heart Failure: Nursing Implications

When possible, treatment involves elimi-

nation of the underlying disease producing the heart failure. For example, surgical correction of a valvular disorder or removal of a calcified pericardium may restore cardiac function to normal and produce a spontaneous diuresis. Unfortunately, most persons with congestive heart failure have irreversible cardiac damage, such as that caused by myocardial infarction. When the primary disease cannot be eliminated, the only alternative is to make the most efficient use possible of remaining cardiac function.

Rest

Rest causes a reduction in the tissue's oxygen need and lightens the burden on the circulatory system. It also produces a physiologic diuresis. Sometimes rest alone is sufficient to alleviate the symptoms of congestive heart failure. The amount of rest required varies with the individual and may range from complete bedrest to only slight restriction of activity.

The prescription of physical rest by the physician must be specific enough to have meaning to the patient. Too often, patients are given ambiguous direction to "rest" or to "take it easy." Such vague statements are not only useless, they may actually be harmful, because each person interprets rest differently. The nurse can help by encouraging the patient to ask the physician specific questions regarding the activity permitted.

Another important nursing responsibility consists in observing such responses of the patient to exercise as pulse and respiratory rate changes. Careful reporting of these observations helps the physician determine the desired amount of activity. Because the patient's condition may fluctuate widely from day to day, the nurse must often use her own judgment in controlling his activity. For example, assume that a patient has been allowed up in a chair for 30 minutes in the morning. Even though this period is permitted, the appearance of dyspnea, chest pain, or a substantially increased pulse rate before the 30 minutes are up indicates that the patient should be put back to bed.

Emotional rest is also important in the management of congestive heart failure. Periods of tension are associated with increased sodium and water retention, while periods of emotional relaxation are associated with diuresis. Nursing efforts should, therefore, be directed toward avoiding emotional problems and achieving a relaxing environment. The importance of emotional rest is not as widely recognized as it deserves to be. A major nursing responsibility is emphasizing the importance of emotional rest to the patient's family and to nonprofessional personnel giving direct patient care. At times, judicious use of sedatives may help promote needed rest and relaxation.

Low-Sodium Diet

Restriction of sodium ions in the diet is a valuable aid in the management of congestive heart failure. In general, the fewer number of sodium ions in the body, the less water is retained.

The degree of sodium restriction necessary to control edema varies with the severity of the heart failure. Many patients can achieve a sufficiently low intake of sodium simply by not adding salt in cooking or at the table and by avoiding high sodium foods, such as salted crackers, bacon, ham, salted nuts, foods with sodium salt preservatives, and so on. As a rule, restriction of the intake of salt to from 2 to 5 Gm. daily instead of the usual 10 Gm. or more in an average diet is sufficient to control edema. But more drastic sodium restriction to less than 1 Gm. a day—even 250 mg. a day or less —may be required for some patients.

The degree of sodium restriction necessary to control edema also varies with other facets of treatment, such as rest and the use of diuretics. For example, an ambulatory patient requires more severe sodium restriction than a patient at bedrest, because rest in itself encourages diuresis. A patient receiving potent diuretics has much less need of severe sodium restriction than a patient not receiving diuretics. Indeed, drastic restriction of sodium intake can be dangerous in the patient receiving a potent diuretic.

Although dietary sodium restriction is simple in theory, it is frequently difficult to achieve. Many patients fail to adhere to low-sodium diets because they mistakenly believe them to be unpalatable; others lack an understanding of the foods allowed and the foods to be avoided. All too often, the only diet instruction given to the patient consists of handing him a copy of his diet on the day of his discharge from the hospital.

The nurse should make every effort to make the diet acceptable to the patient. First of all, she should give him an explanation of why he must be on the diet. Secondly, the dietitian should discuss the diet with the patient and learn what his food preferences are. The possible use of salt substitutes should be discussed with the physician. Additional sessions should be held while the patient is in the hospital in order to increase his knowledge and acceptance of the diet. The nurse should support the dietitian's efforts. In instances where a dietitian is not available, the nurse should carry the full responsibility of diet instruction. For this reason, she should have a working knowledge of low-sodium diets. (See Chap. 10.) Literature concerning low-sodium diets is available from the American Heart Association at the request of the patient's physician. Excellent books on the preparation of attractive low-sodium diets are available. Actually, low-sodium diets can be most appealing and need not decrease the patient's enjoyment of food one whit.

Patients on severe sodium restriction should be observed for symptoms of sodium deficit, especially if they are receiving mercurial or thiazide diuretics, or if they are losing sodium through such routes as vomiting, diarrhea, or repeated paracentesis. The patient should, of course, be instructed to avoid sodium-containing medicines, such as bicarbonate of soda (baking soda).

Digitalis

Cardiac function is frequently improved by the administration of digitalis, which acts by increasing the strength of the heartbeat and the cardiac output. Edema fluid is mobilized by the improved cardiac function, and diuresis results.

Excessive doses of digitalis result in the following toxic symptoms:

- Aversion to food, which usually precedes other symptoms by 1 or 2 days
- Nausea and vomiting
- Diarrhea
- Malaise
- Mental depression
- Blurred vision
- Partial or complete heart block

It is important to differentiate between the anorexia and the nausea of heart failure and that produced by digitalis toxicity. Patients receiving digitalis should have periodic electrocardiograms to detect early the development of digitalis toxicity. Prior to the administration of digitalis, the nurse should check the resting radial pulse. If it is below 60, the apical pulse should be checked. If this is below 60, the dose of digitalis should be withheld, and the physician notified, since the slow pulse may be an indication of impending heart-block due to digitalis overdose.

Symptoms of digitalis toxicity may be induced by potassium deficit, since this deficit sensitizes the heart to digitalis. The patient maintained on digitalis without toxicity can, in the presence of potassium deficit, exhibit arrhythmias typical of digitalis intoxication. An irregular pulse caused by digitalis tox-

icity can usually be corrected by the administration of a potassium salt, either by mouth or, if necessary, parenterally. Magnesium has also been reported to correct the toxic rhythms produced by digoxin.

Patients prone to develop potassium deficit (such as those receiving mercurial or thiazide diuretics, or those with vomiting, diarrhea, or poor food intake) should be observed with especial care for signs of digitalis toxicity. Calcium ions have an action similar to that of digitalis and may precipitate digitalis toxicity. Hence, it is wise to avoid intravenous administration of calcium to digitalized patients.

Diuretics

Diuretics are a valuable aid in the symptomatic treatment of congestive heart failure. The two most commonly used groups are the thiazide and the mercurial diuretics. Both act by increasing the renal excretion of sodium and water. (See the discussion of diuretics in Chap. 10.) Thiazide diuretics are more widely used than are mercurials because of the greater ease of administration.

The mercurials, such as Mersalyl and Mercurophylline, require intramuscular administration. In addition, they have more side effects than the thiazides, including cramps, diarrhea, skin rashes and local pain.

Since diuretics are potentially harmful, as are all drugs, they should be used only when needed. In addition to increasing the excretion of sodium, they substantially enhance potassium loss. Indeed, the chief side effect of potent diuretics such as the thiazides is the loss of potassium. Nearly half of the patients on thiazide diuretics for protracted periods will develop potassium deficit if they are not given an adequate potassium supplement. Prolonged potassium deficit may cause irreversible changes in the cells of the heart and kidney; some authorities feel that it may predispose to chronic nephritis. When diuretics are prescribed in excessively large doses, sodium deficit can develop. Weakness, nausea, vomiting, muscle cramps, even fatal collapse due to severe sodium deficit, can result from overzealous diuretic therapy.

Excessive loss of potassium and chloride

ions during diuretic therapy can be either prevented or corrected by the administration of a suitable potassium salt. An effervescent potassium product, K-Lyte, has been shown to be especially well accepted by patients. The use of diuretics should be decreased when sodium loss is occurring from another route; a low-sodium diet can take the place of diuretic therapy in many persons. It is less expensive, safer and, in many respects, more pleasant.

An acidifying agent, such as ammonium chloride, is sometimes given to enhance the effect of mercurial diuretics in resistant cases of edema. Acidifying agents enhance mercurial diuretic action because of the following facts: Diuretics cause a relatively great loss of chloride ions from the body. This loss of chloride causes a compensatory increase in bicarbonate, hence metabolic alkalosis. Alkalosis decreases the effectiveness of mercurial diuretics; hence, the rationale for acidifying agents. A mild state of acidosis is often induced through the use of these agents in order to promote maximal effectiveness of the mercurial diuretic. Although relatively safe, ammonium chloride may cause gastrointestinal symptoms.

Another type of drug capable of producing diuresis in congestive heart failure is Aldactone, spironolactone, an aldosterone antagonist. It acts by blocking the potent sodium-retaining effect of aldosterone on the renal tubules. Spironolactone should not be given in conjunction with a potassium supplement because of the danger of potassium excess. (Recall that aldosterone causes potassium loss; therefore, its antagonist permits potassium retention.) Spironolactone is especially useful in patients with liver disease in which excessive quantities of aldosterone are present.

Primary nursing responsibilities in the care of the patient with congestive heart failure include keeping an accurate account of fluid intake and output and measuring the weight daily. (See the discussion of both of these procedures in Chap. 8.) The data obtained from these measurements are of inestimable use to the physician as he regulates the dose of diuretics and the degree of dietary sodium restriction.

Fluid Administration

Oral Intake. Water intake is usually not restricted in congestive heart failure unless there is a body sodium deficit or dilution of the serum sodium by the excessive retention of water.

Undue loss of sodium may be caused by the excessive use of diuretics, vomiting, diarrhea, severe diaphoresis, or repeated paracentesis. A drastically reduced sodium intake may predispose to sodium depletion, although persons on low sodium intake for prolonged periods usually develop remarkable sodium conservation, something that does not happen in the case of patients on low potassium intake, since there is no true body conservation of potassium. If the water intake of patients in a mild state of sodium depletion is not reduced, the depressed serum sodium level may become further depressed; a frank state of sodium deficit may then develop. Symptoms of this condition include:

- Weakness
- Abdominal cramps
- Anorexia
- Nausea
- Vomiting
- Inexplicable feeling of impending doom
- Prostration
- Collapse

The operation of abnormal routes of sodium loss should alert the nurse to search for the symptoms tabulated above, especially if the sodium intake is low and diuretics are being given. Although the total sodium content of the body is elevated in congestive heart failure, water retention caused by excessive ADH hormone secretion may dilute the serum sodium concentration to below normal levels. Moreover, part of the extracellular fluid sodium moves into the cells to replace the potassium loss which so often occurs with congestive heart failure. There is no characteristic clinical picture accompanying this state. When it is well developed, however, the usual therapeutic measures fail to reduce the edema that accompanies it.

One of the chief features of intractable

heart failure is the inability of the kidney to respond to the usual diuretics. In such instances, treatment consists of the use of acidifying salts, as described earlier, mercurial diuretics, continued sodium restriction, and restriction of water intake to 1,000 ml. per day.

Intravenous Fluids. The intravenous route for fluid administration may be necessary in critically ill patients with congestive heart failure. Many physicians are hesitant to administer fluids to such patients for fear of causing circulatory overload and pulmonary edema. While there is little doubt that intravenous administration of fluids to a cardiac patient carries some risk of causing circulatory overload, the fear of this complication has been exaggerated to the point that many cardiac patients receive inadequate fluid therapy. The recent increase in the use of venous pressure monitoring devices has done much to alleviate the problem. Frequent checks of venous pressure during fluid administration give early warning of circulatory overload and serve as guides to the safe administration of needed water and electrolytes.

The nurse should pay careful attention to the volume, speed and composition of fluids administered to the patient with congestive heart failure. The response to the fluids should be observed frequently and the flow rate adjusted accordingly. (See Chap. 14 for a more detailed discussion of venous pressure monitoring and nursing responsibilities in intravenous fluid administration.)

Pulmonary Edema. The symptoms of acute pulmonary edema include:

- Restlessness
- Severe dyspnea
- Gurgling respirations
- Cyanosis
- Coughing up of frothy fluid

Welt has pointed out possible causes of pulmonary edema other than administering excessive quantities of fluid or too rapid administration of fluid. Inadequate fluid administration can result in peripheral vascular collapse with tissue anoxia; this condition in itself can precipitate an acute attack of pulmonary edema. Some patients develop

pulmonary edema during venipuncture, or shortly after fluids have been started before there has been time for expansion of the circulatory volume. Pulmonary edema in these instances can be explained as a reaction to fear related to the venipuncture. The following illustrative case was related by Welt:*

A patient with chronic renal insufficiency and hypertensive and arteriosclerotic heart disease with failure despite complete digitalization was admitted to the hospital. It was decided to improve her severe anemia with blood transfusion. The nature of the procedure was not explained to her, she had not been sedated, there was a little difficulty with the venipuncture, and when the needle was successfully introduced into the vein she developed severe acute pulmonary edema. The procedure was discontinued and she recovered from this episode in a few hours. Later that day the nature of and indications for the transfusion were explained to her, she was sedated, and tolerated the administration of 1,000 ml. of whole blood with no untoward reaction whatsoever.

In addition to fear of venipuncture, the patient may interpret the need for intravenous fluids as a grave prognostic sign. This is but another reason to take time to explain to the patient what the intravenous administration consists of and why it is being used.

Occasionally, hypertonic solution of sodium chloride is administered to the cardiac patient to correct a sodium deficit. Great care should be taken to infuse the solution slowly in accordance with the order of the physician. A too rapid administration of hypertonic saline results in a dangerous overloading of the circulatory system.

Acute pulmonary edema constitutes a medical emergency that requires quick, intelligent action by the nurse and the physician. The patient should be quickly placed in a high Fowler's position, and oxygen should be started while the physician is being summoned. Best results are achieved when oxygen is given under positive pressure, since this helps prevent further escape of fluid into the lungs. Preparation should be made for intravenous administration of morphine sulfate. Usually one-sixth to one-half grain is

* Welt, L.: Clinical Disorders of Hydration and Acid-Base Equilibrium. ed. 2, p. 131. Boston, Little Brown, 1959.

ordered in order to relieve the apprehension so characteristic of pulmonary edema. It has also been suggested that morphine may help to reverse pulmonary edema by interrupting reflex arcs set up by the increased venous pressure. The use of alternating tourniquets to obstruct venous return to the heart, or the removal of 200 to 500 ml. of blood by phlebotomy may be tried in order to relieve the work load on the heart and to reduce venous pressure. Rapid digitalization with Lanatoside C improves cardiac function, thus helps relieve pulmonary edema. Diuretics rid the body of edema fluid and thus reduce venous pressure.

NURSING OBSERVATIONS RELATED TO FLUID BALANCE FOLLOWING OPEN HEART SURGERY

This section was prepared by Catherine A. Smith, R.N.. St. Louis University.

One of the most challenging areas of nursing today is the care of the patient undergoing open heart surgery. Due to the magnitude and the severity of the surgical procedure and the emotional trauma endured by both patient and family, a highly skilled nurse is required to adequately meet the demands and requirements that arise.

It is not within the scope of this section to discuss all phases of nursing care of the patient undergoing open heart surgery. Rather, it shall be confined to the nursing responsibilities in relation to disturbances of fluid balance during the postoperative period.

The process of open heart surgery inflicts a tremendous insult upon the body. Extracorporeal circulation is not as effective as normal circulation. The process of hypothermia, together with extracorporeal circulation, affects every organ in the body, producing biochemical changes. Many of these physiological disturbances have not yet been adequately investigated. Those which are known should be familiar to the nurse caring for the patient following open heart surgery.

A good observer is needed at the bedside of these patients, as with any acutely ill patient. There are many symptoms of water and electrolyte disturbances that are apparent to a thoughtful observer. Of all the persons involved in patient care, the nurse is the person in most constant attendance. This places her in the position most favorable to noting beginning changes in body physiology. She has a responsibility to be alert and highly skilled in the observations she makes. It is not her function to diagnose, but rather to be sensitive to meaningful changes and to relate these to the physician.

Acidosis and the Need for Oxygen

Studies have shown that metabolic acidosis frequently occurs following cardiopulmonary bypass and profound hypothermia; this has generally been attributed to hypoxia. This state is manifested by a decrease in blood pH and bicarbonate levels. Therefore, these patients are ideally assessed during the first few postoperative hours with blood pH and bicarbonate studies. The frequency of these determinations is dependent upon the clinical course of the patient.

The nurse, being the person in most constant attendance during the early postoperative period, must be alert for signs of metabolic acidosis. Hyperpnea is a dependable physical sign. It is the increase in the depth of respiration that makes hyperpnea so easy to recognize—there is a tendency to be concerned only about the rate of respiration and to neglect to take note of the depth of respiration. An increase in depth of respiration should be promptly reported to the physician.

The nurse must realize that one of the most common complications following heart surgery with cardiopulmonary bypass is respiratory insufficiency; if untreated, it can proceed to *respiratory acidosis*. These patients are extremely sensitive to oxygen lack; by the time a patient with previously good color exhibits cyanosis, hypoxia may be at a dangerous level. Therefore, the nurse must be familiar with the signs of respiratory distress and respiratory acidosis so that she can promptly communicate this information to the physician and prompt therapy can be initiated. Signs of respiratory distress may include:

- Disturbed facial expression and general behavior of distress

- Shallow, labored, rapid respiration
- Feeble coughing
- Restlessness
- Tachycardia
- Cyanosis

To further facilitate care of the patient following open heart surgery, the nurse's knowledge should include an understanding of the possible causes of respiratory insufficiency and acidosis, which can occur either when the functional capacity of the lungs is reduced significantly or when the patient is unable to perform sufficient respiratory work to provide adequate ventilation. Some of the causes of decreased functional capacity of the lungs include:

- Atelectasis
- Hemothorax
- Bronchospasm
- Pulmonary edema
- Pulmonary infections

Some of the causes of the patient's inability to perform adequate respiratory work are:

- Shallow breathing due to incisional pain
- Respiratory depressant drugs
- Inability of the heart to deliver sufficient amounts of blood to the lungs to permit adequate gaseous exchange

Any of these causes can result in lowered arterial oxygen tension and increased carbon dioxide. Frequent blood studies for pO_2 and pCO_2 are desirable in order to detect early changes and to estimate the progression of recovery processes.

Considering these causes and ever mindful of the preventive aspect of nursing care, it becomes evident that following open heart surgery the patient must be conscientiously engaged in a systematic regimen of turning, coughing and deep breathing. Coughing can do no harm—it should be begun immediately postoperatively while the patient is still somewhat insensitive to pain due to the residue of anesthetic. Coughing is an uncomfortable experience for the patient. The nurse should help the patient perform these exercises in such a manner that they are most tolerable and comfortable for him. Kindness, sympathy and an unhurried manner are important. A pillow held firmly over the site of the incision is reassuring and comforting to the patient.

The state of acidosis, whether respiratory or metabolic, has adverse effects upon the myocardium and affects cardiac rate and rhythm, changes in which should be immediately reported to the physician. Following open heart surgery, arrhythmias are not unusual, but they are less frequent when myocardial oxygenation is adequate. Dammann has stated that above-normal levels of arterial oxygen tension in the early postoperative period are helpful in the prevention of harmful arrhythmias. Such levels can be achieved by intermittent positive pressure or hyperbaric therapy.

For this reason, oxygen is customarily given by nasal tube or tent for the first 12 hours postoperatively. After this period, nasal oxygen is discontinued if the patient's condition is satisfactory. If an oxygen tent is used, it is continued until the second or third postoperative day. Oxygen consumption studies are frequently performed at the bedside to evaluate further the patient's oxygen requirements.

In relation to oxygen requirement, the nurse should realize that metabolic demands for oxygen are increased by certain physiologic states. Such conditions as undue restlessness, shivering and pyrexia can substantially increase the need for oxygen and the requirement on cardiac output. Appropriate nursing measures should be taken to avoid or counteract these conditions.

Daily Weight Measurement

The pattern of daily weights provides an accurate account of fluid loss or retention by the body. The physician relies heavily upon weight changes to prescribe therapy. Candidates for heart surgery are placed on daily weights from their date of admission to the hospital. Daily weights are resumed approximately the second or third day following surgery, after the chest tube has been removed and the movement of the patient to the bed scale is facilitated. (Nursing responsibilities in obtaining daily weight measurements are discussed in Chap. 8.)

Intravenous Therapy

Following open heart surgery, great care and accuracy are required in the management of intravenous fluids. An excessive circulating blood volume can be extremely hazardous; the recently wounded and recuperating heart may be unable to cope with this additional load and pulmonary edema can result. Therefore it becomes evident that intravenous fluid orders must be very clear and specific both to amount and time of infusion. Communication and understanding between physician and nurse cannot be too detailed in this area. Often, however, the physician will order intravenous fluids for a 12- or 24-hour interval. Then it becomes a nursing responsibility to determine the rate at which these fluids should run in order to provide an even distribution over the specified time interval. (See the section dealing with the calculation of flow rate in Chap. 14.)

Each bottle of fluid should be clearly labeled with the time it was begun, the time it is to be completed, and the desired infusion rate. This rate should be checked at frequent intervals—i.e., every 15 to 30 minutes. The importance of the nurse's responsibility in the administration of fluids and the conscientiousness required of her cannot be overstressed.

Urine Output

Since almost every organ system can be affected by the combination of open heart surgery and total body perfusion, deviations from normal urine formation might be anticipated. There is no single factor that will lead invariably to renal complications. Rather, many factors have been noted which singly or in combination predispose the kidneys to serious damage. Among these factors are:

- Extracorporeal perfusion rate
- Length of the perfusion
- Postoperative acidosis

Yeh stated that renal ischemia and nephrotoxins, or their combination, are the most consistent causes of renal failure. He also pointed out that while vasopressor drugs are capable of increasing blood pressure in shock, at the same time renal blood flow, renal plasma flow and urine flow can be severely depressed. To aid in the evaluation of kidney function, the BUN is determined daily.

The rationale and details of accurate urine observations should be basic knowledge to the nurse caring for the patient following open heart surgery. In some cases, a Foley catheter will be in place; and frequent measurements of urine volume, usually hourly, are of utmost importance. Urine volume should be measured accurately, to the milliliter. (See Fig. 82.) A vessel with small calibrations should be used. (See discussion of urinary output measurement in Chap. 8.) A urinary output of less than 15 ml. per hour is indicative of inadequate renal function. When the output falls below this figure, the physician should be immediately notified.

Each time the urinary output is measured, a urinary specific gravity test should be performed. (The procedure for determining the specific gravity of urine is described in Chap. 8.) This information will help to determine the state of hydration, as well as the status of kidney function. The average range of urine specific gravity is 1.010 to 1.030.

Chest Drainage

In caring for the patient following heart surgery, the nurse must have an understanding of the principles of water-seal chest drainage. If she possesses a clear understanding of the mechanics of respiration, she can feel perfectly at ease with the water-seal drainage system. The purpose of the system is to drain excess fluid from the operative area and to re-establish normal intrapleural pressure.

The chest tube must be kept patent by regular milking. This should be done every hour, more frequently if necessary. Milking should begin near the patient's chest and continue down the tubing to the bottle, clearing the tubing of any clots. The tubing should be kept free of any kinks, and care should be taken to prevent looping of excess tubing on the floor.

The nurse must make certain that the bottle *always* rests below the lowest level of

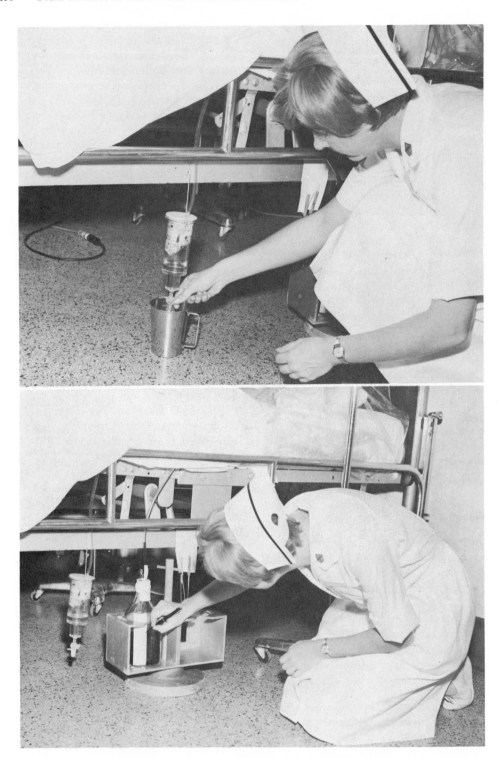

Fig. 82 (*Top*) Measuring urine output with Davol Uri-meter.
Fig. 83. (*Bottom*) Marking chest tube drainage.

the patient's chest. If the bottle is raised to chest level, negative pressure may suck water into the intrathoracic space. The chest bottle should either be kept in a holder or taped securely to the floor. This will prevent accidentally knocking the bottle over and breaking the water-seal system.

All connections must be secure and well taped. If the drainage bottle should be broken or if the water-seal fails for any reason, the tube should be clamped immediately, near the chest. Two clamps should be kept at the bedside for each chest tube at all times.

The water-seal setup should be observed for the amount and character of drainage. Bright red drainage is expected immediately postoperatively, gradually becoming darker, then more serosanguinous. Any sudden change should be reported immediately. To record the amount of drainage, a piece of adhesive tape should be vertically applied to the bottle so that hourly marks can be made, thus giving an accurate account of fluid loss. (See Fig. 83.) In children, the bottle can be placed on a small scale to better indicate small increments of drainage.

The nurse should keep in mind the importance of determining how much the patient has lost in an hour-by-hour pattern.

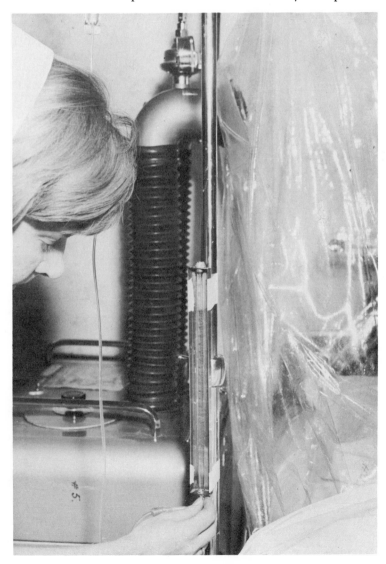

Fig. 84. Measuring venous pressure on a spinal manometer.

For instance, consider these contrasting records:

300 ml.	First hour	400 ml.
50 ml.	Second hour	50 ml.
50 ml.	Third hour	50 ml.
25 ml.	Fourth hour	25 ml.
50 ml.	Fifth hour	25 ml.
100 ml.	Sixth hour	0 ml.
100 ml.	Seventh hour	10 ml.
150 ml.	Eighth hour	5 ml.
Cause for		No Cause
Concern		for Concern

Oscillation of the fluid in the tubing should also be noted. When this ceases, it may indicate that the lung has re-expanded or that a clot obstructs the tubing. The tubing should be checked for patency at this time.

There should be adequate tubing to allow the patient to turn freely in bed. He should be turned every 1 to 2 hours. Turning to the affected side will facilitate drainage.

However, care must be taken that the patient does not occlude the chest tube.

Venous Pressure

All the blood in the body returns to the right atrium of the heart. For this reason, the pressure within the right atrium is known as the central venous pressure. The pressure within the systemic veins depends heavily upon the central venous pressure. If the pressure within the right atrium rises, the pressure within the systemic veins will also rise. Thus, a direct method of measuring peripheral venous pressure gives a reflection of the central venous pressure.

The nurse should realize that venous pressure can be a useful guide in assessing the circulatory status following severe trauma and major surgery. Venous pressure can be affected by several complications:

• *Hypervolemia:* the circulatory system is overloaded and the venous pressure tends to

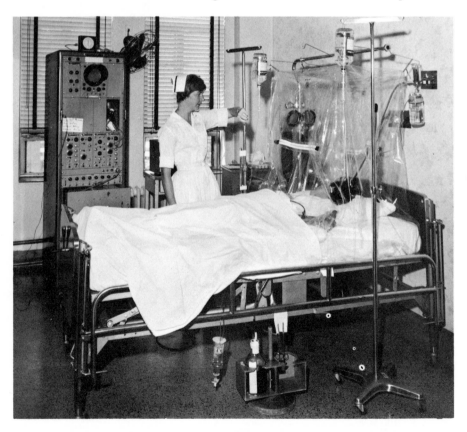

Fig. 85. Fluid gains and losses following open-heart surgery.

be elevated. The work load of the heart is increased. This may lead to peripheral and pulmonary edema and failure of the myocardium.

• *Hypovolemia:* the circulating blood volume is inadequate and venous pressure is decreased. This may be due to vasodilation from rewarming of the body after the period of hypothermia used during the surgical procedure. Hypovolemia more commonly results from postoperative bleeding or shifts in fluid volume between the various compartments.

• *Cardiac Tamponade:* an accumulation of fluid in the pericardial sac causes compression of the heart and an increased venous pressure.

• *Congestive Heart Failure:* the venous pressure will increase.

Venous pressure can be measured by a direct venipuncture and recorded in centimeters of water on a spinal manometer. (See Fig. 84.) Following open heart surgery, the femoral vein is frequently used to obtain these readings. By means of a three-way stopcock, the venous pressure manometer can remain attached to the intravenous fluids that the patient is receiving continuously. Accurate venous pressure readings are dependent upon a good base line. To obtain this base line, the patient must be in a supine position. One must realize that venous pressure is expressed in relation to the level of the tricuspid valve. Therefore, the zero point on the manometer must be on an equal level with the tricuspid valve. This is essentially a midline structure, midway between the anterior and posterior of the body. Initially, this base line will be determined by the physician and the manometer secured at the proper level. The nurse, however, will be responsible for obtaining subsequent venous pressure readings—as frequently as every one-half hour during the immediate postoperative period. For this reason, she should have a thorough understanding of the principles involved in obtaining accurate venous pressure readings. She must realize that any deviation in position of the patient will affect the venous pressure reading. For example, if the patient is turned on his side or the head of the bed is elevated, the venous pressure reading will vary. When using this method, care should be taken not to change the level of a high-low bed once the manometer is in place. Every effort should be made to position the patient so as to obtain an accurate reading. (Venous pressure measurement is discussed in more detail in Chap. 14.)

Chapter 20

Fluid Balance in the Patient With Endocrine Disease

ROLE OF ENDOCRINE GLANDS IN FLUID BALANCE HOMEOSTASIS

The endocrine homeostatic controls include the adrenals, the parathyroids, and the anterior and posterior pituitary glands.

Adrenal Glands

The adrenal mechanism is intimately associated with retention and excretion of sodium, potassium and water. Apparently these effects are exerted through the action of the adrenocortical hormones on the renal tubules.

The primary adrenal cortex secretions are mineralocorticoids and glucocorticoids. Aldosterone is the most important mineralocorticoid; cortisol is the most important glucocorticoid.

The chief function of aldosterone is the control of sodium concentration in the body. Its effect on potassium and sodium is 50 times stronger than cortisol's effect on these electrolytes.

The chief action of cortisol is to promote gluconeogenesis and to deposit glycogen in the liver. It also influences protein catabolism. Other effects of the glucocorticoids include control of inflammation, maintenance of gastric acidity, and a mild mineralocorticoid influence on sodium and potassium concentrations.

Androgenic adrenocorticoids (17-ketosteroids) are also produced by the adrenal cortex. These hormones favor a positive nitrogen balance and they oppose the cata-

bolic effects of the glucocorticoids. Sexual effects of these hormones include promotion of hair growth in the pubic and axillary areas.

Parathyroid Glands

Parathyroid hormone causes an increase in the plasma calcium concentration, primarily by increasing the rate of bone resorption. Any *decrease* in the plasma calcium concentration causes stimulation of the parathyroid glands. Conversely, any *increase* in the plasma calcium level causes parathyroid activity to decrease.

Another function of parathyroid hormone is to increase the renal excretion of phosphate ions and thus to lower the plasma phosphate concentration. The plasma phosphate concentration indirectly influences parathyroid activity, since a reciprocal relationship exists between calcium and phosphate ions—a rise in the concentration of one causing a decrease in the other. Thus, an increase in phosphate concentration causes a reciprocal decrease in the calcium concentration. The decreased calcium concentration causes parathyroid stimulation.

Pituitary Glands

The anterior pituitary gland secretes several hormones. Some of these, such as the growth hormones, exert a direct effect on the metabolism of water and electrolytes. Others exert an indirect effect by stimulating other endocrine glands whose hormones directly influence metabolism. These include thyroid-stimulating hormone (TSH), adreno-cortical stimulating hormone (ACTH), and the gonadotrophic hormones.

The posterior pituitary gland releases a water conserving hormone referred to as the antidiuretic hormone, or ADH. As the name implies, it inhibits diuresis. (It seems more direct to think of it as conserving water.) The release of ADH is influenced by the "osmostat," an auxiliary control located in the plexus of the internal carotid artery. The osmostat is sensitive to changes in osmolarity (electrolyte concentration) of the extracellular fluid.

ENDOCRINE DISORDERS CAUSING FLUID BALANCE DISTURBANCES

It is not within the scope of this chapter to discuss all of the endocrine disturbances causing fluid balance disturbances. A brief discussion of adrenocortical insufficiency and parathyroid disorders is presented. (Diabetes insipidus is discussed in Chap. 21.) Much emphasis is placed on diabetic acidosis because this condition is commonly encountered by the nurse.

Adrenocortical Insufficiency

Adrenocortical insufficiency may be caused by destruction or suppression of the adrenals, or it may be secondary to hypofunction of the pituitary gland. The disease can be either acute or chronic. Symptoms are primarily due to decreased aldosterone and cortisol secretion.

Water and Electrolyte Changes

Water and electrolyte disturbances occurring with adrenocortical insufficiency include:

- Sodium deficit
- Potassium excess
- Extracellular fluid volume deficit
- Mild metabolic acidosis
- Hypercalcemia

Decreased aldosterone secretion is largely responsible for the increased urinary excretion of sodium and retention of potassium,

although decreased cortisol secretion undoubtedly contributes to these changes. Water loss accompanies the increased urinary excretion of sodium and results in extracellular fluid volume deficit. Sodium is lost in excess of water. Decreased cortisol secretion causes a delay in water excretion; decreased glomerular filtration rate contributes to this effect. A loss of bicarbonate ions accompanies the sodium loss and a mild metabolic acidosis may result. Hypercalcemia may also occur with adrenocortical insufficiency.

Other Metabolic Changes

Carbohydrate, protein and fat metabolism are impaired by adrenocortical insufficiency. Lack of cortisol causes decreased gluconeogenesis and depletion of the liver glycogen. Thus, hypoglycemia can occur. Negative nitrogen balance results from the decreased secretion of 17-ketosteroids. Fat metabolism is slowed due to the reduced secretion of cortisol and corticosterone.

Other abnormalities include a reduced cellular response to injury, leukopenia and a decreased number of neutrophils.

Chronic Adrenal Insufficiency

Symptoms of chronic adrenal insufficiency may include:

- Fatigue out of proportion to activity
- Emotional depression and irritability
- Weight loss (due to fluid volume deficit and negative caloric balance)
- Hypotension (particularly pronounced when patient changes from a supine position to an upright position)
- Nausea
- Diarrhea
- Hypoglycemia, noticed several hours after meals (symptoms include hunger, nervousness, sweating, headache and confusion)
- Poor resistance to infection
- Muscle wasting
- Pigmentation of skin, common in adults with primary adrenal insufficiency
- Hair growth retarded
- Dental caries

Treatment consists of daily hormonal replacement therapy. Cortisone is given daily in a dose usually varying between 12.5 and 37.5 mg. This amount must be greatly increased when infection, trauma, diarrhea, inability to eat or other complications occur. Patients should be advised to consult their physician *immediately* when such conditions occur.

A mineralocorticoid, such as desoxycorticosterone or 9-alpha fluorohydrocortisone, is given in addition to cortisone to control sodium and potassium concentrations in the body. Although cortisone causes sodium retention, its effect is too weak to prevent sodium loss during periods of stress. Desoxycorticosterone (DOCA) is available in a long-acting form, Percorten trimethyl-acetate, that may be given intramuscularly every 3 or 4 weeks. Oral therapy with Percorten acetate Linguets allows easy dose adjustment when necessary.

Dietary sodium chloride intake should be consistent with the patient's taste and usually differs little from the average salt content of a normal diet. Salt tablets should be carried to repair sodium loss due to unusual circumstances, such as excessive heat exposure and sweating. Frequent carbohydrate feedings may prevent symptoms of hypoglycemia.

Overtreatment with cortisone may produce unfavorable symptoms such as acne, moon facies, diabetes mellitus, peptic ulcer, bleeding tendencies and hypertension. Overtreatment with mineralocorticoids may cause excessive fluid retention with weight gain and hypertension. The nurse should be alert for these symptoms. Careful recording of fluid intake and output and daily weight measurement are necessary to detect early fluid retention.

The patient should be made aware of the need for systematic medical follow-up in the control of his disease. He should be taught to avoid excessive physical and emotional stress and infections. In addition he should be aware of the symptoms accompanying under- and over-treatment of adrenocortical insufficiency.

Acute Adrenocortical Insufficiency

The nurse should be alert for acute adrenocortical insufficiency, sometimes termed "adrenal crisis," when patients with decreased adrenal function are exposed to stress, such as surgery, trauma, emotional upset or prolonged medical illness. Such a crisis may occur when a patient with chronic adrenocortical insufficiency fails to take his prescribed hormones. (Adrenal crisis as a result of surgery in patients on prolonged adrenocortical hormone therapy is discussed in Chap. 15.)

Symptoms of acute adrenocortical insufficiency include hypotension, thready pulse, nausea, vomiting, confusion and circulatory collapse. The body temperature may rise as high as 105° F.

Treatment consists of the intravenous administration of hydrocortisone as soon as possible. The blood volume should be expanded by the administration of isotonic solution of sodium chloride and glucose, dextran or blood. Vasopressor drugs may be necessary to raise the blood pressure. Sodium deficit should be corrected over a period of several days with hypertonic saline infusions. Glucose should be administered to prevent or correct symptoms of hypoglycemia. Intravenous hydrocortisone replacement therapy is continued until the patient is improved sufficiently to take cortisol intramuscularly, or cortisone when oral intake is tolerated.

The nurse should keep a close watch for changes in the vital signs. A fall in blood pressure and a rapid, thready pulse may indicate inadequate hydrocortisone and fluid replacement therapy. She should also protect the patient from physical and emotional stress, when possible.

Hypoparathyroidism

Underproduction of parathyroid hormone occurs in primary hypoparathyroidism and in the accidental removal of parathyroid tissue during thyroidectomy. Renal tubular damage can interfere with the action of parathyroid hormone and produce symptoms of hypoparathyroidism (pseudohypoparathyroidism). Decreased parathyroid activity results in:

1. Decreased plasma calcium concentration

2. Increased plasma phosphate concentration

Symptoms of hypoparathyroidism are primarily those of neuromuscular irritability produced by a decrease in the serum concentration of ionized calcium. They include:

- Numbness of extremities
- Tingling of hands, feet, and circumoral region
- Mood changes
- Voice changes caused by spasms of vocal cords
- Muscular spasm, induced by compressing blood supply to area
- Abdominal cramps
- Diarrhea
- Carpopedal attitude of hands
- Facial spasm, induced by tapping over nerve course in front of the ear (Chvostek's sign)
- Laryngeal spasms
- Convulsions

Other symptoms of hypoparathyroidism are influenced by the duration of the parathyroid hormone deficiency and the age at which it developed. For example, cataracts or calcification of various body parts such as the basal ganglia of the brain may occur when hypoparathyroidism has long been present. Formation of new teeth is restricted when hypoparathyroidism occurs in a child, although the degree of hypoplasia depends upon the age at which hypoparathyroidism began.

The danger of the accidental removal of parathyroid tissue during thyroidectomy is always present because the parathyroids are small and resemble fatty tissue. Removal of half of the parathyroid glands usually doesn't present symptoms. (Most persons have four parathyroid glands; some have less and some have as many as seven.) However, removal of three out of four causes symptoms of hypoparathyroidism, until the fourth gland is able to hypertrophy sufficiently to fulfill the function of all of the glands. Tetany may be produced by temporary interference with the parathyroid blood supply following thyroidectomy.

The nurse should be alert for symptoms of deficit of ionized calcium during the postoperative care of patients who have undergone thyroidectomy. Such symptoms usually appear a few days after the operation. Early complaints are of numbness and tingling in the hands and feet. Compression of circulation to the hand while checking the blood pressure may cause spasm of the forearm muscles and palmar flexion of the hand. Other symptoms of deficit, such as general irritability or "jumpiness," may be noted. It is crucial to detect calcium deficit early so that appropriate hormonal therapy or calcium replacement or both can be started before the onset of laryngeal spasms and convulsions.

Hypocalcemia due to hypoparathyroidism may be treated by the administration of calcium salts. Calcium gluconate given intravenously may control tetany; calcium gluconate or lactate may be administered orally for the same purpose. An increased dietary intake of high calcium foods will also be beneficial.

Dihydrotachysterol (A.T. 10) is a substance having an action similar to that of parathyroid hormone (parathormone). It increases calcium absorption from the bone and thus causes an increased plasma calcium concentration. It is administered from three to seven times weekly in conjunction with oral calcium replacement. Dihydrotachysterol is less expensive than parathormone and has a longer action. Although parathormone is effective initially, its effects are soon lost, probably due to the development of immune bodies.

Hyperparathyroidism

Overproduction of parathyroid hormone occurs in primary hyperparathyroidism and in tumors of the parathyroid gland. Increased parathyroid activity results in:

1. Increased plasma calcium concentration
2. Decreased plasma phosphate concentration

Secondary hyperparathyroidism may be found in patients with renal disease, which interferes with excretion of phosphate ions and causes the plasma phosphate concentration to rise. Due to the reciprocal action of phosphate and calcium, the plasma calcium concentration drops. The low plasma calcium level causes stimulation of the parathyroids and eventually produces parathyroid hyperplasia, which causes progressive decalcification of the skeleton, sometimes referred to as "renal rickets."

Symptoms of hyperparathyroidism produced by the diminished neuromuscular irritability stemming from calcium excess include:

- Mental confusion
- Loss of memory or mental acuity
- Lethargy
- Weak, sluggish muscles
- Constipation
- Vomiting
- Anorexia
- Abdominal pain (may be the most striking symptom)
- Prolonged cardiac systole

Other symptoms of hyperparathyroidism are produced by the excess filtration of calcium through the glomeruli. Calcium sediment deposits in the kidneys and produces tubular damage. Polyuria occurs, due to the increased renal solute load and to the damaged renal tubules. Polydipsia (excessive thirstiness) follows excessive water loss through the kidneys. Uremia and hypertension may eventually follow the renal damage imposed by calcium excess.

Severe hyperparathyroidism causes excessive bone absorption and eventually produces extensive skeletal decalcification. Decalcified bones are easily broken; on x-ray they show "punched out" areas. The bone disorder produced by hyperparathyroidism is sometimes called von Recklinghausen's disease. There is an increased incidence of pancreatitis and gastric ulcers in patients with hyperparathyroidism.

The treatment of hyperparathyroidism consists of surgical removal of the over-active parathyroid tissue. More than one parathyroid tumor may be present and require the excision of several parathyroid glands. Following surgery, hypoparathyroidism may be present until the remaining parathyroid tissue hypertrophies.

Bone recalcification is rapid following removal of parathyroid tumors; symptoms of calcium excess recede. However, irreversible renal damage and skeletal deformities may have developed.

Severe Diabetic Acidosis

Diabetic acidosis occurs when an insulin lack prevents normal glucose metabolism, and body energy needs are met with the catabolism of fats and proteins. Events often associated with the onset of diabetic acidosis include:

- Omission of insulin
- Overeating
- Lack of carbohydrate, causing increased fat and protein utilization (may be caused by strenuous exercise of prolonged vomiting)
- Failure to increase insulin dosage during times of increased need:
    Infections
    Thyrotoxicosis
    Trauma
    Surgery
    Pregnancy

Diabetic acidosis is a serious condition presenting several water and electrolyte disturbances. The nurse must be aware of the causes and manifestations of these imbalances so that she can detect their early occurrence and cooperate intelligently in their treatment.

Water and Electrolyte Disturbances Prior to Treatment

Insulin must be present for glucose to pass through the cell to participate in cellular metabolism. When insulin secretion is decreased glucose cannot be utilized. Its concentration in the blood stream rises (hyperglycemia). With glucose unavailable, the body must utilize fats and proteins; as the result of catabolism of fats, ketone bodies accumulate. This leads to ketosis (metabolic acidosis).

Cellular and Extracellular Fluid Volume Deficit. Hyperosmolarity of the extracellular fluid is produced by the high glucose concentration. Water is drawn from the cells to maintain osmotic equilibrium. When the glucose concentration in the blood exceeds 180 mg. per 100 ml., glucose is excreted in the urine (glycosuria). Because 10 to 20 ml. of water are required to excrete each gram of glucose, water loss through the kidneys is increased. Since sodium and chloride reabsorption are hindered by the osmotic diuresis, excessive amounts of these ions are excreted in the urine. The metabolic end-products of protein and fat increase the renal solute load, thus increasing the water loss. (Recall that materials must be in solution before the kidneys can excrete them.)

Insensible water loss by way of the lungs may be doubled due to the deep, rapid respiration accompanying acidosis. Although both water and electrolyte loss are increased in diabetic acidosis, water loss predominates. In severe diabetic acidosis there is a deficit of approximately 100 ml. of water per Kg. of body weight. For example, a patient weighing 154 lbs. may have a water deficit of 7 L; water is lost both from cells and from extracellular fluid.

Ketosis (Keto-acidosis). The increased utilization of fat for energy needs causes accumulation of the ketone bodies aceto-acetic acid, beta-hydroxybutyric acid, and acetone. The usual keto acid plasma level is 1 mEq./L.; it may reach as high as 20 mEq./L. in diabetic acidosis. Due to the increased keto-acid concentration in the blood stream, ketones are excreted by the kidneys (ketonuria). The accumulation of an excessive number of H^+, stemming from the keto acids, causes the blood pH to drop, sometimes to as low as 6.9 or even 6.8. The increase in the number of ketonic anions (negatively charged ions) causes a compensatory decrease in the number of bicarbonate anions (also negatively charged), representing the body's attempt to maintain electrical equilibrium. The bicarbonate level may drop as low as 5 mEq./L.

Compensatory Respiratory Alkalosis. A fall in blood pH from the normal to not lower than 7 causes stimulation of the respiratory center and hyperventilation, a compensatory mechanism that increases the excretion of carbon dioxide from the lungs and thus lowers the carbonic acid content of the extracellular fluid. Blood pH increases. If the blood pH drops below 7.0, the respiratory center is depressed rather than stimulated. The acidosis is made more severe, due

to retention of carbon dioxide by the lungs and the resultant increase in the carbonic acid content of the extracellular fluid. Severe fluid volume deficit can reduce the plasma volume sufficiently to induce circulatory shock. The resultant decreased blood flow to the respiratory center can also produce respiratory depression, even though the blood pH is above 7.0.

Effect of Fluid Volume Deficit on Renal Function. The plasma volume is decreased due to excessive fluid loss from the intravascular compartment. Decrease in the renal blood flow interferes with glomerular filtration. Organic acids, sulfates, phosphates, potassium, magnesium and nonprotein nitrogen waste products are retained by the kidneys, intensifying the metabolic acidosis. The increased retention of potassium, plus its liberation from the cells (due to fluid volume deficit and starvation), elevates the plasma potassium level. Oliguria eventually results when the plasma volume is decreased sufficiently to produce circulatory shock; it is associated with increased blood levels of potassium, urea, uric acid, creatinine, ketones and non-protein nitrogen products.

Changes in Electrolyte Concentrations. Destruction of cells releases protein, glycogen, water and potassium. Large quantities of potassium pass from the cells to the extracellular fluid. A cellular potassium deficit exists even though the potassium level of the extracellular fluid may be normal or even elevated. In severe diabetic acidosis, a 154 lb. man may develop a total potassium deficit of approximately 500 mEq.

Deficits of sodium and chloride may develop even though hemoconcentration is present. In addition to their loss with glucose diuresis, these electrolytes may be lost because of vomiting, gastric dilatation and paralytic ileus. Because sodium combines with ketonic anions, its excretion is increased. In severe diabetic acidosis, a 154 lb. man may develop a total sodium deficit of approximately 500 mEq., and a total chloride deficit of approximately 440 mEq.

Magnesium and phosphorus are chiefly cellular electrolytes, having actions similar to potassium. Cellular deficits of these electrolytes probably develop in the same way as does cellular potassium deficit. A 154 lb. patient with severe diabetic acidosis may develop a total magnesium deficit of approximately 56 mEq., and a total phosphorus deficit of approximately 260 mEq.

Recognition of Diabetic Acidosis

The nurse should be thoroughly familiar with the symptoms of diabetic acidosis. She should be alert for their occurrence in any diabetic patient, but particularly in those with poor diet habits who are careless in their administration of insulin and those with infections or other illness. One of the nurse's greatest responsibilities to the diabetic patient and his family is to teach them the early recognition of diabetic acidosis.

Diabetic acidosis is characterized by a number of readily recognizable signs and symptoms. These with their probable causes are listed in Table 43.

TABLE 43. SIGNS AND SYMPTOMS OF DIABETIC ACIDOSIS AND THEIR PROBABLE CAUSE

SIGN OR SYMPTOM	PROBABLE CAUSE
Polyuria	Osmotic diuretic effect of hyperglycemia (Renal solute load greatly increased due to presence of high glucose concentration and to the increased concentration of metabolic end-products of fat and protein)
Polydipsia	Cellular dehydration causes thirst (Water loss causes hyperosmolarity of the extracellular fluid; water is drawn from the cells)
Glycosuria	Blood glucose level exceeds renal threshold (usually 180 mg./100 ml.)
Acetonuria	Excessive accumulation of ketones in the blood causes increased excretion of ketones in the urine (acetone is a ketone body)
High specific gravity of urine	High renal solute load
Tiredness, muscular weakness	Lack of carbohydrate, potassium deficit; loss of protein from muscles
Face appears drawn and flushed	Fluid volume deficit (sharpening of facial features) Acidosis (flushed color)
Dry tongue and mucous membranes, cracked lips	Fluid volume deficit
Deep, rapid respiration (Kussmaul)	Compensatory mechanism to increase extracellular fluid pH by the elimination of large amounts of CO_2 from the lungs with the resultant decreased carbonic acid content in blood
Nausea and vomiting (Vomitus may be dark brown, due to blood)	Atony of the stomach Bleeding from stretched gastric mucosa
Brownish particles on teeth, lips and gums	Deposited there when vomitus is expelled
Weight loss	Fluid volume deficit, inability to metabolize glucose
Acetone breath odor (odor similar to that of over-ripe apples)	Acetone content of body increases; acetone is volatile and is vaporized in the expired air
Gastric dilatation and paralytic ileus	Neuropathy Water and electrolyte loss

TABLE 43. SIGNS AND SYMPTOMS OF DIABETIC ACIDOSIS AND
THEIR PROBABLE CAUSE—(*Continued*)

SIGN OR SYMPTOM	PROBABLE CAUSE
Abdominal pain, rigid abdomen (can simulate appendicitis, pancreatitis, or other acute abdominal problem)	Apparently related to fluid volume deficit (condition improves when deficit is repaired)
Chest pain (may simulate pain of pleurisy)	Apparently related to fluid deficit (condition improves when fluid deficit is repaired); may be due to over-active respiration caused by acidosis
Moaning	Usually associated with abdominal or chest pain
Soft eyeballs, wrinkled cornea	Fluid volume deficit
Low blood pressure	Fluid volume deficit severe enough to decrease plasma volume significantly
Cold extremities, may have purplish appearance	Decreased peripheral blood flow secondary to fluid volume deficit
Body temperature below normal or normal (If fever is present it is almost always associated with the precipitating factor of the diabetic acidosis, such as an infection)	Fluid volume deficit
Oliguria	Fluid volume deficit causes decreased renal blood flow with decreased glomerular filtration rate Atonic urinary bladder may become greatly distended with urine
Rapid, shallow, gasping respiration replacing Kussmaul breathing	Drop in blood pH below 7.0 or significantly decreased blood flow to the respiratory center
Laboratory Findings *Blood sugar:* (Normal is 80-120 mg./100 ml.) Elevated above normal, usually 400-600 mg./100 ml.; may be as high as 2,000 mg./100 ml.	Faulty glucose metabolism causes glucose to accumulate in the blood

Bicarbonate:
   (Normal plasma bicarbonate level is):
      Adults: 25-29 mEq./L.
      Children: 20-25 mEq./L.)
Decreased below normal; may be as low as 5 mEq./L.
	Ketonic anions cause a decrease in the bicarbonate level

Others: NPN elevated White count elevated, but differential normal	Impaired metabolism and glomerular function

Treatment of Diabetic Acidosis

Initial Evaluation. A patient with symptoms of diabetic acidosis should be admitted to the hospital for immediate evaluation and treatment. Often the emergency room nurse spends a brief time with the patient before the physician arrives. She should utilize this time to the fullest advantage to expedite diagnosis and treatment.

While obtaining a voided urine specimen for sugar and acetone tests, the nurse should try to get an account of the events leading to the development of symptoms. If the patient is confused and non-responsive, the information may often be obtained from an accompanying family member. The nurse should ask if any treatment for acidosis was given prior to hospital admission. (Sometimes the physician may instruct the family by phone to give a fast-acting insulin if symptoms of acidosis are present.) The patient should be kept warm with blankets. If a voided urine specimen cannot be obtained, the physician may later request a catheterized specimen. The patient may have a dilated atonic urinary bladder; failure to void should not be attributed to renal failure until the bladder is catheterized to check for this disorder. The nurse should use meticulous technique while performing this procedure; infections are particularly dangerous to the diabetic patient.

The nurse should check and record the vital signs at frequent intervals. A low blood pressure and a rapid thready pulse may indicate severe fluid volume deficit with circulatory failure. A change from deep, rapid respiration to rapid, shallow gasping respiration may indicate a severe drop in blood pH (below 7.0) or impaired blood flow to the respiratory center due to fluid volume deficit and circulatory collapse. A temperature elevation probably indicates the presence of an acute infection; the temperature is usually subnormal in the patient with diabetic acidosis. The patient's level of consciousness should be evaluated at frequent intervals; progressive loss of consciousness indicates increasing severity of acidosis. Other symptoms of acidosis should be searched for and noted. (See Table 43.)

The nurse should notify the laboratory to draw blood; the physician usually requests tests for blood sugar, bicarbonate or blood pH, acetone and blood urea nitrogen. Intravenous water and electrolytes such as hypotonic saline or a balanced hypotonic electrolyte solution (Butler type) may be ordered and started through the same venipuncture. Initial fluids are given to improve the blood volume and blood pressure. Insulin is not usually administered until the blood sugar and urine test results are available. When acetone is found in the urine, or when other pronounced signs of acidosis are present, a dose of quick-acting insulin may be given before the blood sugar test result is obtained. It is imperative that the presence of hypoglycemia be ruled out before insulin is given. Hypoglycemia is characterized by anxiety, sweating, hunger, headache, dizziness, double vision, twitching, convulsions, nausea, pale wet skin, dilated pupils, normal breathing and normal blood pressure.

Insulin Administration. Since the lack of insulin initiates diabetic acidosis, insulin administration is required to correct it. Although the need for insulin is readily recognized by all authorities, there is some disagreement as to how much, when and how it should be given.

Some physicians prefer to give adults approximately 100 units of regular or crystalline insulin intravenously the first hour, and then 100 units intramuscularly every hour for the next 3 or 4 hours. (Factors influencing the insulin dose include the patient's blood sugar, weight and the duration of his diabetes.) Other physicians prefer to give multiple doses of regular or crystalline insulin, such as 50 units every hour, until acetonuria diminishes. There are valid arguments for both methods.

Insulin can be given intravenously, intramuscularly, or subcutaneously. For maximal rapidity of action, regular or crystalline insulin are best, since only they can be given intravenously. Although intramuscular injections are absorbed more quickly than subcutaneous injections, the intravenous route gives the quickest results of all, and is most dependable when there is some question of absorption from intramuscular or subcutaneous injections because of the presence of shock.

The nurse should observe the patient for signs of hypoglycemia, which might occur with the large doses of insulin required to correct acidosis. Other nursing responsibilities include performing urine sugar and acetone tests accurately, checking insulin orders with great care, and measuring the insulin dosage carefully. The orders for insulin are based on the blood sugar and acetone levels and on the quantities of sugar and acetone in the urine. Orders for insulin may be confusing in the early treatment of acidosis; the nurse should take sufficient time to be certain she carries them out accurately.

In a sense, urine values for glucose and acetone tell the attendant less about the patient's current status than about past events. With aggressive treatment one can produce hypoglycemia in the presence of glycosuria and ketonuria.

The large doses of insulin sometimes needed to correct acidosis may be frightening to the nurse if she is unaware that in ketoacidosis an abnormal serum globulin is present which antagonizes the action of insulin. For this reason, larger doses are needed in acidosis than are normally needed to control simple hyperglycemia in the same patient.

Fluid Replacement Therapy

1. EARLY PHASE (FIRST 4 HOURS). After the initial insulin dose has been given, emphasis is placed on re-establishing the blood volume and repairing extracellular and cellular fluid volume deficits. Repair of the deficient blood volume causes improved renal function and allows the excretion of excess organic acid wastes and metabolic end-products. This may be accomplished by the administration of 2 to 3 L. of isotonic solution of sodium chloride or hypotonic electrolyte solutions during the first 2 to 6 hours.

Isotonic solution of sodium chloride (0.9%) is readily available and is commonly used in the treatment of diabetic acidosis. It expands the extracellular fluid volume and helps replace losses of sodium and chloride. The first 2 L. can be given in 2 to 4 hours if the patient has satisfactory cardiac and renal status. It does not, however, provide free water for cellular hydration and the establishment of urine flow. Its chloride content exceeds that normally found in plasma; therefore, if used extensively, it can worsen acidosis by imposing a chloride excess. (An excessive number of chloride ions causes a compensatory decrease in the number of bicarbonate ions.) Usually no more than 3 L. of isotonic saline are given in the first 6 to 12 hours, to avoid making the acidosis more severe.

Since the patient with acidosis loses relatively more water than electrolytes, there is much to be said for the administration of hypotonic solutions. A hypotonic solution of sodium chloride with or without added sodium lactate or bicarbonate can be employed. Or, a balanced electrolyte solution of the Butler type, providing both cellular and extracellular electrolytes, may be given. Another solution sometimes used in the early treatment of acidosis is a mixture of 750 ml. of lactated Ringer's and 250 ml. of distilled water. The use of sixth molar sodium lactate or 1.5 per cent sodium bicarbonate is recommended by some to increase the bicarbonate content of the blood. Unless these solutions are administered cautiously, they may produce alkalosis.

Authorities disagree as to the desirability of using glucose solutions in the early treatment of diabetic acidosis. Some physicians use them from the onset of treatment; others wait at least 4 hours before infusing glucose solutions. Those against the early use of glucose feel that it does nothing more than to add to hyperglycemia and thus increases osmotic diuresis with the resultant water and electrolyte loss from the body. After the first 4 to 6 hours of treatment, danger of hypoglycemia exists, perhaps because the available glucose has been metabolized and there is no glycogen available. Thus glucose may be needed. One liter of 5 per cent glucose in water is usually covered with 25 units of regular insulin.

Fructose has been used in the early treatment of diabetic acidosis because it does not require insulin to be metabolized, thus sparing body fat and decreasing ketogenesis. It does not, however, increase glucose utilization.

Potassium administration is contraindicated in the early phase of treatment, since the plasma potassium level is usually elevated due to the liberation of cellular potassium into the extracellular fluid and to poor renal excretion of potassium caused by decreased urinary output. Potassium excess may cause cardiac arrhythmias; if elevated to two or three times the normal level, cardiac arrest may occur. Potassium solutions are best withheld until the plasma potassium level is normal or below normal. The ECG is used frequently throughout therapy to detect changes in potassium concentration. Signs of potassium excess may appear during this phase, or the ECG may remain normal. Very rarely, a patient shows potassium deficit at this time; if so, it is almost always associated with a severe loss of potassium prior to the onset of diabetic acidosis.

2. SECOND PHASE (4-8 HOURS). Approximately 4 to 8 hours after the onset of therapy the patient is usually much improved and the need for parenteral fluids is decreased. Usually oral fluids may be tolerated by this time. The rate of intravenous infusion can be considerably slowed. If the blood sugar has fallen substantially, glucose may be given orally to combat hypoglycemia; intravenous glucose in water may also be required.

Although potassium deficit rarely occurs this early, the plasma potassium level has usually dropped sufficiently to allow potassium to be given, by mouth or intravenously, to ameliorate the developing cellular deficit. Oral administration is preferable. Fluids of high potassium content include orange juice, grape juice, milk and real meat broth. (Contrary to common belief, consommé cubes are not rich in potassium.) Intravenous replacement of potassium can be accomplished by use of a Butler type solution, or it may be added to a suitable fluid in the form of KCl. (Nursing responsibilities in the administration of potassium solutions are discussed in Chap. 14.)

3. PHASE OF POTASSIUM DEFICIT (8-24 HOURS). Recall that in the early phase of diabetic acidosis the plasma potassium level is normal or elevated, due to the liberation of potassium from the cells during the breakdown of glycogen and protein, and to decreased renal function with excessive retention of potassium. After administration of potassium-free fluids early in therapy, the plasma potassium decreases for the following reasons:

1. The administered fluids dilute the plasma.
2. Re-establishment of the plasma volume improves renal function and increases potassium excretion.
3. Part of the extracellular potassium enters the cells as they take up glucose under the influence of administered insulin.
4. Formation of glycogen within the cells —involving utilization of potassium, glucose, and water—causes further withdrawal of potassium from the extracellular fluid.
5. Potassium re-enters the cells to help repair the cellular potassium deficit.

Because of the great need for potassium during the later stages of treatment, potassium should be added to parenteral infusions during this period.

Potassium deficit becomes obvious after 8 to 24 hours of treatment, most often between the 10th and 24th hours. The plasma potassium level may fall as low as 2 mEq./L. (recall that the normal plasma K+ level is 5 mEq./L.). The nurse should be alert for the symptoms of potassium deficit during these hours, including:

- Weakness
- Flaccid paralysis of skeletal muscles
- Paralysis of respiratory muscles, resulting in shallow, gasping respiration and cyanosis
- Abdominal distention
- ECG changes
- Cardiac failure with ashen color
- Sudden death (most common 8 to 20 hours after therapy is started)

Potassium should be given as soon as renal function improves and the plasma potassium concentration falls to normal. The cellular potassium deficit takes over a week to replace; yet, even small amounts of potassium taken regularly help ward off a severe deficit. Fluids mentioned above should be encouraged. Oral replacement of potassium is safer than intravenous replacement. If the patient tolerates oral fluids better, they can be enriched with potassium additives. K-Lyte, an effervescent potassium preparation, is palatable and well tolerated.

SUMMARY OF FLUID THERAPY AIMS. In the first 24 hours of treatment of diabetic acidosis, the aim is to replace 80 per cent of the total water, sodium and chloride loss. Cellular electrolytes are not assimilated as rapidly as extracellular; therefore, only 50 per cent of the potassium and magnesium deficit, and 25 per cent of the phosphate deficit, are replaced on the first day. In addition to replacing past and concurrent losses, daily maintenance needs must be met.

Gastric Lavage. Some physicians routinely perform a gastric lavage on all patients with diabetic acidosis. Others do so only when the patient has demonstrable signs of gastric dilatation, such as nausea, vomiting and epigastric distress.

Removal of gastric contents makes the patient more comfortable; it relieves abdominal distention, vomiting and nausea. Oral intake is made possible earlier. The danger of aspirating gastric contents is less when the distended viscus is emptied, but the hazard of inducing alkalosis should not be disregarded.

Cleansing Enema. A cleansing enema may be ordered to relieve abdominal distention caused by intestinal atony.

Other Therapy. The patient should be restored to his usual diet as quickly as it is tolerated. After recovery from diabetic acidosis, long-acting insulin can be resumed, with supplemental doses of fast-acting insulin as indicated by urine test results. An excellent opportunity exists for teaching the patient while he is still in the hospital how to prevent future bouts of acidosis.

Nurse's Role in Preventing Diabetic Acidosis

Because the nurse is actively involved in teaching diabetic patients, she is in a splendid position to help prevent diabetic acidosis. She should keep the basic learning principles in mind when teaching self-care to diabetics. The rate of learning of the individual must be considered; so must the knowledge he already possesses concerning the disease. Physicians sometimes present explanations far beyond the patient's comprehension. Rather than risk the embarrassment of asking for a more simplified explanation, the patient may pretend to understand—this can lead to serious difficulties.

It is important for the patient to gain a clear understanding of his condition and of his responsibilities to himself. Time and effort devoted to effective teaching of the diabetic patient pays off handsomely when it helps prevent diabetic acidosis. An excellent instructional book for diabetic patients is *Diabetes for Diabetics* by G. F. Schmidt, Miami, Florida, The Diabetes Press of America, 1965.

Failure to teach the diabetic the importance of (1) taking the prescribed amount of insulin daily, (2) reporting conditions that may alter the need for insulin, (3) adhering to the prescribed diet, (4) performing urine sugar and acetone tests accurately, and (5) seeking medical follow-up as indicated, predisposes to diabetic acidosis.

Insulin Administration. The omission of insulin injections or inadequate insulin doses are common causes of diabetic acidosis. Most nurses devote more time to teaching the mechanics of insulin administration than to any other aspect of diabetic self-care. When one considers the hesitancy of some patients to give themselves injections, plus the dangers of inaccurate insulin dosage, it is understandable why extra time is needed in this area. Equally important, however, is the explanation of factors that may alter the insulin dosage, and what to do when such problems arise.

Much emphasis is properly placed on encouraging the patient receiving insulin to eat all of his food, to prevent a hypoglycemic reaction. However, the patient may come to believe that he has no need for insulin except when he eats. A common cause of diabetic acidosis is the failure of the patient with anorexia, nausea or vomiting, to take insulin. It is not unusual to admit a patient in diabetic acidosis who comments, "I haven't eaten for the past few days and didn't need my insulin injections." He has assumed that when he does not eat he should omit insulin injections. *This common assumption is not true.* The body needs insulin, although in modified dose and perhaps of a different type, even when the patient is not eating.

The nurse should make it clear to the patient that insulin should never be omitted without specific instructions from the physician. When the patient cannot eat, he should contact his physician for instructions. The once-daily injection of long-acting insulin may be temporarily reduced or discontinued, until the patient is able to eat again. Instead, frequent doses of quick acting insulin may be given as indicated by findings of urine sugar and acetone tests. If food intake is decreased for a prolonged period, the patient should be admitted to the hospital for parenteral fluid therapy and observation. It must be remembered that the nausea and vomiting experienced by the patient may be signs of developing diabetic acidosis. If so, failure to take insulin accelerates the development of acidosis.

Diabetic Diet. Eating more than permitted by the prescribed diet is a frequent cause of diabetic acidosis. While this may be due to poor emotional acceptance of the disease, it may also be due to lack of adequate understanding of the diet.

When possible, the diabetic patient should receive his diet instructions during frequent sessions with a dietitian. The nurse should have sufficient understanding of the diet to supplement the dietitian's instructions. Sometimes, in the absence of a dietitian, the nurse must carry the entire responsibility of diet instruction. Few nurses are so well acquainted with diabetic diets that they will not profit from a review prior to teaching the patient.

Urine Testing. Physicians rely heavily on urine sugar and acetone tests to serve as guides in prescribing insulin. If the patient performs the tests improperly or reports them incorrectly, the physician will receive false information and the insulin dose is likely to be incorrect.

Directions accompanying commercial equipment for testing the sugar and acetone content of urine are usually simple and easy to follow. Because the nurse is so familiar with the purpose of the tests, how to perform them, and how to report them, there is a tendency for her to under-teach the patient in their use. Often the nurse performs the test once in the patient's presence, has him repeat the procedure, and considers this area of teaching completed. Problems have arisen from such haphazard teaching. Attention must be paid to details, particularly those the nurse has found confusing to previous patients.

Clinitest tablets are widely used to estimate the quantitative sugar content of urine. Other tests, such as Clinistix and Combistix or Tes-tape may be used. These are enzyme impregnated strips that change color when dipped into a solution containing glucose;

although strips are more sensitive than tablets, they are less accurate quantitatively.

Errors in urine testing that may occur with the use of Clinitest include:

- Use of tablets that have been exposed to moisture or excessive temperature
- Use of improperly cleaned test tube and medicine dropper
- Failure to perform the test as indicated by directions
- Failure to indicate which scale—percentages or plus marks—is used to report the findings

Because Clinitest tablets are extremely hygroscopic, they should not be exposed to moisture. The container should be kept tightly closed. Tablets with blue or black discoloration will not give accurate results.

After 5 drops of urine, 10 drops of water and 1 Clinitest tablet are placed in the test tube, the solution will boil and change color. The reaction should be observed carefully. Fifteen seconds after the boiling has stopped, the solution should be shaken gently and the color compared with the color scale supplied with the set. If the solution changes from orange to brown during the reaction, the solution contains more than 2 per cent sugar.

The color chart supplied with the Clinitest set is divided into six areas representing sugar concentrations of 0.0 per cent (negative), 0.25 per cent (trace), 0.5 per cent (plus 1), 0.75 per cent (plus 2), 1.0 per cent (plus 3) and 2 per cent (plus 4). Occasionally supplemental regular insulin is ordered according to the results of each Clinitest. A typical order might read:

Give 5 units of regular insulin if Clinitest is 1 plus (+)
Give 10 units of regular insulin if Clinitest is 2 plus (++)
Give 15 units of regular insulin if Clinitest is 3 plus (+++)
Give 20 units of regular insulin if Clinitest is 4 plus (++++)

Difficulty can arise with such an order if the patient reports his test results on the percentage scale, but does not indicate he is using that scale. For example, if the patient reports his test results as "2," meaning 2 per cent, and the nurse assumes he means 2 plus, he would receive only half of the desired insulin dose.

When test strips are used, such as Clinistix, Combistix, or Ketostix, the patient should be cautioned not to leave them in the urine too long, since this may cause the chemical reagents to dissolve out, resulting in inaccuracy.

Even more of a problem is the failure of many diabetics to test their urine as frequently as instructed by the physician. While the cause of this may be poor emotional acceptance of diabetes, it may also be due to inadequate emphasis on the importance of urine testing. The nurse should encourage the patient to get into the habit of testing his urine while in the hospital, so that he will continue to do so at home. The need to report findings of acetone in the urine should be particularly emphasized.

Some diabetics go for periods of weeks, months, or longer without testing their urine for sugar or acetone, an exceedingly dangerous omission. The patient should be made to realize that his body's need for insulin is not static, that the insulin dose must be regulated in accord with the findings of blood and urine tests.

Recognition of Diabetic Acidosis. Failure of the patient to recognize the early symptoms of uncontrolled diabetes and early diabetic acidosis leads to delay in instituting treatment. The longer the patient goes without treatment, the less are his chances for recovery.

The nurse should stress the importance of being alert for symptoms of acidosis, particularly when an infection, disease, or emotional upset is present. She should also point out that when such symptoms occur, the attending physician should be notified immediately. Manufacturers of insulin preparations provide excellent literature for diabetics. Many useful facts are contained in these booklets. For example, symptoms of acidosis and hypoglycemia are described in a clear and simple fashion. The patient should be given copies of such literature for use during teaching sessions and for reference at home. A member of the patient's family should also be taught to recognize symptoms of acidosis.

Need for Medical Supervision. The patient should be made to realize that meticulous control of diabetes mellitus helps delay complications, such as the renal and cardiovascular disorders so frequently associated with the ailment.

Chapter 21

Fluid Balance in the Patient With Neurologic Disease

REGULATION OF FLUID BALANCE BY THE CENTRAL NERVOUS SYSTEM

Respiratory Center and pH Regulation

The amount of carbon dioxide given off by the lungs is controlled by the respiratory center in the medulla. Recall that carbon dioxide is crucial in the carbonic acid: base bicarbonate buffer system. Alkalinity and pH of the extracellular fluid increases when an excessive amount of carbon dioxide is exhaled. (Carbon dioxide dissolved in water or in extracellular fluid forms carbonic acid; loss of carbon dioxide decreases the ratio of carbonic acid to base bicarbonate.) Contrary-wise, the acidity of the extracellular fluid increases and the pH decreases when too much carbon dioxide is retained. (The retained carbon dioxide weights the carbonic acid side of the carbonic acid : base bicarbonate balance.)

Chemoreceptors found in the aortic arch and in the carotid sinus send stimuli to the respiratory center. Chemical stimuli that increase respiration include:

- Increased CO_2 content of blood (up to an arterial concentration of 9%)
- Decreased plasma pH
- Hypoxia

The inhalation of carbon dioxide in a concentration of less than 9 per cent stimulates the respiratory center and increases respiration by increasing the concentration of carbonic acid and decreasing the pH of the plasma. If the concentration of carbon dioxide in the inspired air is greater than 9 per cent, however, the nervous receptors are unable to respond. Instead of increased respiration, there is decreased respiration and carbon dioxide narcosis. Clinically, this is of crucial import.

A fall in plasma pH causes an increase in rate and depth of respiration, which blows off excess carbon dioxide; but if the plasma pH falls below 7.0, pulmonary ventilation is depressed, and the acidosis becomes more severe. A reduction in the available oxygen causes hypoxia and increased respiration. Pathologic conditions can cause depression or stimulation of the medullary respiratory neurons and can thus alter plasma pH. (See the section dealing with changes in pulmonary ventilation.)

Influence of Central Nervous System on Osmotic Balance

The central nervous system influences water loss from the kidneys, the skin and the lungs. It controls the desire to drink, as well as the motor ability to do so. Emotions influence water balance by affecting the drinking pattern; for example, neuroses sometimes cause compulsive water drinking.

Aldosterone secretion may be under the control of volume receptors, apparently located in the right atrium, and pressor receptors, perhaps located in the thyrocarotid junction. Afferent fibers from these areas pass to the hypothalamic region. Nevertheless, the main stimulus to increased aldosterone secretion is lowered sodium intake.

Hyperosmolarity stimulates the hypothalamus to release ADH. ADH secretion is also influenced by volume receptors in the left atrium and pulmonary veins.

CLINICAL CONDITIONS

Brain infections, tumors, or trauma can cause a diversity of fluid balance problems, depending on the area of the brain involved. Injury to the hypothalamus and the brain stem presents the most problems, because many metabolic functions are controlled in these areas. Many brain injuries interfere with the patient's ability to recognize thirst, as well as his ability to drink. The desire to eat and the ability to do so may also be affected. Recall that inadequate intake of food and fluids is responsible for a number of fluid imbalances.

Often, water and electrolyte balance is the most critical factor in determining the survival of the neurologic patient. For this reason, the nurse should become acutely aware of common problems so that she can aid in their early detection and correction.

Hyperthermia

The heat control center is located in the hypothalamus. Direct injury to this area, or pressure exerted by edema or masses in other areas of the brain, can cause a body temperature elevation. The extent of the elevation provides an important clue to the seriousness of the brain injury. For example, a slight concussion may result in a temperature of 101° F. or less. A more severe head injury may quickly be followed by a high temperature. Cerebral vascular accidents cause temperature elevations that are roughly proportional to the severity of the accident. A rise in temperature in a neurologic patient is an ominous sign.

Patients who have recovered from encephalitis, or those with cerebral damage from birth injuries, may have faulty temperature regulation. Multiple sclerosis is sometimes associated with low, irregular fever. An injury to the upper cervical spinal cord often results in high, irregular fever. Surgical operations in the area of the third ventricle sometimes cause pronounced hyperthermia.

Fever should be reduced by pharmacologic or physical means. An automatically regulated hypothermic blanket can be most helpful in reducing temperature; sponging with ice water or alcohol is less effective. Fever speeds up body metabolism. (See the discussion of fever in Chap. 10.) Because of the increased energy expenditure, the patient needs more calories and water. Yet, as mentioned above, a neurologic patient is often unable to recognize thirst and hunger. Moreover, impaired motor function may interfere with the mechanics of drinking and eating. Thus, at a time when the need for food and fluids is great, the patient may be unable to respond with increased intake. Because fever resulting from brain lesions may continue for weeks, or even months, careful attention must be paid to meeting the patient's need for food and fluids.

Nursing Implications. Too often, the nurse falsely assumes that all patients experience normal thirst and appetite and are capable of reacting to their needs for fluids and food. She should remember that confused or unconscious patients do not have this capability. She must, therefore, help assess and meet their nutritional needs.

If the patient is unable to take oral fluids, other routes of intake are available. For example, a patient with difficulty in swallowing may not be able to drink sufficient fluids, yet his fluid requirement can easily be met with tube feedings. A patient with nausea and vomiting can neither take fluids orally nor by gastric tube, but he can be provided with parenteral fluids. Keen observations by the nurse help the physician determine which replacement route is best and thus minimize the duration of the period of inadequate intake.

All confused or unconscious patients should be placed on careful intake-output measurements. Fluid loss by all routes, such as sweating, vomiting, or diarrhea, should be carefully recorded. Body temperature checks should be made every 4 hours—oftener if indicated—to detect elevations. Evaluation of fluids lost from the body serves as a basis for fluid replacement. Inadequate fluid replacement eventually results in fluid volume deficit and increased body temperature.

It is often difficult to determine the urinary output of neurologic patients, since many of them are incontinent. Because of time-consuming bed changes, the nursing staff is often misled into thinking that incontinent patients have large urinary outputs. Failure to assess the urinary output accurately may lead to inadequate fluid replacement. To avoid guesswork, seriously ill patients should have indwelling urinary catheters. The insensible water loss caused by fever can be assessed by accurate daily weight measurements, which also give an indication of total fluid balance status. (See Chap. 8 for further discussion of nursing responsibilities in fluid intake-output records and body weight measurements.)

Fever often occurs in a patient with cerebral edema, presenting the physician with a difficult problem: the patient needs fluid replacement, yet the danger of increasing cerebral edema may contraindicate such therapy.

Pathologic Conditions Affecting the Respiratory Center

Pathologic conditions of the central nervous system can cause stimulation or depression of the respiratory neurons, thus altering plasma pH.

Hyperventilation. Neurologic conditions associated with overstimulation of the respiratory center include:

- Meningitis
- Encephalitis
- Brain tumor
- Fever

Hyperventilation results from the overstimulation of respiratory neurones. Increased pulmonary ventilation causes excessive elimination of CO_2, resulting in respiratory alkalosis (primary carbonic acid deficit). A mixture of 5 per cent CO_2 and 95 per cent O_2, breathed for a short period by the patient with cerebral damage, helps relieve the symptoms of respiratory alkalosis.

Hypoventilation. Neurologic conditions associated with depression of the respiratory center include:

- Direct trauma to the respiratory neurones in the medulla

- Pressure on the respiratory neurones secondary to tumor, hemorrhage, or brain abscess
- Bulbar poliomyelitis

Hypoventilation results from the depression of respiratory neurones. Retention of excessive amounts of CO_2 causes respiratory acidosis (primary carbonic acid excess). Hypoventilation, which is far more dangerous than hyperventilation, presents these hazards:

- Hypoxia
- Respiratory acidosis
- Increased CO_2 retention with dilation of the cerebral blood vessels and a rise in intracranial pressure

Hypoventilation due to medullary depression may necessitate the use of a mechanical respirator. Treatment should also be directed at eliminating the cause of the respiratory center depression.

Nursing Implications. The nurse should be alert for changes in respiration. She should check the respiratory rate, depth and rhythm and should watch for symptoms of respiratory acidosis when breathing is suppressed. These include:

- Disorientation
- Weakness
- Coma, if acidosis is severe

The nurse should also watch for symptoms of respiratory alkalosis when the rate and the depth of respiration are increased. These symptoms include:

- Light-headedness
- Numbness, tingling of fingers and toes
- Circumoral paresthesia
- Tinnitis
- Blurring of vision
- Convulsions
- Unconsciousness

Some of the symptoms, such as disorientation, weakness, convulsions, coma and blurred vision, may be caused by other conditions, such as brain tumors or cerebral vascular accidents. Such symptoms should be evaluated in the light of the patient's history and neurologic status.

The physician usually orders frequent pH

and bicarbonate tests to help evaluate the patient's electrolyte status. These tests help distinguish between symptoms of electrolyte disturbance and those of neurologic origin.

Sodium Excess After Brain Injury

Sodium excess is the most frequent electrolyte disturbance following brain injury. It is usually caused by inadequate water intake. Recall that thirst and the motor activities necessary to respond to it are often affected by neurologic trauma.

High protein tube feedings (which are average in sodium content) are contraindicated during the first week after brain trauma. Because of the stress response that follows trauma, the patient is unable to anabolize protein normally. The renal solute load is increased, resulting in excessive water loss, which eventually produces sodium excess. Fever causes additional water loss and further contributes to sodium excess.

Nursing Implications. The nurse should be alert for symptoms of sodium excess when the water intake is deficient or when excessive water loss occurs. Symptoms of sodium excess (water deficit) include:

- Dry, sticky mucous membranes
- Flushed skin
- Oliguria
- Urine specific gravity above 1.030
- Fever
- Plasma sodium above 147 mEq./L.

Fever after neurologic trauma calls for a check of the serum sodium level.

Efforts should be made to supply adequate water, by mouth if possible. If tube feedings are necessary, the nurse should carefully record the amount of water given, plus the total volume of the tube feeding mixture. Few tube feeding mixtures supply adequate water; additional amounts should be given between feedings. The nurse should consult with the physician to determine the desired total intake and to learn of necessary restrictions. The physician may order a specific volume for the 24-hour period in order to prevent or minimize cerebral edema and elevation of the intracranial pressure. If a specific fluid intake is not established, the nurse should give fluids in amounts sufficient to keep the tongue moist and the skin turgor normal.

It may be necessary to use the intravenous route to supply water if the patient is vomiting or has diarrhea. Recall that in Chapter 14, 5 per cent dextrose in water was described as an excellent solution for meeting water needs in most situations. However, any condition likely to be associated with cerebral edema and increased intracranial pressure contraindicates use of this solution. The infusion of an isotonic solution of dextrose raises intracranial pressure, partly because dextrose passes into the cerebrospinal fluid and increases its osmotic pressure. An apparently acceptable solution for supplying water to the brain injured patient is 5 per cent dextrose in isotonic solution of sodium chloride, diluted with an equal amount of distilled water. Electrolytes, even in small quantities, interfere with the elevating effect of dextrose on cerebrospinal fluid pressure.

Sodium Deficit Following Brain Injury

Brain injury may be followed by sodium deficit if excessive water has been given, especially when the patient is perspiring heavily or vomiting. Or, sodium deficit may occur because of cerebral salt-wasting. Water overdose can be corrected by withholding water until the excess water is excreted; cerebral salt-wasting, however, represents a more difficult problem.

Cerebral Salt-Wasting. Cerebral salt-wasting involves the urinary excretion of large amounts of sodium, despite an existing sodium deficit. The mechanism is not known; the salt-wasting may be caused by inappropriate production of ADH, which causes renal retention of water without concurrent retention of sodium and results in sodium deficit through dilution. It is observed most often in patients with cerebral vascular accidents, although it has been seen in patients with encephalitis, brain tumor, head injury and bulbar polio. The frequency with which cerebral salt-wasting occurs is not known. The possibility of its presence should always be considered.

Sodium replacement is required in patients with cerebral salt-wasting; the amount of sodium needed to overcome symptoms of sodium deficit varies with the individual. The salt-wasting may be temporary, since it sometimes disappears when the neurologic condition is relieved.

Nursing Implications. The nurse should be alert for symptoms of sodium deficit when the patient is losing large amounts of sodium and drinking large quantities of sodium-free fluids. Any patient with a cerebral vascular accident, brain tumor, head injury, encephalitis, or bulbar polio may develop cerebral salt-wasting, with the following symptoms of sodium deficit:

- Listlessness
- Absence of thirst
- Loss of appetite
- Nausea and vomiting
- Headache
- Giddiness
- Unless corrected, circulatory collapse with increased pulse rate, decreased blood pressure, pale skin, shock, and death

An important nursing responsibility in caring for patients with salt-wasting is the recording of all routes and types of fluid intake and output.

Diabetes Insipidus

Diabetes insipidus results from interruption of the supraopticohypophyseal pathway by a variety of lesions, so that the posterior pituitary gland no longer secretes ADH adequately. Causes of diabetes insipidus include brain tumor, head injury, encephalitis, syphilis, reticuloendotheliosis, vascular disease and tuberculosis. It is most often caused by a tumor of the hypothalamus or hypophysis. Recent surveys have indicated that primary idiopathic diabetes insipidus and brain tumors account for approximately 75 per cent of the cases.

Symptoms of diabetes insipidus include polyuria and polydipsia. Polyuria is caused by the decreased secretion of ADH; polydipsia represents an attempt to replace the large urinary water loss. The urine volume is usually from 4 to 6 L. per day, although it may be as great as 12 to 15 L. It depends largely on water intake, which remains rather constant from day to day. The specific gravity of the urine is low, remaining between 1.002 and 1.006. The serum sodium level is usually slightly above normal.

The polyuria of diabetes insipidus must be differentiated from that caused by chronic renal disease, diabetes mellitus, and compulsive water drinking. The differential diagnosis presenting most trouble is between diabetes insipidus and compulsive water drinking.

Compulsive water drinking is usually caused by a neurosis; it may, however, be brought about by an organic lesion in an area of the brain concerned with thirst. The primary disturbance in compulsive water drinking is excessive water intake; polyuria occurs secondarily. The water intake depends largely upon the emotional state of the individual, and, therefore, fluctuates greatly from day to day.

Several tests have been devised to help diagnose diabetes insipidus. For example, if water can be withheld long enough to cause concentration of the urine to a specific gravity of 1.010, the patient probably doesn't have diabetes insipidus. However, it is difficult to withhold fluids from the patient with diabetes insipidus, even temporarily, without causing a water deficit or even peripheral vascular collapse. Another test consists of the administration of hypertonic solution of sodium chloride. In the normal individual, this procedure stimulates ADH secretion and thus decreases urinary volume. The individual with diabetes insipidus is unaffected by extracellular osmolar changes; the only mechanism capable of decreasing urinary volume in such patients is the administration of Pitressin, vasopressin. The administration of Pitressin produces a more concentrated urine in the patient with diabetes insipidus than can be achieved with water restriction.

Nursing Implications. The nurse should be alert for polyuria and polydipsia in patients with brain tumor, head injury, vascular disease, or cerebral infection. An accurate intake-output record is helpful in detecting these symptoms—it also reveals the drinking pattern. (Recall that the drinking pattern helps differentiate between diabetes insipidus and compulsive water drinking.)

If diabetes insipidus is present, provision should be made for an easily accessible water supply. In addition, the patient should be as close to the bathroom as possible. Fluid balance is remarkably well maintained in the patient with diabetes insipidus, as long as he has access to as much water as he wants.

Elevated Intracranial Pressure

Causes. Elevated intracranial pressure occurs when the rate of cerebrospinal fluid formation is increased or when the rate of absorption of cerebrospinal fluid is decreased. Brain tumors may produce either or both of these effects. Any irritation to the meninges, such as an infection or tumor, causes large quantities of fluid and protein to pass into the cerebrospinal fluid system; the added volume causes a rise in intracranial pressure. A large hemorrhage can directly increase intracranial pressure by compressing the brain. The formation of arachnoidal granulation, caused by hemorrhage or infection, can interfere seriously with cerebrospinal fluid absorption and thereby increase intracranial pressure. An excessive fluid intake can precipitate cerebral edema and increased intracranial pressure in some patients with cerebral disease or injury. Water, orally or as a 5 per cent dextrose in water solution intravenously, may raise intracranial pressure. Carbon dioxide causes dilation of the cerebral vessels. The increased blood flow resulting from the dilation may produce an abrupt elevation of intracranial pressure; indeed, it may cause papilledema.

Symptoms. The nurse should be alert for the symptoms of elevated intracranial pressure in all patients with cerebral abnormalities. Symptoms of elevated intracranial pressure include:

- Change in level of consciousness
- Dimming of vision, due to papilledema
- Persistent dull headache, most severe in the morning
- Projectile vomiting, often *not* preceded by nausea
- Progressive rise in blood pressure
- Slowed pulse and respiratory rate

Treatment.

HYPERTONIC GLUCOSE. Hypertonic glucose solutions, once commonly used to reduce intracranial pressure, are now used sparingly in most hospitals. Infusion of hypertonic glucose increases the intravascular osmotic pressure, withdrawing water from the edematous brain and from the cerebrospinal fluid space. Although the intracranial pressure is reduced, the reduction is not sustained and the pressure rises again. The reason for this lies in the fact that hypertonic glucose increases the osmotic pressure of the cerebrospinal fluid, causing it to attract water by osmosis. Some authorities feel that hypertonic glucose does more harm than good.

HYPERTONIC UREA (UREVERT). It has been found recently that the intravenous administration of a hypertonic solution of urea produces a significant and well sustained decrease in intracranial pressure in patients with cerebral injury or space-occupying lesions. Not metabolized, urea is rapidly excreted by the kidneys, carrying with it large quantities of water and sodium. It is available in concentrations of 4 and 30 per cent. The 30 per cent solution is designed for the reduction of intracranial pressure.

Urevert is a synthetic lyophilized urea. The maximal dose should not exceed 1.5 Gm./Kg. body weight. Urevert is available in two kit sizes containing 40 or 90 Gm. of urea. Either kit provides 30 per cent urea when reconstituted with the accompanying diluent. A sterile transfer administration set is also provided with each kit. The solution should be prepared immediately before use.

The Urevert administration set delivers 10 drops/ml. The properly diluted solution should not be given at a rate faster than 60 drops/minute for 1 to 2 hours. The desired effect may persist from 3 to 10 hours. Side effects, such as nausea, vomiting, tachycardia, mental confusion and hyperthermia, have been caused by careless administration of Urevert. Because Urevert has a pronounced diuretic effect, an indwelling urinary catheter should be inserted before the infusion is begun; the catheter facilitates accurate measurement of urinary output.

Since Urevert is an irritating hypertonic solution, it may cause phlebitis and pain. Extravasation of the solution causes sloughing of the surrounding tissues. Because venous thrombosis may occur with Urevert administration, the infusion should be started in a large vein, with the needle carefully anchored. Because of the danger of thrombosis, veins in the lower extremities of the aged should not be used.

Contraindications to the use of Urevert include severe renal or hepatic damage, pronounced extracellular fluid volume deficit, or active intracranial bleeding. If the solution is given to patients with impaired kidneys or liver, it should be administered cautiously. Frequent checks of the patient's blood urea nitrogen (BUN) level should be carried out.

MANNITOL. Mannitol is an osmotic diuretic capable of relieving elevated intracranial pressure when given intravenously as a 20 per cent solution. The relatively high total dose is 1.5 to 2 Gm./Kg. of body weight. This amount may be given over a period of 30 to 60 minutes, provided the patient has normal cardiac and renal function. Sometimes mannitol is given less rapidly—500 ml. of 20 per cent mannitol over a 90-minute period, for example. Because of the diuretic effect of mannitol, a catheter should be inserted into the bladder before the mannitol is administered. Although 20 per cent mannitol is chemically stable, it may crystallize when cooled excessively. If this occurs, the bottle should be warmed to 50° C. in a water bath, then cooled to body temperature before being administered.

The nurse should obtain a specific order concerning the rate of administration of the solution. If a large amount of mannitol is given rapidly, the patient may complain of headache, a sensation of chest constriction and chills. The increased intravascular fluid volume, caused by the drawing of water into the bloodstream, may cause pulmonary edema or symptoms of water excess (sodium deficit). (Symptoms of pulmonary edema are described in Chap. 19; those of water excess are described in Chap. 15.) The nurse should observe the patient closely during the administration of mannitol, especially when it is given at a rapid rate. The site of injection should be observed frequently, since extravasation of mannitol can cause swelling and thrombophlebitis.

Chapter 22

Fluid Balance in the Patient With Respiratory Disease

The lungs can be regarded as organs of body homeostasis, since they regulate the carbonic acid level of the extracellular fluid through exhalation or retention of carbon dioxide.

Under the control of the medulla, the lungs act promptly to correct systemic hydrogen ion changes, which are synonymous with acid-base disturbances. Thus, when the ketosis of starvation produces metabolic acidosis (primary base bicarbonate deficit), the medulla signals the lungs to exhale carbon dioxide by means of deep, rapid respiration. When loss of hydrochloric acid through prolonged vomiting produces metabolic alkalosis (primary base bicarbonate excess), the medulla orders the lungs to retain carbon dioxide by means of slow, shallow respiration.

The disruption of normal pulmonary function can produce water and electrolyte imbalances. For example, blockage of the bronchi and of the alveolar-capillary membrane in bronchiectasis results in the inadequate elimination of carbon dioxide from the lungs, with increased carbonic acid concentration in the extracellular fluid and respiratory acidosis (primary carbonic acid excess). High fever, with its associated hyperventilation, causes an excessive elimination of carbon dioxide from the lungs, and a decreased carbonic acid concentration in the extracellular fluid resulting in respiratory alkalosis (primary base bicarbonate excess).

The lungs remove large quantities of water from the body as water vapor. (Recall that the daily insensible water loss from the lungs is about 300 ml., varying with the environmental humidity and the depth and the rate of respiration.) Abnormal conditions, such as sustained hyperpnea, excessive formation of mucous or of purulent secretions, or continued coughing, greatly increase the water loss.

RESPIRATORY ACIDOSIS

Pathologic Mechanism and Symptoms

Respiratory acidosis is caused by any clinical situation that interferes with pulmonary gas exchange, thus producing primary retention of carbon dioxide with a resultant increase in carbonic acid concentration of the extracellular fluid.

Respiratory acidosis may be associated with no obvious clinical signs except dyspnea out of proportion to effort. Hyperpnea at rest may be another sign. Other indications of inadequate pulmonary ventilation include cyanosis and tachycardia, although respiratory acidosis can occur without cyanosis. The hydrogen excess of acidosis leads to loss of cellular potassium. The serum potassium level increases. Conduction blocks and ventricular fibrillation may follow.

The symptoms of respiratory acidosis may be difficult to detect; the nurse should be alert for their occurrence when the patient has a condition prone to be associated with respiratory acidosis.

Chronic Pulmonary Diseases Associated With Respiratory Acidosis

Chronic pulmonary diseases, such as bronchiectasis, asthma, pulmonary fibrosis, or emphysema, may cause respiratory acidosis. A factor common to all these conditions is chronic interference with gas exchange, resulting in primary retention of carbon dioxide with an increase of carbonic acid in the extracellular fluid. Because emphysema is by far the most common cause of respiratory acidosis, it will be discussed as a separate entity.

Emphysema

Pathologic Mechanism and Symptoms. Emphysema involves chronic obstruction to the flow of air into and—even more important—out of the lungs. The chronic airway obstruction causes overdistention of the lungs with air. As a result, the alveoli become enlarged and eventually rupture and coalesce.

Conditions that may contribute to airway obstruction include respiratory infections, smoking, and breathing polluted air. Nevertheless, the precise etiology of emphysema and the exact site of the obstruction are not known. The disease is most common in older persons, particularly males who have done manual labor. Poor ventilation and interference with gaseous exchange at the alveolar level produce hypoxia (inadequate arterial oxygenation) and hypercapnia (excessive carbon dioxide concentration in the extracellular fluid).

Retention of carbon dioxide causes a weighting of the carbonic acid side of the carbonic acid: base bicarbonate balance. As a result, this ratio becomes more than 1 to 20, and the balance is tipped in favor of acidosis. The pH of the blood is more acid than normal. The bicarbonate level is increased since the body retains bicarbonate ions to balance the excessive quantity of carbonic acid. Thus, both the carbonic acid content and the bicarbonate content of the blood increase. If the ratio of carbonic acid to base bicarbonate becomes stabilized at 1 to 20, the pH of the extracellular fluid will be normal. For example, if the carbonic

acid concentration is 1.60 mEq./L. instead of the normal 1.35 mEq./L., and if the base bicarbonate is 32 mEq./L. instead of the normal 27 mEq./L., the pH will still be 7.4—that is, normal—because the 1 to 20 ratio prevails. This condition is sometimes referred to as "compensated respiratory acidosis." However, if the body compensatory mechanisms fail and the 1 to 20 ratio is upset, the extracellular fluid pH will drop below normal. The condition is then referred to as "uncompensated respiratory acidosis." In compensated respiratory acidosis, the plasma pH will be normal. In uncompensated respiratory acidosis, the plasma pH will drop below normal.

The emphysematous patient may fluctuate between compensated and uncompensated acidosis. For example, a respiratory infection may tip his delicate state of balance and precipitate uncompensated respiratory acidosis.

The symptoms of emphysema with respiratory acidosis may include:

- Chronic fatigue
- Dyspnea, first noted on exertion
- Moderate cyanosis, early
- Respiration with a prolonged expiratory phase accompanied by wheezing or a blowing sound
- Large barrel-shaped chest
- A chest that appears to be held in permanent inspiration, so that the shoulders appear elevated and the neck shortened
- Use of accessory respiratory muscles in breathing
- Chronic productive cough
- Dull headache
- Severe cyanosis in the terminal stages
- Coma, if acidosis is severe

Treatment. Ideally, the treatment of respiratory acidosis should consist of eliminating the underlying pulmonary disease. Unfortunately, this is not possible in emphysema. For this reason, treatment is directed toward maximal relief of pulmonary obstruction and the improvement of pulmonary ventilation.

Bronchodilators, such as Isuprel, are beneficial since they reduce bronchial spasms and thus improve pulmonary ventilation. Best results are obtained when the patient first exhales completely and then inhales the medication directly into the respiratory tract. Bronchodilators may be administered by means of a positive pressure device, such as the Bennett or Bird respirator, or by means of a hand nebulizer. The nurse should learn how to use this equipment. She should teach the patient how to continue his treatments after he is discharged from the hospital.

Sputum may be thick in the emphysematous patient and difficult to expectorate. For this reason, an expectorant may be given to liquefy the sputum and make it easier to cough up. Mucomyst acetylcysteine is a safe and effective mucolytic agent that liquefies both purulent and nonpurulent secretions. It is particularly useful in any sort of pulmonary disease in which viscid or inspissated mucous secretions are present. It may be administered by nebulization, by intratracheal instillation, or by direct application. Quibron is a bronchodilator-expectorant combining the effectiveness of theophylline plus the expectorant action of glyceryl guaiacolate. Given by mouth, it is useful for the symptomatic treatment of bronchospastic conditions, including pulmonary emphysema.

An absolute increase in the number of circulating red blood cells occurs in emphysematous patients as a result of hypoxia. In addition, the total blood volume increases. For this reason, phlebotomy may be useful as a therapeutic measure.

Patients with excessive respiratory secretions may be helped by postural drainage, which brings secretions up high enough so that they can be eliminated by coughing. Breathing exercises which utilize the abdominal muscles help the lungs empty and aid in the elimination of carbon dioxide. The nurse should supplement the educational efforts of the physical therapist and the physician, and encourage the patient to practice these exercises.

Antibiotics may be necessary when a respiratory infection occurs. Unfortunately, the patient with emphysema is highly susceptible to such infections, particularly during the winter. Although ideally the patient should move to a mild climate during the fall and winter seasons, this is rarely possible. Hence, the patient should be taught to avoid exposure to respiratory infections, sudden chilling, and unnecessary exposure in damp or cold weather. If, in spite of these precautions, he develops a respiratory infection, he should immediately report that fact to his physician. The secretions of respiratory infections cause further obstruction to pulmonary ventilation in the emphysematous patient. Respiratory acidosis can occur readily, and the patient may become seriously ill in a short time.

Acute Respiratory Acidosis

The development of acute respiratory acidosis demands special measures. Bronchial aspiration may be necessary to rid the respiratory tract of mucus and purulent secretions. A mechanical respirator, used cautiously, may improve pulmonary ventilation. Overzealous use of a mechanical respirator may cause such rapid excretion of carbon dioxide that the kidneys will be unable to eliminate the excess bicarbonate ions with sufficient rapidity to prevent alkalosis and convulsions. For this reason, the elevated carbon dioxide concentration should be decreased slowly.

THAM is an organic buffer capable of reducing the carbon dioxide concentration, increasing the bicarbonate concentration, and increasing the pH of the extracellular fluid. It can be used to treat acute respiratory acidosis in association with mechanical ventilation. However, it depresses ventilation and can cause apnea. For this reason, it should not be used for chronic respiratory acidosis.

Fluid volume deficit accompanying respiratory acidosis may be treated by the intravenous administration of a Butler-type solution containing balanced quantities of extracellular and cellular electrolytes, plus carbohydrate, or with sixth molar-lactate. Oxygen can be administered to relieve severe hypoxia; it should be administered with caution to the patient with respiratory acidosis.

Prevention of Carbon Dioxide Narcosis During Oxygen Therapy

Carbon Dioxide Narcosis. *Carbon dioxide*

narcosis may be produced by excessive oxygen administration to a patient with chronic respiratory acidosis. Chronic elevation of the carbon dioxide content of the extracellular fluid causes the respiratory center to become insensitive to carbon dioxide. (Recall that while the respiratory center is normally extremely sensitive to changes in carbon dioxide concentration and that a slight elevation causes respiratory stimulation, arterial carbon dioxide concentration of over 9 per cent causes respiratory depression.) Hypoxia becomes the main stimulus to respiration when the carbon dioxide mechanism is not functioning. A reduction in arterial oxygenation stimulates respiration, and an elevation of arterial oxygenation removes the stimulus. Thus, if oxygen is administered in sufficient quantities to raise arterial oxygenation, respiration will decrease. Decreased respiration favors carbon dioxide retention. Eventually, carbon dioxide narcosis will result unless the situation is reversed.

The nurse should be alert for the occurrence of carbon dioxide narcosis when oxygen is administered to a patient with respiratory acidosis. Symptoms may include:

- Drowsiness
- Irritability, depression, or euphoria
- Warm, flushed skin
- Respiratory depression
- Tachycardia; arrhythmias may develop
- Hallucinations
- Muscular tremors of face or extremities
- Blood pressure, normal or elevated
- Convulsions
- Paralysis of extremities
- Deep coma

Safe Oxygen Administration. Oxygen therapy should be used cautiously in patients with chronic respiratory acidosis. It is important to give no more than a 30 or 40 per cent concentration of oxygen in air; a higher concentration may produce serious respiratory depression.

Continuous oxygen therapy is dangerous and should be avoided; oxygen is best given intermittently to patients with chronic respiratory acidosis. Best results are obtained when oxygen is administered with an intermittent positive pressure device, which both furnishes oxygen and—more importantly—

increases carbon dioxide elimination. To avoid impending carbon dioxide narcosis, the physician may order frequent checks of the carbon dioxide content of the plasma. If this rises excessively, oxygen should be discontinued.

Acute Pulmonary Conditions Associated With Respiratory Acidosis

Mechanical Obstruction With a Foreign Object

Mechanical obstruction of the respiratory tract with a foreign object prevents air flow into the lungs and results in severe anoxia. In addition, air flow from the lungs is interrupted. The sudden retention of carbon dioxide causes acute respiratory acidosis; it can also cause a mild rise in blood pressure.

Ventricular fibrillation and potassium excess are common causes of death in patients with acute respiratory acidosis. Treatment consists of the intravenous administration of a sixth molar sodium lactate solution, which can be prepared by adding 30 ml. of sterile water to the contents of a 20 ml. container of Ion-O-Trate sodium lactate.

Sudden relief of the obstruction, such as may be produced by tracheotomy, causes hyperventilation and may result in alkalosis and tetany as carbon dioxide is rapidly eliminated from the lungs. The bicarbonate level remains temporarily high. (Recall that the kidneys cannot excrete bicarbonate ions as rapidly as the lungs excrete carbon dioxide.) Rapid correction of acidosis may cause ventricular fibrillation, probably due to potassium excess.

Apnea may also follow the sudden release of a respiratory obstruction through tracheotomy, possibly because of hypotension and decreased blood flow to the respiratory center. The blood pressure should be checked immediately before and also after tracheotomy to detect hypotension. If hypotension occurs, the physician may request that the patient be placed in the Trendelenburg position and that a vasopressor be given.

Other acute pulmonary conditions that may be associated with respiratory acidosis include pulmonary edema, atelectasis, open chest wounds and severe pulmonary infections.

Other Conditions Associated With Respiratory Acidosis

Overdoses of Drugs. Overdoses of morphine, Demerol, or a barbiturate result in depression of respiration and increased retention of carbon dioxide. Before administering a drug of this class, the nurse should carefully check the dose, as well as the time when the drug was last given. In addition, the rate and depth of respiration should be observed before and after administration of the drug.

Pain. Severe pain, particularly in the abdomen or thorax, results in splinting of the chest and shallow respiration. Carbon dioxide is retained and respiratory acidosis may develop. Judicious use of analgesics is indicated to relieve pain and to allow the patient to breathe more efficiently.

Weak Respiratory Muscles. Weakening of the respiratory muscles may be caused by such conditions as poliomyelitis or spinal cord injuries. Adequate pulmonary ventilation is not possible; an excessive amount of carbon dioxide is retained by the lungs, and respiratory acidosis may develop.

Inaccurate Regulation of Mechanical Respirators. Inaccurate regulation of a mechanical respirator may result in excessively shallow and slow respiration. Excessive carbon dioxide is retained by the lungs, causing respiratory acidosis.

Inhalation Anesthesia. The use of inhalation anesthetics, such as Cyclopropane or ether, may be associated with hypoventilation and carbon dioxide retention. Mild carbon dioxide retention may be well tolerated for a while, particularly if hypoxia is not present. However, respiratory acidosis may develop as soon as 15 minutes after the start of inhalation anesthesia; it is most likely to occur in patients with chronic pulmonary disease, such as emphysema.

A patient may have normal color and still develop respiratory acidosis, particularly during an operation when the anesthetized patient is given oxygen. While the use of oxygen therapy to produce tissue oxygenation is good, if measures are not taken to increase the exhalation of carbon dioxide (such as with a positive pressure breathing device), an excessive amount of carbonic acid may form in the extracellular fluid and cause respiratory acidosis. The first indication of acidosis may be the development of ventricular fibrillation, probably due to potassium excess. Carbon dioxide retention potentiates vagus nerve activity so that minor stimuli, such as tracheal suction, may cause cardiac arrhythmias. Positioning the patient on the operating table in such a way that normal respiratory excursions are prevented contributes to the development of respiratory acidosis.

Excessive Carbon Dioxide Inhalation. Inhalation of carbon dioxide in concentrations exceeding 9 per cent depresses the medullary respiratory center and produces an increased alveolar carbon dioxide content. This, in turn, causes an increased plasma carbonic acid level and acidosis. For example, a patient in an oxygen tent from which carbon dioxide is poorly absorbed may breathe excessive quantities of carbon dioxide.

Orthopedic Deformities. Restriction of respiratory excursions by spinal deformities may result in carbon dioxide retention and acidosis, even though the lungs are normal.

RESPIRATORY ALKALOSIS

Pathologic Mechanism and Symptoms

Respiratory alkalosis may be caused by any condition that causes an increased excretion of carbon dioxide through the lungs, with a resultant decrease in the carbon dioxide concentration of the extracellular fluid. Hence, a decrease in the carbonic acid side of the carbonic acid:base bicarbonate ratio occurs.

Symptoms vary in respiratory alkalosis. They may be only those of the underlying disease process, or they may be absent. Sometimes, the patient may appear to be short of breath. He may use his upper chest muscles and accessory respiratory muscles during respiration; he may complain of pain and tenderness of the left side of his chest. Alkalosis may cause increased neuromuscular excitability because of the decreased ionization of calcium. (Recall that calcium ionization is decreased in alkalosis.) Anoxia may occur because alkalosis inhibits the release of oxygen from oxyhemoglobin. The most characteristic clinical picture of respiratory alkalosis is represented by the hyperventilation syndrome:

- Dizziness or light-headedness
- Numbness and tingling of fingers and toes
- Circumoral paresthesia
- Tinnitus
- Blurred vision
- Palpitation of the heart
- Sweating
- Dry mouth
- Tetany

Symptoms of alkalotic tetany are more likely to occur if the respiratory alkalosis developed rapidly. The nurse should be alert for these symptoms in any patient having a condition likely to be associated with respiratory alkalosis.

Conditions Associated With Respiratory Alkalosis

The most common cause of respiratory alkalosis is the hyperventilation that accompanies emotional upsets. Treatment consists in making the patient aware of his abnormal breathing practices. He should be made to realize that this breathing pattern causes his symptoms. He can be shown how to relieve his symptoms by holding his breath or breathing into a large paper bag. Such measures cause an accumulation of carbon dioxide in the lungs and relieve the alkalosis.

Hyperventilation can result from hypersensitivity of the respiratory center, such as occurs with meningitis and encephalitis. Respiratory alkalosis develops because excessive amounts of carbon dioxide are blown off by the lungs. The inaccurate regulation of a mechanical respirator, causing too deep and too rapid respiration, results in excessive carbon dioxide elimination, hence, respiratory alkalosis.

Overdoses of salicylates cause excessive stimulation of the respiratory center and hyperventilation. Alkalosis may occur early in salicylate intoxication. Later, by the time the patient arrives at the hospital, metabolic

acidosis may predominate. Other causes of hyperventilation include high fever, exposure to high environmental temperatures and oxygen lack. If the hyperventilation is prolonged, respiratory alkalosis may supervene.

CARE OF THE NEAR-DROWNED PATIENT

Drowning has increased as water sports have become more popular. Today accidental drowning is a common cause of death in the United States. Drowning is also a common method of suicide. Factors that may contribute to accidental drowning include:

- Fatigue
- Hyperventilation or prolonged breath-holding in order to swim long distances underwater
- Muscle cramps
- Hysteria
- Currents or underwater obstacles
- Intoxication

The nurse should be acquainted with the physiologic changes occurring with drowning and with the treatment of these changes, since she may be called upon to care for near-drowned patients in the hospital or at the scene of the accident.

Sea-Water Drowning

Physiologic Changes. Sea water is strongly hypertonic; when inhaled into the lungs, it causes a diffusion of water from the blood into the lungs. The result is hemoconcentration and massive pulmonary edema. Sodium excess and an elevated hematocrit develop as a result of the large water movement from the intravascular compartment of the extracellular fluid into the lungs. Hypotension and a decreased rate of heart contraction lead to death in asystole.

Treatment. The treatment of sea-water submersion, as outlined by Redding and Pearson,* is as follows:

1. If the patient has breathing movements, is conscious, and is not cyanotic, he can be

* Redding, J., and Pearson, J.: Management of drowning victims. Am. Family Physician, 7:55, 1964.

moved to a hospital for a chest x-ray and hematocrit determination.

2. Time should not be wasted in trying to drain water from the lungs.

3. If the patient is not breathing, he should receive mouth-to-mouth resuscitation until oxygen is available. When oxygen is available, it should be given until the patient arrives at the hospital where positive pressure ventilation with oxygen is possible.

4. Tracheal intubation or tracheotomy makes prolonged positive pressure breathing easier; it also facilitates the removal of secretions by suction.

5. Plasma should be given if the hematocrit is elevated or if the x-ray shows evidence of pulmonary edema.

6. When the hematocrit is normal and the chest x-ray is clear, positive pressure breathing can be discontinued.

7. Antibiotics should be administered if indicated.

Fresh-Water Drowning

Physiologic Changes. Aspiration of fresh water into the lungs results in the entrance of large quantities of water into the intravascular compartment. The blood becomes greatly diluted and massive hemolysis of the red blood cells occurs. Hemodilution results in a decreased hematocrit and sodium as well as potassium deficits. Death usually results from ventricular fibrillation, probably caused by sodium deficit and poor oxygenation.

Treatment. Treatment of fresh water submersion, as outlined by Redding and Pearson, is as follows:

1.-4. Same as listed under treatment for sea-water submersion.

5. Immediate closed cardiac massage, if no carotid artery pulse can be palpated.

6. If no pulse is palpable at the time of hospital admission, 1 ml. of 1:1000 epinephrine solution should be given into the heart.

7. Electrical defibrillation should be performed if an electrocardiogram indicates ventricular fibrillation.

8. The plasma and urine should be checked for hemolysis; a partial exchange transfusion may be necessary if hemolysis is severe.

Chapter 23

Water and Electrolyte Disturbances
from Heat Exposure

INTRODUCTION

Although heat disorders occur most often in tropical zones, the temperate climate of North America can cause heat stress. Many persons living in a temperate climate withstand heat stress poorly, hence the increased number of deaths during heat waves. Another common source of heat disorders is the heat stress imposed by certain occupations.

Industry is often associated with artificially-created hot climates, resulting from or deliberately designed for some industrial process. For example, persons working in the textile weaving and processing industry are often subjected to an artificially induced, warm, humid climate, because these conditions are best suited to textile processing. Certain segments of the glass, rubber, steel and mining industries are also associated with high environmental temperatures. Laundry, construction and agricultural workers are often exposed to heat stress, as are firemen.

Because so many persons in our society may be subject to heat disorders, the nurse should become familiar with their prevention, recognition and treatment.

A brief review of body thermoregulation mechanisms will promote a more thorough understanding of the section concerning specific heat disorders.

THERMOREGULATION IN THE BODY

Mechanisms of Thermoregulation

To maintain thermoequilibrium in the body, the amount of heat lost must be equal to the amount of heat gained. Heat is lost when the environmental temperature is less than body temperature. It is gained when the environmental temperature exceeds body temperature and when body energy expenditures are high. Fortunately, the body has a sensitive and efficient thermoregulation system. Let us consider its elements.

Hypothalamus. The heat control center, located in the hypothalamus, has two anatomically separate subcenters: one is responsible for conserving heat and the other for giving off heat. The heat control center is made aware of body temperature variations directly from local brain temperature changes (secondary to variations in the temperature of blood supplying the brain), and reflexly from afferent fibers of the many cutaneous nerve endings sensitive to hot and cold. Efferent fibers of these nerves are chiefly involved with vasomotor activity and the functioning of the sweat glands.

Circulatory System. The circulatory system bears much of the burden of thermoregulation. The constriction of cutaneous blood vessels occurs when the environmental temperature is lower than the body temperature and when energy expenditures are low. Cutaneous vasoconstriction decreases the amount of blood brought to the surface for cooling and thus conserves body heat. Dilatation of the cutaneous blood vessels occurs when the environmental temperature exceeds the body temperature and when energy expenditures are high. Because more blood is brought to the surface for cooling by radiation and conduction, body temperature is lowered.

Sweating is initiated when the environmental temperature exceeds 82.4 to 86° F. (28 to 30° C.). The evaporation of sweat from the body surface causes cooling of peripheral blood. The cooled blood is returned to core parts of the body and serves to reduce body temperature.

Sweat Glands. Of the body's sweat glands, approximately two million have thermoregulation as their chief function. Sweat is normally a hypotonic fluid containing several solutes, the chief of which is sodium chloride. The concentration of sodium chloride in sweat depends largely on the dietary intake; thus the amount per liter of sweat is highly variable. For example, 5 L. of sweat may contain from 2 to 20 Gm. of sodium chloride. A high salt intake causes an increased excretion of salt by the kidneys and sweat glands. Decreased salt intake, or excessive salt loss, causes renal conservation of salt; the sweat glands similarly conserve salt. The retention of needed salt by the kidneys, and possibly by the sweat glands, occurs in response to increased aldosterone secretion.

Other solutes in sweat include potassium, ammonia and urea. The potassium concentration in sweat may be as high as 9 mEq./L.; excessive sweat losses could conceivably lead to potassium deficiency.

The *maximal* sweating rate for most persons is roughly 2 L./hour; obviously, this rate cannot be maintained for long periods. Individuals accustomed to high heat stress may sweat as much as three or more liters per hour. As much as 20 Gm. of sodium chloride has been reported lost in one day's sweat during high heat stress.

Summary of Bodily Responses to Heat Stress. Exposure of the body to heat stress elicits the following responses:

1. Increased peripheral vasodilatation, to allow more blood to come to the surface for cooling by radiation and conduction

2. Increased sweating, to allow for cooling by evaporation

3. Increased blood volume and venous tone, to improve venous return to the heart

4. Increased cardiac output and pulse rate

5. Increased secretion of antidiuretic hormone, to allow the conservation of body water; the 24-hour urinary output may drop to as little as 300 ml.

6. Increased aldosterone secretion, to allow the conservation of body salt; aldosterone causes sodium retention by the kidneys and may exert a similar effect on the sweat glands

Acclimatization to Heat

It has long been known that individuals accustomed to high temperature, either in a natural hot climate or in their work, tolerate heat stress much better than those accustomed to cool temperatures. Yet, the latter can gradually develop a tolerance for heat when repeatedly exposed to it. This process of physiological adaptation is called *acclimatization*. It is accomplished by a series of physiological changes, which serve to ameliorate the effects of heat stress.

Physiological Changes. Individuals exposed repeatedly to heat stress gradually experience fewer of the disagreeable sensations induced by heat, such as lassitude and general discomfort, because of the physiological changes induced by acclimatization.

The specific changes include a progressive decrease in rectal and skin temperatures, a decreased pulse rate, and increased sweating. The sweat contains a lower concentration of sodium chloride; it may contain a higher quantity of potassium than normal.

Rate of Acclimatization. Most of the changes brought about by acclimatization occur in the first 4 to 7 days of heat exposure; they usually attain their maximum after two weeks of daily heat exposure. A person does not have to be subjected to heat stress 24 hours a day in order to become acclimatized. According to Leithead and Lind, the best way to induce acclimatization is to engage in repeated, uninterrupted periods of 100 minutes work under heat stress. Even a daily heat exposure period of 50 minutes is sufficient to induce an important measure of acclimatization. Short exposures to heat will not induce acclimatization because they present no threat to the body's thermoregulation mechanisms.

HEAT DISORDERS

There are several classifications of heat disorders; that used in this chapter was derived chiefly from *Heat Stress and Heat Disorders*, by C. Leithead and A. Lind, Philadelphia, F. A. Davis Company, 1964.

Prolonged exposure to heat can produce several reactions:

- Heat syncope
- Heat cramps
- Heat exhaustion
     Primary water-depletion (sodium excess)
     Primary salt-depletion (sodium deficit)
- Heatstroke

The clinical picture of each disorder is related to the length of exposure to heat and the individual's peculiar response.

Heat Syncope

Heat syncope is also referred to as heat collapse; it is characterized by a sharp reduction in vasomotor tone after heat exposure, which causes peripheral vasodilatation and a tendency to venous pooling. There are no underlying water or electrolyte disturbances.

Symptoms. The pooling of venous blood in the peripheral vessels in heat syncope causes hypotension and cerebral anoxia. Symptoms may include fainting, lightheadedness, or fatigue. Fainting most often follows an additional stress, such as sudden postural changes, heavy lifting, or prolonged standing. Other symptoms may include pallor, nausea, weakness, blurring of vision, numbness and sensations of hot and cold. The pulse rate is increased at the onset of syncope and then decreases. Breathing is low and sighing. The systolic blood pressure is greatly decreased, the diastolic pressure only moderately. The temperature may be above normal; if the patient was engaged in strenuous activity before fainting, the temperature may reach 102° F. Usually the muscles are flaccid. Perspiration, most evident on the forehead, is present.

Treatment. Symptoms subside when the patient is placed in the recumbent or head-low position; consciousness is regained in a few minutes. Rest for 1 or 2 hours in a cool environment is indicated.

Although diagnosis is usually not difficult, the patient should be examined for more serious illnesses associated with fainting. Other causes of sudden fainting may include epilepsy, heart disease, depletion of sodium or water, and heatstroke. The patient should be checked for urinary incontinence and a bitten tongue; both are indicative of an epileptic seizure. The presence of an arrhythmic pulse rate may indicate heart disease. The specific gravity and salt content of the urine should be measured; both are usually normal in heat syncope because there are no major water and electrolyte changes accompanying this disorder. The presence of a high urinary specific gravity may indicate the presence of heat exhaustion due to sodium excess rather than heat syncope.

Prevention. Persons not accustomed to high temperatures should gradually expose themselves to heat, as described earlier in the section dealing with acclimatization to heat. Strenuous activities in a hot environment should not be attempted until maximal heat tolerance is achieved. Patients with cardiac disease should be cautioned against excessive heat exposure, particularly when exercising.

Heat Cramps

Heat cramps are sometimes called miner's, fireman's, or stoker's cramps. They are painful spasms of voluntary muscles that follow strenuous exercise in hot surroundings, either climatic or industrial, plus drinking plain water. Good health does not preclude their occurrence; even workers well accustomed to their jobs can develop them. Workers in some occupations accept heat cramps as an occupational hazard of no serious consequence; they seldom seek medical help unless severe cramps develop.

There is some doubt about classifying heat cramps as a separate entity rather than including it as a manifestation of heat exhaustion due to sodium deficit. Both are due to a depletion of sodium chloride. However, heat exhaustion is more severe and has a broader symptomatology than heat cramps.

Symptoms. The only symptom in heat cramps is the intermittent cramping of voluntary muscles; usually the muscles involved are the ones most exercised. Cramps may be preceded by a twitching in the affected muscles, which tighten into a hard lump. Pain is excruciating during severe heat cramps and subsides as the spasmodic contractions cease. Most cramps last less than one minute; the patient is comfortable between cramps.

The time of onset is almost invariably toward the end of a day's work. *Heat cramps are always preceded by several hours of strenuous exercise, heavy sweating, and liberal plain water intake.*

Treatment. Analgesics offer little or no relief for the spasms. The specific treatment is salt replacement. One-fourth of a teaspoon of salt may be added to a glass of water and repeated at intervals of 5 to 30 minutes. Severe cramps may require an infusion of one-half to one liter of isotonic saline to relieve immediate symptoms; when cramps have subsided, salt can be given orally. The patient should rest for 24 hours after the cessation of cramps. Muscles are stiff and sore after heat cramps, and several days' rest may be necessary before the patient can return to work.

Prevention. The prevention of heat cramps includes increasing the salt intake or decreasing the plain water intake. The former is much to be preferred. Decreasing the water intake predisposes to more serious heat disorders, such as heat exhaustion due to sodium excess and heatstroke. Acclimatization is helpful.

In addition to the normal dietary salt intake, some workers may need 2 or 3 Gm. of extra salt daily to prevent heat cramps; others require as much as 5 Gm. extra. Tablets of salt are often provided at drinking fountains in factories where excessive sweating is a problem. Some workers can sweat profusely and drink plain water liberally without developing heat cramps. This unexplained fact sometimes causes others to ignore medical advice to take supplemental salt tablets.

Heat Exhaustion Due to Sodium Deficit

Heat exhaustion (sodium deficit) stems from the inadequate replacement of the sodium chloride lost in sweat during prolonged heat exposure. It is often associated with the performance of hard work in high environmental heat.

Even though sweat is hypotonic, a sizable amount of salt can be lost when sweating is excessive. If plain water is drunk freely, without salt replacement, symptoms of sodium deficit become pronounced. Unacclimatized persons are more apt to develop sodium deficit than those accustomed to high heat stress. Sweat glands of acclimatized persons have a greater ability to conserve salt when the body's supply is low. This adaptation process takes place after an exposure period to heat of about 5 to 6 days. The phenomenon may explain why some men, accustomed to working and sweating in hot industries, can pay little attention to salt replacement and drink plain water freely without developing symptoms of sodium deficit. However, it should not be forgotten that anyone exposed to high heat stress is vulnerable to salt-depletion heat exhaustion.

Symptoms. Although both sodium and chloride are lost in heat exhaustion due to sodium deficit, the symptoms are primarily those of sodium deficit. Because sodium is the chief extracellular ion, its depletion causes a fall in the osmolarity of the extracellular fluid. As a result, water enters the cells, diluting their electrolytes and causing them to swell. Equally important, water diuresis occurs and causes a pronounced decrease in the extracellular fluid volume. The decrease of extracellular fluid volume and the increase in cellular fluid volume seems to be at least partly related to all of the symptoms of this form of heat exhaustion. Plasma volume is progressively decreased as sodium deficit becomes more severe; in some cases the volume has been reduced by half.

Symptoms of heat exhaustion due to sodium deficit develop insidiously over 3 to 5 days and include:

- Fatigue
- Headache

- Muscle cramps
- Giddiness
- Vomiting
- Nausea
- Anorexia
- Syncope
- Listlessness
- Constipation or diarrhea
- Circulatory collapse, in last stages

In early sodium deficit, the complaints are of apprehension, weariness and muscle weakness, headache and giddiness. These symptoms persist and are later accompanied by nausea, cramps and vomiting. Painful muscle cramps lasting up to two or more minutes frequently occur in heat exhaustion. Usually the cramps occur in muscles fatigued by exercise. In severe sodium deficit, the legs, the arms and the abdominal muscles may be involved.

Thirst is not a striking feature as it is in heat exhaustion due to sodium excess. The body temperature is usually subnormal or normal; occasionally it may rise to 101° F. The urine is not highly concentrated and contains negligible amounts of sodium chloride. The plasma sodium and chloride levels are reduced. The hematocrit percentage is high, often about 60 per cent.

Only badly neglected persons reach the stage of profound circulatory collapse. The hypotension, oliguria, and shock that result may cause death. Clinically, it is sometimes difficult to distinguish between heat exhaustion due to sodium deficit and that due to water depletion. Table 44 lists a comparison of symptoms to help differentiate between the two.

Treatment. The treatment consists of bedrest in cool surroundings, and a high salt and water intake. The daily salt intake should be approximately 20 Gm. until sodium deficit is corrected. Unlike some animals, man does not crave salt when sodium deficit is present; therefore, a natural drive to consume enough salt to repair the deficit cannot be relied on.

Salt can be palatably replaced by adding it to liquids such as tomato juice or broth. It can also be supplied in oral isotonic saline if nothing else is at hand. Enteric-coated salt tablets should not be used for treatment because they take hours to dissolve in the intestines; they should be used only as a prophylactic measure.

Prevention. Persons working in a hot environment should consume an adequate amount of salt. Most diets contain approximately 10 Gm. of salt; acclimatized men generally need no supplement to their normal dietary salt intake. Unacclimatized men working in hot surroundings may require as much as 5 Gm., and rarely 10 or 15 Gm., of extra salt daily to prevent salt depletion.

TABLE 44. DISTINCTION BETWEEN HEAT EXHAUSTION DUE TO SODIUM DEFICIT AND THAT DUE TO WATER DEPLETION (SODIUM EXCESS)

FEATURES	SODIUM DEFICIT	WATER DEPLETION (SODIUM EXCESS)
Duration of symptoms	3 to 5 days	Often much shorter
Thirst	Not prominent	Prominent
Fatigue	Prominent	Less prominent
Giddiness	Prominent	Less prominent
Muscle cramps	In most cases	Absent
Vomiting	In most cases	Usually absent
Thermal sweating	Probably unchanged	Diminished
Hemoconcentration	Early and marked	Slight until late
Urine chloride	Negligible amounts	Normal amounts
Urine concentration	Moderate	Pronounced
Plasma sodium	Below average	Above average
Mode of death	Oligemic shock	High osmotic pressure, oligemic shock, heatstroke

Adapted from Leithead, C., and Lind, A.: Heat Stress and Heat Disorders. p. 165. Philadelphia, Davis, 1964.

This amount can be reduced after acclimatization has been achieved. The occurrence of other abnormal losses of salt, such as in vomiting or diarrhea, is an indication to increase salt intake.

Since it is difficult to add more than 10 Gm. of table salt to the daily diet without making it unpalatable, salt tablets are used to supplement dietary salt intake. Some salt tablets are merely compressed salt and are designed to add to drinks or food; their only advantage over table salt is that they require less storage space. The most widely used salt tablets are enteric coated; these tablets are available in 5 grain (0.33 Gm.) and 10 grain (0.65 Gm.) sizes. Other tablets are chocolate coated and disintegrate quickly when swallowed.

Patients receiving diuretic therapy should be observed closely for salt-depletion during the hot summer months; physicians sometimes deem it necessary to curtail the use of diuretic drugs during this time. Recall that diuretics cause an increased urinary excretion of sodium, water, and potassium.

Heat Exhaustion Due to Sodium Excess

This form of heat exhaustion is due to inadequate water replacement during prolonged heat exposure and sweating. A high price is paid in sweat to allow successful thermoregulation in hot surroundings. Because sweat is hypotonic, relatively greater amounts of water than salt are lost. Failure to adequately replace the water loss leads to water depletion (sodium excess). This form of heat exhaustion, if uncorrected, predisposes to heatstroke.

Symptoms. Thirst occurs early, and the patient will respond to it unless circumstances prevent. These may include an inadequate or unpalatable water supply, or the inability of infants and extremely enfeebled persons to respond to thirst.

Symptoms of heat exhaustion due to sodium excess depend upon the degree of water loss; three clinical grades can be described, as shown in Table 45.

Generally speaking, a man can survive in a temperate climate for 7 to 10 days without water; he can survive only 1 or 2 days without water when exposed to the extreme heat of the desert.

TABLE 45. HEAT EXHAUSTION DUE TO WATER DEPLETION (SODIUM EXCESS)

CLINICAL GRADE	SYMPTOMS
Early	Thirst Loss of 2% body weight (equivalent to 1.5 L. in a man weighing 70 Kg.)
Moderately severe	Intense thirst Dry mouth, difficulty in swallowing Scanty urine of high concentration Rapid pulse Increase in rectal temperature to about 102° F. Poor skin turgor Loss of 6% body weight (equivalent to 4.2 L. in a man weighing 70 Kg.)
Very Severe	Same as above Marked impairment of mental and physical capacities High rectal temperature Cyanosis, circulatory failure, extreme oliguria or anuria Rapid breathing (hyperventilation may cause tetany) Loss of more than 7% body weight (equivalent to 5 to 10 L. in a man weighing 70 Kg.) Coma and death when 15% of body weight is lost

Adapted from Leithead, C., and Lind, A.: Heat Stress and Heat Disorders. p. 148. Philadelphia, Davis, 1964.

Treatment. The patient should rest in bed in a cool environment. Sponging with cool water may be necessary if the body temperature is greatly elevated. The feet should be elevated to improve blood return to the heart; the arms and legs should be rubbed to stimulate blood flow.

A high fluid intake is indicated; if the patient can tolerate water by mouth, cool fluids should be given at frequent intervals to achieve an intake of 6 to 8 L. in the first 24 hours.

Intravenous infusion of 4 or more liters of

5 per cent dextrose in water may be necessary if the patient is unconscious or otherwise unable to take fluids orally. Renal function should be assessed before a large volume of intravenous fluids is given. The presence of severe oliguria or anuria could cause circulatory overload; or water intoxication can result if large volumes of 5 per cent glucose in water are given to a patient with renal damage. Daily body weight and fluid intake-output records should be kept; further fluid replacement is made as clinical findings indicate.

The plasma sodium level and urinary sodium chloride content are measured daily. Recall that sodium chloride is also lost in sweat, even though the water loss is more pronounced. If a sodium deficit is present after water replacement, isotonic saline may be given.

Prevention. An adequate supply of cool water should be made easily accessible to men working in hot surroundings. Infants exposed to heat should be offered water frequently. Aged or otherwise enfeebled persons should also be offered fluids frequently. Inadequate oral intake should be reported so that another replacement route can be used.

Heatstroke

Heatstroke is the most serious heat disorder and is associated with a high mortality rate. It is characterized by the sudden cessation of sweating following exposure to high heat stress. Its distribution is world-wide, either in naturally occurring hot climates or in artificial hot surroundings, such as occur in some industries. Heat waves in usually temperate climates account for a large number of heatstroke victims.

The exact pathology of heatstroke is not understood; the production of sweat seemingly fails. So long as sweating continues, with water and salt losses replaced, the body can withstand heat stress well. According to Guyton, an individual can tolerate several hours of exposure to a temperature of 200° F. if the air is completely dry and if air currents are flowing to promote rapid evaporation of sweat from the skin surface.

Central nervous system symptoms, failure of sweat formation, and high body temperatures (above 105° F.) are characteristically present in heatstroke.

Predisposing Factors. Certain factors predispose to heatstroke:

- Inadequate acclimatization
- Obese body build
- Pre-existent acute or chronic illness
- Recent use of alcohol
- Inadequate water and salt intake
- Recent use of atropine-like drugs
- High relative humidity
- Extremes in age
- Strenuous physical activity in hot surroundings
- Failure to appreciate the dangers of heat exposure and to take adequate precautions

DISCUSSION. Much evidence supports the thesis that lack of acclimatization predisposes to heatstroke. Malamud, Haymaker and Custer, in 1946, studied the heatstroke deaths of 125 soldiers undergoing intensive training in southern United States. They found that one-fourth of the men who died had been in camp less than 2 weeks, and about one-half had been there less than 8 weeks.

An obese person has less body surface in proportion to body weight than does a person of slight build, hence he has greater difficulty in dissipating heat. Conditions such as myocardial ischemia, arteriosclerosis, and hypertension seem to predispose to heatstroke.

Recent use of alcohol prior to heat exposure may predispose to heatstroke. According to Leithead and Lind, there are probably several reasons why this is true: alcohol causes an increased metabolic load and steps up internal body temperature; it dulls judgment and critical thinking; it causes increased water loss from the body.

Atropine-like drugs cause decreased sweating and thus interfere with the dissipation of body heat. The administration of atropine before surgery has been implicated as a predisposing factor in heatstroke of heavily draped surgical patients in hot operating rooms.

A high relative humidity predisposes to heatstroke because it interferes with the evaporation of sweat from the body. Failure of sweat to evaporate causes inefficient body cooling. The body temperature begins to rise when the relative humidity is 100 per cent and the environmental temperature is above 94° F.

The high incidence of cardiovascular disease in the aged predisposes this age group to heatstroke. Infants are also predisposed to heatstroke; they have an unstable thermoregulatory mechanism, in addition to immature renal function. The infant's renal function, particularly during the first month of life, does not allow concentration of urine when excessive water loss by other routes has occurred. Sodium excess results because of the kidney's inability to conserve needed body water when perspiration losses are great.

Strenuous activity increases the metabolic rate and thus elevates the body temperature; the addition of a hot external temperature subjects the body to two sources of excessive heat and predisposes to heatstroke. Heatstroke has been observed in persons doing heavy manual labor when the environmental temperature was as low as 84.2° F. Of 158 heatstroke patients studied by Gauss and Meyer (1917), the majority were manual laborers, including some firemen or laundry workers. However, it should be remembered that even mild activity in extremely hot surroundings may result in heatstroke.

Failure to appreciate the dangers of heat exposure is often related to the development of heatstroke. The nurse should become familiar with the preventive measures listed at the end of the chapter so that she can offer sound advice about heat disorders to lay persons.

Symptoms. Persons mildly afflicted with heatstroke may have no prodromal symptoms. Others may experience symptoms for a few minutes to 1 or 2 hours before loss of consciousness. These symptoms may include euphoria (associated with a rise in body temperature), headache, dizziness, faintness, numbness, drowsiness, aggressiveness, mental confusion and incoordinated movements.

The onset of heatstroke is usually sudden and is heralded by disturbances of the central nervous system. Symptoms of heatstroke include:

- Disorientation
- Absence of sweating
- Complaint of feeling hot
- Involuntary limb movements
- Skin dry and hot to touch (skin turgor is usually good unless heatstroke is preceded by water depletion)
- Rectal temperature of at least 105° F.
- Convulsions, either localized or generalized
- Projectile vomiting
- Rapid pulse (may be as high as 150 beats per minute)
- Rapid respiration (may be as high as 60 per minute)
- Systolic blood pressure elevated
- Red, blotchy appearance of face (patient may look as if he has been strangled)
- Incontinent liquid feces
- Circulatory collapse
- Petechial hemorrhages in the brain, heart, kidney, or liver (if the patient survives, residual damage to these organs, particularly the brain, may become evident)
- Coma

Most persons suffering with heatstroke are comatose at the time they receive medical attention. Many times the comatose heatstroke patient is mistaken for a stroke victim; the presence of neurological symptoms resembling those of stroke accounts for this confusion.

Rapid breathing in heatstroke may cause respiratory alkalosis (primary carbonic acid deficit) due to the excessive blowing off of CO_2 and result in hypokalemia. This imbalance is less threatening, however, than hyperkalemia, which occasionally occurs. Potassium excess is associated with cellular breakdown due to heat; potassium leaves the cells and enters the extracellular fluid, where it remains because of poor renal function due to circulatory collapse and the cessation of sweating. (Recall that sweat contains potassium.) Potassium excess can cause sudden death in heatstroke victims.

Treatment. *Quick and effective reduction of the high body temperature is essential.* Even a few hours delay may leave the patient with severe neurological deficits. The longer the temperature remains high, the greater the possibility of irreversible brain damage. When the body temperature is above 106° F., damage to cells throughout the entire body occurs; damage to brain cells is particularly critical, because they cannot be replaced. When the body temperature reaches 110 to 114° F., the patient can live only a few hours unless the temperature is rapidly reduced. Regardless of how high the temperature is, it should be reduced to 102° F. within the first hour of treatment. Recovery from heatstroke depends largely on reducing the degree and duration of fever.

The most effective method of cooling is immersion in a bathtub of ice water; this measure may seem drastic, yet the temperature must be rapidly lowered to 102° F. Other methods are not as rapid and sure. They include sponging with ice water or alcohol, and packing the patient in cold sheets. Antipyretics are too slow and do not lower the body temperature sufficiently to be of value in the initial treatment of heatstroke. Because the measures to promote cooling may be frightening to the conscious patient, he should be constantly attended and reassured.

It is especially important that the patient be constantly attended while he is immersed in a tub of ice water. Since the patient may be comatose, or at least disoriented, he must be protected from drowning. The body temperature should be taken every 5 minutes. The temperature is usually taken orally, because special equipment would be necessary to measure it rectally. The nurse should recall that the oral temperature is approximately one-half to one degree less than the rectal temperature. When the temperature reaches approximately 102° F., the patient should be removed from the ice water bath; otherwise, too much cooling could result and cause subnormal temperature and shock. Reduction of the body temperature to 102° F. causes the patient to feel better. Slight paralysis is sometimes relieved by the temperature reduction. After the removal of the patient from the tub, the body temperature should be measured at frequent intervals so that any rise can be noted early; it may be necessary to repeat hypothermic treatment. The blood pressure should be checked regularly during the first few days.

Salt and water losses must be replaced slowly until adequate renal function is established. After 1 to 3 days of intensive treatment, the sweat glands again become functional, although it may be as long as 6 months before they begin to secrete normally. The patient should remain at bedrest for 1 to 2 weeks after temperature reduction.

EMERGENCY MEASURES BEFORE MEDICAL AID IS AVAILABLE. Because time is so vital in preventing fatalities from heatstroke, one should take every measure possible to reduce body temperature as soon as possible. Unfortunately, heatstroke may occur in an area some distance from medical aid; furthermore, facilities for ice water baths or even sponging may not be available. *The following points should be kept in mind to care for the heatstroke victim before medical aid is available*:

1. Move the patient out of the sun to the coolest, best ventilated spot available.

2. Remove most of the patient's clothing.

3. Summon medical aid; if necessary, move the patient to medical aid. The transporting vehicle should have all of its windows opened so that a draft can blow on the patient to promote cooling. If moving the patient entails further exposure to high heat stress, it is better to wait until a more suitable means of transportation is available. Additional heat stress could cause death.

4. Investigate surroundings for *any* immediate means of reducing the patient's temperature until more effective measures can be made available. For example, if heatstroke occurs during an outing near a body of water, the patient may be partially immersed to promote cooling. Or, if a water hose is available, the patient can be sprayed continuously with water. If nothing but a drinking water supply is available, the patient can be sponged with it.

5. Massage the patient's skin vigorously; this maintains circulation, aids in accelerating heat loss, and stimulates the return of cool peripheral blood to the

overheated brain and viscera. Body heat may be lost rapidly in this manner.

Summary of Measures to Prevent Heat Disorders

The nurse has a responsibility to the public to offer sound advice about heat disorders and their prevention. In addition, she should be alert to the prevention of heat disorders in hospitalized patients. Remember:

1. All persons exposed to high heat stress should increase their daily salt and water intake. Heat resistance is developed by replenishing water and salt losses as they occur. Infants should be offered water frequently during hot days, as should enfeebled adults. Salt tablets should be taken to supplement dietary salt intake when excessive sweating occurs, except in acclimated persons and those on low-sodium diets.

2. Strenuous activity should be curtailed as much as possible during hot days.

3. Persons customarily exposed to heat stress should maintain good physical condition. Sufficient rest and proper food and fluid intake help prevent heat disorders.

4. Persons moving from a temperate to a hot climate, or those subjected to heat stress in their work, should gradually build up a tolerance to heat through planned acclimatization. Sudden exposure of an unacclimatized person to high heat stress predisposes to heat disorders. (See section dealing with acclimatization to heat.)

5. Prickly heat should be prevented as much as possible, because it interferes with sweating and dissipation of heat from the body. Persons exposed to heat should wear loose, porous clothing, take frequent cool baths, and keep their rooms well ventilated.

6. Persons particularly susceptible to heat disorders should be protected from hot, unventilated places. Such persons include infants, the aged, persons with cardiovascular disease, and those under the influence of alcohol.

7. Persons taking atropine-like drugs should be protected from excessive heat exposure; atropine causes a decrease in sweating and an increased susceptibility to heat disorders. Such persons should be urged to keep their rooms well ventilated during hot weather, take frequent cool baths, and wear loose, porous clothing.

8. Persons taking diuretics should avoid excessive heat exposure and sweating. Recall that diuretics cause an increased excretion of sodium from the body; if the sodium level is further depleted by excessive sweating, the patient may develop salt-depletion.

9. Persons confined to bed should be protected from excessive bedclothing and hot, poorly ventilated rooms.

10. Potassium deficit has been shown to help cause some heat disorders. Hence, persons prone to develop potassium deficit—those taking diuretics, for example—should guard against potassium deficit in hot weather. Food intake, hence potassium intake, usually decreases in hot weather. At the same time, more potassium than normal is lost in heavy sweating.

Chapter 24

Fluid Balance Disturbances in Infants and Children

INTRODUCTION

Water and electrolyte disturbances occur more frequently in children than in adults. While one recognizes and manages fluid imbalances in children in much the same way he does in adults, there are also important differences. The younger the child, the more pronounced are these differences. The nurse should understand the peculiar problems posed by the child with a body fluid disturbance, so that she can make meaningful observations and can cooperate intelligently in his care.

An obvious and important difference between small children and adults is size. Yet, children are not merely miniature adults, for the child's body composition and homeostatic controls differ from those of the adult. It is helpful to compare the child's body composition with that of the adult and to review the salient characteristics of the child's homeostatic and metabolic functioning.

DIFFERENCES IN WATER AND ELECTROLYTE BALANCE IN INFANTS, CHILDREN, AND ADULTS

Comparison of Body Water Content

The premature infant's body is approximately 90 per cent water; the newborn infant's, 70 to 80 per cent; the adult's, about 60 per cent. The infant has proportionately more water in the extracellular compartment than does the adult. For example,

40 per cent of the newborn infant's body water may be in the extracellular compartment, as compared to only 20 per cent in the case of the adult.

As the infant becomes older, his total body water content decreases, possibly due to a progressive growth of cells at the expense of the extracellular fluid. The decrease is particularly rapid during the first few days of life, but continues throughout the first 6 months. After the first year, the total body water is about 64 per cent (34 per cent in the cellular compartment, and 30 per cent in the extracellular compartment). By the end of the second year, the total body water approaches the adult percentage of approximately 60 per cent (36 per cent in the cellular compartment, and 24 per cent in the extracellular compartment). At puberty, the adult body water composition is attained. For the first time, there is a sex differentiation: females have slighly less water because they have a higher percentage of body fat.

Comparison of Daily Body Water Turnover in Infants and Adults

The infant's relatively greater total body water content does not always protect him from excessive fluid loss. On the contrary, the infant is more vulnerable to fluid volume deficit than is the adult, because he ingests and excretes a relatively greater daily water volume. An infant may exchange half of his extracellular fluid daily, while the adult may exchange only one-sixth of his in the same period. Proportionately, therefore, the infant has less reserve of body fluid than does the adult.

The daily fluid exchange is relatively greater in infants, in part because their metabolic rate is two times higher per unit of weight than that of adults. Due to the high metabolic rate, the infant has a large amount of metabolic wastes to excrete. Because water is needed by the kidneys to excrete these wastes, a large urinary volume is formed each day. Contributing to this volume is the inability of the infant's immature kidneys to concentrate urine efficiently. In addition, relatively greater fluid loss occurs through the infant's skin because of his proportionately greater body surface. The premature has approximately five times as much body surface area in relation to weight, and the newborn, three times, as do the older child and adult. Any condition causing a pronounced decrease in intake or increase in output of water and electrolytes threatens the body fluid economy of the infant. According to Gamble, an infant can live only 3 to 4 days without water, while an adult may live 10 days.

Comparison of Electrolyte Concentrations and pH

Plasma electrolyte concentrations do not vary strikingly between infants, small children and adults. The plasma sodium concentration changes little from birth to adulthood. Potassium concentration is higher in the first few months of life than at any other time, as is the plasma chloride concentration. The serum phosphorus level is higher in infants and children than in adults. The newborn's and the child's bicarbonate levels are lower than the adult's. (See Table 46.)

Because the infant's metabolic rate is high, the rate of metabolic acid formation is also high. Thus, the infant has a tendency toward metabolic acidosis (primary base bicarbonate deficit). Buffer systems are not as efficient in the newborn as they are in older infants and children. A full-term newborn infant is slightly acidotic at birth; however, the pH is usually normal by the second day of life. The premature infant is even more acidotic and may remain so for a few weeks. Because cow's milk has higher phosphate and sulfate concentrations than breast milk, newborns fed cow's milk have a lower pH than do breast-fed babies.

Comparison of Kidney Function

The newborn's renal function is not yet completely developed. Thus, if infant and adult renal functions are compared on the basis of total body water, the infant's kidneys appear to become mature by the end of the first month of life. However, if body surface area is used as the criterion for comparison, the child's kidneys appear immature for the first two years of life. Since the infant's kidneys have a limited concentrating ability and require more water to excrete a given amount of solute, he has difficulty in con-

TABLE 46. COMPARISON OF "AVERAGE" BLOOD (SERUM OR PLASMA) ELECTROLYTE VALUES (MEQ./L.) AT DIFFERENT AGES UNDER VARYING CONDITIONS

	PREMATURES		First Week	NEWBORNS		CHILD 5-20 yrs.	ADULTS	
ELECTROLYTE	"Acidotic"	"Well"		On Breast Milk	On Cow's Milk		Young	Over 70
Sodium	..	..	146	..	..	144	142	144
Potassium	..	6.1	5.8	..	..	4.3	4.5	4.6
Calcium	..	..	4.9	..	..	4.9	4.9	5.2
Chloride	102.6	106	107	107.7	108	103	103	105
Phosphorus	4.2	4.1	4.2	..	..	2.8	2.0	1.7
Organic Acids	20.9	17.8	6	..	..	6	5	..
Bicarbonate (CO_2 combining power)	12.1	16.8	22.1	22.3	20.2	23	26.3	25
CO_2 Content	..	20	23.4	23.6	21.4	24.5	27.6	..

Weisberg, H.: Water, Electrolyte and Acid-Base Balance. ed. 2, p. 334. Baltimore, Williams & Wilkins, 1962.

serving body water when it is needed. Also, he may be unable to excrete an excess fluid volume.

Comparison of Body Surface Area

The infant's relatively greater body surface area is present until the child is 2 or 3 years old. The skin represents an important route of fluid loss, especially in illness. Since the gastrointestinal membranes are essentially an extension of the body surface area, their area is also relatively greater in the young infant than in the older child and the adult. Hence, relatively greater losses occur from the gastrointestinal tract in the sick infant than in the older child and adult. In comparing fluid losses in infants to those in adults, one might regard the baby as a smaller vessel with a larger spout.

Comparison of Water Requirements

Regardless of age, all normal individuals require approximately 100 ml. of water per 100 calories metabolized. Since infants and children have higher metabolic rates than do adults, they need proportionately more water. For example, an infant expends 100 calories per Kg. of body weight; an adult, only 38 calories. An infant needs 100 ml.

of water per Kg., while the adult requires only 38. Water needs for various age groups are listed in Table 47.

NURSING OBSERVATIONS RELATED TO FLUID IMBALANCES IN CHILDREN

Charted nursing observations can be immensely helpful to the physician or can mean nothing, depending on whether the nurse knows what to look for and takes the time to record her observations on the nursing notes. Because small children cannot describe their problems, the pediatric nurse has to be especially observant. Some of the major areas in which observations should be made are described below.

Tissue Turgor

Tissue turgor is best palpated in the abdominal areas and on the medial aspects of the thighs. In a normal person, pinched skin will fall back to its normal configuration when released. In a patient with fluid volume deficit, the skin may remain slightly raised for a few seconds. Poor nutrition can also cause poor tissue turgor. Obese infants with fluid volume deficit often have deceptively normal-appearing skin turgor. An infant with water loss in excess of sodium loss (sodium excess), such as occurs in some

TABLE 47. Mean Ranges of Daily Water Requirements of Infants and Children at Different Ages Under Normal Conditions

Age	Average Body Weight (Kg.)	Total H$_2$O Requirements per 24 Hours (ml.)	H$_2$O Requirements per Kg. in 24 Hours (ml.)
3 days	3.0	250–300	80–100
10 days	3.2	400–500	125–150
3 months	5.4	750–850	140–160
6 months	7.3	950–1,100	130–135
9 months	8.6	1,100–1,250	125–145
1 year	9.5	1,150–1,300	120–135
2 years	11.8	1,350–1,500	115–125
4 years	16.2	1,600–1,800	100–110
6 years	20.0	1,800–2,000	90–100
10 years	28.7	2,000–2,500	70–85
14 years	45.0	2,200–2,700	50–60
18 years	54.0	2,200–2,700	40–50

Nelson, W. E.: Nelson's Textbook of Pediatrics. ed. 4, p. 55. Philadelphia, Saunders.

types of diarrhea, has a firm thick-feeling skin. This same phenomenon is observed in the child who has sodium excess due to an excessive sodium intake, as occurs in salt poisoning.

Mucous Membranes

Dry mouth may be due to a fluid volume deficit or to mouth breathing. When in doubt, the nurse should run her finger along the oral cavity to feel the mucous membrane where the cheek and gums meet; dryness in this area indicates a true fluid volume deficit.

Breathing Rate, Depth and Pattern

The nurse should observe the rate, the depth and the pattern of respiration. Hyperpnea, such as occurs in metabolic acidosis due to diarrhea or salicylate poisoning, can double the water loss by way of the lungs. Accelerated breathing should be reported so that water losses through this route can be replaced. Older children and adults with metabolic alkalosis (primary base bicarbonate excess) have decreased rate and depth of respiration, with irregular rhythm. The young infant may normally have irregular respiration; thus, changes in respiratory rhythm are not dependable in detecting metabolic alkalosis.

Changes in respiratory rate and depth are significant in evaluating the child's response to therapy. For example, a change from deep, rapid respiration to slower, less deep respiration indicates improvement in the child with metabolic acidosis.

Tearing and Salivation

The absence of tearing and salivation is a sign of fluid volume deficit and should be noted on the chart.

Thirst

Avid thirst indicates increased tonicity of the extracellular fluid with cellular dehydration. An infant can be tested for thirst with water, although the presence of nausea may mask this symptom.

Behavior

The child's general behavior is also significant in evaluating the response to therapy of fluid imbalances. When the very ill child begins to display appropriate responses to people, ceases to have irritable, purposeless movements, and is less lethargic, his condition has improved.

General Appearance

A child with a fluid volume deficit has a pinched, drawn facial expression. His eyes appear sunken and are soft to the touch, due to decreased intraocular pressure. If the anterior fontanel is still patent, it may be depressed. A grayish skin color, due to decreased peripheral circulation, also accompanies severe fluid volume deficit.

Nature of Cry

The cry of an ill infant is higher pitched and less energetic than normal. With improvement in his condition, the cry becomes less high pitched and more lusty.

Body Temperature

Fluid volume deficit is often associated with a subnormal temperature because of reduced energy output. Depending on the underlying disease, however, fever can accompany fluid volume deficit. If fever is present, its height should be recorded frequently. The rate of insensible water loss is greatly increased with fever; the amount of water lost depends on the height and duration of the fever. Fever may indicate excessive water loss from the body with resultant sodium excess, or it may be caused by an infection. The extremities are cold to the touch in severe fluid volume deficit—even when fever is present—due to decreased peripheral blood flow.

Urine Output

In addition to noting the number of voidings, the nurse should estimate how much of the diaper is saturated with urine. Occasionally she would do well to weigh a dry diaper and compare its weight with that of the same diaper after the child has voided. The nurse should also note the urine's concentration, as revealed by its color. Failure to record urinary output accurately makes treatment far more difficult.

A child with fluid volume deficit has a decreased urinary output and an increased urinary specific gravity. If the fluid deficit is severe, he may go as long as 18 to 24 hours without voiding and still not have a distended bladder. If a child with a known fluid volume deficit excretes large amounts of dilute urine, he probably has renal damage.

Stools

Again, it is not enough just to chart the number of stools. The quantity of the stool should be estimated as nearly as possible; its character should be described. Thus, if a stool appears normal, it should be so described on the chart. If the stool is liquid, the degree of saturation of the diaper should be noted. Any abnormal contents, such as blood or mucus, should also be recorded.

Vomiting

It is important to chart the number of times the patient has vomited, when he vomited, the quantity of vomitus (approximated if necessary), and the nature of the vomitus.

Merely charting the number of times the patient vomited helps little in planning fluid replacement therapy, since the amount of fluid lost can vary widely from one attack of vomiting to another. Failure to describe the vomitus may make fluid replacement therapy more difficult. For example, if the vomitus is bile stained, one can conclude that it came from below the pylorus. Since fluids from below the pylorus are chiefly alkaline, fluid therapy must be designed to replace alkaline losses, using, for example, an intestinal replacement solution.

Weight Changes

Weight loss can be caused by loss of fluid or by catabolism of body tissues. The weight loss associated with fluid volume deficit occurs more rapidly than that caused by starvation. A mild fluid volume deficit in an infant or child entails a loss of from 3 to 5 per cent of the normal body weight; a moderate fluid volume deficit, from 5 to 9 per cent; a severe fluid volume deficit, 10 per cent or more. If possible, the child's weight before the onset of the illness should be obtained from the parents, or from the family physician, who may have a record of the normal weight from a recent office visit.

If weighing is not performed accurately, it is useless. Even a minor error is important when the patient is small. The child should be weighed at the same time each day, before he has eaten, after he has voided. The same scales should be used each time, and the child should be weighed naked.

Amount and Character of Fluid Lost by Suction or Other Routes

The amount and character of fluid lost by suction, drainage tubes, or fistulas should be recorded. If the fluid loss cannot be directly measured, it should be estimated as accurately as possible.

Fluid Intake

The amount and type of fluids received by the patient, either orally or parenterally, should be recorded.

FLUID REPLACEMENT THERAPY IN CHILDREN

Daily Requirements

The basic requirements of water and electrolytes must be met daily. In addition, one should supply the amounts necessary to correct pre-existing deficits, as well as concurrent abnormal losses, such as those that occur from diarrhea, vomiting, suction drainage, and the like. The normal water requirements per Kg. of body weight at various ages are listed in Table 47. Approximately 2 to 3 mEq. of sodium and potassium are required for each Kg. of body weight to meet maintenance needs. This corresponds to approximately 50 to 70 mEq. of sodium or potassium/sq. m. of body surface/day.

Although the adult can go without food for several days without developing gross ketonuria, infants and children react quickly to the omission of calories. Ketonuria can occur within a few hours after the onset of fasting. For this reason, carbohydrate must be incorporated in fluids designed to meet daily maintenance needs.

Oral Replacement

Water and electrolyte replacement is best accomplished by the oral route for these reasons:

1. Fluids taken into the gastrointestinal tract are slowly absorbed, while parenterally administered fluids pass directly into the circulation; the body is less adversely affected if excessive amounts of water or electrolytes are given by the oral than by the parenteral route.

2. Oral fluid replacement allows the child free movement and activity, as opposed to hours of being restrained during subcutaneous or intravenous infusions.

It should be emphasized, however, that even in the case of the oral route, it is relatively easy to overwhelm the body's homeostatic capabilities, particularly in the case of the infant and small child. For this reason, the dose for fluids administered orally should be calculated with the same care and precision as doses to be administered parenterally. Moreover, although the oral route is far safer than the intravenous route, potassium should not be given by mouth when oliguria or anuria is present.

A child with fever and no major fluid loss from the gastrointestinal tract requires only sufficient water and electrolytes to meet his maintenance needs. Hellerstein suggests a solution for this purpose: dissolve one package (approximately 3 oz.) of gelatin dessert (made by General Foods Corporation, A & P, or Safeway) in 32 oz. of water. Each liter of this solution provides 10 to 20 mEq. of sodium and of chloride, plus 400 calories.

A child with large fluid loss from diarrhea requires additional sodium and chloride. Hellerstein suggests this oral solution: dissolve one package (approximately 3 oz.) of gelatin dessert, 1/2 teaspoon of sodium chloride, in 64 oz. of water. Each liter of this solution provides 30 to 40 mEq. of sodium and of chloride, and 200 calories. After gastrointestinal tolerance is improved, potassium should be supplied. Many physicians feel that oral potassium should be given whenever the patient can tolerate liquids by mouth. Potassium can be provided by orange juice, grapefruit juice and grape juice. A suitable oral solution for providing water, electrolytes and calories is Lytren, prepared by mixing 8 measures of Lytren and 32 oz. of water. Measures should be carefully leveled in accordance with the manufacturer's instructions. Each liter of this solution supplies 25 mEq. of sodium, 25 mEq. of potassium, 30 mEq. of chloride, and 280 calories, plus other ingredients.

Nursing Implications. The nurse should be especially careful in preparing oral electrolyte solutions to follow directions carefully and use precisely the right measurements. The accidental use of a tablespoon when a teaspoon is specified triples the dose of the electrolyte. If sugar is to be added to the solution, great care should be taken to avoid mistaking salt for sugar.

Parenteral Fluid Therapy

Subcutaneous Route. Subcutaneous fluids are easier to start than are intravenous fluids, particularly in infants and small children. For this reason, the subcutaneous route is used fairly widely in pediatrics, even though it has serious hazards and limitations. Subcutaneous fluids are poorly absorbed in the child with a severe fluid volume deficit because of the frequently associated peripheral circulatory collapse. The route, therefore, is not dependable in patients with severe fluid balance disturbances. Another disadvantage of the subcutaneous route is the limitation of the types of fluids that can be administered by this route with even a modicum of safety. (The reader is referred to Chap. 14 for a discussion of which fluids can be given subcutaneously.)

The nurse should check the injection sites frequently and adjust the flow rate so as to prevent painful swelling. Because fluid-

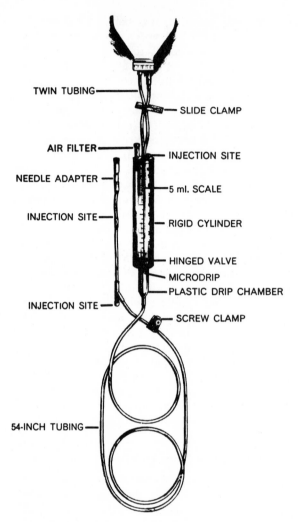

FIG. 86. Soluset administration set. (Abbott Laboratories)

TWIN TUBING

SLIDE CLAMP

AIR FILTER

INJECTION SITE

NEEDLE ADAPTER

5 ml. SCALE

INJECTION SITE

RIGID CYLINDER

HINGED VALVE
MICRODRIP
PLASTIC DRIP CHAMBER

INJECTION SITE

SCREW CLAMP

54-INCH TUBING

logged tissues are fertile sites for infection, sterile cotton dressings should be applied with adhesive strips after the needles are withdrawn.

Intravenous Route. The danger of administering an excessive fluid volume is a real one in all age groups. Infants and small children are faced with special dangers simply because of their small size and the ease of supplying fluids in adult-sized bottles. The accidental administration of an extra 500 ml. of fluid, such as 5 per cent dextrose in water or isotonic solution of sodium chloride, might mean little to the adult, but it can be disastrous to the infant or small child. This group of patients have greater difficulty excreting excessive fluid

volume. Moreover, they are more susceptible to pulmonary edema than are adults.

Measures should be taken to avoid an overdose of intravenous fluids. The volume available in the bottle, which might run rapidly into the patient, should be limited. It has been recommended that a bottle containing no more than 250 ml. be used for children under five years of age, and that no more than 500 ml. be contained in the bottle used for any child.

The development of special administration sets for pediatric use has added a greater margin of safety to fluid administration. The Soluset consists of a rigid plastic cylinder calibrated in units of 5 ml., from 0 to 100 ml. (See Fig. 86.) Any amount of

FIG. 87. Pedatrol Administration Set. (Baxter Laboratories, Morton Grove, Ill.)

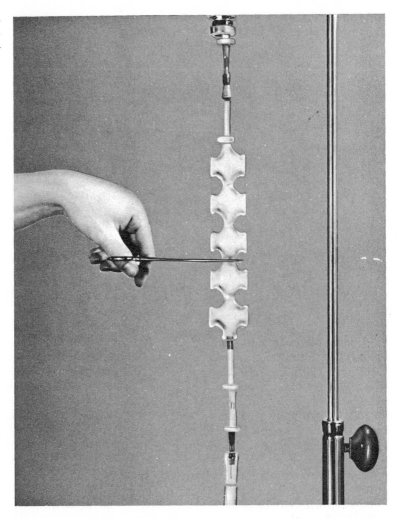

fluid up to 100 ml. can be added to the cylinder from the solution bottle. After the desired amount of solution enters the cylinder, the solution bottle is clamped off. Thus, the only amount that could run in is the amount in the plastic cylinder; when the cylinder empties, it can be refilled. A Microdrip drop adaptor is supplied with this set; approximately 60 drops deliver 1 ml.

Another set designed for pediatric use is the Pedatrol set. It is a flexible plastic apparatus divided into aliquots of 10 ml. each. (See Fig. 87.) By simply moving a hemostat's position on the set, the maximal amount of fluid that could be infused can be limited to 10, 20, 30, 40, or 50 ml. The Minimeter drop adaptor is used with the Pedatrol set

and reduces drop size; approximately 50 drops deliver 1 ml. The Pedatrol set can be refilled when necessary.

The physician prescribes the total volume of fluid to be given over a designated period of time, as well as the desired number of milliliters per hour or drops per minute. When the nurse knows the total volume to be administered in a fixed period of time, plus the drop factor of the set to be used, she can easily check the flow rate by her own computations. (The reader is referred to the discussion on calculation of flow rates in Chap. 14.) Great care should be taken to assure accuracy when the flow rate is calculated.

Even though drop size adaptors and small

containers are used to reduce the possibility of error, the nurse must still keep a close vigil on the flow rate, as well as on the patient's response to the fluids. The flow rate should be counted every 15 minutes and adjusted as necessary. (Factors that can alter the flow rate are discussed in Chap. 14.) A pediatric parenteral fluid sheet should be kept at the bedside of infants and small children to record the observed flow rate, the amount of fluid absorbed each hour and the amount of fluid left in the bottle. Such frequent observations and notations greatly reduce the risk of excessive fluid administration.

CLINICAL CONDITIONS COMMONLY ASSOCIATED WITH FLUID IMBALANCES IN SMALL CHILDREN

Diarrhea

Diarrhea is a common cause of water and electrolyte disturbances in infants and small children. The large loss of liquid stools can rapidly deplete the young child's extracellular fluid volume, especially when it is combined with vomiting. Usually water and electrolytes are lost in isotonic proportions (fluid volume deficit or "isotonic dehydration"). However, water can be lost in excess of electrolytes (fluid volume deficit with sodium excess or "hypertonic dehydration"), and electrolytes can be lost in excess of water (fluid volume deficit with sodium deficit or "hypotonic dehydration"). Because sodium is the chief extracellular ion, its excess or deficit is of primary importance in producing symptoms.

Intestinal fluids are alkaline; therefore, large losses of fluids in diarrhea may result in metabolic acidosis (primary base bicarbonate deficit). Potassium deficit is another frequent accompaniment of diarrhea.

Extracellular Fluid Volume Deficit ("Isotonic Dehydration")

Symptoms. Approximately 70 per cent of patients with severe diarrhea undergo a proportionate loss of water and electrolytes. Symptoms of fluid volume deficit due to infantile diarrhea include:

- History of large quantities of liquid stools
- Weight loss
- Dry skin with poor tissue turgor
- Soft eyeballs with a sunken appearance (due to decreased intraocular pressure)
- Depression of anterior fontanel, if it is still patent
- Skin ashen or gray in color and extremities cold (due to inadequate peripheral circulation)
- Depressed body temperature, unless fever accompanies the diarrhea, such as in an infection
- Lethargy
- Signs of hypovolemic shock if treatment is not started promptly
    Weak rapid pulse
    Decreased blood pressure
    Oliguria

Metabolic acidosis usually accompanies frequent liquid stools. (Recall that the intestinal secretions are alkaline because of their high bicarbonate content. Therefore, loss of alkaline secretions in diarrheal stools results in metabolic acidosis.) Decreased dietary intake contributes to metabolic acidosis; thus, in the absence of adequate food intake, the body utilizes its own fats for energy purposes. The metabolism of these fats causes the accumulation of acidic ketone bodies in the blood, further contributing to the metabolic acidosis caused by bicarbonate loss.

A major symptom of metabolic acidosis is the increased depth of respiration, a body compensatory mechanism that blows off carbon dioxide, thus reducing the carbonic acid content of the blood and influencing the carbonic acid:base bicarbonate balance in the direction of an increased pH. If ketosis of starvation is present, an acetone odor may be noted on the breath. Symptoms of severe potassium deficit include weakness, anorexia, vomiting, excessive abdominal gas, and flabby muscles, like half-filled water bottles.

Treatment. The first goal of fluid replacement therapy is to expand the extracellular fluid volume sufficiently to prevent or correct symptoms of hypovolemic shock. A restored blood volume permits adequate renal blood flow and increased urine formation. Improvement of renal function helps the body eliminate organic acids and thus correct acidosis. Physicians vary in the precise fluid therapy employed. All agree that if kidney function is depressed because of extracellular fluid volume deficit, a special solution should be administered to correct renal depression. Renal depression is indicated by:

- Urinary specific gravity above 1.030
- Oliguria, revealed by the history of voiding less than 3 times during the previous 24 hours
- Anuria, shown by absence of urine in the bladder

Renal depression is assumed to be present when there has been a recent fluid loss of great magnitude, such as occurs with severe infectious diarrhea of explosive onset.

When renal depression is present, the physician administers an initial hydrating, or pump-priming solution to (1) restore the kidneys to normal function if the cause of the depression is extracellular fluid volume deficit, or (2) to discover that the renal depression is not the result of a fluid volume deficit, but rather of serious renal impairment.

Pump-priming solutions have about one-half the electrolyte concentration of extracellular fluid. A typical solution is simply a one-third isotonic solution of sodium chloride in 5 per cent dextrose. Such a solution provides 51 mEq. of sodium and 51 mEq. of chloride. All commercial companies make available such solutions.

With renal flow established, one can then administer a repair solution. Some physicians use lactated Ringer's solution with dextrose and added potassium. Doses of such solutions are usually based on ml./Kg. of body weight.

The water and electrolyte requirements for infants and children, when expressed in units/Kg., vary considerably for children of different ages and weights. For this reason, many physicians prefer to use body surface area as the dose criterion since this is independent of age and weight, except in the case of prematures.

Many physicians prefer to use Butler-type solutions, sometimes known as balanced solutions, so formulated that, when used to correct a fluid volume deficit, they provide electrolytes in such quantities that the homeostatic mechanisms can:

1. Retain those required for normalization of body fluid electrolyte composition
2. Excrete electrolytes that are not needed
3. Provide carbohydrate to combat ketosis and tissue breakdown

Balanced solutions provide both cellular and extracellular electrolytes, including sodium, potassium, lactate, chloride, phosphate, and sometimes, calcium, magnesium, citrate and sulfate. A conventional Butler solution provides 75 cations (or anions) per liter and is designed for administration to older infants, children, and adults. A balanced solution especially designed for infants contains 48 cations (or anions) per liter. It is designed for administration to full-term or large premature to one-month-old infants. An oral balanced solution, Lytren, based originally on the formula devised by Darrow and Cooke, provides 52 mEq./L. All balanced solutions provide added carbohydrate in order to help meet the caloric requirements of the child. Balanced solutions are given at a dose level of 1,500 ml./sq. m. of body surface/day for maintenance. In the presence of a moderate fluid volume deficit, the dose level is 2,400 ml./sq. m. of body surface/day. For a severe volume deficit, the dose level is 3,000 ml./sq. m. of body surface/day. The rate of administration is 3 ml./sq. m. of body surface/minute.

Fluid Volume Deficit with Sodium Excess ("Hypertonic Dehydration")

Symptoms. Approximately 20 per cent of patients with severe diarrhea have suffered a relatively greater loss of water than of electrolytes. If the infant has ingested a high solute-containing formula during his illness or has been inadvertently given an overly-concentrated electrolyte mixture, the renal water loss intensifies the sodium excess already present. Because the infant cannot concentrate urine efficiently, large volumes of water are needed to excrete solutes. The infant's need for water is intensified by the fact that his insensible water loss is great because of his large body surface area.

Symptoms of fluid volume deficit and sodium excess caused by diarrhea include:

- History of large quantities of liquid stools associated with a low water intake, high solute intake, poor renal function, or all three
- Weight loss
- Skin elasticity and turgor not lost; however, the skin has a thickened, firm feeling
- Avid thirst (hypertonic extracellular fluid draws water from the cells, producing cellular dehydration)
- Irritability displayed when disturbed; otherwise behavior is lethargic
- Tremors and convulsions
- Muscle rigidity
- Nuchal rigidity
- Chloride and protein concentration of spinal fluid elevated
- Although signs of extracellular fluid volume deficit are not present for first few days, they eventually occur with symptoms of hypovolemic shock
- Brain injury (may be due to intracranial hemorrhage and effusion into the subdural space)

Treatment. Treatment principles and details are similar to those given under extracellular fluid volume deficit.

Small amounts of electrolytes are used in the repair solutions to prevent a too rapid correction of the sodium excess, since a rapid return of the plasma sodium concentration to normal may precipitate acute sodium deficit (water intoxication).

Symptoms of sodium deficit can result from the abnormal uptake of water by the cells, secondary to the inability of the immature kidneys to maintain the normal relationship between water and solute. Convulsions can result from the too rapid reduction of the sodium concentration in the extracellular fluid; they are less likely to occur when the correction of the sodium excess is carried out gradually. Convulsions occurring in an infant with sodium excess can also be an indication of brain damage, in

which case, phenobarbital may be required to control them.

Hypocalcemia can occur during treatment, possibly caused by the loss of calcium in the stool or by the decreased ionization of available extracellular calcium, which occurs with correction of the metabolic acidosis. Symptoms of hypocalcemia occur less frequently when calcium is included in the treatment solution. The administration of 10 to 30 ml. of 10 per cent calcium gluconate added daily to one of the infusions may prevent calcium deficit from developing.

During repair of water losses, the patient with sodium excess may develop fluid volume excess with edema and, possibly, heart failure.

Fluid Volume Deficit with Sodium Deficit ("Hypotonic Dehydration")

Symptoms. Approximately 10 per cent of patients with severe diarrhea have suffered a relatively greater loss of electrolytes than of water, usually because fluid losses have been replaced with plain water in dextrose or some other electrolyte-free solution, which dilutes the electrolyte concentration of the extracellular fluid. Because sodium is the chief extracellular ion, the primary symptoms are due to its deficit. Symptoms of fluid volume deficit and sodium deficit caused by diarrheal losses include:

- Clammy skin
- Lethargy
- Hypovolemic shock, in severe cases

Treatment. Treatment principles and details are similar to those given under extracellular fluid volume deficit.

Measures to Prevent or Minimize Water and Electrolyte Loss in Diarrhea

1. Hospitalized infants with diarrhea should be isolated so as to prevent infecting other children in the unit. Meticulous attention should be paid to isolation technique.

2. Diarrhea can be caused by infections transmitted to the infant by contaminated formula or equipment. Unless technique is impeccable, this can occur readily in the

hospital. The nurse should see that the mother knows how to prepare the baby's formula safely before she goes home.

3. Water and electrolyte losses can be minimized if diarrhea is reported immediately so that treatment can be started. Mothers should be instructed to report diarrhea as soon as it is noticed.

4. Liquid stool losses are greater if the baby continues to take oral feedings than if his gastrointestinal tract is put to rest temporarily. Mothers should be instructed to withhold formula feedings when diarrhea occurs until they have checked with the physician. Because of the high solute content of skim milk, boiled skim milk that is undiluted should not be used in the treatment of infants with diarrhea. Because of the infant's poor renal concentrating ability, he needs large quantities of water to excrete the large renal solute load presented by undiluted skim milk. Boiled skim milk should never be used unless diluted with at least an equal volume of water, plus added carbohydrate.

5. Mothers should be encouraged to follow the physician's instructions precisely in returning the infant to full formula feedings following a bout of diarrhea. In most cases the infant with diarrhea is given initially an oral electrolyte solution with glucose. When tolerated, a little milk is added each day until full feedings are resumed.

Inadvertent Use of Salt Instead of Sugar in Formula Preparation

Sodium excess without fluid volume deficit occurs when too much sodium is ingested. The accidental substitution of salt (sodium chloride) for sugar in formula preparation results in a disastrously high sodium intake. Unfortunately, such accidents are not rare. The grossly hypertonic formula causes the infant to cry; if his cry is interpreted as indicating hunger, more of the hypertonic formula is given and the condition worsens.

Symptoms. Symptoms accompanying the excessive ingestion of sodium include:

- Avid thirst
- Irritability when disturbed, otherwise lethargy
- Tremors and convulsions
- Nuchal rigidity
- Muscle rigidity
- Elevation of protein and chloride concentrations of the spinal fluid
- Expansion of the extracellular fluid
- Visible edema
- Brain damage in some patients

Treatment. Treatment principles and details are similar to those given under extracellular fluid volume deficit.

Nursing Implications. Table 48 shows the quantities of sodium and chloride ions present in varying concentrations of salt water. When one considers that the child's daily need for sodium is only 1 or 2 mEq. per pound of body weight (50 to 70 mEq./sq. m. of body surface/day), it becomes clear why the accidental substitution of salt for sugar is so dangerous.

The nurse should caution the parents to use great care in the preparation of infant formulas, stressing the harm caused by excessive sodium intake and the simplicity of its prevention. The need to keep sugar and salt in clearly-labeled containers should be stressed. Merely bringing up the subject may

TABLE 48. ELECTROLYTE CONTENTS OF SOLUTIONS OF TABLE SALT

| CONCENTRATION | APPROXIMATE COMPOSITION | |
SALT / 1 QUART OF TAP WATER	NA mEq./L.	CL mEq./L.
⅛ tsp.	10–15	10–15
¼ tsp.	20–30	20–30
½ tsp.	45–60	45–60
1 tsp.	120	120
1 tbs.	350	350

Statland, H.: Fluid and Electrolytes in Practice. ed. 3, p. 201. Philadelphia, Lippincott, 1963.

make the parents more careful in formula preparation.

Vomiting

Hypertrophic Pyloric Stenosis

Symptoms. Hypertrophic pyloric stenosis is a common cause of vomiting in small infants, usually under six weeks old. Because of the repeated vomiting, the infants are poorly nourished. While hypertrophic pyloric stenosis can be corrected surgically, preoperative correction of the water and electrolyte disturbances caused by the prolonged vomiting is mandatory.

Vomiting causes the same imbalances in children as it does in adults. These include metabolic alkalosis (primary base bicarbonate excess), potassium deficit, sodium deficit and fluid volume deficit. Metabolic alkalosis occurs because of the excessive loss of potassium, hydrogen and chloride in the vomitus. Loss of chloride causes a compensatory increase in the number of bicarbonate ions; this occurs because both are anions (negatively charged ions). Total cations must always equal the total anions so that electrical equality can be maintained; if the quantity of one anion is decreased, another anion must increase in compensation. The bicarbonate side of the carbonic acid:base bicarbonate ratio is increased, and the pH increases—that is, becomes more alkaline. Sodium and potassium are plentiful in gastric juice; prolonged vomiting leads to deficits of both. Since water is also lost in the vomitus, fluid volume deficit occurs. Because the losses are sustained over a relatively long period, circulatory collapse is not prominent in hypertrophic pyloric stenosis as it is in severe diarrhea.

The infant with hypertrophic pyloric stenosis presents the following symptoms:

- Difficulty in retaining feedings, which becomes progressively worse during the first few weeks of life; eventually, projectile vomiting follows each feeding
- Appearance of malnutrition
- Symptoms of fluid volume deficit
- Decreased respiration (compensatory

action of lungs to retain carbon dioxide and increase the carbonic acid content of the blood)
- Tetany accompanying alkalosis (due to decreased calcium ionization in an alkaline pH)
- Despite starvation, ketosis does not usually appear
- Palpable pyloric tumor

Treatment. PREOPERATIVE PERIOD. To minimize fluid losses, oral feedings should be discontinued and fluids given parenterally. If gastric suction is used, the water and electrolytes lost by this procedure should be replaced. Treatment principles and details are similar to those given under extracellular fluid volume deficit.

POSTOPERATIVE PERIOD. The young child does not retain sodium after a surgical operation, as do many adults. Sodium should, therefore, be included in the postoperative repair solution. There is excellent rationale for including potassium likewise.

Obstruction Below the Pylorus

Vomiting caused by an obstruction below the pylorus contains alkaline secretions from the intestines, in addition to the acid secretions from the stomach. Vomitus may be bile-stained. If alkaline secretions predominate, metabolic acidosis results. Contributing to the metabolic acidosis is the ketosis of starvation.

Salicylate Intoxication

Unfortunately, salicylate intoxication is commonly seen in children. It frequently results from leaving aspirin in the reach of the small child, particularly flavored aspirin. Accidental ingestion of only two to four times the recommended dose of one grain per year of age will produce toxic effects. Overdoses in the treatment of fever is another common cause of salicylate poisoning.

Salicylates cause the respiratory center to be more sensitive to carbon dioxide; respiration becomes deep and rapid. As a result, excessive amounts of carbon dioxide are eliminated from the lungs; respiratory alkalosis (primary carbonic acid deficit) develops. Symptoms of a deficit of ionized calcium caused by the alkalosis appear. They include numbness and tingling of the face and extremities, positive Chvostek's sign, muscle twitching, and convulsions.

Adults and older children have respiratory alkalosis as the major disturbance. Children under five years of age usually develop a more complicated acid-base disturbance. Quickly following the initial respiratory alkalosis, they develop metabolic acidosis, as a result of inadequate utilization of carbohydrate caused by the toxic doses of salicylates and the resultant increased utilization of body fat. This usually appears within 3 to 24 hours after the salicylates are ingested, probably by the time the child reaches the hospital. Symptoms of severe salicylate intoxication in the child resemble those of diabetic acidosis. They consist of severe hyperpnea, vomiting, acetone odor to the breath and fluid volume deficit. Hyperthermia is common and is manifested by a flushed appearance and sweating. Bleeding may occur, due to disturbances in blood coagulation or to thrombocytopenia. Adults and older children can cope with the impaired metabolism of salicylate intoxication better than can young children.

The blood pH is thus affected by two imbalances—respiratory alkalosis and metabolic acidosis. Sometimes the two imbalances neutralize each other and the pH remains normal. If respiratory alkalosis is more severe than metabolic acidosis, as is frequently the case in older children and adults, the pH is elevated above normal. If metabolic acidosis is more severe than respiratory alkalosis, as is frequently the case in small children, the pH is decreased below normal.

Treatment. Unfortunately, severe salicylate poisoning is sometimes confused with diabetic acidosis, and the child is given insulin. Insulin is not indicated and can produce disastrous effects. Emergency therapy is directed at removing as much of the salicylate from the stomach as possible before it is absorbed. Gastric contents should be evacuated; then the stomach should be lavaged with an isotonic solution of sodium chloride. If more than one hour has elapsed since the ingestion of aspirin, emesis should be induced.

After the stomach contents have been emptied, attention is given to supplying adequate fluids to promote excretion of salicylates by the kidneys, which account for the excretion of about 80 per cent of ingested salicylates. Carbohydrate is administered to prevent or combat ketosis. The amount of fluids required depends largely upon the length of time elapsed since poisoning occurred. Since severe hyperpnea usually accompanies metabolic acidosis, large quantities of water are lost by way of the lungs. Some patients who have not received prompt therapy suffer severe fluid volume deficit, which must, of course, be repaired. Treatment principles and details are similar to those given under extracellular fluid volume deficit.

The urine can be alkalinized as a means of promoting salicylate excretion. This can be accomplished by the intravenous administration of lactate-containing solutions.

Calcium gluconate can be given to relieve symptoms of ionized calcium deficit, such as tetany. Vitamin K_1 can be used to prevent excessive bleeding.

Burns

The treatment of children with burns is essentially the same as that described for adults in Chapter 16. The major difference lies in the calculation of the percentage of the body involved in the burn, since the child's body proportions are different from those of the adult. (See Fig. 88.)

Another major difference between the child and the adult lies in the need for greater accuracy in fluid administration in children, since the child has greater sensitivity to minor errors in fluid administration. Both pulmonary edema and shock develop more quickly in children than in adults.

A child with more than a 10 per cent burn will require parenteral fluid therapy. To evaluate the effectiveness of fluid replace-

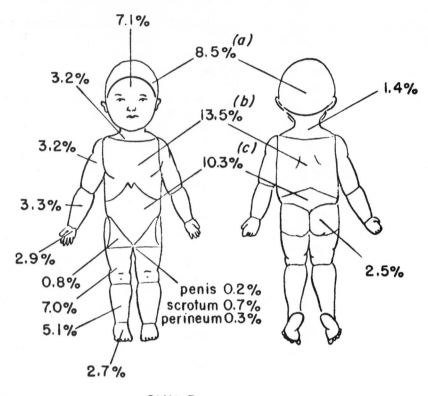

CHILD: one year

Surface areas of the parts of the body (%)

(a) Entire scalp
(b) Entire upper trunk, front and back
(c) Entire lower trunk, front and back

Fig. 88. Surface diagram constructed from Meeh's data. Child of six months to three years. (Moyer, C.: Treatment of large burns. Arch. Surg., *90*:856, June 1965)

ment, it is necessary to measure the urinary output at regular intervals; an in-place urinary catheter may be required. If a catheter is not used, a plastic diaper with the collecting area connected to drainage tubing may be used. A finger cot—with the blind end clipped off—can be used to conduct urine from the penis to the drainage tube, in male infants. A child under one year of age should have an hourly output of from 5 to 10 ml.; a child between one and ten years, between 10 and 25 ml.; or, 10 to 30 ml./sq. m. of body surface/hour, regardless of age.

Milk Sickness

Infants and children who have drunk the milk of cows that have eaten white snakeroot (*Eupatorium urticaefolium*) can develop milk sickness or trematol poisoning. This disease is characterized by a profound acidosis, resembling that of salicylate intoxication or severe diabetic acidosis. The acidosis is peculiarly refractive to therapy and requires vigorous parenteral fluid administration. Cases have been reported as recently as 1963. The disease can occur wherever the white snakeroot grows, that is, in the Midwest and Upper-south. The disease can also occur when cows eat the rayless goldenrod   (*Aplopappus   heterophyllus*), which grows in the Southwest.

Any infant or child (or adult for that matter) who:

1. has a severe acidosis of unknown origin,
2. is free of fever,
3. has drunk milk of carelessly pastured cows

should be suspected of having milk sickness, until the disease is ruled out.

Bibliography

Gauss, H., and Meyer, K.: Heat stroke: Report of 158 cases from Cook County Hospital, Chicago. Amer. J. Med. Sci., *154*:554, 1917.

Malamud, N., Haymaker, W., and Custer, R.: Heat stroke: A clinicopathologic study of 125 fatal cases. Milit. Surg., *99*:397, 1946.

Fuller, R., Johnston, E., and Ebersole, J.: Drowning and the Postimmersion Syndrome. Washington, D. C., Armed Forces Institute of Pathology, 1949.

Gamble, J.: Chemical Anatomy, Physiology and Pathology of Extracellular Fluid. Cambridge, Harvard Univ. Press, 1950.

Moyer, C.: Fluid Balance, A Clinical Manual. Chicago, Yearbook Pub., 1952.

Lowe, C.: Principles of parenteral fluid therapy. Am. J. Nursing, *53*:963-965, (Aug.) 1953.

Ashley, F., and Love, H.: Fluid and Electrolyte Therapy. Philadelphia, Lippincott, 1953.

Womack, N.: On Burns. Springfield, Ill., Thomas, 1953.

Milner, C.: Nursing care of severely burned patients. Am. J. Nursing, *54*:456-459, (April) 1954.

Farr, H.: Fluid and electrolyte balance with special reference to the gastrointestinal tract. Am. J. Nursing, *54*:826-831, (July) 1954.

Wolf, E.: The nurse and fluid therapy. Am. J. Nursing, *54*:831-833, (July) 1954.

Hardy, J.: Fluid Therapy. Philadelphia, Lea & Febiger, 1954.

Luisada, A.: Heart. ed. 2. Baltimore, Williams & Wilkins, 1954.

Frohman, I.: Constipation. Am. J. Nursing, *55*: 65-69, (Jan.) 1955.

Palumbo, L.: Ulcerative colitis: Medical and surgical care. Am. J. Nursing, *55*:311-315, (March) 1955.

Blocker, T., et al.: Nutrition studies in the severely burned. Ann. Surg., *141*:589-597, (May) 1955.

Elkington, J., and Danowski, T.: The Body Fluids, Basic Physiology and Practical Therapeutics. Baltimore, Williams & Wilkins, 1955.

Mayo, C.: Surgery of the Small and Large Intestine. Chicago, Yearbook Pub., 1955.

Wilkinson, A.: Body Fluids in Surgery. Baltimore, Williams & Wilkins, 1955.

Snively, W., Sweeney, M., and Wessner, M.: Systematic approach to fluid balance (Part 1). GP, *13*:74-83, (Jan.) 1956.

———: Systematic approach to fluid balance (Part 2). GP, *13*:74-86, (Feb.) 1956.

Dunning, M., and Plum, F.: Potassium depletion by enemas. Am. J. Med., *20*:789-792, (May) 1956.

Bland, J.: Clinical Recognition and Management of Disturbances of Body Fluids. ed. 2. Philadelphia, Saunders, 1956.

Selye, H.: The Stress of Life. ed. 8. New York, McGraw-Hill, 1956.

Snively, W., and Sweeney, M.: Fluid Balance Handbook for Practitioners. Springfield, Ill., Thomas, 1956.

Snively, W.: Body surface area as a dosage criterion in fluid therapy: Theory and application. Metabolism, *6*:70-87, (Jan.) 1957.

Smith, A.: Nasogastric tube feeding. Am. J. Nursing, *57*:1451-1452, (Nov.) 1957.

Artz, C., and Reiss, E.: The Treatment of Burns. Philadelphia, Saunders, 1957.

Snively, W., and Brown, B.: In the balance. Am. J. Nursing, *58*:55-57, (Jan.) 1958.

Snively, W., and Sweeney, M.: Therapy of imbalances of the body fluids. GP, *18*:74-85, (Aug.) 1958.

Creevy, D., and Tollefson, D.: Ileac diversion of the urine and nursing care of the patient with ileac diversion of the urine. Am. J. Nursing, *59*:530-536, (April) 1959.

Jay, A.: Colitis. Am. J. Nursing, *59*:1133-1135, (Aug.) 1959.

Snively, W.: The body's response to burning. GP, *20*:132-144, (Sept.) 1959.

Litchfield, J.: Low potassium syndrome resulting from use of purgative drugs. Gastroenterology, *37*:483-488, (Oct.) 1959.

Barron, J.: Tube feeding of postoperative patients. S. Clin. North America, *39*:1481-1491, (Dec.) 1959.

Cartwright, M.: Tube feeding by nasal gavage. RN, *22*:55-60, (Dec.) 1959.

Birren, J. (ed.): Handbook of Aging and the Individual. Chicago, University of Chicago Press, 1959.

Brown, A.: Medical and Surgical Nursing II. Philadelphia, Saunders, 1959.

Moore, F.: Metabolic Care of the Surgical Patient. Philadelphia, Saunders, 1959.

Nordmark, M., and Rohweder, A.: Science Principles Applied to Nursing. Philadelphia, Lippincott, 1959.

Pareira, M.: Therapeutic Nutrition with Tube Feeding. Springfield, Ill., Thomas, 1959.

Welt, L.: Clinical Disorders of Hydration and Acid-Base Equilibrium. ed. 2. Boston, Little, Brown, 1959.

Heap, B.: Sodium restricted diets. Am. J. Nursing, 60:206-209, (Feb.) 1960.

Snively, W.: Fluid balance in obstruction of the large intestine. J. Indiana Med. Ass., 53:427-434, (March) 1960.

Grace, W.: Practical clinical management of electrolyte disorders. New York, Appleton-Century-Crofts, 1960.

Snively, W.: Sea Within: The Story of Our Body Fluids. Philadelphia, Lippincott, 1960.

Ziffren, S.: Management of the Aged Surgical Patient. Chicago, Yearbook Pub., 1960.

Chamberlain, J., Welch, K., and Morse, T.: The Management of Burns in Children. Clinical Symposia, Ciba Pharmaceutical Products, Inc., 13:3-24, (Jan.-March) 1961.

Brickman, D.: Some pointers on I.V. therapy. RN, 24:38-47, (Aug.) 1961.

Artz, C., and Hardy, J.: Complications in Surgery and Their Management. Philadelphia, Saunders, 1961.

Guyton, A.: Textbook of Medical Physiology. ed. 2. Philadelphia, Saunders, 1961.

Friedrich, H.: Oral feeding by food pump. Am. J. Nursing, 62:62-64, (Feb.) 1962.

Adriani, J.: Venipuncture. Am. J. Nursing, 62:66-70, (March) 1962.

Collentine, G.: How to calculate fluids for burned patients. Am. J. Nursing, 62:77-79, (March) 1962.

Crouch, M., and Gibson, S.: Blood therapy. Am. J. Nursing, 62:71-76, (March) 1962.

Doberneck, R.: Acute renal failure after open-heart surgery utilizing extracorporeal circulation and total body perfusion. J. Thorac. Cardiov. Surg. 43:441-452, (April) 1962.

Snively, W.: Systematic approach to diagnosis of body fluid disturbances. GP, 25:114-127, (May) 1962.

Wilson, J., et al.: Central venous pressure in optimal blood volume maintenance. Arch. Surg., 85:563-578, (Oct.) 1962.

Dodds, W., and Forseng, A.: Study of acid-base balance in open-heart surgical patients. Canad. Anesth. Soc. J., 9:488-496, (Nov.) 1962.

Harrison, T. (ed.): Principles of Internal Medicine. ed. 4. New York, McGraw-Hill, 1962.

Snively, W. (ed.): Body Fluid Disturbances. New York, Grune & Stratton, 1962.

Weisberg, H.: Water, Electrolyte and Acid-Base Balance. ed. 2, Baltimore, Williams & Wilkins 1962.

Dammann, F.: The management of the severely ill patient after open-heart surgery. J. Thorac. Cardiov. Surg., 45:80-90, (Jan.) 1963.

Winter, C., Roehm, M., and Watson, H.: Urinary calculi. Am. J. Nursing, 63:72-76, (July) 1963.

Hartmann, A., Sr., et al.: Tremetol poisoning—not yet extinct. J.A.M.A., 185:706-709, (Aug. 31) 1963.

Robinson, F.: Nursing care of the patient with pulmonary emphysema. Am. J. Nursing, 63:92-96, (Sept.) 1963.

Stafford, N.: Bowel hygiene of aged patients. Am. J. Nursing, 63:102-103, (Sept.) 1963.

Williams, H.: Pulmonary emphysema. Am. J. Nursing, 63:88-91, (Sept.) 1963.

Rae, N.: Caring for patients following open-heart surgery. Am. J. Nursing, 63:77-82, (Nov.) 1963.

Drummond, E., and Anderson, M.: Gastrointestinal suction. Am. J. Nursing, 63:109-113, (Dec.) 1963.

Blake, F., and Wright, F.: Essentials of Pediatric Nursing. ed. 7. Philadelphia, Lippincott, 1963.

Bland, J.: Clinical Metabolism of Body Water and Electrolytes. Philadelphia, Saunders, 1963.

Bowes, C., and Church, H.: Food Values of Portions Commonly Used. ed. 9. Philadelphia, Lippincott, 1963.

Cooper, L., Barber, E., Mitchell, H., and Rynbergen, H.: Nutrition in Health and Disease. ed. 14. Philadelphia, Lippincott, 1963.

Kark, R., et al.: A Primer of Urinalysis. ed. 2. New York, Harper, 1963.

Krug, E.: Pharmacology in Nursing. ed. 9. St. Louis, Mosby, 1963.

Statland, H.: Fluid and Electrolytes in Practice. ed. 3. Philadelphia, Lippincott, 1963.

Davenport, R.: Tube feeding for long-term patients. Am. J. Nursing, 64:121-123, (Jan.) 1964.

Snively, W.: Toward a better understanding of body fluid disturbances. Nursing Forum, 3:1-17, (Jan.) 1964.

Yeh, T.: Renal complications of open-heart surgery; predisposing factors, prevention, and management. J. Thorac. Cardiov. Surg., 47:79-97, (Jan.) 1964.

Weisberg, H.: Pitfalls in fluid and electrolyte therapy. Symposium on fluid and electrolyte therapy. J. St. Barnabas Medical Center, 2:99-108, (Aug.) 1964.

Sako, Y.: Emergency Management of the Acutely Burned Patient. pp. 5-9. Hospital Medicine,

Wallace Laboratories, Cranbury, N. J., (Oct.) 1964.

Frohman, I.: The adrenocorticosteroids. Am. J. Nursing, *64*:120-123, (Nov.) 1964.

Benz, G.: Pediatric Nursing. ed. 5. St. Louis, Mosby, 1964.

Brunner, L., Emerson, C., Ferguson, L., and Suddarth, D.: Textbook of Medical-Surgical Nursing. Philadelphia, Lippincott, 1964.

Davis, L.: Christopher's Textbook of Surgery. ed. 8. Philadelphia, Saunders, 1964.

Goodhart, R., and Wohl, M.: Manual of Clinical Nutrition. Philadelphia, Lea & Febiger, 1964.

Grollman, A.: Clinical Endocrinology and Its Physiologic Basis. Philadelphia, Lippincott, 1964.

Kottke, F., and Blanchard, R.: Bedrest begets bedrest. Nursing Forum, *3*:56-63, 1964.

Leithead, C., and Lind, A.: Heat Stress and Heat Disorders. Philadelphia, Davis, 1964.

MacBryde, C.: Signs and Symptoms. ed. 4. Philadelphia, Lippincott, 1964.

Redding, J., and Pearson, J.: Management of drowning victims. Am. Family Physician, 7:55, 1964.

Shafer, K., Sawyer, J., McCluskey, A., and Beck, E.: Medical-Surgical Nursing. ed. 3. St. Louis, Mosby, 1964.

Wohl, M., and Goodhart, R.: Modern Nutrition in Health and Disease. ed. 3. Philadelphia, Lea and Febiger, 1964.

Grollman, A.: Diuretics. Am. J. Nursing, *65*:84-89, (Jan.) 1965.

Moyer, C., Margraf, H., and Monafo, W.: Burn shock and extravascular sodium deficiency—Treatment with Ringer's solution with lactate. Arch. Surg., *90*:799-811, (June) 1965.

Moyer, C., *et al.*: Treatment of large human burns with 0.5% silver nitrate solution. Arch. Surg., *90*:812-867, (June) 1965.

Snively, W.: The clinician views potassium deficit. Minn. Med., *48*:713-719, (June) 1965.

Shaffer, J., and Sweet, L.: Allergic reactions to drugs. Am. J. Nursing, *65*:100-103, (Oct.) 1965.

Varvaro, F.: Teaching the patient about open-heart surgery. Am. J. Nursing, *65*:111-115, (Oct.) 1965.

Bordicks, K.: Patterns of Shock. New York, Macmillan, 1965.

Goldberger, E.: A Primer of Water, Electrolyte, and Acid-Base Syndromes. ed. 3. Philadelphia, Lea & Febiger, 1965.

Schmitt, G.: Diabetes for Diabetics: A Practical Guide. Miami, Diabetes Press of America, 1965.

Smith, D., and Gips, C.: Care of the Adult Patient. Philadelphia, Lippincott, 1966.

Snively, W., and Dick, R.: Computer approach to diagnosis of body fluid disturbances. J. Ind. S. Med. Assn., *59*:233-246, (Mar.) 1966.

Snively, W.: Potassium salts and intestinal ulcer. J.A.M.A., *195*:977, (Mar. 14) 1966.

Westerman, R., and Snively, W.: Potassium deficit: clinical aspects, GP, *33*:85-93, (June) 1966.

Snively, W., and Furbee, L.: Discoverer of the cause of milk sickness. J.A.M.A., *196*:103-108, (June 20) 1966.

Snively, W.; Montenegro, J.; and Dick, R.: Quick method for estimating body surface area. J.A.M.A., *197*:208-209, (July 18) 1966.

Coburn, J., and Reba, R.: Potassium depletion in heatstroke: a possible etiologic factor. Mil. Med., *131*:678-687, (Aug.) 1966.

Snively, W., and Westerman, R.: Serum potassium determination. J.A.M.A., *197*:151, (Aug. 15) 1966.

Index

Italicized Numbers Indicate Illustrations.